SCREEN
ACTING

****

How to Succeed
in Motion Pictures
and Television

SCREEN
ACTING

---

*How to Succeed
in Motion Pictures
and Television*

BY

BRIAN ADAMS

LONE
EAGLE

SCREEN ACTING

Copyright © 1986, 1987 by Brian Adams

LONE EAGLE PUBLISHING CO.
2337 Roscomare Road, Suite Nine
Los Angeles, CA 90077-1815
310/471-8066 • FAX 310/471-4969

Printed in the United States of America

Cover design by Gloriane Harris

First Lone Eagle Printing, December 1987
Second Printing, December 1989
Third Printing, March 1992

This is an authorized reprint of an original hardcover edition published by Image Book Company, Sydney, Australia.

Library of Congress Cataloging in Publication Data

Adams, Brian
    SCREEN ACTING

      1. Moving Pictures Acting — Vocational Guidance
2. Acting for television — Vocational Guidance
I. Title
PN1995.9.A26A3   1987   791.43'023   87-29682
ISBN 0-9589512-0-9
ISBN 0-943728-20-7 (pbk)

96 95 94 93 92

10 9 8 7 6 5 4 3

Gratefully dedicated to my parents . . .

An actor should take lessons from the
painter and the sculptor. Not only
should he make attitude his study, but
he should highly develop his mind by an
assiduous study of the best writers,
ancient and modern, which will enable
him not only to understand his parts,
but to communicate a nobler colouring
to his manners and mien.

– GOETHE.

ACKNOWLEDGEMENTS

I would like to thank the following persons and companies for permission to reproduce stills . . .

Basil Appleby
Terry Bourke
William Brown – World Wide Pictures, Inc.
Crawford Productions
Tom Greer – Grundy Television
Di Holmes – John Sexton Productions
Patricia Lovell – Pavilion Films
Lionel Midford – Greater Union Film Distributors
Leonard Webb – United International Pictures
Fiona Wingrove – McElroy & McElroy
United Telecasters – Channel Ten, Sydney

And to . . .

Peter Banki – Copyright Council
Buddy Basch
Bruce Davis – Academy of Motion Picture Arts and Sciences
Christopher Drake for illustrations
Robert Frederick
Robert Greenberg for explanatory photographs
Ilsa Konrads – Vogue Australia
Weidenfeld Publishers Limited
World Book, Inc.

And to the following actors for explanatory photographs . . .

Maria Dujany
Karen Lennox
Tony Partridge

HOW THIS BOOK CAN ENHANCE YOUR PERFORMANCE SKILLS

★★

Acting, either as a part-time interest or as a full-time career, has universal appeal. During the years I worked in Hollywood, about one in every three persons I came in contact with claimed to be an actor, rather than a waitress, salesperson, teacher, banker, lawyer, accountant, drycleaner, receptionist or whatever it was they were doing at the time I met them. Even my dentist moonlighted as an actor. His receptionist once told me: 'Doctor can't take any appointments next week, he'll be in rehearsal.' Such is the popularity of acting. I'm of the opinion, if every acting hopeful in Los Angeles received a casting call on the same day, the city would come to a standstill.

I find no fault with the desire to express creativity through acting. I contend that given the opportunity, the vast majority of humans would rather be in *showbusiness* than any other business. And why not? It's fun. It's glamorous. It's exciting. It's creative. And, it's financially rewarding, providing you hit the top.

Shakespeare wrote many passages about the stage and its relation to people. Perhaps if the television receiver and the screen camera had been around in his time, he might have used the words *clamoring to be players* instead of *merely players* when he wrote:

> All the world's a stage
> And all the men and women merely players.

The human need to perform well before others is inherent in us all. For some, there is an insatiable need to proceed beyond mere social acceptance, to test dramatic instinct and express, through professional performance, the thoughts, feelings and needs of stage characters.

1

The testing place of *dramatic instinct* is center stage. Here, the dialogues of scriptwriters and the concepts of production-makers come into being through the interpretive and creative skills of the players.

The knowledge to become a professional player, to achieve proper interpretation of script, to portray a stage character true to the author's intent before the screen camera, is what this book is about.

Screen Acting is a practical manual of performance techniques written with simplicity and dramatic clarity in mind; it is a treasury of information on *what* to do and *how* to do it. Its chief aim is to bring to the beginner, to the teacher of drama as well as to the professional actor, performable techniques to develop creativity and enhance performance levels.

For the careerist actor, this book explains the requirements, functions and practices of theatrical agents, managers, publicists, casting directors and industry unions. It outlines how to assemble composites, presentation and publicity materials and audio/video audition tapes. Other valuable information includes:

- What to request when entering into contracts with producers
- How to select an agent
- How to find a worthwhile school of acting
- How to overcome stage-fright and develop stage-confidence
- How to project a highly-individual personality
- How to get your acting career moving
- How to handle auditions and screen tests

This book covers the elements essential to television and motion picture presentation. Those actors trained in theatre performance will find this work a natural extension of their knowledge. Acting for camera and acting before a theatre audience differ only in the dynamics and style of the performance, not in the assemblage of words and the development of a stage character.

Screen acting places certain limitations and restrictions on the actor. Facial animation, gestures and general movement of the body require toning down. Exaggerated movement of the eyes and mouth are magnified when projected onto the screen. Video and motion picture cameras mercilessly record performance insincerity. In addition, there are limiting factors to voice levels. Sensitive microphones do not require over-vocalizing of dialogue.

This book is a psychological survey of acting, clearly defining the differences between mechanical, physical acting-out of words and inspirationally-guided performance. The reader will discover how to detect and better understand human motive factors which greatly affect attitudes and determine actions and how to apply this knowledge when developing a screen character. Performance techniques include: *attitude-action playing, subtext analysis, subconscious impression playing, dialogue realism, kybernetic*

2

*attack, who-what-when-where-why-how theory, rhythmic movement, inner
and outer scenic environment adjustment,* etc.

This book gives practical advice on how to overcome the many
challenges, difficulties and problems which face the actor trying to
establish a career. It takes more than acting competence to reach and stay at
the top. Knowledge, experience and constant use of motivational techniques are the time-tested ways to gain success. This book includes easy-to-
understand principles of self-motivation which bring success in accordance
with the degree of their application.

Importantly, this book will influence you to attain a deeper understanding of the processes of human thought and feeling. This knowledge will
guide and inspire you to bring about well-balanced personal thought and
emotion patterns, resulting in a far happier and more creative way of life.

The benefits to be obtained from a study and practice of acting are not
reserved exclusively for professional actors. They are available to all
persons willing to devote time and effort to the application of the necessary
principles. If you are a person who is timid and withdrawn, you will find
acting a wonderful way to remove inhibitions and an excellent 'release
valve' for frustration, worry and anxiety. Stifling inhibitions and pent-up
emotions are personality detractors. They are barriers to social enjoyment,
creative self-expression and general well-being.

This book should be read systematically and regularly. Apply the
techniques and you will release the force of creativity within you. Tap your
hidden talents, exploit them and you will attract the success you desire. The
important thing is to begin *now*. Involve your attention steadily in the
acting project of your dreams. *Whatever holds attention determines action.*
And be reminded of Shakespeare's passage about those who fail to reach
their full potentiality:

> *Life's but a walking shadow, a poor player*
> *That struts and frets his hour upon the stage*
> *And then is heard no more.*

Determine your goals – what you want to *be* and *do*. Don't strut and fret
your hour upon the stage of life and then be heard no more. If acting is the
thing you love to do, then do it. When you are expressing your creativity
and giving of your talents to others, you are on the path to true and *lasting*
success.

BRIAN ADAMS

OSCAR
© A.M.P.A.S. ®

Since their inception in 1927, 'Oscars' have become the most respected of film awards anywhere. Members of the Academy of Motion Picture Arts and Sciences award them based solely on artistic and technical achievement. Best Actor and Best Actress Oscars for 1927-28 were awarded to *Emil Jannings* and *Janet Gaynor*.

THE PRINCIPLES
IN ORDER OF APPEARANCE

★★★

1: PRESENTATION

2: DEVELOPMENT

3: PERFORMANCE

John Seale, an AFI cinematographer award winner, lines up a crane shot with the Panavision 35mm motion picture camera. Seale gained valuable experience as a camera operator before advancing to director of photography status and his job of making actors look good on film through clever lighting. (Photo Ian Potter)

1:
PRESENTATION

★★★

COMMENT ...

I was introduced to showbusiness during my teen years in Australia. The excitement of setting that 'first foot' on a theatrical stage has never left me. My training as an actor and the greater part of my showbusiness experience came about in the hyper-active cities of Toronto, New York and Hollywood. As a young actor attempting to climb aboard the golden merry-go-round, I was quickly and some-what dramatically made aware of two essential requirements for screen success: carefully-prepared talent and meticulous personal presentation. The following five chapters are about *preparation and presentation.*

Actress checks schedule with floor manager during lull in production of television serial. (Photo Grundy Television)

THE PROFESSIONAL ACTOR *AND* ACTING AS A CAREER

SCENE 1

Practical Ideas in this Chapter . . .

- An Insight Into The Alluring World of Acting
- The Pros and Cons of Acting As A Career
- What Peter Sellers Had To Say About An Acting Career
- What An Acting Career Has To Offer In Positive Terms
- From Amateur To Professional – To Be Or Not To Be?
- How To Know Your Decision Is The Right One
- Get Your Worrying Done *Before* Not After You Decide
- A Word About The Amateur Actor
- From Amateur Actor To Extra Player
- The First Plateau – Achieving Professional Status
- Comments By Professionals On Professionalism
- Think Your Way To Professionalism
- 20 Personal Attributes Required To Join The *Professionals*
- Don't Waste Time – Be Ready When Opportunity Knocks
- Rod Steiger Changed His Life When Opportunity Knocked
- How To Cut Loose From Indolence And Spark Self-Action
- Summary of Ideas To Review

10

SCENE 1

★★★

1. AN INSIGHT INTO THE ALLURING WORLD OF ACTING

Hope – fortune's cheating lottery,
where for one prize, a hundred blanks
there be.

— COWLEY.

Hollywood, in spite of its decline over recent years, is still recognized as the movie capital of the world. It has another distinction – dubious though it might be – of possessing the world's largest burial ground of the hopes, wishes, dreams and expectations of countless unlucky acting aspirants.

The truth is, for every player contracted for a role on the screen, twenty, fifty, a hundred or more others lose out. And losing out more times than winning, facing constant rejection, being turned down without being told why, are just a few of the heavy burdens professional actors must learn to live with in order to survive in one of the most competitive of all professions.

A condition prevalent among actors, no matter where they may reside, is that at least 90 per cent of them are without acting employment at any given time. Stage actors are harder hit than screen actors, as theatre struggles to survive financially. How actors manage to survive both emotionally and financially during their periods of non-employment is a seldom-reported aspect of the profession. Many are forced to take jobs washing dishes, cleaning, serving in restaurants and general laboring. All of which can greatly erode an actor's confidence.

It's surprising how many acting aspirants embark upon a screen career without knowledge of the work problems and the stringent requirements of the industry they hope to conquer. Also, far too many lack proper training, bother to set career goals or have substantial reasons for wanting to become professional actors. The glamorous aspect of the business often dulls the harsh realities, hence the thousands of annual casualties.

There is a good deal more to the establishment of a career in acting than often meets the eye of the uninitiated. The requirements are demanding and the sacrifices constant. There are numerous pitfalls for the novice – as many an innocent has sadly discovered. Charlatans lurk at every corner eager to corrupt and exploit the unwary, naive person.

Acting is mentally strenuous and physically-exhausting work. Sometimes the rewards aren't commensurate with the time and energy expended. Wages can be pitifully low in proportion to the expertise demanded. An actor's life is not always to be envied. A great deal of time, effort and money needs to be spent on training, agent hunting, making the rounds of casting offices for interviews and attending auditions. Presentation materials need to be produced and clothes must be properly maintained. Mental and physical stamina is vital, a determination to succeed is essential.

Perhaps I've painted a bleak picture of the business of acting. It isn't totally so, but it is partly so. Beginners should be aware of the drawbacks before blindly leaping into an industry of doubtful rewards. There are no guarantees of success, no office-type employment structures where one advances more predictably in position and salary with each year of service.

There aren't too many people prepared to make the sacrifices acting as a career demands. It is best to understand, acknowledge and accept the rules of the game at the very beginning to avoid wasting precious time on a shot-in-the-dark chance at acting success. Apply the age-old maxim: *be sure you are right, then go ahead.*

2. THE PROS AND CONS OF ACTING AS A CAREER

Students who aspire to professional screen careers must face the fact that they will have a most difficult and challenging time ahead of them. Every year thousands of hopefuls try, very few succeed.

You may believe that in your case things will be different. You may feel that you will be discovered quickly and be offered roles immediately you turn professional. This is seldom the case. Most professional actors have to work years to gain even moderate success in terms of pay, industry acceptance and audience following.

Competition is fierce among the thousands of professionals who already have a head start on you. It is not encouraging to report that there are more actors than acting jobs and those who do secure roles receive no guarantee that when one job finishes another will be forthcoming.

The Screen Actors Guild often quotes in its publication *Screen Actor*, depressingly low incomes for the majority of its members. Approximately

90 per cent of actors under SAG jurisdiction earn less than $15,000 per annum. On the other hand, there are several hundred members who earn well in excess of $150,000 per annum and a select number receiving in excess of $500,000 per annum. There are stars who command one million dollars per picture or receive one million dollars or more per year as leads of successful television series.

Those actors who reach featured player or star status can and do become exceedingly wealthy and famous. Stardom brings benefits most people dream about. There will always be a need for star players. Perhaps your name will one day grace a theatre marquee. That's looking on the bright side. No one can deny that opportunity for success does exist for the *trier*. The point I make is: *nothing ventured, nothing gained*.

3. WHAT PETER SELLERS HAD TO SAY ABOUT AN ACTING CAREER

Film star, the late Peter Sellers, when asked by a television interviewer to give his views on acting as a worthwhile career replied: 'Fame comes at a price. You can be a middle-of-the-bill actor all your life, but if you want to make it and be a success, you have to pay the price acting demands. An actor requires patience, a strong constitution to withstand the hardships and setbacks. You have little privacy. You have to think twice before going anywhere. It's easier if you have confidence. I am an insecure person. It hasn't helped. Acting is hard work.'

Fame came to Peter Sellers. He worked hard to achieve it. He deserved it. Peter Sellers was a creative person – but so are you. You too can make your own unique creative contribution, be it large or small. But you must be prepared to make the sacrifices demanded of you if you want to reach the top.

4. WHAT AN ACTING CAREER HAS TO OFFER IN POSITIVE TERMS

Acting as a profession – a highly respected one – offers the careerist performer an opportunity to display talents, to contribute to a worthy art form, to join an elite group of skilled communicators and motivators, an opportunity to 'make good' as a creative individualist.

Then there's public adulation and large amounts of money. Wherever films are produced, stars are made. The monetary and other benefits of stardom are enviable. Two million dollars *plus* per picture is not an uncommon salary in today's movie-market for actors with world-wide appeal. Huge salaries attest to the value placed on star performers by producers.

One of the more appealing aspects of acting is the creative satisfaction which can come through performance. To create a living character from words supplied by an author is a wondrous experience. Every actor who works creatively adds something, no matter how small, to the art form. And this factor alone can bring a worthwhile feeling of artistic achievement.

5. FROM AMATEUR TO PROFESSIONAL – TO BE OR NOT TO BE?

Now, to the question: 'should I make acting a career?' A decision of this importance must, by necessity, be arrived at carefully and rationally. Commonsense must prevail. Emotion and ego need to be dispensed with. An analysis of your present *circumstances*, *needs* and *desires* must be thorough.

If you are holding a secure, well-paid position, cutting off your source of income could have disastrous consequences, particularly if you are a beginner without an agent, without training and experience. More to the point is the question of your talent. Do you possess the basic acting talent to develop into a top-ranking actor?

The sensible course to follow is to take your time. Enrol in a worthwhile school of acting and discover whether you are 'cut-out' for acting. Don't burn your bridges. Leaving a secure job too early in your career won't advance your cause.

Do not 'trust-to-luck' or listen to the advice of persons unqualified to advise you. Your future is at stake. It is too important to be guided by non-professional informants feeding you worthless information. Talk to professionals in the business of acting. Mix with working actors and question them as to the best trainers, agents and work opportunities. You will need the best information available in order to arrive at a sensible decision.

6. HOW TO KNOW YOUR DECISION IS THE RIGHT ONE

There are five questions you should analyse before deciding upon becoming an actor. They are:

(1) Do I have a basic talent for acting which can be developed?
(2) Am I willing to accept the rigorous demands, disciplines, disappointments and challenges an acting career involves?
(3) Am I willing to devote time, energy and money to study and professional training?
(4) Am I willing to move to another city or country if there aren't sufficient work opportunities where I reside?
(5) Do I now have or can I obtain sufficient financial backing to sustain my needs while establishing an acting career?

If you answer all five questions in the affirmative, chances are you can rest easily if you decide to become a professional actor. But remember, those who turn professional receive no guarantee of success when they receive a guild card.

7. GET YOUR WORRYING DONE BEFORE NOT AFTER YOU DECIDE

The American philosopher William James pointed out that, 'There is no more miserable human being than one in whom nothing is habitual but indecision.' It is necessary and prudent to take a reasonable amount of time when deciding on important issues, but do not allow yourself to fall into the habit of procrastination.

If you must worry at all, get it over *prior* to making a decision. The rule of proper decision making is to search for the facts, weigh the pros and cons, decide, then stick to the decision you've made. Worrying over a decision once made, won't change the outcome. Worry is no dissolver of problems. It can be a perpetuator of them. Arrive at a decision then forget *possible* consequences. It's done and that's that. Now focus your attention and give your energy to getting on with what has to be done.

8. A WORD ABOUT THE AMATEUR ACTOR

There are many consumers of drama who desire to be on the fringe of the business or who are content to take up acting as a hobby or for social reasons. Acting is an excellent outlet for frustration, for developing personality and securing self-confidence. It is a dignified way to meet new friends. Amateur community theatre is an avenue to explore if you do not desire to become a professional actor.

Commercial television programs and motion pictures do not have a place for the amateur actor. There are community centers that house television and film workshops where the amateur actor and director may take advantage of the equipment and training offered. A phone call to your local government office is the best way to locate these community facilities.

The deepest satisfactions for the amateur actor are often found through participation in a dramatics club and involvement in community theatre. A dramatics club usually conducts regular meetings to discuss drama and related subjects, produces one-act plays, gives play readings and organizes group attendance at professional productions. Sometimes a dramatics club will cast only from within its membership.

Community theatre often attracts a wide variety of talented people interested in drama production. Participating in community theatre is an excellent way to increase your dramatics experience by sharing your knowledge with other members. Casting for each production is, as a general rule, open to the general public. Local newspapers and libraries often carry announcements re casting and membership in community theatre groups.

9. FROM AMATEUR ACTOR TO EXTRA PLAYER

If you desire to gain first-hand knowledge and limited acting experience in television and films before making a decision to become a professional actor, then consider extra work. There are part-time extra players and professional full-time extra players. The professional extra can often make a reasonably good living if he or she lives in a major production center such as New York or Hollywood. Extra players require union membership.

Extra work is fairly well paid. The long hours spent on interior sets and exterior locations can be boring and energy draining. Extra players require patience and must be physically well to withstand the endless hours of standing around waiting to perform. Reliability is essential.

Directors like to work with professional full-time extras. Their experience is invaluable. They know when to 'come alive' and when to be inconspicuous in a scene. They know not to upstage line players. But one thing to keep in mind is this, in Hollywood, at least, if you begin your career as an extra, chances are it will end there. Few players who start as extras move out of extra work.

Extras work through agents or casting offices. A phone call to a theatrical agent will bring information as to pay scales, commissions payable, union requirements and work opportunities.

10. THE FIRST PLATEAU – ACHIEVING PROFESSIONAL STATUS

The first plateau of acting success is the rise from amateur to professional status. It's said that the only thing distinguishing an amateur actor from a professional actor is a piece of paper called a union card. In order to turn professional, that is, make money at it, it is necessary to hold membership in a theatrical union. However, a union card is no guarantee that the bearer is a 'professional' in the true sense. A union card offers the holder the right to seek work within the acting profession.

True professionalism begins as a state of mind. It is a specific attitude which dictates particular courses of action. Its roots are deeply embedded in an individual's attitude toward himself, toward things and toward people. It encompasses a willingness to watch, listen and to learn. It requires a selflessness, a dedication to perfecting the job that has to be done, of being conscious of the feelings of others, of being neither too obsequious or too arrogant, of not being frightened of failure or success.

A professional actor must be more than the holder of a union card seeking employment. The status which ought to be sought is to be recognized by peers as a true professional, a person who reliably does the job he/she was hired to do. No matter where you pursue your acting career, whether in Hollywood, New York, London, Sydney, Toronto, Paris, Rome, Madrid or your home town, your reputation travels ahead of you or follows you, but most assuredly always puts a *label* on you. Therefore, establish from the beginning of your career that you are going to be a competent, forthright, honest and uncomplicated actor dedicated to perfecting your talents.

The acting profession is an open door to those who qualify. There will always be a place for well-trained, well-adjusted, well-presented and talented actors. The goal is to achieve *professional status*. Once this has been accomplished, industry personnel in a position to assist, will be eager to do so.

11. COMMENTS BY PROFESSIONALS ON PRO-FESSIONALISM

Over the years, I've kept a written record of comments on professionalism I've overheard or read that have been made by all-time industry greats. Worth quoting are the following:

INGRID BERGMAN: It seems to me, an actor must dedicate his life to loving what he does. I've worked with a great many professionals and I admire them for being that.

HUMPHREY BOGART: Respect your trade. Perfect your work. Show up on time and know your lines.

CHARLES BRONSON: Know yourself. Don't be superficial. Present yourself to advantage on the screen. Play by instinct, but give your best. Be reliable. Be ready so you can grasp opportunity when it comes.

RICHARD BURTON: The camera is relentless, you have to know what you are doing. Get involved. Be the first on the set, word perfect.

JAMES CAGNEY: Take it all very seriously. Don't take advantage of others. But don't let others take advantage of you.

BETTE DAVIS: Actors must care about what they are doing. If it's worth doing then it's worth doing well. Don't hesitate to give acting all you've got. Work hard at it.

KIRK DOUGLAS: Acting is a heart-breaking business. You're using your emotions. You have success, you have failure. Each is difficult. Sometimes success is more difficult to handle. Develop some kind of humility, some kind of modesty. Acting is as disciplined as a piece of music. Be professional in everything you do – know what you are doing and why.

GREER GARSON: It's necessary to be conscious of the feelings of others. Selfishness isn't good in our work. Actors need to help fellow artists and crew members. We rely on one another.

SIR JOHN GIELGUD: Strip your work of its affectations. It is now a more realistic world. Play for realism. Build strong relationships. Contribute what you can in the best way you can. Be confident. Play without fear, without caution. And listen to others.

HELEN HAYES: Professionalism is doing what is expected of you well. Establish an air of friendliness and helpfulness. Give to others. Professionals are people who are a joy to work with.

KATHARINE HEPBURN: Behave with self-control. Show impeccable manners. Know your craft. Acting is a business requiring discipline. Seek absolute truth in your work. But don't take yourself too seriously. Develop so much energy you don't seem ever to get tired.

LOUIS JOURDAN: Searching for the truth should be every actor's occupation. I think discipline contributes to professionalism.

WALTER MATTHAU: I never say anything I don't mean.

LAURENCE OLIVIER: Flair, practice, determination, courage, dedication – that's professionalism. Acting great parts devours you. To be a star you've got to have a certain edge, a flair for acting in any medium. Don't be tiresome, difficult or temperamental.

GREGORY PECK: This profession means a lot to me, because acting is a profession and not a flash-in-the-pan thing. It requires dedication. A promise to yourself to do the best you can.

NEHEMIAH PERSOFF: Find an involvement with real life, establish relationships with other members of the cast.

ANTHONY QUINN: It's dedication, morality, being discreet, bold, confident. Be willing to learn, to listen. That's professionalism.

DIANA RIGG: Get an appetite for work. Acting is an art. To be lucky enough to be successful in it is a gift and you must keep working at it. But it is a question of getting your balance right. That is, have interests other than acting.

BARBARA STANWYCK: Become a superb technician. Do not bring your problems to the set. They can create problems for others.

JOHN WAYNE: Acting is damned hard work. It's not something to fool around with. Too many people come to rely on you, put their trust in you. Professionalism is not letting them down.

12. THINK YOUR WAY TO PROFESSIONALISM

It is obvious from the foregoing statements of stars past and present that professionalism is very much a way of *thinking* and *acting* which contributes not only to your own welfare but to the welfare of others.

Build into your consciousness a set of values which become your guide for all you say and do. If you display a personality which lacks discipline, shows little respect for others, then others will see you as an actor who is *less* than professional and not want to hire you or work with you.

Think of yourself as a professional in every respect. Treat others as you wish others to treat you. Be fair, just, honorable, reliable, conscientious and respectful. Develop confidence about yourself as a performer. You need the very special self-confidence displayed by professionals – confidence to offset discouragement, setbacks, unkind press stories and reviews, turn-downs by agents and producers – as you seek stardom. A professional attitude allows you to get on well with people. It is your defence against negative circumstances should they arise.

13. DON'T WASTE TIME — BE READY WHEN OPPORTU-NITY KNOCKS

Wasted time often means wasted opportunity. Careerist actors cannot afford to mark time, wait around to be discovered or do precious little to develop their talents. People who 'loiter' in life seldom achieve anything worthwhile. Success has a habit of by-passing indolent people. It has a habit of bestowing its blessings on active people.

Charles Dickens, showing great insight, wrote: *of all the swindlers of the world, there is none greater than the self-swindler, robbing the self of time, opportunity, creativity.* It's a wonderful statement worthy of typing on a

20 PERSONAL ATTRIBUTES REQUIRED TO JOIN THE

PROFESSIONALS

- ☐ 1. DEDICATION TO YOUR CRAFT
- ☐ 2. UNSELFISH ATTITUDE
- ☐ 3. DISCIPLINED THOUGHTS AND EMOTIONS
- ☐ 4. CO-OPERATIVE WITH FELLOW ARTISTS
- ☐ 5. PUNCTUAL AT *ALL* TIMES
- ☐ 6. PERSONABLE AND COURTEOUS
- ☐ 7. SINCERE AND TRUTHFUL
- ☐ 8. DECISIVE
- ☐ 9. COMPASSIONATE
- ☐ 10. IMAGINATIVE
- ☐ 11. AMBITIOUS
- ☐ 12. SELF-ASSURED
- ☐ 13. PERSISTENT
- ☐ 14. KNOWLEDGEABLE
- ☐ 15. WELL ORGANIZED
- ☐ 16. TALENTED AS A *CREATIVE* ARTIST
- ☐ 17. COURAGE OF CONVICTIONS
- ☐ 18. SENSE OF HUMOR
- ☐ 19. SOCIALLY REFINED
- ☐ 20. EFFECTIVE COMMUNICATOR-MOTIVATOR

 Place a check-mark alongside each attribute you believe you possess. A score of 20 makes you a front-runner in the acting stakes.

3 x 5 card to be read each time indolence rears its head.

It's been said that screen stardom is 'in the lap of the gods'. I believe stardom rests with each individual who seeks it. The reason many actors fail is because they are not prepared to invest time, energy and money in what is expected of them. They seek something for nothing. As Dickens said, they are 'self-swindlers'. Actors who desire true expression and recognition of their talents must be prepared to make sacrifices, to work hard to succeed. The lazy way may be the easy way through life, but it is not the way to high achievement.

Seldom does opportunity give warning as to when and where it will present itself. The important thing is to be ready when it comes. It rarely knocks twice. Start *now* and involve your time and attention steadily on your desire to become a professional actor. Don't waste precious time. To be truly active and productive is to be always developing and building toward success. Life will take on new meaning when you become *involved* in worthwhile pursuits.

14. ROD STEIGER CHANGED HIS LIFE WHEN OPPORTUNITY KNOCKED

Rod Steiger faced a bleak period in his life when 'certain problems' created a deep state of depression. He experienced ill-health, underwent heart surgery, then volunteered for psychiatric therapy.

'I was in bad shape,' he said. 'It was affecting my confidence and ability to remember lines. I needed to talk to somebody. That's why I went to an analyst. He reminded me of my past successes and convinced me that I could enjoy new ones if only I would allow myself to get active again. I have learned to stop feeling sorry for myself.'

Steiger, on the suggestion of his analyst, was urged to take up counseling. Having played an analyst in *The Mark*, it was put to him that he should play one in real life. He was excited by the idea. Here was an opportunity to help himself and at the same time help others in distress. Boredom, loneliness and idleness gave way to mental stimulation, joy and productive activity. Rodney Stephan Steiger's life changed quickly, dramatically and beneficially.

15. HOW TO CUT LOOSE FROM INDOLENCE AND SPARK SELF-ACTION

Inactivity is a breeding ground for loneliness, fear, anxiety and depression. These negative states of mind take the shine off personality, thwart ambition, destroy creativity and encourage laziness. Failure isn't far behind.

Booker T. Washington, the most influential black leader and educator of his time in the United States, wrote: *No idle person is ever safe, whether he be rich or poor, white or black, educated or illiterate.* Get yourself moving in life. Idle days are wasted days. *Go forward!* Don't mark time. Get active in something — *anything*. Become totally absorbed in planning your career, in

20

study and training, in preparing yourself for acting opportunities and in helping others on a voluntary basis. Honest activity cannot hurt you in any way. Chances are, it will do a great deal of good for you when you least expect it. When you contribute to the welfare and success of others, the good you do boomerangs.

It is your right to be whatever you choose to be. You are on this earth to express yourself in a creative and successful way. You are here to fulfill your dreams and ambitions, to lead the abundant life and to be happy, well and free. You cannot achieve these things if your mind and body are indolent. You've got to get your life into high gear, make something of yourself, contribute something so that life has a special meaning for you.

All your experiences, events, circumstances, actions, are but the reflections and reactions to your thoughts, feelings and beliefs. An affirmative, *active* consciousness produces faith, confidence and expectancy. It knows no defeat. It doesn't let you down when the going gets tough. The happiest man, the creative man, the successful man is he who is active, dedicated, striving to grow, develop and improve.

Cut loose from indolence. Don't sit passively waiting for miracles to occur in your life. If you do, you'll live more by reaction instead of gearing your life to success through affirmative self-action. Charge your mind with self-motivating thoughts. Be full of praise, encouragement, good-will and optimism. *Get on fire!* Fall in love with life. *Be productive!* Success won't be far behind.

> *Indolence is the dry rot of even a good mind and a good character; the practical uselessness of both. It is the waste of what might be a happy and useful life.*
> — Tryon Edwards

SUMMARY OF IDEAS TO REVIEW

1: An acting career demands a great deal of mental and physical stamina. Don't let the glamorous aspect dull the harsh realities.

2: Some actors get rich. Most do not. It may take several years to establish a worthwhile career. Don't rely on overnight stardom.

3: Peter Sellers said, 'Acting is hard work.' Be prepared to work hard.

4: A positive aspect of acting is the creative satisfaction which can come through performance. This, plus a reasonable income are the rewards.

5: If you desire to move into the professional acting ranks, be sure to fulfill the requirements. Seek the best training. Determine your talent and its potential.

6: Ease into the profession by working as an extra, but only for a short time until you get a 'feeling' for the business. In Hollywood, if you begin your career as an extra, it could end there.

7: The first plateau to reach is professional status. Professionals are reliable, talented, considerate, courteous, pleasant people.

8: Don't waste time. Become involved in achieving your aims. Opportunity seldom knocks twice. Be ready to make your mark should opportunity arise.

9: Rod Steiger faced a bleak period in his life but learned to stop feeling sorry for himself. He became active — mentally and physically. It changed his life. Change your life. *Get on fire!* Go after what you want.

10: Inactivity is a breeding ground for loneliness and depression. Cut loose from indolence and motivate yourself to productivity. You can achieve a lot by spending your time wisely, by preparing for the career you desire. Lazy people seldom win. You are on this earth to express yourself in a creative way. You were born to succeed.

LAYING THE FOUNDATIONS FOR A REWARDING SCREEN CAREER

SCENE 2

Practical Ideas In This Chapter . . .

- Prepare A Personal Study Program
- Study Allied Arts To Complement Your Acting Knowledge
- Brando Studied Many Subjects To Improve His Acting Ability
- How To Use This Book To Reap The Most Benefit
- How To Increase Reading Speed Without Loss of Comprehension
- How To Improve Retention of Study Material
- *Five* Suggestions To Make Study Periods Productive
- *Two* Indispensable Aids To Assist in Your Study of Acting
- A Personal Library Puts You In The Company of Great Minds
- Suggested Reading Material
- Library Starter List 1
- Library Starter List 2
- Extend Your Knowledge of the 'Theatre of Life'
- *Five* Valuable Self-Training Aids (Chart)
- Scrapbook And Files — Your Personal Encyclopedia
- Education And Specialized Acting Training
- Acting Workshops And Drama Schools
- The First Step To Getting What You Want
- Architect's Advice Is Valuable For Career-Minded Actors
- The Marx Rule-of-Thumb Theory Is Funny But Impractical
- A Goals List And Action Plan Help Materialize Your Dreams
- The *Action* Plan (Chart)
- Affirmations Inspire Confidence For High Achievement
- Actress Used Affirmation Technique To Win Role
- You Go Where Your Vision Is
- Remain True To Your Goals — Don't Be Swayed By Others
- Summary of Ideas To Review

SCENE 2

★★★

1. PREPARE A PERSONAL STUDY PROGRAM

Learning the ways and means of acting places a definite burden on the monetary resources, the energy and the *time* of the learner. The task is a challenging one. It is hard work. It doesn't come free. But it's worthwhile if taken seriously.

Study and learning, to be useful, should be undertaken with a sense of positive expectation and enthusiasm. It should be regular and organized. A lazy, haphazard, disinterested approach is time wasting. Therefore, if you earnestly desire to join the ranks of the professionals, then approach the learning process with this goal in mind: *to absorb as much as possible, as quickly as possible, the theory of acting.*

The reason many actors fail to get ahead is because they aren't qualified to handle complex roles. Don't waste time dreaming about stardom. Don't postpone study and training. Begin today — *now*! Become active in seeking ways to develop your mind, expand your knowledge and improve your talents.

Prepare a personal study program. Set aside a specific period each day for reading, note-taking, voice and speech development and physical exercise to improve movement. Even one hour per day *every* day will bring noticeable results almost immediately. It will help to stimulate your mind and body, safeguarding them from negative thoughts which produce destructive emotions and rob the body of vitality. Do not break your daily routine of study and exercise. Your untiring efforts to gain knowledge and improve your talents will not go unrewarded when opportunities come your way.

2. STUDY ALLIED ARTS TO COMPLEMENT YOUR ACTING KNOWLEDGE

The contents of this book are designed not only to present acting methods, but to guide, challenge and motivate you to seek a greater awareness of life and of human experience. This task of search and enquiry ought not to begin and end with the reading of one book, but should relate to the reading and study of other works, other subjects and the development of interests other than acting. Don't confine your knowledge and experience to just one sphere of life.

Begin a study of the allied arts: music, dance, art, sculpture, literature, architecture, interior design, costume design, directing. Expansion of your knowledge will bring greater appreciation and easier application of the acting principles outlined in this work. It will help to actualize your acting goal, give you a keener understanding and appreciation of art and humanity and improve your taste and judgement generally.

3. BRANDO STUDIED MANY SUBJECTS TO IMPROVE HIS ACTING ABILITY

Marlon Brando is intensely interested in subjects other than acting. Interested in human beings, their problems and causes, he donates his time and large amounts of money to movements which appeal to his social conscience, like the rights of American Indians, famine relief, UNICEF and UNESCO. He lives the life of the inquisitive, knowledge-seeking actor seven days a week. He likes to absorb everything around him, some say in a child-like way.

During his early acting years in New York, Brando took courses in psychology, graphology, the history of art, French, in addition to acting lessons with Stella Adler, Elia Kazan and at The Dramatic Workshop of the New School for Social Research. He loves to travel. It gives him the opportunity to meet and study people, soak-up new experiences and appreciate different cultures.

Asked by a British journalist to give his views on acting and suggestions helpful to newcomers, Brando replied: 'Acting is as old as mankind. It wasn't invented with the theatre. If you want to bring truth to acting you've got to study mankind, know the psychology of mankind. Human nature, the behavior of people, they've always fascinated me. Actors must observe and I enjoy that part of it. I could sit all day and just watch people go by. You learn so much. I study the allied arts. I spend a lot of time reading philosophy and psychology. Actors should do this.'

Brando is a controversial figure in the profession. Few would oppose his approach to acting study. He admits that without an insight into the human psyche, he wouldn't have been equipped to give the shatteringly poignant character portrait in *On The Waterfront*, for which he received an Oscar.

4. HOW TO USE THIS BOOK TO REAP THE MOST BENEFIT

In his book *Make The Most of Your Time,** J. Maurus writes: *For the mind's nourishment, reading is essential. Minds feed on minds. You read a man's book and you grow with its riches.* Reading books can pay handsome dividends providing there is understanding of the content. In order to grow in knowledge and wisdom through reading, absorb, digest and retain what you read. Put your knowledge to work.

Use this book as a reference manual. Read and re-read it, often. Do not skim-through the pages. Read carefully. Ideas sink in slowly. Superficial learning is not lasting. Concentrate as you read. Discover the techniques and ideas valuable to you and allow your mind sufficient time to absorb all that you read.

The first reading of this book should be completed without interruption. Subsequent readings can then be of specific chapters in a precise study of the ideas, suggestions and methods of acting each chapter contains. *Think* about what you read. *Evaluate* it. Can the techniques be individualized to your own specific needs? Personal development comes about through understanding and *practice* of acquired knowledge.

5. HOW TO INCREASE READING SPEED WITHOUT LOSS OF COMPREHENSION

An average reader's rate is about 200 to 300 words per minute. A trained reader can read at the rate of 1,500 to 2,000 words per minute with equal comprehension. Methods to increase reading speed without undue loss of comprehension include:

1: Take in several words at a single glance instead of reading word-by-word.
2: Look for *key words* in a sentence which give clues to meaning.
3: Look for *key ideas* within a paragraph which indicate meaning.
4: Reduce the amount of lip movement as you read silently.
5: Don't go back over what you have read. Train your eyes and mind to read at a steady rate continuously.
6: Discipline your mind to *concentrate* on what you are reading. This negates the practice of going back over material just read because you aren't paying sufficient attention to your reading.
7: Adjust your rate of reading to different kinds of material. Novels can be read at a faster rate than text books.
8: Use a ruler to isolate each line. It restricts the eyes to reading one line at a time, thus avoiding 'skipping' of lines.
9: Do not force yourself to read study material when you feel unwell.
10: Clear your mind of worries before you settle down to absorb study material.

*Make The Most of Your Time, J. Maurus. Better Yourself Books

6. HOW TO IMPROVE RETENTION OF STUDY MATERIAL

Some actors admit to possessing a 'poor memory'. If your mind is healthy, there is no such malady. Poor memory is usually an excuse for loss of concentration due to lack of mind discipline.

Your mind's memory banks are superior to the largest and most sophisticated computer. In a lifetime it is estimated that an individual's long-term memory can record and store up to one million billion separate pieces of information. IBM's largest computer is capable of storing 256 million pieces of information. The mind of man is a colossal instrument, much undervalued and grossly underused.

Memory is a range of processes which includes impression, recognition and recall. Your memory will function brilliantly when you become *involved, interested in, absorbed* and *moved* by the things you see, hear and read.

Don't admit to yourself that you suffer from so-called poor memory. The key to remembering what you see, hear and read is discipline of thought movement. Don't allow random thoughts to enter your consciousness when your total attention is required to absorb important information. Become mentally alert. Really *listen* to others when they speak to you. Really *see* what needs to be viewed and retained and really *absorb* information contained in material you read.

7. *FIVE* SUGGESTIONS TO MAKE STUDY PERIODS PRODUCTIVE

Quite often we spend time reading and later forget much of what we have read. Unproductive reading time can be avoided by focusing the attention on study material without a lapse in concentration. Some factors related to poor concentration are: tiredness, noise distractions, ill health and boredom.

When studying a text where knowledge of the subject matter is to be retained, the important and time-conserving things to do are:

(1) **CONTROL THE MOVEMENT OF YOUR THOUGHTS:** focus total attention on what you are reading. Do not allow unrelated thoughts to criss-cross your consciousness. When the mind is not alert, is inattentive, reading information is not absorbed into the subconscious, the storehouse of all our knowledge and experience.

(2) **PLACE YOURSELF IN ISOLATION:** distractions cause reading delay and loss of concentration, resulting in less comprehension of the material being read. Sit comfortably in a quiet place. Do not have radio, television or recorded music playing. Music played even at low volume can distract your train-of-thought, causing you to daydream.

(3) **READ SYSTEMATICALLY:** do not skip or skim over pages. Read paragraph-by-paragraph, page-by-page, chapter-by-chapter. You

will find that this method is best for comprehension of the text.

(4) **UNDERSCORE WORTHWHILE IDEAS:** underscoring saves searching through chapters to find passages you wish to re-read. Use a colored marker to underline or to score through important text passages.

(5) **WRITE DOWN YOUR INTERPRETATION OF TECHNIQUES:** use a loose-leaf book to compile key formulas. Use your own phraseology instead of copying word-for-word key ideas. This gets your mind engrossed in what you are studying and helps you to quickly grasp the meaning of the text

8. *TWO* INDISPENSABLE AIDS TO ASSIST IN YOUR STUDY OF ACTING

For the five hundred most commonly-used words in the English language, the dictionary lists approximately 14,000 meanings. Words are the basic *tools of trade* of the writer and of the actor. As an actor's job is to interpret the ideas suggested by the words of a writer and then articulate them in a precise and meaningful way, a study of words needs to be undertaken to grasp their meaning and correct pronunciation. This ensures that the actor communicates to the listener the *exact* meaning of the writer's work.

Two important aids an actor may consult to bring about correct pronunciation and clear understanding of words are:

1: a *dictionary*
2: a *thesaurus* of English words and phrases

A thesaurus is a reference book of words grouped by ideas. With a dictionary you know the word and need to find its meaning so it is listed alphabetically. With a thesaurus you have the idea and you want the right word to express it, so all the words and phrases are classified according to ideas. A thesaurus gives a range of synonyms (words that have similar or related meanings) and this is helpful in improving oral communication. Misuse of words is minimized by thoughtful and constant use of a dictionary and thesaurus.

9. A PERSONAL LIBRARY PUTS YOU IN THE COMPANY OF GREAT MINDS

You will find it helpful in continuing your studies to have a personal library of good books and plays to which you can refer as frequently as desired. Good books and plays present an opportunity to meet great minds and share in their wisdom and knowledge.

Begin immediately to build your personal library and commence a regular reading program. Reading books and plays is one of the most productive and self-satisfying ways to spend your leisure hours.

10. SUGGESTED READING MATERIAL

If your budget restricts the purchase of many books, borrow them from a public library. Thousands of excellent books have been written on drama and the allied arts. Visits to community libraries will turn up many of these volumes including everything from translations of the ancient Greek and Roman dramas to the latest Broadway and London plays.

Start your personal library with hardcover, thumb-indexed editions of a dictionary and thesaurus. Paperback editions may tempt you because of their lower cost, but they have fewer entries and their binding materials seldom can withstand prolonged use. Gradually add textbooks on acting, play production, television and motion picture production, writing and directing. As soon as possible add the works of Shakespeare, a history of the theatre, biographies and autobiographies of actors, directors, famous people in history, anthologies and good novels. Be sure to include works on the allied arts and time-tested plays.

Actor Louis Jourdan maintains that actors should engage themselves in a 'quest for truth' to be found in good books. 'I read books that I know I can re-read. They must be serious books, ones that will teach me something of life. I'm searching for the truth. That's my present occupation,' he says.

Vincent Price is another actor who believes that good books help to make life more meaningful, exciting and successful to those dedicated to reading. Mr. Price is an actor of diverse talents and interests. He is a scholar, author, chef, lecturer, raconteur and art collector. 'It is possible to explore every facet of life through books. Actors need them,' he feels.

My personal library is extensive and I use it for research not only for acting roles but for the writing, directing and lecturing I do. When I hosted *Adams at Noon* (USA), *Adams After Noon* and the *Tonight Show* (Australia), it was necessary to do a great deal of research in connection with the interviews I conducted. Knowledge of a wide-range of subjects was essential. Books were an invaluable aid. For the talk-back radio show and the television series *Around The World*, which I wrote and hosted, reference books were the backbone of both shows. I could not have performed in a competent way without them.

An extensive personal library requires a sizeable investment. Perhaps if you are experiencing a shortage of funds, a word dropped to family and friends that books would be welcome as gifts on special occasions, will lessen the burden on your finances.

The larger the collection of good books and the more you read and absorb the information they contain, the more knowledgeable and wiser you are likely to become. And, as a bonus, you will be able to communicate and argue from a substantially better base of information than the less than well-read person. Good books are a *good* investment.

LIBRARY STARTER LIST
1

ACTING:
Actors On Acting — Toby Cole – Helen Krich Chinoy
An Actor Prepares and *Building A Character* and *Creating a Role* — Constantin Stanislavski
How To Make It In Hollywood — Wende Hyland & Roberta Haynes
The Dynamics of Acting — Joan Snyder
Training The Speaking Voice — Virgil Anderson
Working Up A Part — H. Darkes Albright

ALLIED ARTS:
A Treasury of Art Masterpieces from The Renaissance to the Present Day — Thomas Craven
Borzoi Book of Modern Dance — Margaret Lloyd
The Music Lovers Handbook — Elie Siegmeister

PRODUCTION – DIRECTION — PLAYWRITING:
A Practical Manual of Screen Playwriting — Lewis Herman
A-Z of Movie Making — Wolf Rilla
The Art of Dramatic Writing — Lajos Egri
The Director in The Theatre and *Constructing A Play* — Marian Gallaway
The Film Director — Richard L. Bare
The Five C's of Cinematography — Joseph V. Mascelli
The Technique of Television Production — Gerald Millerson

NOVELS:
For The Term of His Natural Life — Marcus Clarke
Les Misèrables — Victor Hugo
Raymond Chandler (6 novel volume) — Raymond Chandler
Rudyard Kipling (6 novel volume) — Rudyard Kipling
The Grapes of Wrath — John Steinbeck
The Novels of Dashiell Hammett — Dashiell Hammett
The Sun Also Rises — Ernest Hemingway
The Sound and the Fury — William Faulkner
Ulysses — James Joyce
War and Peace — Leo Tolstoy

OTHER:
Emerson's Essays — Ralph Waldo Emerson
Five Great Dialogues — Plato
History of The Film — Maurice Bardèche – Robert Brasillach
How To Succeed — Brian Adams
Olivier — Logan Gourlay
On Film Making — King Vidor
Run-through — John Houseman
The Name Above The Title — Frank Capra
The Screen Arts — Edward Fischer
The Theatre - 3000 Years of Drama, Acting & Stagecraft — S. Cheney
Theatre Handbook and Digest of Plays — Bernard Sobel

LIBRARY STARTER LIST
2

PLAYS:
A Doll's House — Henrik Ibsen
A Man For All Seasons — Robert Bolt
A Taste of Honey — Shelagh Delaney
Ah, Wilderness — Eugene O'Neill
Arsenic And Old Lace — Joseph Kesselring
Barefoot In The Park — Neil Simon
Blithe Spirit — Noel Coward
Born Yesterday — William Inge
Bus Stop — William Inge
Cheaper By The Dozen — Perry Clark
Cyrano De Bergerac — Edmond Rostand
Deathtrap — Ira Levin
Death of A Salesman — Arthur Miller
Detective Story — Sidney Kingsley
Dinner At Eight — George S. Kaufman – Edna Ferber
Elizabeth The Queen — Maxwell Anderson
Films Scenes For Actors — Edited by Joshua Karton
I Remember Mama — John Van Druten
Laura — Vera Caspary – George Sklar
Little Women — John D. Ravold
Look Back In Anger — John Osborne
Morning Becomes Electra — Eugene O'Neill
My Sister Eileen — Joseph Fields – Jerome Chodorov
Of Mice And Men — John Steinbeck
Our Town — Thornton Wilder
Pygmalion — George Bernard Shaw
Stage Door — Edna Ferber – George S. Kaufman
Streetcar Named Desire — Tennessee Williams
The Barretts of Wimpole Street — Rudolph Besier
The Cherry Orchard — Anton Chekhov
The Children's Hour — Lillian Hellman
The Diary of Anne Frank — Frances Goodrich – Albert Hackett
The Glass Menagerie — Tennessee Williams
The Hasty Heart — John Patrick
The Importance of Being Ernest — Oscar Wilde
The Little Foxes — Lillian Hellman
The Man Who Came To Dinner — George S. Kaufman – Moss Hart
Who's Afraid of Virginia Woolf? — Edward Albee
Wuthering Heights — Randolph Carter
William Shakespeare volume of complete works:
All's Well That Ends Well, Antony and Cleopatra, As You Like It, A Midsummer Night's Dream, Coriolanus, Cymbeline, Hamlet, Henry IV (parts I and II), *Henry V, Henry VI* (parts I, II, III), *Henry VIII, Julius Caesar, King John, King Lear, Love's Labour's Lost, Macbeth, Measure for Measure, Much Ado About Nothing, Othello, Pericles, Richard II, Richard III, Romeo and Juliet, The Comedy of Errors, The Merchant of Venice, The Merry Wives of Windsor, The Taming of the Shrew, The Tempest, The Two Gentlemen of Verona, The Winter's Tale, Timon of Athens, Titus Andronicus, Troilus and Cressida, Twelfth Night.*

11. EXTEND YOUR KNOWELDGE OF THE 'THEATRE OF LIFE'

Since it is difficult to convey to an audience something which you yourself may know little, you require, as an actor, knowledge and appreciation of a wide-range of subjects: history, politics, science, medicine, religion, electronics, economic trends, sports, current events, as well as the arts. The *theatre of life* covers people, places and things of importance.

Katharine Hepburn maintains that acting is a business requiring tremendous discipline and a great deal of knowledge on the part of actors. 'There are,' she says, 'so many thrilling things to learn. Things we actors must know of and use in our performances. I regret I have wasted a certain amount of time. Time I could have used in studying life.'

Carry out a program of study and research through reading. Attend evening college extension courses. Keep informed by reading newspaper editorials, magazine articles. Subscribe to trade and business journals. Watch television current events programs, documentaries and travel programs. Attend lectures, film screenings, plays and concerts. Know something of many subjects to gain a broader appreciation of the world around you. By looking at the world with a 'dramatic eye' and understanding it a little better, you build a reservoir or material from which to draw your many stage characters.

One of the best general reference tools available to an actor is an encyclopedia. I have found *The World Book Encyclopedia** an invaluable research tool, particularly the section on 'how to do research'. It includes advice on planning an assignment, locating information, the right books and articles to read, conducting an interview, writing a report, giving oral reports, lists of audio-visual materials available and other significant information.

12. FIVE VALUABLE SELF-TRAINING AIDS

There are five helpful *career assistants* worthy of purchase. The cost of these self-training aids — when ammortized over a period of several years — is relatively inexpensive in relation to their value. They are:

(1) metronome
(2) audio recorder
(3) video recorder
(4) video camera
(5) typewriter

METRONOME: this is a clock-work device with an inverted pendulum that beats time at a rate determined by the position of the sliding weight on the pendulum. It is used to help maintain regular tempo when practicing music. An excellent actor's assistant to help regulate tempo and pace of dialogue as it is practiced.

*World Book-Childcraft International, Inc.

AUDIO RECORDER: beneficial to the development of voice and speech. A recorder allows recording and playback of speech exercises to detect incorrect sounds, pronunciation, emphasis and meaning.

VIDEO RECORDER: training programs, documentaries, current events programs, commercials, teleplays and motion pictures can be recorded (copyright permitting) for study purposes. Current and classic motion pictures are available for hire or purchase on video cassette.

VIDEO CAMERA: when used in conjunction with a video recorder, a camera allows visual coverage of audition pieces and scenes to be rehearsed for analysis during replay.

TYPEWRITER: typing skill is valuable for several reasons:

(1) A character you are to play is required to be seen typing. It is best that the character appears to actually type rather than pretend to type.

(2) Letters, lecture notes, resumès, biographies can be self-typed, rather than having to pay others to type them.

(3) Extra income can be earned at home by typing for others.

A typewriter can be an efficient work-tool as well as an income producer. Stage and screen actress, Ruth Cracknell, says typing is a skill all actors should acquire. 'I've never regretted learning to type,' she admits. Her typing ability produced much needed income during her beginning years in acting.

13. SCRAPBOOK AND FILES — YOUR PERSONAL ENCYCLOPEDIA

In order to make available for continuing study, lecture notes, articles, pictures, play programs, reviews and kindred subject matter that you collect, it is advisable to keep a scrapbook, a notebook and card files. In short order you will have a valuable source of study material.

Your scrapbook can be as simple or as elaborate as your pocketbook allows. A large loose-leaf book is suggested. Newspapers and magazines are the basic sources from which you will collect your file material. Feature stories on stage, screen and TV performers, reviews of plays, teleplays and films are worthy of collection.

Notebooks should be loose-leaf and divided into sections such as: performance ideas and techniques, reports on lectures, personal reviews of plays and films, new words, their meaning and correct pronunciation, books to be read, etc. A 3 x 5 card filing system is also suggested. Give each card a heading such as: speech exercises, personality traits observed, success affirmations, playing techniques, etc.

Your permanent records should not only be a source of well-organized information on the performing and allied arts, but a source of pleasure and pride. The ultimate value of your material will be determined by how carefully it has been selected and classified and how often it is used.

— FIVE VALUABLE SELF-TRAINING AIDS —

(1) Metronome

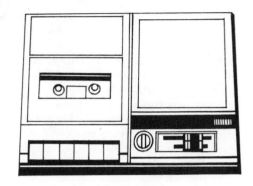

(2) Audio Recorder

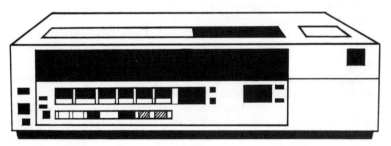

(3) Videotape Recorder

(4) Video Camera

(5) Typewriter

14. EDUCATION AND SPECIALIZED ACTING TRAINING

It is not necessary to hold a university degree in order to become a professional actor. It *is* necessary to have a well-rounded education — self taught or otherwise — in order to become a knowledgeable, intelligent actor. Illiteracy is a definite handicap in the profession of acting.

The English actor-manager, Sir Herbert Beerbohm Tree, is reported to have said: 'An actor should know something of everything and not too much of anything.' It is not expected that an actor be either a genius or stupid, but it is expected that an actor be both knowledgeable and intelligent. A broad, general background of knowledge and interests should be acquired and intelligently applied.

Plays, teleplays and screenplays refer to people and events in history, music, literature, philosophy, science, medicine, religion, politics and current events. The more you know of these fields of endeavor and of people, places and things, the better equipped you will be to understand and play the roles you hope to be offered.

In addition to a certain amount of formal education, you will require specialized training in acting. Speech and dialogue lessons, movement and dance lessons, acting theory and scene-study classes, video and film camera training are readily available through commercial acting schools in most cities. Selecting a legitimate acting school is important. Beware of the school that promises work. Phone a talent agency, talk to a working actor, call your local actor's union and ask their advice as to suitable training establishments.

Specialized schools of acting and allied performing arts schools exist in every city. If you are unable to receive a recommendation to a school, consult a telephone directory to obtain addresses and telephone numbers of drama schools in your area. Visit them and inspect their facilities. Talk to their instructors and students. Study their curricula, then make up your mind as to the school which best suits your needs. If it is possible to monitor classes before joining, then do so. This is the best way to judge the merits of an acting school and its teachers.

If, eventually, you wish to become a teacher of drama at a college or university, an academic qualification is necessary. Nearly all universities offer a program in theatre arts. Some universities gear their courses toward careers in professional theatre. Select a university that is recognized by theatre and industry professionals as being of high standard. Those schools without a good reputation in drama do not carry much influence with producers, directors and casting people. For the actor, a drama degree, as worthy as it may be, does not mark the bearer as a front-rank actor. However, the training received should prove to be beneficial.

15. ACTING WORKSHOPS AND DRAMA SCHOOLS

It is impossible to list here, all universities and commercial acting schools that show promise. A list of that nature would require a book in itself. I can offer a personal recommendation to those who wish to train in New York.

Having studied at *The Neighborhood Playhouse*, I know its attitude toward discipline and training of the actor and therefore place it high on the list of worthy schools. One of the best teachers in speech is Robert Neff Williams who (at the time of writing) teaches at the *Juilliard School.*

Acceptance to the better schools is via personal interview and audition. Write a letter to the registrar enquiring as to the prescribed procedure for enrolment. A short list of schools is offered taking in the cities of New York, Los Angeles, London and Sydney.

DRAMA SCHOOLS

NEW YORK:
Actors Studio
Stella Adler
American Academy of Dramatic Art
Herbert Berghof – Uta Hagen
Wynn Handman
Juilliard School
The Neighborhood Playhouse School of the Theatre
LOS ANGELES:
Film Industry Workshops Inc.
Vincent Chase Workshop
The Nina Foch Studio
Tracy Roberts
Lee Strasberg Theatre Institute
LONDON:
Royal Academy of Dramatic Art (RADA)
SYDNEY:
Australian TV Film Industry Workshop
Ensemble Theatre School
National Institute of Dramatic Art (NIDA)

UNIVERSITIES AND COLLEGES USA

Carnegie – Mellon University, Pittsburgh PA
Los Angeles City College, Los Angeles, CA
New York University, New York, NY
Northwestern University, Evanston, IL
The Juilliard School, New York, NY
The University of California Los Angeles, Los Angeles, CA
University of Iowa, Iowa City, IA
University of Southern California, Los Angeles, CA
Yale Drama School, New Haven, CT
NOTE: *Consult the annual directory of the American Theatre Association (ATA) for a complete listing of schools that offer degrees in theatre arts. Most libraries carry this publication.**

*USA only. In other countries direct enquiries to a US Consul office.

16. THE FIRST STEP TO GETTING WHAT YOU WANT

It isn't so-called luck that attracts success but well-organized plans and hard work. Actors who count on luck to bring them good-fortune seldom do more than wait for something to turn up. It hardly ever does. In place of achievement comes boredom, frustration, fear, anxiety, worry and dissipation of energy and time.

To attract success in any field of endeavor, it is necessary to know in precise terms *what* is desired. It is also necessary to draft plans to help achieve desired goals. To do so is to lay a foundation stone upon which to build your future — a solid future. Your goals, simply stated, are what you wish to become, what you desire to accomplish and what you would like to have: *to be, to do, to have.*

When you know what you desire in life and have a strategy to achieve it, you bring order into your affairs, establish a sense of purpose, a reason for living and succeeding. You become master of your life, not slave to it. Your strategy — achievement plans — inspire you to move forward in the direction of success. The important first step to high achievement is to know what you want in specific terms, why you want it and how you intend to achieve it.

17. ARCHITECT'S ADVICE IS VALUABLE FOR CAREER-MINDED ACTORS

Requiring professional advice on how best to implement ideas for the development of a commercial property I owned, a friend suggested I speak to an architect he knew. A meeting was arranged with George Lee. I was impressed with the advice George gave me and I present it here because of its value to actors.

'The ultimate satisfaction and success of your undertaking is relative to the plans that are prepared and the manner in which these plans are carried out. Well-laid plans save time, energy and money. Establish what you desire to achieve, then I can draft a master plan to bring it to reality,' George Lee advised me.

Plans — good ones — show the way. They are guideposts to the achievement of whatever they represent: building, journey, career. No right-thinking builder would construct a building without a set of plans. No sensible traveller would begin a journey without knowing the destination and no intelligent actor should attempt to crash New York, Hollywood, or London without a properly-conceived plan of action. A plan of action means less frustration, fewer wrong moves, detours, wasted time, money and energy.

18. THE MARX RULE-OF-THUMB THEORY IS FUNNY BUT IMPRACTICAL

I remember reading that Groucho Marx's father, a tailor, measured his customers by the rule-of-thumb method rather than with a tape measure.

Fittings weren't suggested. It was Chico's job to deliver the garments on completion. He seldom engaged customers in conversation. He collected the money and bolted. Needless to say, few customers were happy, for Mr. Marx's suits weren't what they'd expected. The rule-of-thumb method is unreliable. Inevitably, any haphazard job approach must result in disappointment, frustration and failure.

19. A GOALS LIST AND ACTION PLAN HELP MATERIALIZE YOUR DREAMS

Don't use the rule-of-thumb method — haphazard approach — if you seek an acting career. You'll waste precious time. Your hopes, dreams, wishes for acting success won't happen of their own accord. You must support them with positive plans and positive action. The important thing to do is to start planning and involving your attention on chosen projects. In short, *select your targets and take action.*

Make a list of goals to achieve. Be specific. Write goals down in detail. Place a time limit on their completion. Reduce major goals to a couple of sentences so they are clear in your mind and appear practical. Reduce your goals into subgoals to bring small, quick successes. Think of goals within easy reach, those things you know you can accomplish quickly. Each small success will inspire you to move ahead to major success.

When your goals list has been completed, draft an *action plan* — a written report on how you intend to achieve each goal. Your plan should include ways of earning extra income to help pay for a library of books, training aids, new clothes, pictures and acting lessons. Include a list of acting schools, agents to approach, friends and associates in a position to help you or who can introduce you to influential people. Don't bury your blueprint to success. Place it where is can be read *every* day.

20. AFFIRMATIONS INSPIRE CONFIDENCE FOR HIGH ACHIEVEMENT

Moment-by moment, day-by-day, it is possible to draw success to you by the thoughts you hold, the ideas you contemplate and the goals you have planned. There is no block to your success save in your thought-life and mental imagery. The Roman philosopher Marcus Aurelius, said: 'A man's life is what his thoughts make of it.' Success is a state of mind. It must begin *within* before it can materialize *without.*

Calmly dwell on what you want in life. Declare firmly and repeatedly that what you desire is realistic, worthy and available to you. Impress upon your subconscious mind that your goals will materialize. *Believe it!* Affirmations of this kind are thought-lifters. They bolster your confidence and general well-going. They allow no room for negative ideas to creep into your consciousness, robbing you of self-assurance and creative success.

Type the following affirmation on a 3 x 5 card. Carry the card with you and at frequent intervals during the day read it.

THE *ACTION* PLAN
CHART

Name: _____   Date:_____

Major Goals List: To Be Completed By:
1: _____   _____
2: _____   _____
3: _____   _____
4: _____   _____
5: _____   _____

Sub Goals:
1: _____   _____
2: _____   _____
3: _____   _____
4: _____   _____
5: _____   _____

Plan of Action:
Goal 1: _____
Goal 2: _____
Goal 3: _____
Goal 4: _____
Goal 5: _____
Goal 6: _____
Goal 7: _____
Goal 8: _____
Goal 9: _____
Goal 10: _____

Progress Reports:
1st 3 months: _____
2nd 3 months: _____
1st year: _____

Action Group (persons in a position to assist your career):
Name: _____
Name: _____
Name: _____
Name: _____
Name: _____

Goals Achieved:
1 ☐   2 ☐   3 ☐   4 ☐   5 ☐   6 ☐   7 ☐   8 ☐   9 ☐   10 ☐

21. ACTRESS USED AFFIRMATION TECHNIQUE TO WIN ROLE

A young actress attended a metaphysics seminar I give on occasion for actors and directors. She complained about her lack of self-confidence and panic during casting sessions and rehearsals. 'I fall apart. My knees knock. My palms sweat and my voice quivers,' she told me.

It was clear that her trouble was created by her conscious expectancy of failure. Her negative *idea* of failure attracted failure. The more failure she experienced the more she believed that her acting career was coming to an end. I instructed her to hold an image in her mind of the confident actress she wished to be and to supplant fear, doubt and anxiety with thoughts of confidence, faith, poise, control. I typed an affirmation on a card for her and suggested that she focus her mind on its truths at frequent intervals throughout the day.

A couple of months later, her agent arranged a screen test for her. She told me in a phone conversation, following a successful outcome of the test, that she had given the best performance of her career. 'I memorized the affirmation you gave me and the spiritual truths neutralized the negative patterns of fear and self-doubt. I believed that the screen test would be successful. I had belief in my ability as an actress and was full of faith and confidence. I got the part. But more importantly, I no longer suffer from knocking knees, sweaty palms and quivering voice. My confidence has returned and it's changed my life,' she told me.

22. YOU GO WHERE YOUR VISION IS

Become conscious of your true worth. If you feel inferior and lack self-confidence then you are dooming yourself to failure. Believe in yourself and your ability to succeed. Contemplate victory, high achievement and that is where your vision will take you. You were born to triumph over obstacles. It is essential to change negative mental images, to remove all thoughts of failure if you wish to succeed. Picture the things you *want* and the way you wish to *be* in your mind. There is a law of mind which responds to what you decree, good or otherwise. The law is no respecter of persons. It can't be swayed. It follows *your* orders — *your* thoughts, feelings and beliefs. *It is done unto you as you believe.*

Look beyond appearances and contemplate the reality of successes hoped for and you will make the seeming impossible possible. Accept your good fortune *now*. Give thanks in advance of it taking place. Live in the expectancy of the best occurring in your life and the best will materialize. All your circumstances and events develop out of your attitudes and beliefs. Create a vision on the screen of your mind of *successful* circumstances and hold to the belief that they will come to pass.

23. REMAIN TRUE TO YOUR GOALS — DON'T BE SWAYED BY OTHERS

While travelling by plane from Rio de Janeiro to Buenos Aires, an elderly English gentleman sitting next to me told me that his early ambition had been to act on the stage. 'My family talked me out of it,' he said. 'It's been my one regret in life.'

All of us have been influenced, at one time or another, by the suggestions of others. You can easily recall how parents, relatives, friends, teachers, during early years, attempted to control you, instill fear into you, sway you from your objectives. If you analyse many of the things said to you, you will discover some of it was beneficial, much of it was in the form of propaganda and brain-washing.

Now that you are of an age where you should be thinking for yourself, do not allow others to sway you from your objectives. Question the motives of those persons who attempt to deflect you from your goals, put you down or want you to think and act as they think and act. Be pleasant but firm. Don't become involved in argument with them. Turn a deaf ear to the suggestions: 'You're not the type.' 'You'll fail.' 'Don't waste your time.' 'You're too old.' 'You're too fat.' 'You'll never amount to anything.' 'Actors are drunks or drug addicts.' 'You don't stand a chance.' 'It's who you know.' 'You haven't the talent.'

If your ideal is to serve humanity through the expression of your talents then remain true to your desire. Do what *you* consider is right for you, not the bidding of others who want to distort your life pattern, making the development of good habits and talents difficult. You are the only true thinker in your inner world. Listen to the still, small voice within — intuition. Do not allow others to do your thinking for you or you block your own good, thereby inviting lack, limitation, fear and frustration into your life. The suggestions of others in themselves have no power over your life except the power that *you* entrust to them through your thoughts. Give no person the power to upset you, change you, enslave you mentally, emotionally, spiritually and physically.

Finally, brethren, whatsoever things are true, whatsoever things are honest, whatsoever things are just, whatsoever things are pure, whatsoever things are lovely, whatsoever things are of good report; if there be any virtue, and if there be any praise, think of these things.
PHIL. 4:8

SUMMARY OF IDEAS TO REVIEW

1: Actors often fail because they aren't qualified to handle complex roles. Absorb as much as possible, as quickly as possible, the theory of acting. Use this knowledge as you gain experience.

2: Study the allied arts: music, dance, painting, sculpture, writing, directing, architecture, interior design, costume design, etc. Extend your awareness of life's finer things.

3: Use this book as a reference manual. Study it often and evaluate what you read. Increase your reading speed without loss of comprehension.

4: Don't admit to yourself that you have a poor memory. Mental discipline is the remedy for forgetfulness — *concentrate*.

5: Your best learning aids include a dictionary and a thesaurus in addition to an encyclopedia. Build a library of good books.

6: Use your library of books to increase your general knowledge as well as your acting knowledge. Spend time each day reading.

7: Use the five valuable training aids: *metronome, audio recorder, video recorder, video camera, typewriter*. Organize a scrapbook and files as a source of appropriate study material to which you may refer.

8: Spell out your goals in life. Nothing happens by chance. Draw up a *goals list* and an *action plan*. Know precisely *what* you want and how to achieve your desires.

9: Use *affirmations* to inspire self-confidence. You go where your vision is. Feel and believe that you are capable of success as an actor.

10: Remain true to your goals. Don't be swayed by others from what you desire. Allow no person to upset you, change you, enslave you mentally, physically, emotionally and spiritually.

INDIVIDUALISM:
INNER QUALITIES FROM WHICH
WHICH
STARS ARE MADE

SCENE 3

Practical Ideas In This Chapter . . .

- **How To Project A Highly Individual Personality**
- **Personality Defined**
- **The Two Aspects of Personality**
- ***Three* Steps To Acquiring A Dynamic Personality**
- **Be Your Own *PR* Counsel — Sell Yourself**
- **How To Ascertain How Others See You**
- **Personality Appraisal Chart**
- **Your Personality Package Must Incorporate Inner *And* Outer Qualities**
- **The Actor And Patterns of *Thinking***
- **How The Mind Works: The Conscious Mind — The Subconscious Mind**
- **The Actor And Patterns of *Feeling***
- **The Actor And Patterns of *Believing***
- **The Actor And *Self-Respect***
- **The Actor and *Self-Assurance***
- **The Actor And *Self-Discipline***
- **Discipline Your Mind With *Affirmative Thought Chasers***
- **The Actor And *Decisiveness***
- ***Five* Steps To Effective Decision Making**
- **The Actor And Honesty of *Character***
- **The Actor And *Enthusiasm***
- **How To Light Your Personal Marquee**
- ***Ten* Practical Ways To Generate Enthusiasm**
- **The Actor And *Perseverance***
- **The Actor And *Loyalty***
- **The Actor And *Ambition***
- **The Actor And *Imagination***
- **Stanislavski On Imagination And The Actor**
- **Individualism Gives You Power And Dominance In Your Affairs**
- **Instantly Felt *Inner* Personality Package (Check List)**
- **Summary of Ideas To Review**

SCENE 3

★★

1. HOW TO PROJECT A HIGHLY INDIVIDUAL PERSON-ALITY

'That actor has something.' You say it and you *feel* it. You haven't quite put a label on it but nonetheless you are affected by it and you wish you had it too. *That* actor impressed you with an individual power, a magnetic presence, a dynamic personal presentation, a highly individual personality.

When you develop a highly individual way of presenting yourself, your personality is seen and felt the moment others come in contact with you. It has a highly hypnotic effect. It makes people center their attention on you; it makes them react to you in the way in which you want them to react. This special 'appeal' is called *presence* and it is the ingredient from which stars are made.

A pleasant, expressive, *different* personality is undoubtedly one of the most desired for attributes of people everywhere. Because it breeds popularity, enticing others to enjoy a certain bond with you, it is within reason to say that personality is a tool for social captivation. As an actor desirous of public acclaim, that is the kind of personal power you want and should work hard to develop. It is a behavioral tool capable of winning the acceptance of others and achieving personal goals through them.

2. PERSONALITY DEFINED

A distinctive personality, to some, is a mysterious quality capable of giving one person a distinct advantage over another. This mysterious 'something' is difficult to define because, while it can be seen and felt, it cannot be touched.

47

Personality is best described as expressing the true qualities of the 'self' in such a way as to make an impression on others — pleasant or otherwise.

Habitual patterns of behavior begin as habitual patterns of thought, feeling and belief about the self, people, places and things. Inner convictions and values reflect themselves in moods and actions. Also, these values show up in the standard of dress, grooming, posture and movement of an individual. Clearly then, an individual's *attitude* or concept about the self and life in general, is the major contributing factor to his/her *quality* of personality.

3. THE TWO ASPECTS OF PERSONALITY

It is generally accepted that man has *one* personality with *two* aspects: adequate and inadequate. One is valued, the other value*less*. A fortunate few live within the confines of an affirmative consciousness which creates a pleasant personality, an evenness of moods and properly balanced actions. A majority of people are a mixture of both adequate and inadequate personality: pleasant one day, moody and unpleasant the next, rational one day, irrational the next.

An *adequate* personality is achieved when a proper value is placed on the self producing self-respect. There are no divisions within the self when there is respect *for* the self. An evenness of temperament is the result.

An *inadequate* personality is a reflection of deep-seated resentment and hostility toward the self and toward life in general. The inner convictions are: 'I hate myself. 'I'm no good.' 'I can't get along with others.' 'Why is life so mean to me?' This condemnation and self-abuse arises because self-values are warped. A new, affirmative set of values is the means to an adequate, well-balanced personality.

4. *THREE* STEPS TO ACQUIRING A DYNAMIC PERSONALITY

Residing within you is everything necessary for dynamic personality projection. You begin with what you have and what you are and build from there. Your *self* presentation is expressed through your day-to-day thoughts, feelings and beliefs. These inner aspects determine your physical actions. It is both a mental and a physical thing.

The strength of your individual personality is derived from a combination of markedly-distinguishing inner and outer qualities. These qualities must be seen, setting you apart from people in general. Three steps to achieving a dynamic personality are:

STEP 1 — RECOGNIZE YOUR WORTH: you are a worthy human being. Stop saying 'I'm a nobody.' Place a *value* on yourself.

STEP 2 — TAG YOUR ASSETS: make a list of your *plus* factors such as talents, education, general knowledge, languages spoken, dress sense, posture, physical fitness, pleasant smile, good grooming, etc. Display your good points. *Sell them!*

STEP 3 — TAG YOUR WEAK POINTS: make a list of your *minus* factors such as sloppy dress, poor posture, negative thinker, envious nature, low self-esteem, etc. *Eliminate them!*

5. BE YOUR OWN *PR* COUNSEL — SELL YOURSELF

Public relations people — good ones — are in high demand. They are in the business of selling a better image of people, places and things. Take on your own *PR* and sell others on what you can do. Be concerned with co-ordinating your assets to your public relations capabilities. Find the very best in you, enhance it and then make others aware of it.

Developing a dynamic personality is as important as developing your acting talent if you desire to be a high achiever. If people don't like you, refuse to help you, won't do business with you, then your talent is going to suffer. Use your personality to sell people on liking you and wanting to help you.

Through a well-executed program of distinctive behavior you will be in a prime position to guide the course of your career in the direction you want. By your own concentrated efforts you can move out of the shadow of mediocrity and into the spotlight of eminence, surrounding yourself with a personality aura of success. But remember, you must think, feel and act *as* a successful person in the presence of others, not act *like* one. Insincerity of thought, feeling, belief and action will mark you as a fraud, thus negating your efforts along with your talent.

6. HOW TO ASCERTAIN HOW OTHERS SEE YOU

The easiest way to see yourself as others see you is to take a long, hard look into the mirror of self-appraisal. Analyse the reactions of others to you. If you do not command the respect of others then you must discover why. It could be your manner of dress, your mannerisms, your speech, your lack of confidence, your lack of integrity, your unreliability — any number of things. There is little about your personality that people miss. Therefore, you must discover what is positive about you and what is detrimental to your career advancement.

Use the *Personality Appraisal Chart* and list your affirmative and negative personality traits. Be frank and honest but not unfair to yourself. Don't overestimate or underestimate what you think you are, what you feel you show to others. When your personality inventory has been completed, examine it carefully, then immediately begin making the necessary changes. This is the hardest part. It takes courage to face up to personality and character change. Some people prefer to stay as they are rather than make a conscious effort to change and grow.

When you learn something about your own personality you learn something about the personalities of others and this helps you to adjust to their attitudes when you socialise and work with them, You become more understanding, tolerant, rational and less prone to confrontation with others. The stature of your personality will rise in the face of others. You will be singled out as someone different — someone going places.

PERSONALITY APPRAISAL CHART

Name: _____   DATE:_____

AFFIRMATIVE TRAITS:

1. _____
2. _____
3. _____
4. _____
5. _____
6. _____
7. _____
8. _____
9. _____
10. _____

NEGATIVE TRAITS:

1. _____
2. _____
3. _____
4. _____
5. _____
6. _____
7. _____
8. _____
9. _____
10. _____

COMPLIMENTS I HAVE
RECEIVED:

1. _____
2. _____
3. _____
4. _____
5. _____

CRITICISMS I HAVE
RECEIVED:

1. _____
2. _____
3. _____
4. _____
5. _____

TRAITS I DESIRE:

1. _____
2. _____
3. _____
4. _____
5. _____

CHANGES I MUST MAKE:

1. _____
2. _____
3. _____
4. _____
5. _____

AFFIRMATIVE MOOD
PATTERNS:

1. _____
2. _____
3. _____
4. _____
5. _____

NEGATIVE MOOD
PATTERNS:

1. _____
2. _____
3. _____
4. _____
5. _____

7. YOUR PERSONALITY PACKAGE MUST INCORPORATE INNER AND OUTER QUALITIES

Your personality package incorporates both inner and outer attributes — good, bad or indifferent, they are on display for all to see and judge. People react to you according to what they see, hear and feel. Your personal performance is judged on your physical look — dress, grooming, posture, well being — your attitudes and responses and your manner of speaking, reflecting your education, knowledge and social background. This mental and physical package, according to the way you present it, can appear interesting and exciting or dull and inferior.

The assembly and presentation of an attractive, instantly visible and people-pleasing personality package is as important for the actor as it is for the club and concert performer, because acceptance or rejection are determined by employers *and* audiences. Performers must not only *sound* good, they must *look* good.

When your thoughts are in order your body follows suit — a well-groomed mind is housed within a well-groomed body. An affirmative consciousness produces affirmative actions. When your thoughts reside in the gutter of your mind, self-respect is lost. A person who lacks self-esteem seldom worries about personal appearance. A down-at-the-heel mind is married to a down-at-the-heel body. The two are inseparable. The result is a negative personality package relegating the bearer to a less than desirable future.

Many talented people are professional flops because they are unable to make suitable impressions on people — they have an inability to capture the imagination and the attention of others. There is a lack of 'showmanship' in the way they present themselves. Personality *showmanship* reaches out and *moves* people in an emotional way. It is an instant thing. It hits hard. It makes people sit up and take notice. It is a projection of mind and body dynamics. It is a way of talking, acting and looking that instantly grabs and holds the attention of people.

8. THE ACTOR AND PATTERNS OF *THINKING*

If you genuinely want to make the most of the creative potential within you, then you will need to know something of the workings of your conscious and subconscious mind. The more you know *how* to use the power of your mind, the better will be your sense of direction in life, the more dynamic your individualism and the faster the accomplishment of your goals.

The means to a worthwhile lifestyle can be found within an affirmative consciousness — powerful, affirmative thoughts. Emerson wrote: *Thoughts are things. Thoughts have an in-dwelling power.* The way you *think* governs all phases of your life. You shape, guide and direct your life through your attitudes. When you take charge of your *pattern* of thinking — eliminating negative concepts, substituting them for affirmative ones — you begin to enjoy life as never before. Conditions and circumstances improve. You hold the key to your future. The key is the pattern of your thought — what you *think*, you become.

9. HOW THE MIND WORKS

There is one mind. But it functions through the conscious level (the thinker) and the subconscious level (memory). Whatever ideas your conscious mind habitually dwells on, your subconscious brings to pass. Every *thought* is a *cause*, every *condition* is an *effect*. Thus, the mind works according to the law of *cause and effect*.

THE CONSCIOUS MIND: it is the 'thinker', the objective mind. It has the ability to rationalize but not to remember. It is also called the *male principle*, the *surface self*. Your conscious mind is the leader of your team representing your body, your environment. It gives the orders governing your actions based on decisions it makes after rationalizing information fed to it by your five senses. Whatever the conscious mind decides it passes to the subconscious for attention and action.

THE SUBCONSCIOUS MIND: it is the storehouse of all your thoughts, feelings and beliefs. It keeps your body functioning while you sleep through processes independent of your conscious mind. Your subconscious accepts whatever is impressed upon it. It takes thought forms from the conscious mind and molds them into future events. It works without bias, accepting whatever it is given, obeying whatever demands are made. It acts upon negative ideas in exactly the same way as it acts upon affirmative concepts. It does not reason things out. Your subconscious is the seat of your emotions. It is the *female principle*, subjective and creative. Whatever it accepts, it projects as circumstances and events in your life.

The greatest discovery you could make is the discovery of the power of your mind to attract *good* in your life. Think good and good follows. Think evil and evil follows. Affirmative thoughts produce an apparent strength of attitude which every person desirous of high achievement must possess.

10. THE ACTOR AND PATTERNS OF *FEELING*

Acting is not about actors, it is about people. The feelings, beliefs and actions of people from every walk of life. Acting encompasses the study, understanding and playing of characters of all ages and types. It requires interpretation of *feelings* of characters and the expression of those feelings to bring about performance realism.

In order to understand the emotional patterns of others, it is necessary to understand your own patterns of feeling. This is not an easy task. However, every actor should set aside a period of time on a regular basis to try and understand the 'self' to analyse his/her soul. If, like so many actors I know, you are a victim of your moods, then this study won't come fast enough.

The next time you feel lonely, depressed, anxious, fearful, down-at-the-mouth, ask yourself, 'why do I feel this way?' Try to discover the *cause* of your moods. It should become obvious to you that your moods form out of your thoughts. If you are tough on yourself, hate yourself, then those negative ideas work against you to produce negative actions. When your thoughts are affirmative, your mood pattern is pleasant and you feel 'uplifted' and happy.

Actors would be wise to work toward mental and emotional balance. Excessively high and low mood patterns are personality detractors. A moody person is often an unreliable person. When the spirits are up things are fine, but when the spirits are down mental and emotional stress and strain create personality problems. The cure for a depressed state of mind is to *change* negative thoughts. Replace them with affirmative concepts — high-spirited thoughts produce high-spirited feelings.

A daily reading program of books on psychology and philosophy will help to reveal why people (including yourself) act and react under various circumstances. As you explore, discover, analyse and understand this most beneficial information, your new-found knowledge will lead you to a better understanding of yourself in addition to helping you to better understand the many complex stage characters you may be asked to portray.

11. THE ACTOR AND PATTERNS OF *BELIEVING*

The law of life is the law of belief. Your belief in personal success helps to attract success. The same principle applies to your belief about failure. Whatever you believe to be true eventually comes true. By belief, I'm talking about a deep-down conviction, a dominant idea held fast and foremost in your subconscious mind. When you truly believe in your ability to become a successful actor, you set in motion the creative law of mind, its response to you is automatic. *Believe that I am and I will be.*

You must cease the practice of believing that you are unattractive, untalented, unworthy of success, unwanted and doomed to mediocrity in all that you undertake in life. This self-condemnation strips you of poise, vitality and confidence — the very qualities you need to support your acting talent. Your self-beliefs promote or tear-down your personality.

Your *personality*, your *thoughts* and your *talent* are the keys to acting success. In a clearly visible way, your personality is an expression of your beliefs. Believe that you can *do* what you desire to do and *become* what you desire to become through strong belief in your abilities.

12. THE ACTOR AND *SELF-RESPECT*

You are a highly creative human being with limitless potential for artistic success if artistic success is your dream. You were born to win. It you do not believe that it is possible to express yourself fully in whatever artistic endeavors you so choose, then you are denying yourself a *gift* of life.

Do not under-value you abilities. Do not hold the concept that you are born to fail. Do not endorse inferior feelings and ideas about yourself. Respect yourself. Place a *value* on what you are and what you can become.

Self-respect is essential to success. Lack of it ruins your personality and kills the urge for artistic accomplishment.

A sense of self-esteem puts a shine on your personality and motivates your behavior in a positive way. Self-respect is the path to balanced, harmonious human behavior. No person can be truly happy or successful without adequate liking of the self. Performers, especially, need to feel that they are needed, respected for their abilities and are contributing to the joy and well-being of their audiences. If a person does not value his or her own self, then others quickly sense this lack of self-esteem and respond accordingly.

Your basic desire is to secure your true place in life. You accomplish this task faster and easier when you cease self-condemnation, unwarranted criticism of the self and replace it with genuine self-respect.

13. THE ACTOR AND *SELF-ASSURANCE*

The different degrees of success experienced by performers often lie in the goals they set and the actions they take to accomplish them. Some performers are timid in their approach to the profession. Others boldly move forward, gamble on their ability to succeed and confidently progress from one success to the next. Those actors — the self-assured ones — seldom miss opportunity when it arrives.

Missed opportunity is when you see it coming but take no action. People in general do this quite a lot because they lack the drive and confidence to take a chance, to test their judgement. They fear the possibility of failure, therefore, it is safer to do nothing. Unfortunately, they develop the art of losing. Performers require a high degree of self-confidence because they must learn the art of winning, not develop the art of losing.

Self-confidence or self-assurance means having faith in your very being. It is a strong belief that you are capable of performing the tasks presented to you in life. Faith in the outcome of all your deep-down ideals, wants, convictions and inspirations motivates you to take on challenges and score opportunities as they arise.

Self-assurance is a mind relaxer. It allows your creative mechanism to perform freely, easily and comfortably. It replaces tension, anxiety and fear of failure with energy, peace of mind and enthusiasm for successes hoped for. Self-assurance challenges you to get on with life and make the most of what it offers. It gives you control over what you say and do and adds a bright spark to your personality. To develop your level of self-assurance follow these two rules:

RULE 1: IMMOVABLE FAITH — take a gamble on yourself. The only chance you get in life is the chance you give yourself. Don't deny yourself the opportunity to succeed. Back your desires with *faith*. Don't give in. One failure doesn't mean permanent failure. You have the power to win.

RULE 2: MENTALLY RELAX — take it easy! Don't clutter your mind with 'things' negative. Allow your creative mechanism to flow freely, harmoniously, without apprehension and tension by clearing your mental slate of trauma-producing ideas. Psychic traumas make you a bundle of nerves. Control and direct your thinking. The *effortless* way is the right way. Pursue every project joyfully, wisely and easily without submitting to pressure or fear. A tension-free mind produces a tension-free body. Be still. Return to the *center* within, for here is harmony and tranquility, a place where you live beyond time and space. It is a place to revitalize your soul — a place where the negation of others cannot reach you.

14. THE ACTOR AND *SELF-DISCIPLINE*

Discipline means to maintain order in all that you do, to control your life and to guide it in the ways of your choosing. Self-discipline begins with the control of your thoughts. An orderly, undisturbed mind steadies the emotions, produces well-being, generates enthusiasm for life, encourages and inspires you to press ahead with the goals you have chosen. When your artistic 'feelings' are ignited, they attract relevant, spontaneous actions.

Thoughts which run riot stifle or cripple the creative process. Negative ideas inhibit the personality and intimidate self-confidence. By holding to affirmative thought patterns, more productive time is available to devote to goal directions in personal, social and professional areas of your life. Also, you will enjoy unimpeded use of your five senses with which to study, plan, create, overcome problems, meet challenges, experience new friendships and greatly improve all phases of your life. A disciplined state of mind reduces — if not eliminates — periods of moodiness, listlessness, loneliness, boredom and depression. You won't have to rely on pills, alcohol, drugs or stimulants to restore and maintain mental and physical balance. Discipline is a powerful tool with which to set your life in order.

Self-discipline paves the way for proper order in other valuable ways such as being on time for appointments, completing tasks, keeping promises. It supports self-confidence and strengthens your backbone to stand up for what you feel is right instead of continually giving in to the opinions and demands of others. It gives you the ability to think selectively in a given area, opens a stream of consciousness where the mind is fixed on priority matters instead of inconsequential things. Mental tidiness produces clear, rational reasoning, unblocks the emotions, allows better concentration, spontaneous inventiveness and right action. Discipline your thoughts. Keep them affirmative and you will continue to move in the direction of success, happiness and creative fulfillment.

15. DISCIPLINE YOUR MIND WITH *AFFIRMATIVE THOUGHT CHASERS*

Affirmative thought chasers are mental tranquilizers. They help to restore thought balance, they stem fear, stop panic, control nerves and bring peace of mind. They help you to become master of your mind.

Keep in readiness a host of thought chasers to stem the tide of negative ideas should they creep into your consciousness. *The good destroys the bad.* Make up your own thought chasers and add them to the following list:

- I AM DETERMINED TO WIN.
- I KNOW WHERE I'M HEADED IN LIFE.
- I WILL COMPLETE EVERY TASK I UNDERTAKE.
- MY CREATIVE DESIRES ARE BEING ACHIEVED.
- THE POWER TO SUCCEED IS WITHIN ME.
- MY THINKING IS DISCIPLINED AND HELPS ME TO SUCCEED.
- I AM POISED, BALANCED, SERENE AND CONFIDENT.
- I AM UNAFFECTED BY THE OPINIONS OF OTHERS.
- I AM TALENTED AND USE MY TALENTS BENEFICIALLY.
- I STAND FIRM IN MY CONVICTIONS.
- I HAVE FAITH IN MY FUTURE.
- I GET ALONG WELL WITH FRIENDS, ASSOCIATES, FAMILY.
- I AM ENTHUSIASTIC, FRIENDLY AND HELPFUL TO OTHERS.
- I GIVE AND I RECEIVE.
- MY MIND IS OPEN TO ALL THINGS WORTHWHILE.

16. THE ACTOR AND *DECISIVENESS*

There is an aphorism which states: *It is man's decision that shapes his life.* All through life we are faced with the task of decision making. Few persons can be certain that any decision, at the time it is made, is going to be beneficial, is going to be right or wrong. There is an element of risk associated with decision making. The degree of risk is relative to the information at hand at the time a particular decision is made. The more facts readily available for analysis, the less risk there is of making an incorrect decision.

Every decision will carry with it responsibility for its outcome. For this reason, many persons shy away from making important decisions or allow others to make decisions for them. By placing the burden of responsibility on the shoulders of friends or professional advisors, blame, also, can be passed to them if the decision is a poor one.

Never allow others to make important decisions on your behalf. Courageously decide on a definite course of action, then follow it through to completion — win, lose or draw. It takes strength of mind to make decisions on personal matters concerning problems, events, situations and purchases. Don't be a staller. Don't be a weak-minded person. Decide for yourself the appropriate steps to take on matters of importance and have faith in the right outcome.

Tackle problems rationally, not emotionally. Draw your own conclusions after collecting the facts. Don't rely on hearsay, gossip or the opinions of others. The advice given by others may not be based on careful analysis of the facts or given with your best interests in mind. Decision making and problem solving* are do-it-yourself operations. Don't shirk your responsibility. Train yourself to be a decisive person. It's an admirable trait.

17. *FIVE* STEPS TO EFFECTIVE DECISION MAKING

As an actor you will want to come to the right decision about many important matters concerning your career. Areas of immediate importance will include: choosing an agent, selecting an acting school, purchasing a new wardrobe, deciding on a flattering hairstyle, choosing a part-time job, whether or not to move to a larger city or to travel overseas, the choice of associations and friendships. Your decisions will be easier to make and less prone to error if they are made without fear of the outcome and once made, are acted upon promptly. Five helpful steps are:

STEP 1: *GATHER THE FACTS* — weed out half-truths, less than reliable opinions of those who may want you to act in *their* best interests, not your own.

STEP 2: *WRITE IT DOWN* — put all decisions to be made in writing and in the order in which you wish to dispose of them. Reduce each problem to a single sentence if possible to pinpoint the situation, thus avoiding confusion, distortion and exaggeration of the problem.

STEP 3: *GO IN EASY* — never make an important decision when you are ill or emotionally disturbed or angry. Free the mind of pressure and tension.

STEP 4: *VISUALIZE THE OUTCOME* — express onto the screen of your mind the outcome you desire. See yourself taking the right action, achieving what you desire. *See* it! *Feel* it!

STEP 5: *DON'T STALL* — it's possible that you won't be right all of the time, but if you make enough prompt moves you will increase

*See Chapter 10 *How To Succeed*, by Brian Adams.

your ability to strike-it-right. Don't be a procrastinator. With sheer boldness make decisions then act on them, knowing that you have done all in your power to bring about the results you desire.

18. THE ACTOR AND HONESTY OF *CHARACTER*

The true value of a person can be seen in that person's honesty. An honest person is a dependable, truthful, sincere, loyal, trustworthy, honorable person. A person who is free of deceit. You are wondering, possibly, if such person exists.

In our present-day society, many of the commendable values of our forefathers are absent. A great many people behave quite badly in their social and business dealings with others. They make a mess of their lives because they lack personal integrity, preferring to lie, cheat and steal rather than be honest and forthright. Not all of our forefathers were pillars of society, but many took pride in their sense of rightness, justice and honesty. In these difficult times, society needs more people of good character.

I've listened to actors' complaints about producers, directors, casting directors and agents who have falsely raised their hopes with promises of work, knowing that their promises couldn't or wouldn't be kept. Such acts are inexcusable and patently dishonest.

I've listened to the complaints of producers, directors, casting directors and agents about actors who lie to them about their credits in order to obtain work. Such lies are inexcusable. The practice is dishonest.

An actor I worked with in Hollywood, told me that when he arrived in Los Angeles from New York, he told an agent that he had worked in many top New York-based productions. The agent signed him to an agency contract and immediately sent him to see a studio casting director. 'Tell me what you've worked in recently,' the casting director enquired. The actor mentioned a particular show and talked at great length about his role in it. The casting director showed more than casual interest and pressed for more details. When the actor had finished speaking, the casting director said to him: 'You are a liar. I cast that show and you weren't in it. Please leave my office at once.'

Some would-be actresses, eager to gain stardom, compromise their morals. They sell their souls like common merchandise. While it might seem appropriate to engage in indiscreet acts at certain times, past folly has a habit of haunting the offender when least expected and least desired.

Building a valuable reputation in acting is a goal worth striving to achieve. Never compromise ideals and morals. The actor who desires to make it to the top and stay there should give attention to the development of a strong, forthright, honest and highly-moral character. Personal integrity commands respect — always.

19. THE ACTOR AND E~

When I first met Robert Wagner a~
long been married. My first meeting w~
where Robert was making a film. I was imp~
one another, for their high-spirited attitude~
boundless energy applied to their work as actors. b~
pleasure. Their magnetic personalities, confidence ar~
positive aura which spread to others, making them feel g~

Enthusiasm is an effervescent tool of communication. It gets
up. It motivates others to want to join our cause, fight for us and
us. Enthusiastic leaders attract enthusiastic followers. The interest or
people in us can be used as a criterion of the strength of our enthusiasm.

Enthusiasm is motivated energy. Motivated energy inspires us to get
things done, to become number one. Enthusiasm and action are marriage
partners. Enthusiasm overcomes inertia, dispels procrastination, urges
positive action by stimulating ambition and promotes well-being. It brings
you enough power and persuasion to win friends and the things you desire.

Enthusiasm breeds winners — persons far above the 'maddening crowd'
who plague the offices of agents, casting directors and producers. In the
rush for fame, enthusiastic and talented people survive. It's not always
what you say that impresses others but *how* you say it and *why*. It's the
method and the *approach* that makes or breaks those who seek personal
career assistance of agents and producers.

Enthusiasm is an effective *persuasion* tool. It is a positive method of
establishing an immediate rapport with others when first meeting them.
Enthusiasm helps to neutralize anger or resentment that others may bear
toward us. It produces for us warmth, friendliness, charm, humor, energy
and a look of success which others respond to and remember. Enthusiasm
is a most useful personality trait for the exploitation of personal factors. It
creates an *individualism*, an all-over beauty and genuine personality
appeal.

20. HOW TO LIGHT YOUR PERSONAL MARQUEE

Enthusiasm can do so much for you mentally, emotionally, spiritually
and physically. It is potent medicine, especially when used on a day-to-day
basis. It can 'light-up' your life like the great white way of Broadway and
bring your personality and talents into focus in living color. Displays of
enthusiasm put your name on the marquee of life.

Enthusiasm helps to balance and harmonize your day-in day-out
feelings. It's a fast antidote for loneliness, morbid moods and boredom. It
rapidly dissolves feelings of anger, envy, jealousy, resentment, hate and
fear. In their place it attracts feelings of peace, happiness, benevolence,
respectfulness, confidence and love. Enthusiasm aids digestion, improves
metabolism, stimulates circulation, fires-up energy, enhances muscle
function, relieves tension and calms the nervous system. It doesn't cost a

ottle of pills. It's *free*. Try it!

_ used to control our own emotions as well as the
_ others when problems arise, when difficult decisions are to be
 made and when circumstances are less than favorable. It is a wonderful
performance aid when a difficult role is to be acted or a public appearance is
e made. It's a sure way to attract the attention of others so that they see
s important and special. Enthusiasm is showmanship *plus*. Cultivate it!
erate it! Project it every day of your life. It's an actor's magic wand to
; health, happiness and acting success.

21. *TEN* PRACTICAL WAYS TO GENERATE ENTHUSIASM

Enthusiasm is manufactured by *you*. There are many ways to produce it.
The following approaches should be tackled *every* day until they become
an integral part of your personality output. The degree of your enthusiasm
is always in direct proportion to the amount of *interest* you put into it. Get
interested in and practice the following enthusiasm generators:

1: *OBLITERATE DISINTEREST* — it smothers enthusiasm for people,
places and things and creates boredom.

2: *THINK OPTIMISTICALLY* — don't be a pessimist. Think the best
and the best will occur.

3: *ACT DECISIVELY* — be courageous in your actions. You have
nothing to fear if you *plan* before you act.

4: *RECOGNIZE YOUR VALUE* — you are a creative human being
worthy of the best. Don't demean yourself or your talents.

5: *RESPECT OTHERS* — both the beggar and the king are human
beings needing love and respect. Show kindness to *everyone*.

6: *SMILE* — the world loves the happy person. Laughter breaks
tension, helps people to relax and be happy.

7: *DON'T GOSSIP* — no human being is perfect — not even you. Don't
speak unkindly of others, demean their talents or be critical of them.

8: *REPEL CRITICISM* — people are going to say unkind things about
you, perhaps slander you, particularly when you gain public favor.
Turn the other cheek. It isn't *what* is said that matters, it's your
reaction to what is said that counts.

9: *EAT WELL* — a healthy mind requires a healthy body. Watch your
diet. Eliminate junk food, tobacco, alcohol and drugs. You'll look
better, feel better and live longer to enjoy your career.

10: *EXPAND YOUR HORIZONS* — go looking for new experiences, new
interests and new friends. Keep active, both mentally and physically.

22. THE ACTOR AND *PERSEVERANCE*

There is no success for the individual who gives up without a fight for the
things he/she desires in life. During the years I've been an acting coach and
director, I've witnessed the rise and quick fall of a vast number of acting

aspirants. Many of them failed because they lacked perseverance. When the going got tough they opted out, because quitting was easier than succeeding.

Actors are expected to be *extraordinary* people not mediocre people. Generally speaking, mediocre people lack the drive to succeed. They are content to settle for the status quo because being 'one-of-the-mob' requires little effort. It takes 'guts' to win, to hang on when the going gets tough. Quitters can't win high achievement. An actor cannot afford to be a quitter if the desire is to achieve stardom.

In my own theatrical career, I've experienced more cancelled contracts, more program axings than I care to remember. I can truthfully say, I've allowed none to phase me, to break my spirit or to keep me from trying again. I've had my share of press criticism, too. And I've become immune to the vindictiveness of media critics. Actors cannot expect to have problem-free careers. That would be dull. Actors must learn to accept the good with the bad. It's important to know that when one door closes, another is about to open. The pendulum of life balances life by moving to-and-fro, not tilting to one side. Life is neither all thorns or all roses. Humans can't expect to have *everything* go their way. We need to experience some failure in order to grow and to appreciate success when it arrives.

In every field of human endeavor, the person who wins is the person who is *determined* to win, the person who is courageous, loyal to the self, has integrity and carries on in the face of adversity. A temporary defeat can be turned into a wonderful staging ground to strengthen character and to reaffirm the will to win.

23. THE ACTOR AND *LOYALTY*

You will need helpers to propel you up the ladder of artistic success. These helpers must be believers in your talent. They must be loyalists to your cause, genuine supporters working in your best interests. Agents, casting directors, directors, producers, trainers, production secretaries, scriptwriters, bankers, accountants, lawyers, family members and friends *all* have an important part to play in your climb to acting success. In each instance and at every level, you want your helpers to respect you, stand by you and open up opportunities for you.

As you seek the help of others, you must be ready and willing to return favor-for-favor, kindness-for-kindness and loyalty-for-loyalty. Many a would-be-actor has made the mistake of taking advantage of the generosity of others in his or her mad scramble to succeed in acting. Using others for selfish reasons may work once, seldom works twice and nearly always results in a negative reputation for those who are guilty of it.

Agents, in particular, are often subject to acts of disloyalty by actors. The late Sonny Shamberg, a Hollywood agent who represented me some years back, told me when I joined his client list, 'I expect loyalty from my clients. I have to spend enormous amounts of time selling a client. I'm paid when the client is paid. I want clients to stay loyal to this office.' Sonny had experienced his share of actor disloyalty. I remember his disappointment when an actress he had groomed and worked hard to promote left him and signed with another agent. It wasn't just the financial loss to his agency that bothered him, it was more her hurtful act of disloyalty.

Many actors behave in a despicable way, messing up not only their own lives and careers but the lives and careers of others. Don't join the disloyalty club. In the short term, disloyal acts may seem to be the expedient way to get to the top. In the long term, disloyal acts come back to defeat you. Achieve success through the diligent application of your talents, offering them in an honest way. Reward the efforts of others who work on your behalf with a show of respect and loyalty. Make loyalty another aspect of your individualism. It is a character trait admired and respected by all decent, honorable human beings.

24. THE ACTOR AND *AMBITION*

Ambition is not a bad thing. It is a good thing. Without ambition man would accomplish little. Ambition is a generating force which fires-up the imagination, motivates energy for tackling big goals with enthusiasm and confidence. Actors need to join ambition to talent if they expect to win.

If you cannot generate enough interest to chase after the things you desire then be content with what you are and what you now have and leave it at that. Save your time, energy and money. This will free you from possible disappointment, hard work, perhaps ridicule from family and friends and the spending of money on training and work tools. If, however, you truly desire to achieve, to make something of yourself, then put your heart-and-soul into an ambitious program to succeed as an actor. And keep in mind: *no one finds true success by stepping on others, being disloyal, dishonest, lazy and selfish.*

25. THE ACTOR AND IMAGINATION

Some years ago, in Jefferson City, Missouri, I worked with a New York actress who told me that when she was a young girl in school she played onto the screen of her mind her ambition to become a successful actress. 'Before drifting off to sleep each night I imagined myself on a stage playing to a large and appreciative audience. It was a mental movie of the goal I wanted to win. I began to feel the reality of my dream. Since leaving school, I haven't been out of work as an actress,' this talented artist told me.

There is a *power* within man which will bring forth his dreams if only he will understand and use it. This power is the *workshop* of the mind. It is both interpretative and creative in nature. It is called *imagination*. It knows no restrictions or limitations except those placed on it by faithless, ignorant, apathetic and pessimistic thinkers. Great things are done when man's faculty of imagination is put to work. All the wonderful and commanding achievements of man have come from his imagination in the initial form of ideas, desires and needs.

Your ideas of what you wish to do and desire to become reside in your deeper mind waiting to be acted upon. They take the form of images. They have their own shape, form and substance in another dimension of mind. They are the cause of feeling and action as your faculty of imagination projects them on the screen of space. When you attach confidence and faith to your mental images, they blossom into reality.

The giant oak slumbers in the tiny acorn, the bird sleeps in the egg, the human form grows within the body of its mother and your creative desires are in your imagination awaiting birth. You can become what you desire for yourself. When the idea and feeling unite, action takes places. Your day-to-day ideas and feelings create your circumstances, events and actions as well as construct your character and personality. Use your imagination *constructively* to bring forth and eventually achieve your dreams. *Trust* in the law of life. Have *faith* in the power of your mind. Infinite Intelligence which guides the planets also guides you unless you block it, mistrust it and deny its value and wisdom.

26. STANISLAVSKI ON IMAGINATION AND THE ACTOR

An actor can use his imagination not only to project on the screen of space his own life but the lives of stage characters he is to play. The imagination of the actor must grace the words of the writer with ideas and concepts drawn from his/her own experience and knowledge. Without imagination there can be no creativeness.

Constantin Stanislavski drew to the attention of his students his 'magic if' technique. While calling upon the power of imagination, the student of acting should ask himself what he would do 'if' the events and circumstances in the play were actually occurring to him. This technique helps to bring forth a sincerity of emotions. To put the technique into practice the actor must create an imaginary life with the help of *inner* visual images. He must then place his own feelings into the mind of the stage character, thus better understanding the actions of the character.

From the depths of the mind ideas spring, mental images form and sensations are felt. A role that does not pass through these imagination spheres can never become spellbinding. One of the principal creative forces in the art of acting is the use of artistic imagination.

27. INDIVIDUALISM GIVES YOU POWER AND DOMINANCE IN YOUR AFFAIRS

Now that you are aware of the inner qualities which produce a highly-pleasing personality, put them to work to win people to your cause. This does not mean that you should force your will upon others. To do so would be quite wrong. Your individualism can be used to impress others, to create around you an air of appeal which draws people to you.

A display of personality appeal gives you power and dominance in situations and events you involve yourself in. You are more at ease. You exude a radiance, an individualism which people who catch sight of you notice instantly. You look different, you feel different and you act differently to others because you *are* different. All it takes to achieve personality appeal is your willingness to *change* what has to be changed.

CHECK LIST

INSTANTLY FELT *INNER* PERSONALITY PACKAGE

YES✓	NO✓	QUALITIES
☐ ☐ ☐	☐ ☐ ☐	*Affirmative* pattern of thinking *Affirmative* pattern of feeling *Affirmative* pattern of believing
☐ ☐ ☐	☐ ☐ ☐	*Total* self-respect *Total* self-assurance *Total* self-discipline
☐ ☐ ☐	☐ ☐ ☐	*Continually* decisive *Continually* honest *Continually* enthusiastic
☐ ☐ ☐	☐ ☐ ☐	*Always* persevering *Always* loyal *Always* co-operative
☐ ☐ ☐	☐ ☐ ☐	*Constantly* ambitious *Constantly* imaginative *Constantly* individualistic

NOTE: if you have more than 10 'yes' qualities your character and personality are strong. Add to this package of *plus factors* your talents and you have everything necessary to win career success.

SUMMARY OF IDEAS TO REVIEW

1: An expressive, *different* personality breeds popularity, entices others to enjoy a bond with you, want to help you. Place a value on your *self*.

2. The easiest way to see yourself as others see you is to look into the mirror of self-appraisal. Discover what you are. Make a list of your own personality and character traits. Change negative traits.

3. Study how to best use the awesome power of your mind. Thoughts are things. They govern all phases of your life. Think, feel and believe in your ability to succeed as a performer.

4: Take a gamble on your talents, back your gamble with faith.

5. Discipline your life. Maintain order in your affairs. Control the pattern of your thinking. Discourage negative ideas. Encourage affirmative concepts.

6: Be decisive. Don't procrastinate. When you've made a decision hold to it, support it with confidence. Persevere until you win.

7: Enthusiasm motivates energy. Motivated energy gets things done. Get interested in and enthusiastic about people, places, things.

8: Actors need helpers. Be loyal to those who assist you: agents, casting directors, producers, directors, family and friends.

9: Ambition is a good thing. Put your heart and soul into an ambitious program to succeed.

10: Use the power of imagination to see yourself as you wish to be, to feel the reality of acting success. Use artistic imagination to understand the thoughts, feelings and actions of stage characters.

DYNAMIC IMPRESSIONS: OUTER QUALITIES CONTRIBUTING TO STARDOM

SCENE 4

Practical Ideas In This Chapter . .

- How To Enhance Your Personality With *Showmanship*
- The Actor And A Distinctive Manner of Speaking
- Why People Don't Always Respond Favorably
- How To Get Through To People With The *AIDA* Formula
- How To Develop An Effective Vocal Presentation
- Strong Vocal Presentations Create Strong First Impressions
- How To Eliminate Speech Detractors
- Positive Phraseology Attracts Positive Circumstances And Events
- Vocal Style Is Major Trademark of Stars
- Establish Your Own Vocal Trademark
- How To Remedy Poor Vocal Presentation
- An Impressive Vocal Presentation Can Make You Rich
- How To Establish Credibility And Respect When You Speak
- How To Make Greetings And Responses Above The Ordinary
- Extend Your Vocabulary — Words Are Actors' Tools of Trade
- A Tip From John Barrymore On Word Expression
- Use Words As *Carrots* Not Clubs
- Vincent Price The Master Word-User
- How To Impress Others By Not Saying A Word
- How To Learn while You Listen
- Vital Information On Listening For The Actor
- On Marlon Brando And Listening
- How To Win The Admiration of Your Director
- How To Become A Good Communicator
- Good Communication Raises Your Social And Professional Status
- How To Get The Right People To Assist You
- *Five* Ways To Influence People
- Effective Communication Brings Positive Motivation
- Fulfill Needs of Others And You'll Win Them
- Audiences Seek Intellectual And Emotional Fulfillment
- Communicating Personality Through Body Language
- Body Language And What It Signifies
- How To Look At Others In A Positive Way
- How To Get Others To Instantly Warm To You
- How To Get Others To Look At You In A Positive Way
- The Actor And Physical Fitness
- *Tobacco* And The Actor
- *Alcohol* And The Actor
- *Drugs* And The Actor
- *Dress* And The Actor
- Dress Flair Marks You As Someone Special
- Cary Grant's Advice On Dress Sense
- *Grooming* And The Actor
- Instantly Felt *Outer* Personality Package (Check List)
- Summary of Ideas To Review

SCENE 4

★ ★

1. HOW TO ENHANCE YOUR PERSONALITY WITH SHOWMANSHIP

Having analysed the 'inner' aspects contributing to an individualistic personality, let's now discover the 'outer' factors which strike others instantly, marking you as someone 'special'.

Psychologists tell us that upon meeting others for the first time, there is an impression-gathering period when others judge us by the things we say, how we say them, the way we listen, our posture, movement and gesture, the mode of our dress and the state of our health.

Leading Australian psychologist, Dr. Lyn Barrow, told me during an interview on my Tonight show, 'The measurement of a person's appeal lies in the impressions he or she creates in the minds of others. Some people are shy, lack personality assertiveness, speak poorly, move awkwardly, dress sloppily and these impressions create negative reactions in others.'

Renowned Beverly Hills speech pathologist, Dr. Lillian Glass, maintains that personalities spend fortunes on the way they look and what they wear but 'people judge us on what we say and how we speak.' She feels actors in particular must learn to make the most of their voices. 'Concentrate on speech first and looks second. Learn to put more life into the voice and do away with speech monotone,' Dr. Glass says. It was she who taught Dustin Hoffman how to make the vocal transition from male to female in *Tootsie*. She says she'd like to work on altering the speech of several Hollywood actors to 'improve communication ability' which many of them lack.

The measurement of an actor's public appeal lies in the impressions he/she creates. Lack of personal showmanship — personality assertiveness — coupled to poor speaking ability, inattentive listening, poor posture, ungraceful movement, unkempt appearance and poor health, result in negative impressions being formed in the minds of agents, producers and audiences. A truly effective personality presentation must combine an individual's inner and outer qualities. People must *see* and *feel* your 'presence' as being above the ordinary. Develop a strong character and let the world be touched by your personal attributes and special talents.

2. THE ACTOR AND A DISTINCTIVE MANNER OF SPEAKING

There are several ways of projecting individualism capable of impressing people and arousing their interest in you. One sure way is to project a distinctly different manner of speaking and conversing which attracts and holds the listener's attention.

Your job as an actor is to speak and act well on stage. It will be helpful to you to develop the habit of speaking well, not only on stage, but in your everyday social and business conversations, particularly if you are speaking to persons who are able to promote your career.

Your individuality dulls or shines every time you open your mouth and speak. Using stock phrases, conventional greetings and responses, mumbling, speaking too loudly, mispronouncing words, using words in wrong context, imperfect grammar, are speech handicaps detrimental to success in acting.

A pleasant-sounding voice, expressive in presentation, can be developed by implementing a regular, systematic program of speech-voice exercises and by paying particular attention to the correction of imperfect speech patterns and habits. This is best done under professional guidance and supervision.

Because good vocal presentation is an indispensable tool-of-trade, improving it should be given priority when acting training begins. As Bernard Shaw mentioned in *Pygmalion,* a person's social standing and educational background are judged by the way he talks. Since drama is one of the arts of communication, speech and drama classes are valuable ways of improving voice clarity, accuracy in the presentation of words and communication in general.

Concentrate on developing an impressive manner of speaking and conversing from an ever-changing inventory of phrases and material. Don't slur words, mumble, speak too softly or too loudly. Speak up! If you can't be understood you won't be listened to and if you aren't listened to you might as well give up any thought of public performance.

3. WHY PEOPLE DON'T ALWAYS RESPOND FAVORABLY

The main reason people you talk to don't always do the things you ask of them or respond to you in a way you'd like, is because you aren't successful in breaking through their personal preoccupation. Their interest and concern are with *their* ideas, needs and objectives, not yours — unless you influence them otherwise.

Your major goal as an actor is to develop yourself into a dynamic communicator-motivator. This means that you have to become proficient at getting people to *listen* to you and to *respond* to you in a positive way. When you have mastered the art of *getting through* to people you will be in a position to motivate them so that they respond to you as you desire.

4. HOW TO GET THROUGH TO PEOPLE WITH THE *AIDA* FORMULA

Professional salespersons use a method of communication-motivation called the *AIDA* formula.* This technique can be used by actors with equal success. It is a positive way to grab and hold the attention of those you speak or perform to. The letters AIDA represent:

A ttention
I nterest
D esire
A ction

This formula is a useful step-by-step method of opening, building and closing a sales presentation, speech, business negotiation, stage performance and general expression of personal thoughts and ideas to an audience of one or more. It is an excellent technique to develop the art of social conversation.

ATTENTION: it is of little advantage to continue a conversation unless your listener is giving full attention to your message. Before presenting an idea, submitting a request or offering information, capture the full attention of your listener. Begin your conversation by using the name of your listener. Very few people can resist responding to the sound of their name. When you have gained the full attention of your listener, proceed to the next step.

INTEREST: it is essential to make your message interesting, exciting, stimulating and appealing and this is accomplished by selecting the right combination of words and then presenting them in a dynamic way. Make what you say seem important in a general or in a personal way which arouses the interest of your listener.

DESIRE: this is created when the listener feels that your message or request carries *mutual* benefit. Remove from your dialogue the word 'I'. Substitute 'we' or 'us' or 'you' as often as possible. One-sided requests seldom bring positive response. If you *want* something, *offer* something.

*See chapter 9 *Sales Cybernetics* by Brian Adams.

ACTION: there is an *automatic* response by the listener if you can successfully gain his/her attention, build interest and create a desire for your proposition. The action you receive may not always be the action you want. However, it will prove to be positive more times than negative if you prepare what you want to say and then follow it through with an effective vocal presentation.

5. HOW TO DEVELOP AN EFFECTIVE VOCAL PRESENTATION

Your words and their presentation create an image in the minds of those who listen to you speak. Your patterns of speech are indicative of your level of intelligence. What you say and how you say it are true confessions of your weaknesses, your strengths, your failures, your successes, your education, your social background and ambitions in life. The *way* in which you speak labels you and reveals the *inner* you.

Many people try to hide their feelings of inferiority by saying little, others, by saying too much. Either way, lack of self-assurance is detectable. Directors, particularly, look for a display of confidence in the actors they cast. Therefore, it is extremely important that your choice and use of words are spoken in a manner which indicates that you are a person who is poised, in control and self-confident. When directors see you as a self-assured actor, it gives them confidence to hire you.

It is up to you as you speak to be sure that your vocal presentation is impressive so that any judgement made of you is favorable to you. Establish in your mind that, with practice, you can become a confident conversationalist, public speaker, actor and communicator. Several suggestions to assist you in this regard are:

- Don't be afraid to speak your mind. Always speak clearly, concisely and calmly. Be firm, forthright.
- Think out in your mind exactly what you desire to communicate. Avoid stammering, hesitation, umms and ahhs, speaking too quickly. Don't put a strain on the listener.
- Keep your message simple, short and speak with a sense of authority on subjects you know something about. Avoid exaggeration or falsehood.
- Hold eye contact with those you address. Do not fidget, nervously move about. Be still, poised, at ease and exude confidence.
- Modulate your voice tone, change with the rise and fall of thinking. Place emphasis correctly. Avoid shrill, nasal or rasping voice qualities. Drop the pitch of the voice to strengthen sounds. Use proper breath control. Don't suck air in through the mouth. Push out on the abdomen when taking in air through the nose or through the mouth. Don't heave-up the chest or lift the shoulders as you breathe.
- Omit slang expressions and profanity from your speech. Don't smoke or chew while talking to others. These habits can be annoying to others

destroying your personal presentation. Use your voice as a showcase to impress others with your correct manners and knowledge.

6. STRONG VOCAL PRESENTATIONS CREATE STRONG FIRST IMPRESSIONS

One of the most difficult things to do when meeting people for the first time is to make a favorable impression. First meetings with others often result in unfavorable impressions being made. First impressions are seldom forgotten. No performer can afford to offend others on first meeting by saying the wrong things, speaking incorrectly, producing a voice-tone which is emotionless and monotonous-sounding.

A word out-of-place, a belligerent attitude, voiced self-pity, repetition of stock phrases, evasiveness, lying, giving conversations a sex connotation, scratching while talking, poor diction, etc, are annoying habits which destroy personal appeal. Your vocal presentation must push toward winning, influencing and controlling others. People you come into contact with must see you as an above-average person.

Except when in idle conversation, people use communication — talking — as a means of establishing or accomplishing something. When listening, people sit in judgement of the speaker. A weak, toneless voice, coupled to incorrect grammar and poor diction are detrimental to good communication — putting across ideas, impressing people and influencing them to respond in a favorable way.

Your first objective when meeting people for the first time, is to stimulate their thinking. You must speak correctly and make what you say seem important. Also, people are sensitive to voice sounds. Easy-to-listen-to voice sounds catch and hold the attention of listeners. Harsh, squeaky voice sounds usually irritate listeners. Make your conversations interesting and informative and 'color' your sounds in a pleasant, melodious way.

Laughter relaxes and brings happiness to those who partake of it. A humorous story injected into a social or business conversation can be an excellent impression-building technique and help to relax the person you are speaking to. Personalize conversations by peppering them with the listener's name. Don't place a wall between you and your listener. Be friendly, warm, polite, charming and *smile* when it is appropriate to do so.

7. HOW TO ELIMINATE SPEECH DETRACTORS

Actors are among the worst offenders when it comes to speech negativism. The reason, I believe, is because of the uncertain nature of acting as a profession. Actors are unsure of 'what's ahead', causing them to worry, fret and become fearful of the future. Little wonder so many actors slip into negative habits of thinking and speaking. Negative phraseology easily ranks as the most damaging of personality-dampening habits one may acquire.

Successful people avoid whingers, pessimists and bad-mouths. If you desire to join the winners' circle, think and speak optimistically. Reverse negative catch-phrases. Speak well of fellow actors, your agent, producers and directors — the very people you wish to work with and *need* to advance your career. The examples of negative phraseology which follow, indicate a speaker lacking in self-confidence.

- I can't make it. I don't have the talent to succeed.
- I can't be bothered. I'm too tired to study.
- What's the use? I'm hopeless at everything I try.
- I can't afford it. I'm broke.
- I'm too fat and ugly to get anywhere.
- My agent is hopeless.
- People don't seem to like me. No one will help me.
- The business is rotten. There's no opportunity.
- I'm unlucky. I know I'll fail.
- I don't know the right people.

8. POSITIVE PHRASEOLOGY ATTRACTS POSITIVE CIRCUMSTANCES AND EVENTS

Project confidence through your greetings, social conversations and business discussions. Establish yourself as an optimistic thinker and speaker. Demonstrate self-confidence in your ability and general attitude to life by speaking and acting in an affirmative manner. Let your words be a positive affirmation of your hopes and desires. Positive phraseology helps to attract positive circumstances, events and attracts others to your cause.

9. VOCAL STYLE IS MAJOR TRADEMARK OF STARS

Many of the older generation of stars distinguished themselves not only by performing with a visible individuality, but by speaking and voicing sounds in a different and appealing way. Their voices became for them a *trademark*, easily identifiable, setting them apart from hundreds of ordinary actors.

An excellent example of vocal style, clear diction and expressive delivery is supplied by actor Jack Palance as narrator and presenter of the television series *Ripley's Believe It Or Not*. Palance melodiously 'colors' words, stretches the vowel sounds, articulates consonants and speaks clearly, softly but most effectively. His voice is a finely-tooled instrument of communication.

Stars — past and present — with an instantly apparent distinctive individuality of voice and speech include:
Judith Anderson, Lauren Bacall, Ingrid Bergman, Humphrey Bogart, Charles Boyer, Yul Brynner, Richard Burton, James Cagney, Leslie Caron, Lee J. Cobb, James Coburn, Gary Cooper, Joseph Cotton, Joan Crawford, Bing Crosby, Bette Davis, Kirk Douglas, Melvyn Douglas, Henry Fonda, Errol Flynn, Joan Fontaine, Glenn Ford, Clark Gable, Ava Gardner, James

Garner, Greer Garson, John Gielgud, Cary Grant, Sydney Greenstreeet, Katherine Hepburn, Charlton Heston, Leslie Howard, Trevor Howard, Walter Huston, Victor Jory, Otto Kruger, Alan Ladd, Burt Lancaster, Vivien Leigh, Jack Lemmon, Lee Marvin, Fredric March, James Mason, Raymond Massey, Adolphe Menjou, Robert Mitchum, Laurence Olivier, Edward G. Robinson, Ginger Rogers, Margaret Rutherford, Barbara Stanwyck, Rod Steiger, Spencer Tracy, John Wayne, Orson Welles, Loretta Young, Robert Young.

10. ESTABLISH YOUR OWN VOCAL TRADEMARK

Your voice accounts for approximately 20 per cent of your personality. It projects your attitudes and exposes your emotions. It can be a stimulant or a depressant. Your voice has the power to impress people, to entice them to see you as *extra*ordinary.

Establish a vocal trademark for yourself. Use your voice to sell your talents in an expressive, authoritative, distinct and pleasant way. A well-modulated voice is pleasing to the ear. A carefully-trained voice enhances your overall personality appeal, marks you as an above-average person. A finely-tuned voice is the key to making others sit up and take notice of you when you speak.

11. HOW TO REMEDY POOR VOCAL PRESENTATION

Begin an immediate course of action to correct voice and speech faults. The best aid will prove to be an audio recorder. This will allow you to hear yourself as others hear you. Cultivation of a vocal trademark will take time and lots of practice and attention to your speech faults. Results won't appear overnight.

The best method of detecting speech faults is to read aloud editorials from newspapers, record what you read and then playback your efforts, noting faults to be corrected. From newspaper editorials progress to reading novels, poems, Shakespeare, the Bible. Read slowly. Reading too quickly is a common fault. It is also a speaking fault with many actors.

Compare how you speak with the articulation and presentation of professional broadcasters. Is your rate of delivery too slow or too fast? Do you stutter, mumble, use wrong emphasis, incorrect inflections? Do you ennunciate, speak clearly so that others hear and understand what you say? Is your speech overloaded with stock phrases and shopworn conversational material which sounds commonplace? Is your accent unattractive to the ear?

A helpful exercise to attain more musical expression, more light and shade, more rise and fall, is to sing what you read up and down the scale, emphasizing key words as you go. This exercise helps to eliminate single-tone, monotonous-sounding speech patterns.

A deep (resonant) voice quality adds to vocal appeal. This quality can be developed by stretching the vowel sounds A-E-I-O-U and lowering the pitch of the voice. Reduce the rate of delivery. A too-rapid delivery of words thins-out voice sounds, reduces the effectiveness of key words and makes listener comprehension more difficult. Sing the sounds of *mmmm* – *nnnn* – *ing*, to enhance resonance, to eliminate a weak, timid-sounding voice quality. Resonance is the vibrant tone produced when sound waves hit the chambers of the throat, head, nose and mouth.

12. AN IMPRESSIVE VOCAL PRESENTATION CAN MAKE YOU RICH

Actors aren't the only people in the business of marketing their voices. Lawyers, sales persons, ministers of religion, politicians, advertising and public relations persons and professional seminar speakers rely heavily on their ability to present themselves in an impressive way.

Clear, well-modulated, resonant voices are literally worth their weight in gold. Take the case of professional communicator John Casson. He earns up to $1,000 a day for his lectures to businessmen on how to communicate effectively. He draws freely on the theatre world to dramatise his speeches.

The son of one of British theatre's most famous husband-and-wife teams, Sybil and Lewis Casson, John did a stint as director of the Glasgow Citizens' Theatre, then as resident director with Australia's J.C. Williamson's Theatres.

What makes John's speaking ability worth $1,000 a day? He admits it isn't necessarily his knowledge on communication, because *what* he says 'holds nothing new.' It's more in the *way* he puts his message across. 'I know how to do that,' he says.

John points out that there are things one learns in the theatre to grab and hold the attention of an audience: 'Firstly, when I speak I use my voice without affectation. Secondly, I control my nerves. Thirdly, I get on with the job of communicating my message instead of spending time protecting and promoting my ego.'

Earning sizeable sums of money as a professional speaker does require specific subject knowledge, but coupled to knowledge is an important factor — *how* to present it. Not every knowledgeable person wants to become a professional speaker. However, I feel sure that many *many* more than there are would be in there pitching if only they knew *how*.

Actors do not necessarily have to have impressive looks to succeed as actors, but they do require an impressive vocal presentation. Your voice can make you rich — acting, presenting, public speaking — if you develop it and use it in an unusual and dramatic way.

13. HOW TO ESTABLISH CREDIBILITY AND RESPECT WHEN YOU SPEAK

Establishing an immediate rapport with people you meet is absolutely essential if you want them to work on your behalf, to like you and to be impressed by what you say and do. Those you meet must see you as a *genuine* person, not a selfish person, a conceited person or an insincere person.

Success does not come easily or freely. It is earned. You become successful by giving as well as receiving. If you seek the help of others and ask them to give you their time, their talents, their experience, their knowledge, their friendship, then you must be prepared to give something in return — especially your 'thanks'.

Your credibility is established and respect earned when your actions correspond to your spoken desires, feelings and beliefs. What you say must tally with what you feel. It is unwise to utter insincere remarks, offer insincere flattery or attempt to lie and cheat your way through interviews and casting sessions. Be receptive, be appreciative, flatter and charm, but be genuine. Speak the truth. Far too many people are guilty of insincerity, which brings into question their reliability and credibility.

If help is required from an important person then be forthright and say so, giving the reason why you seek assistance. Don't hedge or present half-truths. Gain the respect of those you want to assist you.

14. HOW TO MAKE GREETINGS AND RESPONSES ABOVE THE ORDINARY

The moment you focus your attention on your greetings and responses you become aware of how routine they sound. Such well-worn phrases as: 'How are you?' 'I'm fine.' 'What's new?' 'Nothing much.' 'How's your job?' It's allright.' Those and other equally mundane expressions are devoid of individuality. They do little to establish your personal appeal.

Whether you are conscious of it or not, you, like everyone, have developed the habit of injecting into your greetings and conversations stock phrases and hackneyed expressions. One of the most commonplace is: 'You know?' Count the number of times you and others use it in general conversation.

There are several ways to avail yourself of new greetings, responses and conversational material. The following five suggestions will get you started on a new course of conversational individuality. The purpose of this exercise is to make you aware of what it is you intend to say and then saying it minus commonplace expressions.

1: Instead of the customary 'hi there, how are you?', inject into your greeting the other person's name: 'John Aston, good morning to you.' 'Mrs. James, good afternoon.'
2: Make opening remarks a statement instead of a question: 'Jean, you look exceedingly well this morning.'
3: Use an interest teaser: 'Tony, I'm glad we've met. You've reminded me of an important matter this morning. Thank you.' Naturally, people you greet with this teaser will be curious as to what you mean and likely to respond with, 'What is it?' Conceive a purposeful answer relating to something you need to accomplish or to a forthcoming appointment.
4: Replace stock phrases with silence. A pause mid-sentence or following a question put to you will serve to draw attention to you.

5: Select topical and interest-arousing tidbits of news gathered from the media and use them as openers or within your conversations: 'Jack, I thought of you this morning when I heard on the radio that interest rates are up one per cent.' 'Joan, I was reading an article on Hong Kong. You were there recently. What impresssed you about the place?'

15. EXTEND YOUR VOCABULARY — WORDS ARE ACTORS' TOOLS OF TRADE

Words are our major means of communication. If your speech is to be an asset rather than a liability you must improve your choice of words via an extension of your vocabulary. It will prove beneficial to develop a special word skill so that the words you speak shade your meanings more accurately toward what is on your mind. This brings an added dimension to your personal presentation.

A dictionary is the best source for learning new words. Start with words beginning with the letter 'A' and work your way through to the end of the dictionary. Select a minimum of five new words each day. Write them down in a note book along with their definitions. Inject them into conversations at social and business meetings and when conversing with family and friends. Be careful in the selection of words. Too many unfamiliar words — difficult to pronounce and to define — won't aid your communication effectiveness. Your speaking aim is to sound natural, to use words easily and comfortably not artificially or in a too theatrical way. People aren't impressed by vocal affectation.

When you read or hear words you do not understand, take note of them, check the definitions in a dictionary and then add them to your word-building list. Should you require other than ordinary words to convey a story or to express an idea, then consult a thesaurus. You do have to sell yourself to others, therefore, use persuasive and descriptive words to put your message across. But remember: refrain from using words in a manner which sounds unnatural or in a condescending way.

Creating dynamic impressions requires the use of understandable speech, not confusing speech. Your communication ability — using words — must have a ring of sincerity as well as authority about it. *Word-skill* is a powerful attention-getter that can put your ideas and your personality across in three vivid ways: *easily, confidently, impressively.*

16. A TIP FROM JOHN BARRYMORE ON WORD EXPRESSION

Actor John Barrymore was taught how to use words in a most effective way by voice coach Margaret Carrinston. She instructed the actor to take hold of a piece of fruit and to describe to her what he was holding. 'I'm holding a big red apple,' he replied in an expressionless tone of voice.

Carrinston made Barrymore recite that line for three weeks until he made that apple sound the most delicious piece of fruit ever grown. It was a lesson Barrymore never forgot. He became a master word-user, thrilling audiences with his dramatic presentations. 'That woman taught me to make love to words. It's a lesson in word skill actors should learn,' Barrymore said.

Make love to words. Use them meaningfully, appealingly, confidently and eloquently to make your performances 'come alive' and to establish another aspect of your personality and talent appeal.

17. USE WORDS AS *CARROTS* NOT CLUBS

The words you speak can be an effective means of winning friends and influencing people. Words improperly used and harshly presented can cause people to turn against you, to dislike you and to refuse to help you. It is better to use words in the form of carrots — enticements — when seeking the assistance of others rather than as clubs in an attempt to bully them into accepting your viewpoints, proposals or requests.

Words are your personal vocal agents selling you in a positive way or destroying your credibility and opportunity for success. They become mirrors reflecting your thoughts, feelings, beliefs and proposed actions. Use words with careful consideration as to their effect. Use them as a bridge to common understanding and friendship. When your listener's communication channel is open it gives you an opportunity to make your mark, to persuade and then to win.

Delete from your conversations words with a negative ring. Where possible, always use positive-sounding words. In the wake of what you say people are left happy or sad, friendly or hostile, agreeable or antagonistic toward you. The attentiveness you receive, the encouragement you get and the help you are offered are determined by your choice of words and how you present them.

18. VINCENT PRICE THE MASTER WORD-USER

Theatre critic, Harry Robinson, writing in the Sydney *Sun-Herald* on the performance of Vincent Price playing Oscar Wilde, pointed out: *Oscar Wilde and Vincent Price. Two remarkable people. Together at the Theatre Royal. Price is a great actor, terrific style, beautiful diction — he can put sixteen syllables into the word "evening". We are very fortunate that he is here.*

Price, as the master communicator-motivator, succeeds because he projects thoughts and feelings through his lines and does it with the utmost clarity and sincerity. The audience hears every word, understands every word and believes everything said. Price twists words around his little finger in a carefully-orchestrated way to make them sound interesting and pleasurable to listen to. He knows how to move audiences in a highly-emotional way. He is an impressive and technically proficient actor.

19. HOW TO IMPRESS OTHERS BY NOT SAYING A WORD

One half of communication is talking. The other half — perhaps the more important half — is listening. The art of conversation goes hand-in-hand with the art of listening. A good listener indicates personal interest in us and our ideas. A good listener pays us a compliment.

Some people talk far too much and listen too little. Silence can be a form of conversation. Sometimes silence speaks louder than words and says more. Good first impressions can be created by closing the mouth and opening the ears.

A good listener always gives the other person a chance to take center stage. It makes the other person feel important. It pays the other person a compliment. It makes the other person more apt to pay attention when it's his or her turn to listen. Learn to be silent when silence is vital. When you're listening, you're learning. *Silence is golden.*

20. HOW TO LEARN WHILE YOU LISTEN

There are three aspects to learning while you are listening. They are:

1: LISTEN for ideas, facts, important information.
2: LISTEN for directives, points of view.
3: LISTEN to the very end before evaluating and passing judgement on the speaker and his or her message.

21. VITAL INFORMATION ON LISTENING FOR THE ACTOR

Know when silence is golden, when it is to your advantage to stop speaking and begin listening. Listen to the speaker without interruption. Concentrate on what the speaker is saying. Concentration is a potent listening weapon. There is an opportunity to learn as you listen. There is a chance that something of importance may not be said if you monopolize negotiations and conversations. Thus, non-listening can be disadvantageous to you.

Good listening requires strict concentration and discipline of the emotions to avoid the mind blanking-out incoming information. Clear the mind of insignificant thoughts when conversing with others. This is particularly important when receiving blocking and performance directions from a director or appointment times and dates from an agent. When the mind is disciplined to *accurate* listening, it is able to absorb all that it receives. When the message, the command, the direction is understood, misinterpretation or time-wasting retelling is avoided. Accurate listening eliminates poor communication. Good acting develops from good listening.

22. ON MARLON BRANDO AND LISTENING

Silence is golden is not the rule always adhered to by Marlon Brando. He is a person intensely preoccupied with his own thoughts, feelings, and the public causes he supports. Like so many of his contemporaries, he tends not to listen when others are talking unless the direction of discussion is firmly in his court.

In the book *Brando*,* the writers Joe Morella and Edward Z. Epstein quote Brando as saying: 'People around me never say anything. They just seem to want to hear what I have to say. That's why I do all the talking.'

Director Lewis Milestone was subjected to Brando's non-listening during the making of *Mutiny on the Bounty*. Brando spent hours arguing over script changes and how scenes should be played. According to Milestone, 'Brando wouldn't listen to directorial suggestions. He tried to take charge of the production and humiliated me in front of the crew.'

According to an actor friend who worked on the film, Brando was more concerned with arguing *his* concepts rather than listening to the points-of-view of Milestone, producer Aaron Rosenberg and writer Charles Lederer. My friend summed it up this way: 'Had Mr. Brando talked less and listened more, there would have been far less argument, fewer frayed nerves, less time and money squandered and a lot better picture produced. It was an energy-draining, stressful experience and I blessed the day it finished.'

According to MGM, Brando cost the company a great deal of money because of the extra months of shooting. Milestone quoted a figure of 'at least $6 million.' Brando claimed the extra costs were due to 'poor executive operation.' The final budget hit $27 million. It was a massive financial headache for Metro-Goldwyn-Mayer.

When working in a production, it is the responsibility of the actor to make a concerted effort to co-operate with fellow artists, crew members and especially the director. Less self-preoccupation, more attentive listening and less arguing must surely bring better personal relationships and a more relaxed performance atmosphere.

23. HOW TO WIN THE ADMIRATION OF YOUR DIRECTOR

It's a fact that talkers take-in little, listeners take-in a lot. I've worked in many productions where directors have had to repeat their instructions because of inattentive actors and crew members. It's a frustrating and time-wasting exercise to have to keep telling people what they are to do. Misunderstandings and arguments could well be avoided and mistakes minimized if more time were devoted to listening than talking.

The cure for non-listening is simple: stop talking when you should be listening and pay attention to the speaker's message or directive. Clear your mental slate so that it is capable of absorbing ideas, dates, facts, opinions and commands.

24. HOW TO BECOME A GOOD COMMUNICATOR

Communication is a two-way exchange of understanding. Therefore, talking is one part of communication and listening the other. The two basic reasons humans fail to understand one another are:

1: We fail to use in an efficient way the *language* we know.
2: We fail to *listen* in a satisfactory way.

Brando Crown Publishers Inc.

Don't be guilty of either of the foregoing communication faults. Understand the words you use and put them together in a logical sequence of ideas so that your listeners can grasp what is in your mind. Don't talk *at* your listeners. Talk *to* them. *Listen* to them. Harmonious human relationships are based on understanding not *mis*understanding. There must be a free-flow of ideas from one person to the next to bring about comprehension and appreciation of each speaker's point-of-view.

The art of good communication is to express ideas and opinions in a forthright way so that your listeners will be impressed by your knowledge, your sense of conviction to your ideals, your background, your presentation and your personality.

Prior to attending a social or business appointment, casting session or professional engagement, ask yourself the following questions:

(a) What message do I wish to impart?
(b) What do I want my listener or audience to think and feel?
(c) Will I know when to stop talking and start listening?
(d) Have I adequately researched and prepared my presentation?
(e) Am I confident I can create the right impression?

25. GOOD COMMUNICATION RAISES YOUR SOCIAL AND PROFESSIONAL STATUS

Your social, business and professional attendances and performances will improve when you eliminate annoying habits of speech. You must become acutely aware of personal communication faults. Be aware of speech habits such as: mumbling, grunting, gasping due to improper breath control, choking sounds, stuttering, stammering or stumbling over words.

Good vocal communication helps to stamp you as a dynamic individualist. If you are guilty of negative vocal habits you are putting up your own barriers to social, business and performance acceptance.

Work on getting people to like you, accept you, want to help you through a dynamic expression of words clear in meaning, friendly in tone, expressively phrased and confidently communicated. When people are *moved* by what you say and how you say it, they want to hear *more* from you. When people listen to you an opportunity arises to impress them, to gain their admiration.

26. HOW TO GET THE RIGHT PEOPLE TO ASSIST YOU

Your habits of speech, your attitudes and actions, your personality and character are the reasons people accept or reject you. Unless you make a positive impression on others you cannot expect them to help you. Your talents will not see the light of day if agents, directors and producers decide that you are unworthy of assistance.

Work on getting people to like you through your friendliness and general presentation. Naturally, you won't get every person you meet to like you, but if you work at it, you will get a majority of the people you meet to take a shine to you and lend you their support. This can be accomplished by taking the initiative when you meet others. Greet them with an open mind, with a firm handshake and with enthusiasm. Communicate honest thoughts and feelings. You have nothing to fear from any person if you are honest of thought, feeling and action.

27. *FIVE* WAYS TO INFLUENCE PEOPLE

As a professional actor your job will include meeting people socially as well as professionally. You will be expected to help with publicity and promotion and this means dealing with newspaper, radio and television interviewers. The force and clarity of your communication ability, the effectiveness of your personality appeal with bring judgement on you in a positive or negative way. The advancement of your career will depend on your talent and the judgements shaped on you by those who see you oh the screen and meet you in person.

Your effectiveness will be enhanced in many ways by improving not only your talents but your personal presentation. Five ways to influence others, are:

1: *INFLUENCE* others with the way you *THINK.*
2: *INFLUENCE* others with the way you *SPEAK.*
3: *INFLUENCE* others with the way you *LISTEN.*
4: *INFLUENCE* others with the way you *ACT.*
5: *INFLUENCE* others with the way you *REACT.*

28. EFFECTIVE COMMUNICATION BRINGS POSITIVE MOTIVATION

COMMUNICATION is the ability to express your ideas, opinions, directives and interests in a clear, rational and precise manner in addition to being able to express the ideas, opinions, directives and interests of others in like manner.

MOTIVATION is the result of effective communication. It is getting things accomplished through our own drives (self-motivation) or inciting others to act and react in the way we want them to act and react (persuasion). Communication and motivation go hand-in-hand.

The art of successful *communication* includes the ability to:

DEVELOP   valid ideas and opinions.
EXPRESS   valid ideas, opinions, directives, interests.
LISTEN   to the ideas, opinions, directives, interests of others.
RETELL   accurately the ideas, opinions, directives, interests of others.

The art of successful *motivation* includes the ability to:

SWAY   with valid ideas, opinions, directives, interests.
CONVINCE   with valid ideas, opinions, directives, interests.
CHANGE   with valid ideas, opinions, directives, interests.

Motivating others to a particular course of action is not a matter of forcing them to do your bidding. Mental coercion and physical bullying bring resentment, hostility and hate in addition to stubborn resistance on the part of those it is used against. A subtle approach, a gentle urging with promise of mutual benefit is the best method to entice others to do your bidding in a spirit of helpfulness and friendliness.

29. FULFILL NEEDS OF OTHERS AND YOU'LL WIN THEM

Every human being has four basic needs which he or she seeks to fulfill. These needs are:

1: *Physiological* needs.
2: *Social* needs.
3: *Psychological* needs.
4: *Creative* needs.

If you want others to give you a job, take you on as a client or to respond to your performances in a positive way, offer incentives which in some way fill *their* needs.

Personal motive is the power which operates on the will of all humans causing them to respond. Put another way, motive is an 'I want a reward' attitude. Failure to present a suitable motive — a reason to respond — is a sure way to be denied what you seek.

30. AUDIENCES SEEK INTELLECTUAL AND EMOTIONAL FULFILLMENT

Audiences give of their time and money to satisfy intellectual and emotional needs when they attend a live performance or watch a teleplay or motion picture. Actors have the power to *move* audiences, to make them laugh or cry, to have them experience fear or contentment, to inform them, educate them, stimulate them, motivate them and to entertain them. These things are nothing less than audiences expect from performers and they will respond in a positive way if given a reason to do so. If performers do not *pay-off*, then audiences feel cheated and respond in a negative way.

Good actors are those who create and present characterizations so that an audience is aroused in an intellectual and emotional way in accord with the dictates of the writer's story. Good actors work for the benefit and the enjoyment of an audience.

Sir Tyrone Guthrie instilled into the minds of those actors he coached and directed, the importance of 'stimulating' the feelings of an audience

84

through acting communication and persuasion. He put to them the proposition that people go to the theatre to be thrilled, sometimes to be educated, but mostly to be entertained and the duty of every actor is to see that they aren't disappointed.

Good actors must learn the art of proper communication and motivation, not only to present their own ideas and needs in a winning way, but to be in a position to present the ideas and concepts of writers in the best way possible.

31. COMMUNICATING PERSONALITY THROUGH BODY LANGUAGE

The way you walk, sit, rise, shake hands, hold your head, fold your arms, gesture, can reveal a great deal about you — particularly about how you feel. The moods and feelings that you try to lock within yourself burst out in physical ways which become a part of your personality and shape the way you present yourself. It's called *body language.*

When you attract the attention of others it is because they 'feel' there is something unusual about you — unusual in a negative or positive sense. Your body language, though you might not be conscious of it, could be revealing things you do not wish to be revealed. Your secret thoughts and feelings about others might not be as secret as you have imagined. Therefore, become aware of your body language. Take control of it. When you attract the attention of others be certain that you are indicating through your words what your body language is revealing.

Your body language holds meaning to the person watching you. Don't alienate that person with offensive mannerisms. Undertake a study of body language — what it represents and how it can be read — and use its positive effects to enhance your personality.

32. BODY LANGUAGE AND WHAT IT SIGNIFIES

The following examples of body language should be assessed against your own physical responses so that, henceforth, you are consciously aware of what you are communicating to others in a non-verbal way.

THE HEAD: a sudden look up, indicates a desire to learn more, to be convinced that what is being said is true. Also indicates expectation and hope. Head down, indicates the listener is contemplating the subject under discussion. Shows weariness, loneliness, a shrinking away from the gaze of others. Head angled to one side, means the listener requires convincing or disbelieves the speaker.

THE EYES: steady eye contact reveals a self-assured type, a person with nothing to conceal, nothing to fear. Eyes reveal true feelings. Poor eye contact reveals lack of self-assurance, shyness, perhaps the speaker or listener has something to hide. Shifty, darting eyes reveal an uneasiness, tension, anger or frustration.

POSTURE: tall, erect, shoulders back, indicates well-being, a person with vitality. Slumped posture indicates poor health, weariness, laziness, lack of ambition and a negative thinker.

THE ARMS: gestures away from the body indicate a forthright person, a quick-thinking individual, candid, confident, demanding, ambitious and an extrovert. Inward gestures (toward the body), indicate a self-centered person, an introvert. Arms folded across the chest reveal a stubborn, persistent, arrogant, power-hungry type. Could suggest a covering up of insecurity. Excessive gesturing while talking indicates an intense, emotional rather than a rational-thinking person.

HANDS: hidden hands indicate a secretive, un-co-operative, non-compromising type. Hands clasped indicate a thoughtful type but prone to procrastination. A person with an analytical mind.

THE HANDSHAKE: strong grip indicates ambitious, confident type, high in self-value. A strong mind and forthright. A weak grip shows timidity, a person lacking in positive self-image values. The handshake is a reliable guide to human personality.

33. HOW TO LOOK AT OTHERS IN A POSITIVE WAY

Hold the head at a straight, *level* angle and maintain eye contact when talking to people. Don't allow the eyes to dart about, drop to the floor or rise to the ceiling. The eyes are the mirror of the soul, revealing attitudes, emotions and degrees of self-confidence.

During the years I've worked as a television interviewer, I've always made a point of studying the eyes of interviewees. In an instant the eyes reveal self-assurance or lack of it, whether or not a person is likely to blank-out, hedge on questions or is being totally honest with answers to probing questions. Eye contact is the best method of 'reading' people, while at the same time establishing in the minds of others your own strengths.

34. HOW TO GET OTHERS TO INSTANTLY WARM TO YOU

When meeting another person, particularly for the first time, use a warm, friendly smile and hold the thought, 'I like this person'. Regardless of how unfriendly others may be toward you, never project resentment or let them feel that you are hostile toward them. When you generate goodwill toward others it's hard for them to remain chilly toward you. A firm handshake and pleasant smile take the emphasis off aggressiveness and anger, helping to 'soften' the attitudes of others.

35. HOW TO GET OTHERS TO LOOK AT YOU IN A POSITIVE WAY

Good posture is a personal attribute that adds to every actor's social and career progress. It is also a factor in maintaining good health.

Stand tall, the shoulders back, lift the chest and chin. Don't allow the shoulders and head to pitch forward. Good posture improves the fall of clothes and appearance generally. [This subject is treated in more detail in chapter ten.]

36. THE ACTOR AND PHYSICAL FITNESS

If you desire to succeed in acting and become a big money earner, you'd better stay alive long enough to enjoy the fruits of your labor. If you heap abuse on your body — eat junk foods, avoid exercise, use drugs, smoke and drink alcohol — you are in for a short life.

Stomachs overloaded with inferior, hard to digest foods cause a chemical imbalance in the system. Food is a source of energy which should not only sustain, it should satisfy without overloading the system. Stay away from highly-processed foods, fad diets and foods with additives. If you want to lose weight and stay slim discover a sensible diet and exercise. Reduce intakes of salt, sugar, fats and foods which heavily-add calories. Eat plenty of natural foods with an emphasis on fresh vegetables and fruits. Worthy of reading is the book *Nathan Pritikin Diet and Exercise*. If you are in doubt as to a diet that won't damage your health, consult a doctor, but in the meantime, discipline your eating habits and embark upon a regular exercise program.

37. *TOBACCO* AND THE ACTOR

Tobacco is ruinous to the stomach, lungs and throat. Actors Dick Powell, William Talman, Ray Collins, Bill Hopper and Humphrey Bogart, singer Nat King Cole, broadcaster Edward R. Murrow, producer Walt Disney and writer Quentin Reynolds, all died from lung cancer, attributed to inveterate cigarette smoking. And former matinee idol, Stuart Granger, admitted: 'Health? I've ruined mine smoking.'

Cigarette smoking is a disgustingly-smelly, dirty habit, costly in terms of money and health. It can be deadly. If you desire good lung power, freedom from wheezing and coughing in addition to a pleasant-sounding voice, don't smoke. In truth, it's the cigarette that smokes — you're just the *sucker*.

Actress Linda Darnell had beauty and talent. She made strong impressions in the films *The Mark of Zorro, Blood and Sand, Summer Storm, My Darling Clementine, Forever Amber* and *A Letter to Three wives*, among others. She died at forty-four after falling asleep with a lighted cigarette that set fire to her bedroom in a friend's house in Chicago. I spoke to her the night prior to her leaving Los Angeles. I was putting together a film package and discussed with her the possibility of her playing one of the major roles. 'I'll meet with you on my return,' she said. Unfortunately, that was not to be. An accident, attributable to smoking, brought a tragic end to the life of this talented performer.

Cary Grant, a smoker for thirty years, kicked the habit. 'I won't have anybody near me who smokes. I don't go to night clubs because they are full of sick people smoking and drinking. I can't stand the smell of cigarette smoke,' Grant said.

Stars who never smoked or who have given up smoking, include: Pat Boone, Doris Day, Bob Cummings, Julie Andrews, John Forsythe, Lorne

Greene, Danny Kaye, Andy Williams, Fred MacMurray, Paul Newman, Joanne Woodward, Michael Jackson. Why not protect your voice, preserve your throat, stomach and general heath and add your name to the non-smokers list?

38. *ALCOHOL* AND THE ACTOR

The number of actors whose careers and lives have been damaged or ruined by alcohol is a matter of public record. John and Dianna Barrymore, Errol Flynn, Tom Conway, Judy Garland, Veronica Lake, Alan Ladd, Spencer Tracy, William Holden and Richard Burton experienced a personal battle with alcohol. Actor Dana Andrews fought and overcame the problem.

Peter Finch, Laurence Harvey, Robert Shaw, Patrick Magee, Peter O'Toole, Oliver Reed and Richard Harris, over the years, all built a reputation as 'hard-drinkers' and 'hell-raisers'. Richard Harris says he hasn't touched a drop since 1981 and the few who are left of the 'old drinkers brigade' have reformed. 'I remember speaking to Burton and we decided that we'd spent one-third of our life getting drunk, one-third getting over being drunk and one-third sleeping. Now that he's no longer with us, it makes you think about death,' Harris said.

Gene Autry, screen cowboy hero of the 'thirties, 'forties and 'fifties, admitted that his health suffered because of his drinking problem. 'It creeps up on you slowly so you don't notice it until it's too late. No one wins against an excessive drinking habit,' the former matinee idol said.

39. *DRUGS* AND THE ACTOR

Mental depression is a common malady among actors. It is sometimes brought on through rejection and criticism. Whether mild or severe, it seriously damages an actor's self-esteem. Unable to cope, some actors become emotional cripples and turn to drugs.

Drug taking is an insidious practice. In the long run, it brings untold misery, financial hardship, ill health — even death. Drug taking to cure emotional problems is a cowardly and stupid practice. It is indicative of a weak-minded and self-centered person. Don't fall into its ruinous claws. Don't become one of the 'mindless breed', addicted to man's foulest enemy.

40. *DRESS* AND THE ACTOR

'Male and female actors,' said the late Edith Head, Hollywood costume designer, 'must learn to wear clothes with complete ease. Audrey Hepburn and Sophia Loren are two attractive actresses who know how to wear clothes with ease. And of the men, Cary Grant will always be my favorite. He wears clothes superbly and in a way you'd expect of a true superstar.'

Another Hollywood costume designer, Anthea Sylbert, feels there are very few people around who have the fashion presence of the 'thirties and 'forties, except perhaps Jack Nicholson. 'He loves to wear good clothes. He likes being a movie star,' she says.

'Many of today's up-and-coming stars want to make a million dollars, but don't want to bother with looking like a movie star,' and, according to Anthea, 'Faye Dunaway is one of the few female stars who makes an effort to look glamorous.'

New York-based costume designer, Theoni Aldredge, who won an Oscar for her work in *The Great Gatsby*, maintains: 'Clothes are important to the actor, both on and off the screen. I feel men should worry about their clothes and how they look as much as women.'

41. DRESS FLAIR MARKS YOU AS SOMEONE SPECIAL

Elegant clothes worn with flair are an asset to the image of every performer. The public sees screen stars as extraordinary people. They expect them to dress in an extraordinary way, expressing their status and mode of living.

Fashion flair is a certain feeling for clothes which complements your physical look (physique) and personality. It is very much a question of good judgement and taste. When you are elegantly dressed you feel better and more self-confident. It is important to take pride in your appearance, to look your best on *and* off the screen.

42. CARY GRANT'S ADVICE ON DRESS SENSE

I first met Cary Grant in 1958. I interviewed him for a series of stories I was writing on Hollywood. I was impressed with his dress sense and told him so. 'What's the secret of your being included on so many "best-dressed" lists?' I asked him. 'I dress to please myself. I don't buy trendy clothes. They date too quickly. Simplicity is the essence of good taste. I prefer well-cut, quality clothes that aren't flashy and I look after my clothes,' he told me.

Avoid fad styles, flashy colors, poor quality materials and poorly-cut garments. High style is *elegant* style using quality materials. Dress to suit your personality, your physique and your coloring. If you desire to become a screen star, begin by dressing like one. And remember Cary Grant's advice: *simplicity is the essence of good taste.*

43. *GROOMING* AND THE ACTOR

Good grooming and personal hygiene are essential when working with others. Actors who fail to recognize this fact aren't likely to make a positive impression or endear themselves to others.

I've worked with actors who seemed unaware of science's miraculous discovery — deodorant. During the making of a telemovie, the wardrobe mistress told me that one of the male actors she had just dressed had 'terrible body odor'. After completing two scenes with this actor, I had to agree with her. It was offensive and I felt quite ill working alongside him.

The rules of good grooming are: wash hair regularly. Clean and manicure nails. Be sure the breath does not reek of offensive food or liquor odors.

Shower *twice* each day. Polish shoes. Try to have a healthy-looking face tan. This can be accomplished even during the winter months by spending 30 minutes in the sun each day. Good grooming takes extra time, but it's worth the time if you desire to present yourself as an extraordinary personality.

CHECK LIST

INSTANTLY FELT *OUTER* PERSONALITY PACKAGE

YES✓	NO✓	QUALITIES
☐ ☐ ☐	☐ ☐ ☐	*Distinctive* manner of personality projection *Distinctive* manner of speaking and vocalizing *Distinctive* manner of greeting people
☐ ☐ ☐	☐ ☐ ☐	*Positive* way of establishing credibility *Positive* way of listening to others *Positive* way of communicating to others
☐ ☐ ☐	☐ ☐ ☐	*Confident* way of motivating others *Confident* way of fulfilling needs of others *Confident* way of expressing body language
☐ ☐ ☐	☐ ☐ ☐	*Striking* eye contact while looking at others *Striking* mental and physical fitness *Striking* dress and grooming habits

NOTE: if you have more than 10 'yes' qualities your outer personality package is strong. Add to these your *inner* personality group of qualities *plus* your talents and you are well on your way to career success.

SUMMARY OF IDEAS TO REVIEW

1: Personality appeal — true individualism — is highly visible. It comes across in the way in which you speak, listen, move, dress and via your state of well-being. Spruce-up your *outer* self.

2: Your pattern of speech, the words you use, are indicative of your intelligence, your weaknesses, your strengths and your social background. Omit slang expressions and profanity from your speech.

3: Eliminate negative phraseology. Be positive in all you say and do.

4: Extend your vocabulary. Find new words and inject them into your conversations.

5: Silence is golden. Know when to stop talking and start listening. Listen for ideas which could help your career. Listen to your director when he is giving instructions. Listen to fellow actors.

6: Actors need to be good communicators and motivators. Learn the best way to get your ideas across to others. Offer incentives. Fulfill the needs of audiences and you'll win them.

7: Communicate positive body language and know what you are indicating to others through body language. Hold eye contact. Stand tall. Use a firm grip when shaking hands. Don't gesture unnecessarily.

8: Smile when meeting people. Hold the thought: 'I like this person.'

9: Reduce excess weight. Diet. Eat foods that are easily digestible and vitamin enriched. Eliminate tobacco, alcohol and drugs.

10: Dress with flair and elegance. Your appearance is important to your image. Good grooming is essential. Hair, nails, body and clothes must be clean and neat at *all* times.

HOW TO GET
YOUR SCREEN
CAREER MOVING

SCENE 5

Practical Ideas In This Chapter . .

- Establishing A Market Place To Sell Your Talents
- Making An Impact In Hollywood, New York or London
- How To Assemble Effective Presentation Materials
- Sample Resumè
- Mailing Presentation Materials To Studios
- Mailing Presentation Materials To Agents
- Mailing Presentation Materials to Producers Upon Request
- The Star Makers
- The Role of The Agent
- How An Actor Can Help An Agent
- Finding A Suitable Agent
- How To Influence An Agent To Accept You
- Signing An Agency Contract
- An Agency Contract Is No Guarantee of Work
- An Agent Is The Best Person To Negotiate Player Contracts
- What To Request In Contracts
- The Personal Manager
- Watch Out For The Charlatans
- Sound Advice From Phillip B. Gittelman
- The Accountant-Business Manager
- Stewart Granger On Spending Too Much Money
- Cher And Extravagance
- The Press Agent
- Sarah Bernhardt Knew The Value of Being Talked About
- How George Hamilton Created An Image To Crash Hollywood
- Develop An Image Says Publicist Robert Frederick
- Don't Rely On Publicity Alone Cautions Buddy Basch
- Lend A Hand Advises Irwin Zuker
- Keep A Record Of Your Notoriety
- Handling Casting Interviews And Auditions
- Screen Tests
- Preparing Scenes For Casting Directors
- The Use Of Thank You Notes
- Various Categories of Work In Screen Drama
- Union Affiliations
- Securing Part-Time Employment
- Breaking Into The Lucrative Commercial Field
- The Television Commercial Interview
- Dressing For A Commercial Casting Session
- Narrative And Voice-Over Work
- Audio Audition Tapes
- Salaries (Salaries Chart)
- The Work Procedure
- Professional Courtesy On The Set
- The World of The Stunt Actor
- Facing Up To Humiliation
- Extending Your Marketability To Television Hosting
- Rehearsal Schedule (Chart)
- Work Call Sheet (Chart)
- Summary of Ideas To Review

SCENE 5

★★

1. ESTABLISHING A MARKET PLACE TO SELL YOUR TALENTS

Hollywood, New York and London are no longer the exclusive centers of creative opportunity they once were. Many large cities in the US are now promising fields for starting a theatrical career. And recently, Australia has emerged as an important producer and exporter of films and television programs. Sydney, closely followed by Melbourne, are major production centers offering actors screen opportunities. Toronto offers young Canadian actors a chance to gain experience in television and film acting.

Hollywood, most likely will still remain the goal of a great many ambitious actors. In spite of the dwindling opportunities and rapidly increasing band of actors attempting to gain a foothold, there are many advantages in being there. Prominent agents, producers, directors, writers and screen stars still locate there. Big-budget television drama series carry the 'made-in-Hollywood' tag and multi-million dollar budget motion pictures are mostly cast and produced there. Also, success in Hollywood means world-wide success and audience recognition.

Deciding whether to stay in your home town or head for overseas will depend on your financial situation, your family ties and the level of your talent and experience. If there are opportunities for employment in your area then it might be wise to stay at home. Perhaps not permanently, but for two or more years or at least until you have some experience and training upon which to build a career overseas. Producers and casting directors in

Hollywood will want to see a sample of your work, either on film or on video tape. Worthwhile roles in local productions are an excellent calling card. The more you have to show, the easier it will be for your agent to sell you.

Some actors find it advantageous to train in New York, Hollywood or London and then return home to seek employment. There are many first-class schools in each of these cities in addition to private coaches in special fields ready to add polish to every facet of an actor's talent.

Young people, especially, are not encouraged to come to Hollywood or New York, where work prospects are bleak for the untrained and inexperienced. In both places, the cost of living is high. Without sufficient capital or a job, *any* job, chances of survival are slim.

2. MAKING AN IMPACT IN HOLLYWOOD, NEW YORK OR LONDON

Those actors determined to crash one or all three of the top centers for television and film production should arm themselves with all the necessary qualifications upon which success in these centers depends. Exceptional talent is only *one* of the requirements, others have been discussed in previous chapters. The *essential* assets include:

(a) a determination to succeed.
(b) sufficient capital to live on for one year.
(c) a minimum of one year's training in acting.
(d) acting credits in television, film, theatre.
(e) personal magnetism or 'charisma'.
(f) well-presented physically: dress, grooming, manner, posture.
(g) presentation materials: pictures, resumè, biography, audio-video tapes or film of your work.
(h) an ability to sell yourself to agents, producers, casting directors.
(i) good health.
(j) self-confidence based on superior talent.

Very few actors possess *every* qualification necessary to attain screen stardom. If you do consider yourself to be among the few, by all means set your sights high and make an all-out attempt to crash Hollywood, New York, Toronto, London or Sydney. Armed with good presentation materials, a guild card(s), a determination to succeed, good timing and an effective agent to sell your superior acting talents, you stand an excellent chance of making it to the top.

3. HOW TO ASSEMBLE EFFECTIVE PRESENTATION MATERIALS

Your presentation materials are your calling cards. They are professional selling tools. Therefore, they must be properly produced. Presentation materials should include:

(a) good head-shot photographs.
(b) resumè of experience, training, personal data.
(c) biography.
(d) re-prints of publicity materials and reviews of roles performed.
(e) audio-video tapes or film segments of work.

Actors can be notoriously mean when it comes to self-investment. The standard of personal presentation materials is quite low. Some actors do not see the benefit of investing money in professional photographs, typing or printing resumès and producing audio and video tapes of their talent. 'I can't afford to do it,' is the usual excuse. Yet, I've seen actors squandering money on cigarettes and alcohol. They would be better denying themselves these dubious luxuries and spending their money on career benefits. Pictures and background information are essential. Without them you're not only wasting your own time but the time of others when you show up for interviews. They are the tools of trade *all* actors must possess.

PHOTOGRAPHS: seek a professional *theatrical* photographer. They are to be found in cities where actors work. If there isn't a showbusiness photographer in your home town then travel to the nearest city which has one. The business section of the telephone directory is the first place to look. Call a theatrical union, an agent, an actor friend or an advertising agency for a recommendation to a good photographer. Don't waste your money on pictures taken by a friend or amateur photographer showing you in your backyard. They won't do. And usually, nor will pictures taken by hometown wedding photographers. When you have a few names of *theatrical* photographers, visit them and inspect their work. Enquire as to charges, whether they shoot indoors or outdoors or both, how many prints are included in the basic fee, how many rolls of film they would shoot. Select a photographer whose work you admire and with whom you have a rapport. Seek advice as to wardrobe, hairstyle and if female, makeup to apply. Professional-looking pictures are essential.

THEATRICAL HEAD SHOTS 8 x 10 in black and white are standard. It is best to have a variety of shots from which to choose the one or two head shots you ultimately use. Color shots for actors aren't necessary. As your agent will need a constant supply of photographs, *printing* them in runs of 100 or more is the most economical procedure. Each print can then include your agent's name and phone number as well as your own name printed along the bottom of the picture. If your press kit is to be given to newspapers and magazines, black and white *glossy* prints are acceptable by newspapers and color *transparencies* by most magazines, although print media like to shoot their own photographs for feature stories.

THEATRICAL COMPOSITES are used for TV-commercial submissions. They differ to head-shot pictures. Several poses are printed on the *one* 8 x 10 and these should depict whatever *type* you are or can be: sporty-looking, business executive, housewife, gangster, etc. Don't include too many poses, here wearing a funny hat, there a false beard and glasses. Show yourself as a *character* not a caricature causing you embarrassment. A kaleidoscope of odd characters is not the real you. The best composites show an actor representing the types he/she best portrays.

Your pictures will be used by your agent to 'sell' you to those who haven't met you. Therefore, they must be representative of your true look, encouraging the viewer to want to meet you. When selecting prints, seek the advice of your agent and photographer as to the best shots to use. You will require new head shots every one or two years. Casting people want to see you as you are *now*, not as you were ten years ago.

RESUMÉ: this is an important inclusion in your presentation file. Include: personal details such as height, weight, age range, credits, guild memberships, training, agent's name, address, telephone number. If you do not have a private number, invest in an answering service. Agents often call clients on the same day an interview has been arranged. Type or print resumè sheets. Do not hand-write them.

BIOGRAPHY: this is useful to the news media. It should provide a condensed history of activities, education, skills, awards, quotes from reviews of your work, theatrical highlights, interesting incidents and goals you seek to achieve. It is not a credit list but a synopsis of your past and present activities and future hopes. Keep your biography to a single page unless you have a most interesting story to tell.

PUBLICITY MATERIALS-REVIEWS: include re-prints of press reviews and news articles relating to your showbusiness activities. This information indicates that there is a degree of importance about you.

AUDIO-VIDEO TAPES AND FILM CLIPS: these work aids are essential because they allow your agent-manager to present your work to casting directors, producers and directors so that they can assess your acting ability. An audio and a videotape recorder come into their own in this regard. Your performances can be recorded when they appear on television and radio work can be recorded onto audio tape. Film clips, because of their cost and difficulty in obtaining them, are being replaced by less-expensive easy-to-use videotapes. Most feature films are released on home video and this gives actors easy access to their work. Agents and casting directors have or will have access to audio recorders, videotape machines and 16mm film projectors for viewing the work of actors.

THE PRESENTATION FILE: place your printed or typed material and photograph within a cover. It can be an inexpensive plain folder or expensive cover with your name and photograph printed on it. Whichever you choose, your file must look professional in its assembly. Print a sufficient number to last one year. Up-date your file at the end of each year or when you need to insert new credits and information.

PRESS KIT: essentially, an actor's press kit will include the foregoing items with the exception of audio-video tapes and film clips. Press kits are used by studio publicists and press agents to send to media reporters on behalf of a studio player or actor-client prior to a pre-arranged interview.

SAMPLE RESUMÈ

ACTOR'S NAME (ANSWERING SERVICE NUMBER)

AGE RANGE:	30 to 40	AGENT:	name
HEIGHT:	5'10"		address
WEIGHT:	155lbs		phone
EYES:	hazel		
HAIR:	brown	UNIONS:	SAG – EQUITY
SUIT:	40 reg (or dress)	SHOE:	9E
WAIST:	33	GLOVE:	7½
INSEAM:	34	HAT:	6⅞
SHIRT:	15/34 (or blouse)		

STAGE CREDITS:
   Mr. Roberts (Doc) Toronto Playhouse   1985
   The Shrike (Jim Downs) New York Off Broadway   1984

TELEVISION CREDITS:
   Hotel (Johnny) "The Inside Man"   1985
   Dallas (Tallon) "Boom Days"   1985
   Prisoner (Armstrong) "Breakout"   1984

FEATURE FILMS:
   Day of the Phoenix (Slade) Briad Film Prod's   1986
   Roadhouse (John Franks) Aries Films   1985

RADIO CREDITS:
   Canadian Playhouse (13 shows – lead)   1985
   Starlight Mystery Theatre (26 shows – lead)   1984

TRAINING:
   Neighborhood Playhouse (2 yrs) New York
   Canadian Theatre School (3 yrs) Toronto
   TV-Film Industry Workshop (4 yrs) Sydney

SKILLS:
   Surfing, horseback riding, karate, dancing, skating.
   Speak French, German, Spanish. Excellent at dialects.

Actor *Tony Partridge* has good 8 x 10 head shot capturing strong character look.

Actor, TV commercial performer *Robert Greenberg's* 8 x 10 glossy captures bright personality.

Actress *Jane Hamill's* head shot is effective for drama and TV commercial representation.

Gordon Nilsson's 8 x 10 is good example of what casting directors expect to see.

▲ *Ruth Gregson* is seen regularly in TV commercials.

Liz O'Neill presents attractive look in 8 x 10 glossy ▲

▲ *Jean Fahey* has impressive (printed) head shot.

Karen Lennox's 8 x 10 is effective for ▲ drama work.

The information allows the interviewer to study the background of the person to be interviewed. If an actor hires a press agent, the cost of producing and mailing press kits is borne by the actor. In the case of a studio contract player, the studio covers all publicity and promotion costs related to the actor.

4. MAILING PRESENTATION MATERIALS TO STUDIOS

Major studios receive hundreds of pictures of work-hopeful actors in the mail every week. In nearly all cases these pictures are discarded. In some cases, where a stamped, self-addressed envelope is included, a picture may be returned. Therefore, mailing a presentation folder to a television or film studio is a waste of time and money. According to Hoyt Bowers, well known Hollywood casting director, 'Composites that come to studios by mail end up in the wastebasket, as do letters requesting interviews. We interview actors by appointments arranged by agents.'

Professional actors don't send their pictures and resumès through the mail to studios and producers. Their agents submit them for them. Writing to studios requesting an interview marks you as a beginner, an amateur. Initially, use your presentation materials to secure an agent.

5. MAILING PRESENTATION MATERIALS TO AGENTS

Before mailing your picture and resumè file to every agent listed in the yellow pages, call a few of them on the telephone first. Find out who are taking on new clients. Suggest an interview. If it is not granted ask if you can mail your presentation file and follow it up with another phone call in a week or so.

If your file is professionally presented and your picture and background information interesting, you could receive a call inviting you to an interview. But don't take it for granted that an agent will automatically acknowledge your material or send it back to you if he/she isn't interested. One or two might, most won't.

A short (typed) letter should accompany your file. Don't write cute, boring, ridiculous, insulting letters. They will be thrown out with the trash. If you have been recommended to an agent by one of his/her clients, then by all means use that person's name to open a door for you. Always include in your letter a telephone number where you can be contacted. It is less time consuming for an agent to pick up a phone and call you than it is to write you a letter if he/she wants to see you.

6. MAILING PRESENTATION MATERIALS TO PRODUCERS ON REQUEST

Producers, like casting directors of major studios, interview actors by appointments arranged by agents. However, if you have heard about or read in the press that a certain producer is looking for a *new* face to play a particular role and you feel you qualify, then mail your file along with a letter. Set out why you feel you should be granted an interview. Keep your message brief and to the point. The same rule applies to independent casting directors and the casting departments of advertising agencies who make it known that they are seeking new faces for a particular role or commercial to be made on behalf of a sponsor. A picture and resumè arriving on their desks at the appropriate time could result in an interview(s) *and* work.

If you are represented by an agent then allow the agent to make *all* submissions and requests for appointments. If you are new to the business, your agent will introduce your presentation materials to the studios, producers, independent casting directors and casting departments of advertising agencies.

7. THE STAR MAKERS

The people who contribute to an actor's success are many. The people who help to launch an actor are few. They include:

AGENT
MANAGER
PRESS AGENT

Sometimes an actor is helped to stardom by one person – his/her agent. Where a trusted friendship and business bond have been established, success isn't far behind. Such is the case with Hollywood agent Meyer Mishkin and two clients in particular, Richard Dreyfuss and Lee Marvin. Mishkin has genuine friendships with many of his clients and there is a sense of loyalty between them. Star-builders need talented, loyal clients and actors need loyal, honest, friendly agents.

8. THE ROLE OF THE AGENT

A theatrical agent is the *link* between client and producer. An actor employs an agent. An agent doesn't employ an actor. An agent doesn't work on salary but on a commission basis. It is the role of the agent to find the *right* roles for a client, to haggle over fees, billing and perks and to do everything necessary to keep a client employed.

In Hollywood, it is customary for an agent to sometimes accompany a *new*, promising client on important interviews. Where an audition is held in a casting director's office, the presence of the agent is unnecessary. For general casting calls, an agent does not accompany a client.

Good agents – dedicated, hard workers – will have many contacts in the business: writers, directors, producers, casting directors, publicists, press agents. Agents who represent stars nearly always hear about new projects before run-of-the mill agents and without going through the regular casting channels.

An agent will introduce a new client to his/her best contacts first. In most cases, a new client will receive a goodly amount of time and attention during the first few weeks of signing an agency contract.

An agent's knowledge of parts on offer will come from several sources: producer's office, casting director's office, trade journals, media reports, personal contacts and even from clients. In Hollywood, *Breakdown Services* puts out a list each day of television shows and films about to be cast. Details include the types of characters required, names of the producer and director, projected production date and to whom submissions should be sent. The Hollywood trade papers – *Hollywood Reporter* and *Daily Variety* – are also excellent sources of information on upcoming productions. A valuable casting source is *The Australian Film Review*, a trade paper giving production information on upcoming TV shows and films.

9. HOW AN ACTOR CAN HELP AN AGENT

Pictures and resumès are the sales tools used by an agent to help sell the talents of his/her clients. It is customary to print the name and telephone number of an agent at the bottom of photographs and at the top of resumè sheets. Many agents prefer to personally select a client's head shots. Others are happy to use whatever pictures are supplied, providing they are of professional quality. The cost of presentation materials is borne by the actor, not the agent.

Video clips or film clips of an actor's work are a necessity in today's competitive showbusiness market place. Casting directors will nearly always call for 'film' if they do not know an actor's work. A newcomer without a sample of his/her work has to rely on the expertise of the agent to convince a casting director to 'chance' a small role. Sometimes an agent will convince a casting director or producer to 'test' a client. Today, the trend is to shoot these on videotape for instant playback. Video and film clips are an expensive necessity. However, they are the quickest means of finding work in the industry.

Agents expect their clients to 'list' themselves in a casting directory. The cost is moderate compared to the benefit to be gained. An actor's listing includes a photograph and any credits he/she wishes to include, plus the agent's name. A casting directory is a bible to producers, directors and casting directors. In Hollywood, the *Academy Players Directory* is published three times yearly by the Academy of Motion Picture Arts and Sciences. In London *Spotlight* is the casting reference. In Sydney, *Showcast* is published yearly with separate books for male and female players.

A good agent is a busy agent. A busy agent doesn't have time to waste on clients calling to ask 'what's happening, why aren't I working?' If an agent's clients don't work then the agent doesn't earn money. Agents *want* their clients to work or why would they retain them on their books? If you have a valid reason to call your agent, get to the point quickly and make the call brief. Don't arrive at your agent's office without first phoning to make an appointment. And if you're kept waiting, be patient.

One of the busiest agencies in Australia is Bedford-Pearce Management operated by Martin Bedford and Shirley Pearce, two very likeable and hardworking people. I asked them how best an actor can assist his/her agent. 'A client should call the agent after each interview to give the result. Whenever an actor leaves town, even for a few days, a contact point should be left with the agent. It's a good idea to have an answering service or an answering machine which can be checked regularly for messages if an actor is away from home during the day,' Martin advised.

'It is the obligation of an actor to conduct him/herself in a professional way when going on interviews and jobs. Arriving late, being ill-mannered, dressing sloppily, badgering casting receptionists for information, forgetting to take along picture and resumè are things to avoid if an actor wants to make friends and influence people in the business. Unprofessional behavior is apt to bring swift actor/agency severance and little chance of success for those guilty of it,' said Shirley Pearce.

A client can work with an agent he/she isn't particularly fond of but who is a first-rate agent. While there does not have to be a close personal relationship there needs to be a professional working relationship or both parties will suffer. The best actor/agent relationship is where both parties like and respect one another. It's easier to talk positively about someone you like than it is to talk positively about someone you dislike.

Many actors prefer to sign with a big agency rather than a small one because the large agencies are able to offer better protection and aren't so eager to push a client into anything that comes along because they need the commission. Some actors prefer a small agency because they feel they can receive more personal attention and won't get 'lost' in the agency's client list. Walter Matthau is quoted as saying agents are 'promoters and hustlers' who don't particularly 'do any work'. Maybe some are in this category. However, an agent is a necessary tool in an actor's climb to stardom. Let the foregoing be a guide when selecting and working with an agent.

10. FINDING A SUITABLE AGENT

It's been said that finding a good agent is much like finding a good marriage partner – both are extremely difficult to achieve. The success of your dealings with an agent you select will depend on the personal relationship with the person who handles you. In a small agency this is not a problem. In a large New York or Hollywood agency each agent is responsible for a single area of the business such as legitimate theatre, television, motion pictures and variety work. In this situation a different agent represents you for each type of job. It is essential to establish a good rapport with one person in particular who can advise you of various matters concerning your career and follow up on all jobs for you.

In Hollywood and New York (as in all major US cities) agents are franchised by the various craft unions. Lists of all franchised agents are available from *Screen Actors Guild*, 7750 Sunset Boulevard, Los Angeles, CA 90046 or their New York office at 551 Fifth Avenue, New York City, NY 10017.

In London contact *British Actors Equity Association*, 8 Harley Street, London W.1. Agents are franchised by the Department of Trade and Industry.

In Sydney contact *Actors And Announcers' Equity Association of Australia*, 32 Orwell Street, Potts Point, NSW 2011. Agents are franchised by the Department of Industrial Relations. (For the address of Equity in other major Australian cities, consult a phone directory.)

11. HOW TO INFLUENCE AN AGENT TO ACCEPT YOU

Enticing an agent to take on a newcomer is difficult unless the newcomer has exceptional talent and appearance. Helpful advice for inexperienced newcomers comes from a well-known agent I know in New York. He advises: 'An actor's personality is a very saleable commodity. On meeting an actor, an agent needs to see personality first, then talent. If an actor wants an agent to represent him he must glow with personality, have a magic presence. Talent without personality is hard to sell. I'm quite disappointed if the actors I see don't have that "spark" when they enter my office.' And that's the key: exude an *individualistic personality* when asking an agent to accept you. It's hard to reject a person with charm and appeal.

12. SIGNING AN AGENCY CONTRACT

In New York, an actor might *list* himself with but not *sign* himself to one particular agent. He might have several agents working on his behalf. This arrangement is changing in favor of one agent for television commercial representation and one for TV and film drama *or* one agent representing both fields. In Hollywood, the arrangement is for an actor to *sign* an agency contract with one agent to represent him in a particular field – sometimes in all fields. Actor-variety artists use two and sometimes three agents to cover them for drama, commercials and club work.

In the US, agent-actor contracts are covered by the various guilds giving protection to both parties should a dispute arise. Signing a contract gives an agent the 'exclusive' right to seek work for the client. In most of these union contracts, the actor is protected by a clause providing that if an agent does nothing for the actor over a specified period, then the actor may terminate the contract by a notice in writing to the agent. The agent is protected by certain stipulations giving the actor limited rights on refusing roles.

In television and motion pictures, an agency contract covers all work secured by an agent. When the agent and client are mutually satisfied, contracts are renewed, involving nothing more than re-signing for a specified period. It is wise to consult with a union before signing an agency contract if you have any doubts as to your responsibilities.

13. AN AGENCY CONTRACT IS NO GUARANTEE OF WORK

When an actor signs an agency contract, the agent is under no legal obligation to secure work for the client. An actor should not feel that the agent deserves commission – 10 per cent of the gross fee paid to the actor – only if the agent has secured the job in the first place. There are numerous incidental expenses involved in representing a client such as telephone calls, mailings, trips to studios and luncheon meetings with casting people and producers. It is easy for an actor to forget or ignore the endless hours of effort put forth on his/her behalf by an agent. Quite often, the time and expense result in no return to the agent. Be patient and be grateful for the efforts of an agent on your behalf.

14. AN AGENT IS THE BEST PERSON TO NEGOTIATE PLAYER CONTRACTS

The job of an agent is to negotiate all player contracts on behalf of clients. Problems of salary, billing, conditions, etc, are handled far more capably by an agent than by an actor. An agent is in a better position to make demands such as dressing room facilities, transport, billing, hotel accommodation and other client requirements. Any unpleasant feelings a producer might have towards an actor's demands during negotiation can be directed at the agent rather than at the actor, thus protecting the actor from any unpleasantness.

Allow your agent to function for you. Never discuss money matters with a producer or casting director. Most producers won't even bring the subject of money into discussions with an actor, but a new, inexperienced or suspect one might. Even though you might feel qualified to handle money matters, problems could surface at a later date and if you have to bring in your agent to repair the damage you've done, it could prove embarrassing to both of you.

15. WHAT TO REQUEST IN CONTRACTS

As you move forward in your career your agent will seek for you better roles with more prominent billing and higher salary. Your agent will discuss with you the fees he thinks you should receive. The size of the role, the budget and the status of an actor are criteria for arriving at sensible fee structures. Obtaining a weekly contract is a better proposition than a guarantee of two days with a possibility of three more should shooting not go according to schedule. The current trend is for casting people to hire actors on a per-day basis, it works out less expensive for them in the long run. Because it's a buyer's market, some casting people fix a salary on a take-it-or-leave-it basis. Whether to accept or reject is then up to the actor.

Sometimes an agent will suggest to a client that he/she accepts a role for a lower fee because the role is likely to lead to good notices and more work and it is possible to elicit better conditions and amenities making up for the lower fee. It is logical that an actor should want better roles and higher fees as he/she develops as a performer. However, each opportunity to act should be evaluated separately. Consider all aspects in a careful and rational way. If an opportunity presents itself to work in a good film that pays less than a previous role, consider the role itself and judge whether it could bring career advancement. It is foolish to reject work on the basis of salary alone.

If your agent lands a role for you in a (US) television series as a running lead or as a lead in a motion picture, the opportunity to ask for a pleasing salary, good billing and other benefits has arrived. Conditions you should discuss with your agent prior to signing a player contract for a major role, include:

(a) The term of the contract. One year is better than three months if you've been selected to work in a series.

(b) An agreed starting salary with increases each three or six months to the end of the term.

(c) Billing arrangements.

(d) Publicity and promotion arrangements.

(e) A car supplied, pick-up service or limousine service to and from locations.

(f) Permission to retain wardrobe at completion of shoot.

(g) Single dressing room facility with refrigerator and phone.

(h) At liberty to accept work which doesn't interfere with production arrangements or sponsorship if working in a TV series.

Stars, of course, sometimes ask for the moon – and get it. Some stars have percentages attached to their salary arrangements. If the film does well at the box office they share in the proceeds. Some stars insist on script, director and co-star approval. Some make silly, time-wasting demands that are difficult to bring about. If the producer thinks the star is worth the extras and expense, they'll be granted. It is my personal view that actors should not price themselves into oblivion and should be conscious of budget factors during salary negotiations. Be fair, reasonable and sensible. By all means place a hefty value on your talents and seek adequate compensation for your work, but allow mutual benefit.

16. THE PERSONAL MANAGER

An actor does not require a personal manager until he/she has achieved star status or unless the artist is capable of working in several fields not adequately covered by an agent. As an example: actor-author-lecturer *or* broadcaster-writer-actor *or* actor-singer-musician. Most managers operate in the variety field managing singers, comics, sight-acts who perform in clubs, on television and who make records. A personal manager does not take the place of an agent, the manager works in conjunction with an agent to promote the interests of clients.

A manager handles every aspect of a client's career. He will urge the agent to seek specific work, he will arrange, either himself or through a press agent, publicity for his client, advise on wardrobe, hair styles, pictures and presentation materials required. He will spend more time with a client than will the agent because his client list will be smaller than the client list of the agent. A personal manager is indispensable to a busy and successful performer.

A contract between a personal manager and a client is not covered by a theatrical union. Before signing a management contract, consult a lawyer or an agent. Don't sign a contract extending beyond one year and insert a 'let-out' clause allowing you to terminate after 90 days if things do not go as desired.

A manager's commission, which is in addition to the commission paid to an agent, ranges from 15 to 25 per cent of the gross fee paid to an artist. Under certain circumstances it could be more. If a manager advances money to a client or runs-up expenses on behalf of a client, he will want those amounts reimbursed. Commissions and expenses are deducted from each pay check a client receives.

Managers require total control over their clients' careers. It is usual for a client to give a manager power of attorney to collect pay checks from agents and to have the final word on contract negotiations conducted by an agent. Peter Gormley is a London manager of several top recording stars and performers and he has a reputation for total control over the artists he handles. 'There are so many things to be thought of, so many decisions to be made. Someone has to take control,' he maintains.

Discover for yourself whether you really need a manager. Unless you are earning a big salary or have the potential to be a big money earner – a star – a manager will be of little benefit to you.

17. WATCH OUT FOR THE CHARLATANS

There are charlatans pretending to be legitimate personal managers. They sign as many artists as they meet, hoping one will 'click' giving them a steady income. Be wary of any manager who promises to make a star of you in short order, flatters you, promises you the world, asks for a weekly retainer and wants to sign you to a five or ten year contract. Don't let ego get in the way of commonsense. A manager who 'discovers' a newcomer, spends time and money to develop, promote and support a new find, is rare indeed. Don't be taken in by insincere flattery.

18. SOUND ADVICE FROM PHILLIP B. GITTELMAN

Phil Gittelman, a top Hollywood personal manager highly respected in the industry, offers the following advice to newcomers: 'Get your act together before you approach an agent or manager. Study, improve your abilities, expand your knowledge, improve your personality, develop self-confidence. Performers must give agents and managers a commodity to sell. We're in the business of promoting talent — professional talent. We're not in the business to tell lies, sell turkeys or insult the intelligence of casting directors and producers. We wouldn't survive. And that's where it's at.'

Phil is constantly on the go. He works like a beaver for his clients. He advises them, nudges agents for them, charms producers for them and does everything in his power to raise their morale, keep them motivated and moving ahead. Phil is the kind of manager every manager-seeking actor dreams about. Unfortunately, there are too few dedicated, hard-working and talented managers around.

19. THE ACCOUNTANT-BUSINESS MANAGER

Some actors aren't good at handling their own business and financial affairs. As soon as they get money, they spend it. Any actor who earns large sums of money who is a spendthrift, should consider a business manager to take care of banking, bill paying, investments, taxation and other financial matters. Some business managers put their clients on a weekly allowance to curb any tendency to overspend.

Business managers are best found through recommendation. Taking pot-luck by searching through the telephone directory is *not* suggested. It's important to know the reputation of any person you entrust money to. Use caution in this regard.

20. STEWART GRANGER ON SPENDING TOO MUCH MONEY

Former screen idol Stewart Granger told a London columnist that 'greed' ruined his life. 'I was always spending more money than I had and doing films I didn't want to do to pay my debts. I've been rich and lost it all.' The rule: be astute in money matters.

21. CHER AND EXTRAVAGANCE

Singer-actress and superstar, Cher, it's been reported, spends a 'small fortune' to overcome beauty problems, keep her emotions in order and refurbish her personal wardrobe.

Cher estimates that, from time-to-time, she has spent $2,000 a month on beauty needs, abut $900 a month on regular sessions with her psychiatrist and about $6,000 a month on her personal and professional wardrobe in addition to normal expenditures relating to her business affairs and personal living expenses. She posed the question to a friend: 'If I'm ever in the position where I can't afford it, what will I do?' A shrewd business manager would have an answer to her question. However, this talented performer's career is moving from strength-to-strength, so I do not expect that she will experience money worries in the future.

22. THE PRESS AGENT

Independent press agents are hired by actors on a fee or on a percentage basis to publicize up-coming television shows and feature films and generally, to keep their names before the public.

Studio publicists are employed to promote productions prior to, during and following their completion. This is achieved via media stories, pictures and interviews with the stars of the shows. Television interviews, as a general rule, are supported by film or video clips of the show being promoted. Publicists and press agents use every avenue open to them to exploit their programs and clients.

23. SARAH BERNHARDT KNEW THE VALUE OF BEING TALKED ABOUT

'If you are to succeed in this business,' Sarah Bernhardt, the French actress once said, 'people must talk about you. They may talk well or ill, but they must talk.' She was talented, eccentric and arrogant – the world's first superstar. Bernhardt was the most talked-about actress of her time, a theatre idol of the world. Through her 83 years, she earned astronomical amounts of money which she gave away to friends and to her legion of lovers.

Sarah Bernhardt knew the value of publicity. Wherever she went, scandal was close by. In addition to her many love affairs, she surrounded herself with exotic animals. People talked about her in whispers, were in awe of her, shocked by her antics, but they flocked to her performances to get a look at her. She was box-office magic.

It isn't necessary to follow too closely in the footsteps of Miss Bernhardt, but it is necessary to develop an interesting and colorful showbusiness image to entice the news media and public to take notice of you. Reporters and television interviewers love controversial and exciting personalities to write about and interview. They shy away from dull, uninteresting, timid and uncommunicative persons.

During the days of the big Hollywood studios, publicists often created interesting backgrounds for uninteresting contract players being groomed for stardom. In some instances, outright lies were told about a particular actor's past. It didn't seem to matter. Fan magazines eagerly printed whatever was given them by the studio publicity people. Today, the news media and the public are too wise to accept trumped-up publicity stories about actors. Therefore, actors must now *be* interesting and colorful and at all times articulate in presenting themselves.

You can enrich your career as well as your social life by developing a magnetic personality, a special way of looking, talking and acting that will draw people to you, make a solid impression on them, get them to write about you, interview and talk about you. Remember the advice of the world's first superstar, Sarah Bernhardt: 'If you are to succeed, people must talk about you.'

24. HOW GEORGE HAMILTON CREATED AN IMAGE TO CRASH HOLLYWOOD

Screen star George Hamilton maintains that somewhere along the line all actors start becoming the parts they play. 'I started playing into my image and my image fused with me. It's the value of style. It doesn't matter whether you have money or you're broke, it is important to look as though you are rich if you are selling a glamorous image.'

Hamilton looked the part of a wealthy actor when he arrived in Hollywood at the age of 18. Inspired by the image created by Errol Flynn he decided to create his own. Arriving for his screen test he dressed up like an old-fashioned screen star, giving the impression he had wealth. He rented a Rolls-Royce and with an out of work gardener at the wheel masquerading as his chauffeur, drove onto the studio lot. He passed his screen test and was offered 500 dollars a week. He told them it wasn't enough, that he couldn't possibly exist on less than a thousand dollars a week.

His performance resulted in a contract on his terms which gave him the down payment for a new Rolls-Royce of his own. The right image was cast for George Hamilton and he's been living it ever since.

25. DEVELOP AN IMAGE SAYS PUBLICIST ROBERT FREDERICK

Warner Bros. studio publicist Robert Frederick, a friend of many years, advises actors to develop a saleable image for themselves. 'It's important that actors appear to be more than run-of-the-mill types if they want the press to write about them. Television interviews in particular, show the world what an actor is like — how he looks and what he represents off the screen. An actor must appear articulate, talented, intelligent, knowledgeable and of course personable when dealing with the media. It's easy to get publicity for an actor who has those qualities,' he says.

Robert Frederick helps to publicize many top films and hundreds of regular artists and stars. He knows the ingredients needed to reap good media coverage for them. One of the secrets of publicity success is casting the right *image* whether it be for a film, a writer, a producer, a director or an actor. And actors can help the 'image builders' by developing a colorful, confident, charming, sincere and *electric* personality to attract more and better publicity to further their careers.

26. DON'T RELY ON PUBLICITY ALONE CAUTIONS BUDDY BASCH

A friend of long standing, former New York publicist and now syndicated travel writer, Buddy Basch, advises actors to base an acting career on 'things substantial' rather than attempting to crack-the-scene via gimmicks and false stories concocted by a press agent.

When Buddy operated his publicity office he handled the press relations and publicity arrangements for many top actors and performers. Over a pleasant dinner at the New York Friars Club, Buddy told me: 'I built my business and reputation by promoting what I believed to be the truth about my clients. I wrote about the things they had accomplished and the things they were about to accomplish which were not only newsworthy but accurate. An actor should hire a publicist when he has something worthwhile to tell the world. Publicity alone won't make a dud actor into a star.'

27. LEND A HAND ADVISES IRWIN ZUKER

Hollywood press agent, Irwin Zuker, one of the nicest men in the business, is an active publicist who has helped the careers of actors, recording stars and authors. He feels that actors should 'lend a hand' if they hire a publicist to promote them.

'I brief my clients prior to media interviews, advise them to do their homework and properly prepare themselves before talking to the press or appearing on television. They must help me, the interviewer and themselves if they want advantageous publicity. They must think about possible questions and the answers they'll give. The better a client handles the interviews the more interviews I can get for him,' Irwin told me.

28. KEEP A RECORD OF YOUR NOTORIETY

Maintain a press book to house your publicity stories and performance reviews. A record of your career is useful to your agent and to a press agent who may be hired at some time in the future. A large loose-leaf book can be purchased from any stationery store for this purpose.

If you hire a press agent and he or she is successful in getting you a lot of press on a national scale, it is advisable to engage a press-cutting service to collect your publicity stories for you. It's easy to scan local newspapers but nigh impossible to know what has been printed about you in papers and magazines across the country.

29. HANDLING CASTING INTERVIEWS AND AUDITIONS

Actors spend a lot of time attending interviews and auditions. Auditioning is a basic element in the actor's craft. If an actor fails at this stage, there is small chance of future success. Interviews are a bridge to work. An actor must learn to build successful interview bridges.

Interviews are held by casting directors either to 'get acquainted' with a newcomer or to 'read' an actor for a specific part. Directors and producers interview actors for specific parts and if they are impressed will sometimes request actors to read or 'test' for various roles.

Impressions are all-important. Dress and grooming play an important part of good impression-making. Jeans — a badge of office for many actors — are fine, providing they fit well, aren't torn and are *clean*. Personal cleanliness is essential.

It's a good idea to dress as close to the image of the character as you can. Ask your agent for character details. If the character is a sports person, a business person, a politician, a taxi driver, a nurse, secretary, school teacher, gangster, it is not difficult to 'look the part'.

Don't overdo impression-making. Be yourself. You must feel comfortable if you are to exude confidence. Be charming, friendly, exude vitality, speak well. Don't chew gum, light up a cigarette, interview the interviewer, avoid eye contact or fidget. *And* be punctual.

The first question that a director, producer or casting director will ask you is likely to be: 'Tell me about yourself.' Other questions you are likely to be asked are: 'What have you been in lately?' – 'Are you studying at the moment?' – 'Why have you chosen acting as a career?' – 'Are you a union member?' Prepare answers to these general questions *prior* to your interview. If you are asked to read for a part, don't get nervous. Compose yourself. When the script is handed to you, read it through *slowly* to yourself to grasp its meaning.

The secret of good cold readings is to know exactly *what* it is you are saying. Establish in your mind the mood of the scene, discover the motives behind the character's words. Don't read too quickly. Take your time. Hold the script at eye level and to one side of your face to avoid masking your face. Don't attempt to physically 'act out' the part. Speak conversationally. It's nigh impossible to produce a perfect performance at a reading. The development of a well-rounded performance takes time and rehearsal. The objective is to *sound* like the character and *look* like the character, giving an indication that you are right for the part and have the ability to play it well.

30. SCREEN TESTS

Don't be frightened by a video or a film camera. Treat them correctly and they'll bring out your magic screen qualities — providing they are there. Tests are now being done on videotape rather than on film in order to save time and money. Some casting directors test actors in their offices. It's quite informal and takes only fifteen minutes or so.

If you are invited to screen test by a casting director, director or producer, you will be given a script prior to the day of the test. Know your part. Be word perfect. Remove from your mind that the test is a do-or-die situation or you will be a bundle of nerves and very likely botch a golden opportunity. Remember: you have nothing to fear but fear itself. The more confident you are the better will be your performance and the less traumatic the experience.

You will be asked to stand or to sit in front of the camera. Don't look directly into the camera lens as you deliver your dialogue unless requested to do so. Take your eyeline to your reading partner. Don't be facially animated. Don't move about. Be still but relaxed as you speak. Keep the voice level up but not higher than a normal conversational volume. Don't speak too rapidly to avoid stumbling over words. However, keep the pace of the scene moving. Don't let it drag or it will become boring. Tightly butt cues to avoid unwarranted, lengthy pausing between your lines and the lines spoken by your partner. Before you commence take a few deep breaths to dispel 'butterflies' hovering around in your tummy. Think, feel, listen and react truthfully. Now, with sheer boldness, go forth and conquer.

31. PREPARING SCENES FOR CASTING DIRECTORS

A casting director may request you to prepare a scene with a partner and to play the scene in his or her office. An audition scene should last from three to five minutes — seven at the most. Select a partner who will complement you, not overshadow you. Select a scene from a fairly recent *modern* play, not a period play. Select something representing your own age range and personality. Something you will feel comfortable playing. Be word perfect. Know your part. Restrict movement and gestures. Remember, you will be judged on your suitability to play before the camera, not before an audience on a theatre stage.

32. THE USE OF THANK YOU NOTES

I have made it a practice to send a brief 'thank you' note or card to agents, producers, directors and others who have been kind, considerate and helpful to me. A short note should express your sincere feelings of appreciation. It is unwise to send gifts unless you are on very close terms with your helpers. Your motives could be misunderstood and the gifts considered to be bribes to obtain further work or assistance.

33. VARIOUS CATEGORIES OF WORK IN SCREEN DRAMA

Work categories for actors in *television* are: extra roles, bit parts, feature roles, co-starring roles, series recurring roles, series co-starring roles and series starring roles.

Work categories for actors in *motion pictures* are: extra roles, bit parts, day players, feature roles, co-starring roles and starring roles.

34. UNION AFFILIATIONS

The performers' associations are trade unions who work to protect the rights of performers in a given field. All persons who desire to work as professional performers must join a theatrical union(s).

In the US the *Screen Actors Guild* (SAG) has approximately 40,000 members. It has jurisdiction over all performers working in feature films, filmed television commercials and filmed television programs as well as filmed industrials.

The *American Federation of Television and Radio Artists* (AFTRA) has approximately 25,000 members and has jurisdiction over live and video-taped programs and commercials for television, taped industrials, transcriptions, phonograph records and radio shows and commercials. At the time of writing, SAG and AFTRA are exploring becoming *one* union as has been the case with SAG and the Screen Extras Guild (SEG).

The *American Guild of Variety Artists* (AGVA) has jurisdiction over club singers and performers, clowns, skaters in ice shows and performer-presenters. (Other than musicians.)

Actors Equity Association (AEA) is the oldest of the guilds and has jurisdiction over all performers appearing in theatrical stage presentations.

It is not easy to obtain membership in any of the US guilds. Joining fees are quite high and annual dues have a small percentage figure tacked on when a performer reaches a certain income bracket.

In Gt. Britain, the union having jurisdiction over all acting fields is *British Actors Equity Association* (incorporating variety artists).

In Canada, the *Association of Canadian Radio and TV Artists* presides over all fields of acting.

In Australia, *Actors Equity of Australia* has various divisions representing actors, announcers and dancers in all fields.

The quickest way to obtain a theatrical union card is to entice a producer or casting director to hire you and then to have either one request the appropriate union to grant you membership.

35. SECURING PART-TIME EMPLOYMENT

Sufficient funds should be available or obtainable to support you while you establish your career. You cannot live on water and air. There is no crystal ball that can forecast when and where success in acting will overtake you. Therefore, you should have training in areas other than acting which will enable you to obtain part-time work to pay your rent, buy clothes, food, cover transportation costs and training.

There are few actors who have not earned a living 'between assignments' working as waiters/waitresses, ushers/usherettes, typists, taxi drivers, nurses, salespersons, etc. Establish contacts in several work fields which are fairly certain to have openings for employment when you require it.

36. BREAKING INTO THE LUCRATIVE COMMERCIAL FIELD

Acting in television commercials is a good way to be 'discovered' and to earn large amounts of money. Both Barbara Feldon and Sandy Dennis were discovered by Hollywood after they appeared in TV commercials — and they earned good money at it.

A Hollywood friend earned in excess of $200,000 during the early part of 1985. His 'windfall' came in the form of two nationally released television commercials. He got both jobs within two weeks of signing with a new commercial agent. He maintains it was 'luck'. Timing, appropriate type and talent, perhaps. But certainly not luck. Casting directors, directors and agency people buy specific 'types' to appear in commercials, not just attractive faces. I know several actors who have been trying to crack the commercial market for five years and more. None, so far, has made it.

Featured players and stars are paid small and large fortunes to lend their talents and names to 'selling' products and services on television. Some stars won't accept television commercial work. Others, such as James Garner, Robert Morley, Laurence Olivier, John Gielgud, James Coburn, Robert Young, Cheryl Ladd, Karl Malden and Orson Welles, have found it quite advantageous to do so.

Residuals* are paid to an artist for more than one screening or after a specified number of screenings of a commercial. This means that each artist appearing in the commercial will be paid whenever the commercial is screened following its contracted and specified run. Residual payments can run into hundreds, even thousands of dollars. For a *program commercial*, an artist is paid a performance fee for a single run, an additional amount for a second run, then further amounts for additional runs on a declining scale. *Spot commercials*, are used between programs during station breaks. A flat

*Fees and residual payments differ, country to country.

fee is paid for unlimited use each 13 week period. Fees, of course, are negotiable and depend on the status of the performer, the number of runs and whether the commercial will screen locally or nationally.

In the US, there are commercial agents who represent performers only in the commercial field. These agents deal with casting directors of advertising agencies and independent casting agents. Casting is done by 'type' and age: a young, sporty-looking male; a 60-year-old businessman; a trim, pretty secretary in her late twenties; a genuine grandmother about age seventy, etc. Casting directors phone agents with the types they seek, requesting the agents to phone them back with a list of 'possibles' for each role being cast. Actor directories are used in this regard to give the casting director and agency people an idea of the 'look' of the actors who have been submitted by agents. Interviews are then conducted to *look* at and *read* those who have been called in.

37. THE TELEVISION COMMERCIAL INTERVIEW

Interviews with casting people for TV commercials follow the same basic pattern as interviews for drama work. The casting director, either an independent or an employee of an advertising agency, will at the interview be flanked by the agency account executive, the director and possibly the sponsor or his representative. Usually, they are a friendly bunch who try to make the difficult task a pleasant one for the actor. After introductions, the casting director or the director will explain the 'story' ask what other commercials you've been in lately and, hopefully, ask you to read for the part.

If the commercial doesn't require the actor to speak lines, the casting director could ask you to 'play out' the situation. Several years ago, an agent sent me on an interview for a tissue commercial. The agency man asked me to climb up onto a window ledge and to pretend that I was catching 'falling tissues from heaven.' The assembled agency people studied my mime, huddled in confab, then announced with undue seriousness: 'Sorry, you don't have the look we want.'

I've come to the conclusion that actors fronting for TV commercial interviews shouldn't take them too seriously. Having once worked in an advertising agency, I am of the opinion that no matter what agency people may say in regard to knowing what they want at a casting session, most of them are in a complete fog. It's quite often a case of trial and error or being impressed on the spot by the 'look' and 'presence' of a performer.

Don't get upset if you miss out on commercial calls. Hundreds of actors try and hundred of actors fail at commercial interviews. Smile. Perhaps at your next casting session the fickle finger-of-fate will point in your direction and you'll experience the excitement and rewards of being selected for a television commercial.

If the commercial you have been cast in doesn't require you to speak but to be seen, it is called a *fifty-percenter*. If you are required to be heard but not seen, it is called a *voice-over*. If you are both seen and heard, it is called a *hundred-percenter.* If you are endowed with beautiful hair, shapely legs, magnificent eyes or lovely hands, those parts of you could be 'bought' to be seen in a commercial.

38. DRESSING FOR A COMMERCIAL CASTING SESSION

In the US, theatrical unions forbid producers requesting actors to attend casting sessions 'dressed' to suit the part. This does not restrict any actor from dressing as he or she desires when attending interviews. Therefore, quiz your agent for character details and if you feel that you can enhance your chance of winning a role by dressing to look like the character, then by all means do so.

A few years ago, I attended a casting session dressed as a gangster. The role was for an Al Capone type. I wore a pin-stripe suit, black shirt, white tie and a snappy cream-color hat. When I read for the role the casting people exclaimed, 'He's it, by George!' However, I didn't accept the role. My agent wouldn't agree to the paltry fee offered.

Looking the part is the first requirement of being successful at casting sessions. Talent, of course, must support appearance. Acting talent is necessary in television commercial work. Commercials are mini-dramas. Performances must have a ring-of-truth about them, characters must have 'appeal' and be convincing in presenting the sponsor message. Commercials cost enormous amounts of money to produce and to screen. Sponsors expect production expenditures to be returned via increased sales. The *quality* of the sales message is therefore important. This is the reason sponsors hire professional actors to 'sell' their products and services . . . actors who *look* right, *sound* right and are convincing in performance.

A word of caution on dress: feel comfortable. Don't dress in an outrageous way just to try and impress casting people. Avoid making a spectacle of yourself. If a clown is required, they'll hire a professional one. Dress to *look* like the character but only if your dress doesn't bring you and those at the interview embarrassment.

39. NARRATIVE AND VOICE-OVER WORK

Documentaries, some feature films, television dramas and news programs often require a voice track laid in over the action to describe events taking place, to tell a story or to give a lead-up to the action shown. The symbol designating this work is 'V.O.' meaning *voice-over*. Actors or announcers who specialize in voice-over work are also called *narrators.*

Voice-over work in television commercials is quite lucrative, but it is not for the amateur player or inexperienced actor. It is a highly-skilled field and extremely difficult to break into. In the US, top voice-over specialists can earn $250,000 a year. Along with proper voice training and experience, a voice-over actor requires a distinctive, unique vocal presentation in addition to an ability to interpret commercial copy. He or she must be able to read copy in a variety of ways, using different inflections and emphasis to bring 'alive' the sponsor-message. The professional copy reader knows how to pace delivery of the text, when to pause, when to use emphasis without being obvious. It encompasses an ability to tell a story in a believable and natural-sounding way.

Documentary narrative is another specialized area requiring good voice qualities plus an ability to read well. Articulation and especially good pronunciation are necessary. There is no room for a strident, monotonous, badly-articulated voice.

The voice-over field includes: television commercials, animated cartoons, movies (including voice dubbing and post syncing), movie trailers, documentary programs, television promos (usually read by station booth announcers), film segments for news and current events broadcasts and all areas where a performer is *heard* but not seen.

40. AUDIO AUDITION TAPES

Voice-over actors do not require pictures or composites. They can be short, tall, fat, skinny, handsome or ugly. They are not subject to the physical requirements of the 'on-camera' performer. More often than not, they work alone in a studio and their faces are unknown to the public.

If you are an experienced actor and feel that your voice is distinctive and you read well, make a voice tape encompassing the following three areas:

(1) Commercial presentation
(2) Documentary narrative
(3) Cartoon voices

Record the three styles of presentation on a master tape and make at least a dozen dubs. With each copy, include a resumè. It is useful to have dubs on reel-to-reel tape as well as on cassette tape. Some agents will have both reel-to-reel and cassette recorders, but some might not. Offering a choice is helpful and not a costly proposition. Again, I suggest a phone call to a small number of agents prior to mailing tapes to ensure that those agents you have selected represent actors in voice-over work and are willing to listen to audition tapes. Always include a stamped, self-addressed envelope and a request that your tape be returned if it proves unsuitable.

COMMERCIAL PRESENTATION: record a 30 second commercial read three different ways: hard sell, soft sell, neutral sell.

DOCUMENTARY NARRATIVE: select several paragraphs from a text book or a magazine article (interesting subject matter) and record the text. Running time should be about 90 seconds.

CARTOON VOICES: record as many different voices as you do well. Use dialects if you are good at them. Running time should be about two minutes.

Do not include explanations on audition tapes, just your name and agency representation. Your tapes should be short, simple, professionally produced and a good representation of your talent. Agents will not spend time listening to an endless, boring, poorly-made audition tape.

41. SALARIES

Superstar salaries are sometimes mind boggling. Elizabeth Taylor, Robert Redford, Paul Newman, Marlon Brando and others, have or still ask several million dollars for each film engagement. This is made up of salary, a percentage of a film's income and personal amenities as stipulated in a star's contract.

Others on the big-money list include Sean Connery who received a whopping $5 million for his James Bond role in *Never Say Never Again* and Roger Moore, who is reported to have earned slightly less — $3 million — for his appearance in another Bond film *Octopussy*.

Sylvester Stallone's picture price is said to be $4 million plus. With emphasis on the plus. His agent, its been reported, once received an offer of $12 million for Stallone to star in a film.

Behind the cute image of Goldie Hawn lies an astute business mind. She commands $2.5 million for a film role. In addition to her acting roles she is a producer, proving that Hollywood is not a male's domain when it comes to opportunity and making money.

Elizabeth Taylor has earned millions of dollars for her appearances in films. When she appeared on Broadway in Noel Coward's play *Private Lives*, her salary, it's said, was $70,000 a week. Her co-star, the late Richard Burton, is reputed to have earned as much. Film actors with 'name' value do very well financially when they work in theatre. Producers are willing to pay high salaries to box-office attractions.

And human actors sometimes compete with animal actors in the salaries and amenities race. CJ, an ape who starred in his own television series in Hollywood, was paid $100,000 a year salary in addition to other considerations such as a special dressing room of superior quality and an unlimited supply of fruit when he worked.

Despite all this, the present state of the profession in regard to work and income, as I've already mentioned, is less than encouraging for a newcomer. As further evidence, British Equity says that of the approximate 26,000 actors on its books, roughly 3 per cent work fairly regularly. And actors belonging to Screen Actors Guild in the US earn on an average less than $8,000 a year. Actors Equity in Australia says the 'average' income of a working actor puts him/her on the breadline.

It isn't hard to work out that a person selling shirts behind a counter in a department store has a better chance of earning a decent living than a professional actor who hasn't reached featured-player or star status. Actors in countries other than those mentioned face an equally bleak earnings picture. Now is a good time to reconsider your decision to enter the profession of acting.

However, if you are genuinely hooked on acting as a career and determined to crash Hollywood, the salary figures listed in the salaries chart are broad examples of what you might expect to earn in the USA should you be fortunate enough to join the ranks of that small, elite, 'in demand' group of working professionals.

SALARIES CHART*

MOTION PICTURE WORK

CATEGORY:	INCOME:
Superstars	$3,000,000 *plus* per picture
Stars	$1,000,000 *plus* per picture
Co-stars (2 or more films in year)	$ 500,000 *plus* per year
Featured-role players (3 films in year)	$ 150,000 *plus* per year
Day players (40 days work in year)	$ 18,000 *plus* per year
Bit players (40 days work in year)	$ 8,000 *plus* per year

TELEVISION SERIES WORK

Series stars (established series)	$1,000,000 *plus* per year
Co-stars (established series)	$ 500,000 *plus* per year
Guest stars (2 guest shots in year)	$ 80,000 *plus* per year
Day players (30 days work in year)	$ 10,000 *plus* per year
Bit players (30 days work in year)	$ 5,000 *plus* per year
Series lead (unknown player) TV pilot	$ 5,000 *plus* per week

*Salaries based on fees paid to US actors.

42. THE WORK PROCEDURE

You have been successful in securing an agent, he's sent you on an interview and the casting director, after reading you, has selected you to play a minor role. You've been granted a union card and now are ready to take on your first professional acting assignment.

SCRIPTS: Your agent will be sent your script and (sometimes) a work call sheet. Some production offices send scripts directly to artists by courier, particularly if they are required on set or on location at short notice. It is a good idea to keep in close contact with your agent during an engagement in case work call times and locations are changed and the changes do not reach you via normal studio channels.

WARDROBE FITTINGS: times are usually phoned to you via your agent or directly to you from the wardrobe department. You will be given specific times to report for fittings or a request might be made to bring in some of your own clothing from which the wardrobe people can make a selection. For a feature film, wardrobe appointments are usually well in advance of your production call. For television, it could be a day or so prior to your production call. Don't be difficult should you be given a wardrobe that doesn't please you. The function of the designer and the wardrobe

121

department are to create a *character*, not a clothes horse — unless of course the role calls for it. You will be dressed by experts to create a specific 'look'. Allow them to do their job.

WORK CALLS: initially, these are phoned to your agent who will contact you with the necessary information. Sometimes they are phoned directly to you from the production office. Once production has begun, work calls are usually handed out at the end of each day's shoot. A call sheet includes: date of call, location, cast required, scenes to be filmed, directions to locations and transport arrangements, etc. Also called a *location schedule* or *production schedule*.

MAKEUP CALLS: you will be given precise times to report for makeup. When you arrive at the studio or on location report to the first assistant director (film) or to the floor manager (television). You will be directed to the makeup department or area set aside for the makeup artists and hairdressers. Refrain from telling the makeup artist his or her job.

WARDROBE: you will be told whether to visit makeup first or wardrobe first then makeup. Make every effort to keep your wardrobe clean and wrinkle-free. Chances are, you will share a dressing room with several other actors. If you have valuables (watch, ring, money), do not leave them in the dressing room. As in every profession, some people are honest, others aren't. If you are lucky enough to be given a private dressing room, it is still advisable to carry valuables on you.

43. PROFESSIONAL COURTESY ON THE SET

There is a strict protocol on a film set or on a studio floor that novice actors are well to understand and observe. Good manners apply when addressing fellow actors and crew members. There is a pecking-order which separates extras, day players, major-role players and stars. The rules to follow include:

- Never argue with the director or with players or crew members.
- Never give acting directions to a fellow player. If you have a complaint then take the director aside and discuss it with him or her.
- Do not sit in a chair assigned to the director or stars.
- Do not photograph actors while they are filming. Taking pictures of actors on a set is frowned upon.
- Do not annoy the stars or your director. If they engage you in conversation, fine, but keep your distance.
- Never touch the property of cast or crew members.
- When actors are rehearsing or a scene is being shot, don't stand within the eyeline of players or close to the set. Stay in your dressing room or in the Green Room if there is one.
- Never move furniture on the set or touch hand props unless they are part of your playing action. Placing or replacing props is the job of the property person.
- Keep quiet during rehearsals and during shooting. Whispering can be

distracting to actors working.
- Don't try to use people you meet on a shoot.
- Keep your opinions to yourself. Don't gossip. Don't criticize other actors.
- No crude language, please. And no alcohol while you are working.
- Speak and act as a professional actor.
- Thank those who have been helpful to you.

44. THE WORLD OF THE STUNT ACTOR

Screen stunt actors are a small, elite group working in a highly specialized and dangerous performing field. Established stunt performers are in demand. They are highly paid — as indeed they should be — for the risks they take in front of the camera. Stunt work is not for the amateur — no matter how brave or physically fit he or she may be.

Any dangerous action called for in a script is assigned to an experienced stunt actor. A few stars, Charles Bronson and Burt Reynolds to name two, sometimes do their own stunts. This is not a wise practice, for obvious reasons. Falling from galloping horses, parachuting from planes, crashing speeding cars, being set alight, beaten up in fight scenes, leave no room for error. It's a dangerous business to be in and stunt actors have scars to prove it.

Stunt acting requires persons with physical stamina, rigid self-discipline, nerves of steel and an ability to handle a wide assortment of equipment such as cars, buses, trucks, motorcycles, boats and guns. It requires a sound knowledge of working safely with fire, explosives, animals etc. It is advantageous to be experienced in scuba diving, hang gliding and the martial arts.

If this area of the business interests you, then training is your first step to becoming a stunt artist. There aren't too many stunt-training schools. Call a local production company or a theatrical union and ask them to recommend one.

45. FACING UP TO HUMILIATION

As I have already pointed out, acting is not a very reliable profession to be in. One success doesn't necessarily guarantee permanent success. An Australian actor, star of two films, is, as I write this book, driving a taxi to earn a living. Sometimes his passengers recognize him and are amazed that a movie star can be a celebrity one day and a taxi driver the next. I have an actress friend who starred in a television series for three years. She now earns a living as a pool typist with an insurance company. 'At first it was humiliating. But I need money to live. There are far too few acting jobs to support me so I have to earn an income as a typist,' she told me.

In 1968, I attended a gala premiere of a motion picture starring a young TV series actor. Several months later, a newspaper columnist reported that the actor was unable to get acting work so had taken a job driving a truck.

In the late fifties, a good friend was signed by MGM to star in a feature film. It was the chance of a lifetime he thought. He enjoyed his star status for a couple of years after the release of the film. However, further acting work didn't materialize. He became despondent. Finally, in order to pay bills, he took a job delivering telephone directories. It's a fickle and highly competitive business, indeed.

It seems quite wrong that experienced actors who reach the top are given no assurance that they will retain the positions they've earned. Some achieve stardom and retain it — some don't. Some rise to the top quickly and fall just as quickly. This is the reason actors are advised to have a secondary skill to fall back on.

I admire those actors who aren't content to sit around moaning about 'bad times', who bite-the-bullet and take secondary jobs — no matter how humiliating the experience. It indicates strength of character.

Another worrying area for an actor is scene cutting by an editor. For any number of reasons, a scene can be shortened or eliminated entirely, leaving an actor to be seen fleetingly or not at all. An actor whose dialogue has been lopped from a scene has no greater prominence than an extra and this can be career damaging when the production is viewed by casting directors. Unfortunately, it's a hazard many actors have to live with.

In spite of the work problems, is an acting career worth fighting for? I believe it is. Television shows and feature films are being produced every day in all parts of the world, providing employment to thousands of actors and technicians — the fortunate ones. The decision to quit or to go on when the going gets tough is a decision all actors face *once* or more times in their careers. The decision is a personal one. It needs to be decided very carefully after weighing up the facts. It's not always a question of talent, mostly it's a question of available work in your area. You can only succeed as an actor by acting. To fight for the chance to become one, to work and earn a living as one, can be a most frustrating and humiliating experience.

An actor's life is not an easy one. It is a life filled with traumas, difficulties, hard work and disappointments. To rise above them, an actor needs an iron will, a high degree of discipline and persistence. Because success in acting brings such high rewards, many actors feel that the tough run-up to it is well worth the effort.

46. EXTENDING YOUR MARKETABILITY TO TELEVISION HOSTING

Television hosting can be a lucrative, creatively-satisfying and exhilarating experience. An actor's background and experience can often enhance his/her chance of success as a television presenter. Self-confidence before an audience and the camera, an ability to communicate ideas, to speak and personally present well are attributes essential to the TV host. While acting and hosting are usually two distinctly-separate careers, they can be and often are successfully combined.

I began my theatrical career as an actor, earned extra income and experience as a reporter, radio broadcaster, television interviewer and host.

Hosting television shows has opened many doors. It hasn't greatly affected my acting opportunities and I've thoroughly enjoyed the experience, not to mention the income.

I know of actresses who host daytime television shows and actors who work as news reporters. The more involved they are in these activities the less time they have to devote to acting. However, it is an excellent chance to gain on-camera experience, to meet important people in the industry, to earn a healthy income while at the same time continuing their study of acting at evening and weekend drama classes.

There will be some actors who will baulk at the thought of TV hosting. There will be others who would like to take it on but who lack the expertise and confidence to do so. And for the others, those who are attracted to the television 'personality' scene, my suggestion is to discuss the possibility with your agent to ascertain your suitability for news reporting, game-show hosting or television interviewing.

For Women Only! Adams at Noon ◎2

Brian Adams with provocative questions and opinions for women every weekday!

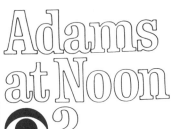

Now!!
Today is more exciting

ADAMS AFTER NOON

TODAY'S GUESTS INCLUDE

★★★★★★★★

The Premier of
NEW SOUTH WALES
Mr. NEVILLE WRAN

★★★★★★★★

TREVOR WHITE
Star of
Jesus Christ Superstar

★★★★★★★★

Today at noon, Channel TEN proudly presents ADAMS AFTER NOON! It's 90 minutes of live provocative, topical entertainment and interviews with the stars, the celebrities, and the personalities who make today's scene so exciting — all presented in Brian Adams' up to the minute new live television show.

12 NOON
MONDAY TO FRIDAY

TV hosting can be good diversification for an actor, offering opportunity to meet interesting and important people as well as to earn sizeable income. The author (L) introduces leading politician *Neville Wran* to studio audience for a 'live' telecast of an *Adams After Noon*. Show was seen on the Ten Network, Australia. ▶

hosting can be hazardous. The author ceived a cream pie in the face from *Sue odes* who was displeased with negae comments the host made concerning r book *Now You'll Think I'm Awful* on *Town Tonight,* Chan 10 Sydney. ▶

in-depth interview was conducted th *Leslie Shaw,* who, in the mid-sixties, aded an agency to bust-up gangs in s Angeles. *Adams at Noon* was proced at the studios of KNXT Channel 2, s Angeles. ▶

REHEARSAL SCHEDULE

"DAY OF THE PHOENIX"   MONDAY OCTOBER 16

PRODUCER: Harry Baume
DIRECTOR: Bill Banks
1ST ASS'T: Bob Anthony

LOCATION: Buring Rehearsal Studios
22 Sunset Blvd.
Hollywood, Cal.
232-222

CAST:
1000	Jordan	Bill Rolfe
1000	Helen	Jean Harvey
1100	Jack	Tom Johnson
1100	Sylvia	Janet James
1130	Debra	May Brown
1130	Henry	Sam Logan
1200	Sacha	Jane Smith
1200	Brian	Harry Lovelock

SET	SCENE	PAGE	DUR'N	CAST
HOTEL LOBBY	17	50	1'06	Jordan/Helen
OFFICE	22	60	1'18	Jack/Sylvia/Debra
SURGERY	25	63	3'18	Jordan/Jack/Debra
BAR	33	90	2.24	Henry/Sacha/Brian
STREET	34	94	1'93	Henry/Sacha/Brian
CAR	35	97	2'02	Sacha/Brian
BUS STOP	36	99	1'00	Henry

NOTE: Parking is difficult. Public parking available at 23rd Street and 6th
Avenue.

128

WORK CALL SHEET

NOTE: CLOSED SET – NO VISITORS

''DAY OF THE PHOENIX''   WEDNESDAY OCTOBER 18

PRODUCER: Harry Baume
DIRECTOR: Bill Banks
1ST ASS'T: Bob Anthony (232-222)
LOCATION: Studio 3, Briad Studios – 44 James Street, Studio City.
DAY: 1st
UNIT: 1st

CAST CALLS			
JORDAN	BILL ROLFE	0630	M/UP & W/R
HELEN	JEAN HARVEY	0630	M/UP & W/R
JACK	TOM JOHNSON	0730	M/UP & W/R
SYLVIA	JANET JAMES	0730	M/UP & W/R
DEBRA	MAY BROWN	0730	M/UP & W/R
5 NURSES	EXTRAS (TBA)	0800	M/UP & W/R

SCENE	TIME	DURATION	CAST	LOCATION	SET
17	D4	1'06	Jordan	Studio	Hotel Lobby
			Helen	Studio	
22	D5	1'18	Jack	Studio	Office
			Sylvia	Studio	
			Debra	Studio	
			5 nurses	Studio	

CATERING: Morning tea – lunch – afternoon tea provided.
NOTE: Wardrobe and makeup required on set.

SUMMARY OF IDEAS TO REVIEW

1: Don't head for Hollywood, New York or London unless you want to train in one of those cities or have sufficient experience upon which to build a career in a major acting center.

2: Prepare a professional presentation file to sell your talents: photos, resumè, biography.

3: Don't waste time and money mailing presentation materials to studios. Secure an agent. Your materials will reach the right people.

4: Select an agent you get on well with. Help your agent by supplying good pictures, tapes or film clips of your work. Place a listing in an actor's directory. Keep your agent informed as to your whereabouts. Engage an answering service.

5: Allow your agent to handle all negotiations. Be sensible in demands.

6: Auditioning is a basic element in the actor's craft. Impressions are important. Improve your personality. Be well dressed and groomed. Exude confidence. Hold eye contact. Be punctual.

7: Interviews for television commercial work follow the same pattern as interviews for drama work. Retain a sense of humor. Don't get anxious, frustrated if you do not click quickly. It's a percentages game. You'll win some, lose some. Maybe you won't win any. But have fun. You'll need acting talent. Commercials are mini-dramas.

8: Voice-over work is lucrative but restricted to experienced, trained actors who read and speak well.

9: There is a *protocol* on the set. Observe the rules.

10: Is an acting career worth experiencing frustration, humiliation? You must decide for yourself.

2:
DEVELOPMENT

★★

COMMENT . . .

Acting is an ancient art. Like all the arts, it is to be studied, understood and practiced. Natural talent is a wonderful gift, but talent without training and development is of little use if the aim is high achievement. One *learns* to play the instrument before joining the orchestra. One *learns* to act before acting professionally. There are many people who are of the opinion that there is little more to acting than the memorization of dialogue. One may as well assume that memorization of a few text books on medicine is sufficient to begin a medical practice.

The instrument of the actor requires development. It must be finely-tuned and responsive to every command during performance. The next five chapters are devoted to theories and techniques for developing the *instrument* of the actor.

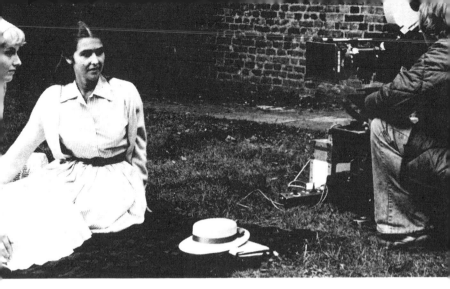

Belinda Carroll and *Lucy Appleby* positioned for close two-shot with camera set at eye-level height for the film *No Longer Alone.*

Lucy Appleby receives her final hair check as boom operator positions microphone and camera is readied for wider and different angle of scene. Film was produced by *Frank Jacobson*, directed by *Nick Webster* for World Wide Pictures.

UTILIZING THE VARIOUS THEORIES AND SYSTEMS OF ACTING

SCENE 6

Practical Ideas In This Chapter . . .

- The Theory of Acting And Its Value
- *Four* Points On Acting Theory To Apply
- Various Theories of Acting
- Aristotle
- William Shakespeare
- The Best Drama Instructor of All Time
- Constantin Stanislavski
- Is Stanislavski To Blame For The Mumblers?
- Stanislavski's System
- Stanislavski's Advice To Students On Technique
- How Not To Be A Pseudo-Method Actor
- The Classic Technique School of Acting
- Early Technique Actors Lacked Naturalism
- Noted Exponents of Modern Technique
- Noted Exponents of The System
- Method or Technique?
- Background On The Actors Studio
- Further Thoughts On Approaches To Acting By Actors
- Other Forms of Acting
- Become A Dedicated Craftsperson
- Summary of Ideas To Review

SCENE 6

★★★

1. THE THEORY OF ACTING AND ITS VALUE

Bringing a stage character to life involves more than being able to speak and move well before an audience. The task of character portrayal is a challenging one, requiring a great deal of knowledge of the theory of acting in addition to practical acting experience. Actors need to learn how to analyse a script to discover underlying meanings, be able to pinpoint character and story exposition and to comprehend the author's intent. Actors must examine their own feelings and responses in order to understand and portray the feelings and responses of stage characters assigned to them. Understanding the concept of performance naturalism is another requirement. Stage characters must be presented as having human attributes and qualities transmitted to audiences by body and vocal expression in a believable way.

In order to better understand the theory of acting — knowledge of how to realistically express the thoughts, feelings and actions of stage characters — let's discover the meaning of the word 'theory'. Webster's *New World Dictionary* describes theory as: ... *a looking at, contemplation, a mental viewing, an idea or mental plan of the way to do something, a systematic statement of principles involved ... a formulation of apparent relationships.*

The true value of theory is seen in its application. Knowledgeable people do not automatically become successful people just because they have stored a great deal of knowledge. To be beneficial, knowledge must be used. It's value can then be determined in its application. A knowledge of acting theory is no guarantee of acting success no matter how much information has been acquired. Acting theory must be applied, joined to acting experience, then its worth becomes evident. An actor having studied acting theory is better able to express creativity because he/she knows *what* to do and *how* to do it.

2. *FOUR* POINTS ON ACTING THEORY TO APPLY

The value of *applied theory* is evident in the four points which emerge from the analysis of the word itself, for they present a positive means to accomplish the stage task. The four points are:

1-CONTEMPLATION: study the overall meaning of the script. Analyse the story and dialogue and come to a conclusion as to the author's intent: *why* he/she wrote it, *what* the characters seek to accomplish via their attitudes and actions.

2-MENTAL PLAN: formulate a plan as to your approach to the role. Discover the purpose and objectives of the character's actions and how best they can be presented. What is the character saying and why?

3-PRINCIPLES: to establish performance professionalism it is necessary to apply acting principles in a systematic and subtle way.

4-RELATIONSHIPS: formulate in your mind apparent relationships between the character you play and other characters, places and things involved in the story.

3. VARIOUS THEORIES OF ACTING

Down through the ages many famous playwrights, producers, actors, acting teachers, critics and philosophers have had *theories* of acting. Aristotle made his analysis of drama back in the third century B.C. William Shakespeare, before his death in 1616, had a great deal to say about actors and acting. Both Aristotle and Shakespeare were expert thinkers who had an extraordinary understanding of human nature. Shakespeare understood people as few other artists have. He created characters that have meaning beyond the time of his astonishing 37 plays. In recent times we've been awakened to the acting theories of Constantin Stanislavski. But much of what he had to say, Shakespeare and Aristotle said before him.

4. ARISTOTLE (384-322 B.C.)

Aristotle, the greatest teacher of his period and perhaps the greatest teacher of all time, was the very first drama critic. He loved drama as an art form. He had much to say about it for he believed that it encouraged freedom of thought, freedom of speech and freedom of expression. He used his brilliant mind to analyse drama, giving the world his *Poetics*, a set of dramatic principles used to this day by playwrights and critics.

Aristotle reasoned that stage characters must be motivated by goals and personality traits. They must *seem* to be real beings with hearts and minds. They should be brought to the spectators of drama in an interesting, spirited and believable way. In *Poetics*, he wrote: *Every play, one may say, admits of spectacle, character, fable, or plot, diction, melody, and thought.* *Poetics* has probably been the single most influential work in all literary criticism.

5. WILLIAM SHAKESPEARE (1564-1616)

English playwright, poet and actor, Shakespeare is considered the greatest dramatist the world has known. He could see in a dramatic situation the qualities that relate to all human beings. He had a deep insight into the nature of man. As an actor, Shakespeare knew his theatre. He wrote many passages about the stage and its relation to people. He used words with great skill to suggest sounds, motion and color. He was a member of several repertory companies, the most famous being the Lord Chamberlain's Men. He had his theory of acting and it comes through in Hamlet's speech to a band of travelling actors before their performance at the court.

(*HAMLET*, 111, 2.)

HAMLET: Speak the speech, I pray you, as I pronounced it to you, trippingly on the tongue; but if you mouth it, as many of your players do, I had as lief the town-crier spoke my lines. Nor do not saw the air too much with your hand, thus; but use all gently: for in the very torrent, tempest, and (as I may say) whirlwind of passion, you must acquire and beget a temperance, that may give it smoothness. O! it offends me to the soul, to hear a robustious, periwig-pated fellow tear a passion to tatters, to very rags, to split the ears of the groundlings; who, for the most part, are capable of nothing but inexplicable dumb shows, and noise: I would have such a fellow whipped for o'er-doing Termagant; it out-herods Herod; pray you avoid it.

Be not too tame neither, but let your own discretion be your tutor: suit the action to the word, the word to the action, with this special observance, that you o'erstep not the modesty of nature; for anything so overdone is from the purpose of playing, whose end, both at the first, and now, was, and is, to hold, as 'twere the mirror up to nature; to show virtue her own feature, scorn her own image, and the very age and body of the time, his form and pressure. Now this overdone, or come tardy off, though it make the unskilled laugh, cannot but make the judicious grieve; the censure of the which one must, in your

allowance, o'erweigh a whole theatre of others. O! there be
players, that I have seen play, and heard others praise, — and
that highly, not to speak it profanely, — that neither having the
accent of Christians, nor the gait of Christian, pagan, nor man,
have so strutted, and bellowed, that I have thought some of
nature's journeymen had made men, and not made them well,
they imitated humanity so abominably.

PLAYER: I hope, we have reformed that indifferently with us.

HAMLET: O! reform it altogether. And let those that play your clowns,
speak no more than is set down for them: for there be of them,
that will themselves laugh, to set on some quantity of barren
spectators to laugh to; though in the meantime some necessary
question of the play be then to be considered: that's villainous,
and shows a most pitiful ambition in the fool that uses it.

6. THE BEST DRAMA INSTRUCTOR OF ALL TIME

Hamlet's speech to the players is one of the best lessons in dramatics ever
expressed. The standards Shakespeare formulated so many years ago are
current today and will remain so for as long as Shakespeare's works are
read. The principles modernized are:

- Speak the dialogue as written, *clearly*, with *understanding* of meaning.
- Eliminate artificial gestures. Use *energy* smoothly to build to an
  emotional climax.
- Resist extreme action and noise to impress unintelligent spectators.
- Don't be dull. Allow your understanding of the role to guide your
  playing. Suit the action to the word and the word to the action.
- Bring out the virtues and the faults of the character in a believable way.
- Never overact to squeeze laughs from an audience. Do not insult the
  intelligent few whose criticism outweighs that of all the rest of the
  audience.
- Do not imitate humanity badly. Show resemblance to the characters you
  portray.
- Never insert extemporaneous lines, particularly in comedy roles, even
  though the lines are smart enough to raise laughs. Such action draws
  attention away from the center of interest, smothering important lines.
  It is unprofessional.

7. CONSTANTIN STANISLAVSKI (1863-1938)

Stanislavski was the stage name of the famous actor and director. Born
Konstantin Sergeyevich Alexeyev in Moscow, Stanislavski established the
Moscow Art Theatre with Vladimir Nemirovich-Danchenko. The theatre
became famous for its realistic performances of plays by Chekhov, Gorky,

Turgenev and others. Stanislavski's direction of *The Sea Gull* in 1898 gave Chekhov his first success as a dramatist.

The acting theories of Stanislavski have been more publicized than any others. They've been more controversial than any others. He shares the distinction of causing a great deal of controversy while being less read and certainly less understood than is desirable. Many acting students are guilty of imitating Stanislavski's acting techniques believing that they can use his theories after watching renowned system actors perform, rather than spend time in serious study.

There are traditionalist actors who feel that the Stanislavski school is to blame for much of the inaudibility and acting sloppiness seen on the stage and before the screen cameras today. The followers of classic *technique* acting or *representational* acting, argue that too many method actors deny the existence of an audience, refuse to hold sufficient eye contact with other performers, mumble their lines, scratch themselves during performance and play in an introverted and isolated way. This performance method is insulting to an audience, they claim.

The proponents of the method school counter that use of low voice, becoming totally involved in the character's actions produces a naturalism. *Feeling* the character's emotions does away with mechanical, forced acting. It's an elementary fact, claim the technicians, that the actor's job is to *act* and to make the audience *feel*. If the actors deny the existence of the audience then it has no part of the play. It simply overhears it and is lucky indeed if it does so. The argument continues adinfinitum.

8. IS STANISLAVSKI TO BLAME FOR THE MUMBLERS?

I cannot agree with those critics of Stanislavski who maintain he is at fault for today's annoyingly inarticulate, no eye contact, backside scratching, 'to hell with the audience' breed of actors professing to be of the method school. Surely these common acting faults are due to inexperience, stupidity and misinterpretation of Stanislavski's theories.

I know of several actors who meet regularly to read the plays of Shakespeare. They profess to be admirers of his work. Yet, their dismal renditions would cause the master dramatist to turn in his grave if he could hear them. Not one member of the group seems to understand let alone follow the advice of Hamlet. The group totally ignores Shakespeare's theories on acting. I do not condemn William Shakespeare for their feeble efforts.

9. STANISLAVSKI'S SYSTEM

Stanislavski was not only an excellent actor-director, he was a metaphysician, a psychologist, a philospher, a person with great insight into the human mind and heart. He was a wonderful teacher with a remarkable intellect, an excellent education and a superior understanding of acting. His books are valuable reading, not only for actors and directors, but for painters, musicians, writers, dancers, sculptors, teachers, doctors, lawyers, analysts and those who desire to gain a better understanding of human emotions. His writings deal with the human experience, offering clues to the freeing of inhibitions, the reducing of tensions and the expansion of personal creativity.

Stanislavski's acting theories reveal the way to acting naturalism, the path to truthful performance and the discovery of the source of stage believability. In his directing of actors, he worked to bring about true, living, emotional creativeness by having them study the inner and outer lives of their stage characters as if they were real people. The striving of his actors to 'live the role' became known as Stanislavski's 'soul technique'. Stanislavski referred to it as the 'system'.

The *system* encompasses an *inner* grasp of the story, text and characters. It is a method of integrating a stage character's thoughts, feelings and acts and performing them free of external interruption and of establishing various units and objectives which provide a *through line of action* to the *super-objective*. In every play there is a main theme and this must be firmly fixed in an actor's mind throughout the performance. It instigated the writing of the play. Therefore, it should be the main source of the actor's artistic creation. *Inner grasp, through line of action* and the *super-objective* are the basic elements of Stanislavski's teaching.

The new method of acting also taught overcoming physical tenseness, control of the mind and body, concentration, memory recall, mental communion with other players and the study of people, places and things to sharpen awareness and perception. Actors were taught that stage posturing leads to mechanical and shallow performance. They were cautioned against false gestures, unjustified movement and facial animation to represent a character's feelings.

Stanislavski's aim was to remove artificiality and to replace it with realistic performance. He pointed out that everything that happens on the stage must be convincing to the actor himself, to the other players and to the spectators.

10. STANISLAVSKI'S ADVICE TO STUDENTS ON TECHNIQUE

Before becoming a drama teacher, Stanislavski was an experienced actor with a well-trained voice and body. When he started the Moscow Art Theatre in 1898, he was working with a company of actors well-grounded in basic acting techniques. They knew how to move and speak well. They were prepared for the new experience into which Stanislavski was to lead them.

Stanislavski insisted that all students joining his school should first study voice production and movement. They were to engage in regular activities to develop the instrument: singing, gymnastics, dancing, fencing. The development of the human body requires systematic and thorough exercise over a long period, he explained.

Students were introduced to inner techniques such as *emotion memory* and the *magic if* and taught how to coax the imagination into play. They

140

were advised to 'link up' with fellow players and objects on stage, to hold 'communion' with them in order to avoid mental lapses which ruin the continuity of a performance. He pointed out that with a grasp of 'inner acting techniques' it is possible to 'live' every moment of every scene, to 'feel' every emotion in each and every performance.

11. HOW NOT TO BE A PSEUDO-METHOD ACTOR

Far too many so-called method actors distort Stanislavski's techniques and in so doing insult the master's work. In restricting themselves to internal techniques alone, they miss the premise upon which the *system* rests. Follow the advice of Stanislavski and study *external* as well as *internal* techniques of acting. Prepare your acting instrument so that you can achieve a true inner creative state.

It is not my belief that the woeful inarticulation of some present-day method actors is a situation that Stanislavski would approve were he alive. Mumbling, scratching and lack of communion would not be tolerated. He stressed proper voice placement and good projection. Stanislavski demanded discipline of his students. This is an attribute not often found in today's new breed of get-rich-quick performers.

12. THE CLASSIC TECHNIQUE SCHOOL OF ACTING

In contrast to the Stanislavski method is the classic *technique* style of acting which utilizes conscious technique rather than total emotional involvement as its base. Technical actors are sometimes referred to as mechanical-external performers and representational actors.

Stanislavski's *system* uses both externals and internals but with the emphasis on internal techniques — emotional responses — so that an actor actually weeps, suffers and triumphs before his audience. The *technique* school stresses absolute control of the actor's instrument allowing no emotional response to interfere with the conscious artistry which is responsible for the performance results. The actor does not attempt to 'live' his part but acts it so well that the *illusion* of living is maintained. The technical actor *assumes* the personality of the character in contrast to the method actor who attempts to *become* the character, experiencing all that his character does.

The technical actor trains his voice, body and mind. He uses both externals and internals equally. The *technique* theory holds that the actor should experience the true feeling of the emotion of each scene at least once, but having done so, can project the feeling to the audience by repeating the voice and body movement of the primary experience. The technique is to *act* and make the audience *feel*. Many theatre actors rely on representational acting to bring about a consistent level of performance. It would be exhausting to feel every emotion in every scene night after night. The technical actor may feel the emotions of his role once or on numerous occasions during rehearsals and performance. The more times the better, but the primary experience is the important thing for the 'feel' of the scene can be set and *assumed* for each performance.

13. EARLY TECHNIQUE ACTORS LACKED NATURALISM

The classic technique school of acting grew up in the theatre. During the 'eighties, the French theatre was regarded as the pinnacle of acting achievement. Actors of this period devised elaborate methods of gesture and movement, sweeping or minute, together with attitudes and tones of voice which well-suited the plays of the time, particularly the dramas of Racine and Molière. Stage characters were types — heroes or villains — rather than individuals. In plays full of stock characters, stylized acting was inevitable. Many of the actor-manager-stars of the day had plays tailored to suit them and the remaining players and the production as a whole were of little importance. Acting teamwork was discouraged. The star made sure he was never upstaged.

With the emergence of the Moscow Art Theatre, declamatory acting gave way to naturalism in the theatre. Being revolutionary, it met with bitter opposition from many of the self-indulgent personality actors. Eventually, French, German and English actors refined classic technique, taking the best from the old and the new. Instead of imposing themselves on a part, technique actors began studying and interpreting it in order to inject real emotion into it. The change was none too soon in coming. A new naturalistic style of playwriting was surfacing. Declamatory acting was unsuited to the works of Chekhov, Ibsen, Shaw and others who introduced modern social problems into their plays in a realistic way. The new realistic style of writing required a new approach to acting.

14. NOTED EXPONENTS OF MODERN TECHNIQUE

The *technique* school has among its exponents many fine English actors. Past and present theatre and film players include: Max Adrian, Harry Andrews, Richard Burton, Noel Coward, Edith Evans, Albert Finney, John Gielgud, Alec Guinness, Leslie Howard, Vivien Leigh, John Mills, Laurence Olivier, Joan Plowright, Michael Redgrave, Ralph Richardson, Flora Robson, Maggie Smith, Sybil Thorndike.

15. NOTED EXPONENTS OF THE SYSTEM

Stanislavski's *system* or *method* school of acting as it is referred to today, has produced a large number of excellent American stage and screen stars. Many of them have trained at the Actors Studio under Lee Strasberg or with other teachers expounding this system. They include: Marlon Brando, Ann Bancroft, Jill Clayburgh, James Dean, Robert De Niro, Robert Duvall, Sally Field, Julie Harris, Viveca Lindfors, Karl Malden, Marilyn Monroe, Paul Newman, Jack Nicholson, Geraldine Page, Estelle Parsons, Mark Rydell, Eli Wallach, Christopher Walken, David Wayne, Gene Wilder, Shelley Winters.

16. METHOD OR TECHNIQUE?

Since the beginning of the twentieth century there have been two distinct schools of acting. Each approach has had and will continue to have strong supporters and critics. A careful study of both *technique* and *system* reveals quite clearly that both approaches aim for naturalism, believability and truth of performance.

Stanislavski pointed out that his system was *a* system not *the* system. Sir Tyrone Guthrie, English theatre director and producer, noted for his imaginative staging techniques, especially Shakespeare's plays, was of the belief that classic technique is the most powerful, skilful, effective and economical method of accomplishing the stage task. 'Few can be genius actors, but everyone can become a competent craftsman through applied technique,' was his view.

The Royal Academy of Dramatic Art in London and the Actors Studio in New York have turned out excellent examples of *technique* and *method* acting. The former stresses the importance of developing the acting instrument via technical exercises: physical culture, dancing, fencing, voice placement and dialogue delivery. The latter inclines toward the emotional side of creativeness, calling the mind (conscious and subconscious) into action, stirring the will and feelings in order to create truthfully and freely. There is much to be said for both approaches to acting. The ideal, it would seem, is to make use of both systems in order to bring about a creative and high standard of playing.

17. BACKGROUND ON THE ACTORS STUDIO

Founded in 1947 by Elia Kazan, Cheryl Crawford and Robert Lewis, the Studio in its original form was a private workshop where working actors could develop their craft. Located on West 44th Street in New York City, the Studio now has more than 500 members, many of them stage and screen stars who attend classes run by a variety of famous actors/moderators.

In 1951, Lee Strasberg was made artistic director. He ruled with absolute power. He was a demanding teacher who put students through painful emotional memory exercises to trigger the imagination and exploit feelings. A remote person, he found it difficult to relate to people outside acting, but he possessed a unique ability to assist actors to create from their inner selves. Noted actors and teachers from around the world came to watch him teach his interpretation of Stanislavski's system of acting. The Moscow Art Theatre sent representatives to see what he offered students. Some say Strasberg was pure genius. Others, like Helen Hayes and Olivier, who observed one of his classes, thought it all boring stuff and a waste of energy. Strasberg's most famous pupil was Marilyn Monroe. She attended his private classes as well as being an 'observer' at the Studio.

Strasberg died in 1982 at the age of 80. Soon after his death, Ellyn Burstyn and Al Pacino were voted in as the new codirectors of the Studio.

Membership to the Actors Studio is gained by audition. The selection process is made extremely difficult. About 1,000 actors audition each year. Three to ten are chosen. However, once you're a member, you're always a member. Classes are free. Many of its members do contribute, which along with private grants keeps the Studio operational.

18. FURTHER THOUGHTS ON APPROACHES TO ACTING BY ACTORS

HARRY ANDREWS: Be eager to try out new ideas, new ways of performing on the stage and before the camera. Be a master of the technique of screen acting. Dedicate yourself to becoming a good actor rather than a star. Stardom, in the Hollywood sense, is seldom related to great acting. Always do what you think is right professionally.

ANNE BANCROFT: One's mind must be mature before it is possible to understand formal training. Treat study seriously. Research every role. Free the instrument for a more relaxed performance. Avoid being phony. If the character must cry then cry, don't pretend to cry. Keep control of your performance. Do not become "lost" in your character. There is a certain truth in life, a reality of being. Strive to express this truth through your rules.

SIR JOHN GIELGUD: Relaxation is the secret to really good acting. Free the voice, the body, the mind. Stress, anxiety, tension, are the robbers of creativity and the free expression of acting techniques. Give attention to every detail. Have complete assurance in your conception of character. Be an actor of integrity.

HELEN HAYES: Learn as much as possible about people. Use acting techniques to interpret character. Learn as much as possible about acting then get on stage and act rather than try to analyse what it's all about. Too many actors get muddled when they sit around and analyse instead of getting on their feet and working it out. Develop an ability to be absolutely truthful. Make the character seem real, a part of life.

GREGORY PECK: Tracy said it all when he advised actors to learn the lines and what's underneath them. Actors are story-tellers so they have to be good interpreters. As far as acting techniques go, learn detachment and concentration. Discipline is so essential, particularly in working before the camera. Screen acting requires a stillness. Learning to be still isn't easy but it's necessary.

19. OTHER FORMS OF ACTING

It has been said that no teacher can make a student into a creative actor, no matter what method of instruction is used. The student must discover a method best suited to his or her temperament and personality, one which helps to achieve what is desired to be achieved. However, it is an accepted fact that a teacher can enhance an actor's ability by exposing the actor to a particular system and then guiding the actor in ways to make the system work.

Three additional acting 'styles' are presented, although they are not representative of a particular theory of acting and no endorsement of their use is given.

144

IMPULSE ACTING: generally associated with untrained and amateur actors who may have great enthusiasm but little adroitness and delicacy of performance. Impulse actors rely on physical force to pound their way through a performance. Having no technique to rely on, they act by impulse, 'mug', overplay emotions, over-gesture. The glamor and excitement of acting by impulse has greater appeal than training and playing via traditional methods. The impulse actor is usually insecure in performance, artistically unreliable and prone to solo performance rather than team spirited.

STEREOTYPE ACTING: usually associated with actors who have a basic knowledge of acting techniques which are used to *imitate* what has been observed rather than trying to create something new and fresh. They are imitators of 'style' who resort to tricks of gesture, facial expression and patterns of vocal delivery. They love to copy bits of 'business' they have seen other actors successfully accomplish. Stereotype acting is predictable, mechanical and usually lacks truth of emotion. It is easy to fall into the habit of stereotype acting — of working mechanically, without feeling.

PERSONALITY ACTING: a tag placed on many screen actors. The personality actor is sometimes dubbed an 'exhibitionist'. He/she is more interested in calling attention to him/herself rather than merging the 'self' into the character being played. Personality actors use charm. They try to 'look good' via the parts they play. Appearance is important to them — a near-to-perfect image is essential. They suit themselves to the characters rather than the characters taking on individual or different, perhaps unglamorous aspects of which they disapprove.

Personality playing brings charm and appeal to performance but little inventiveness. This criticism is not leveled at all screen actors, for many are highly-trained, experienced, dedicated professionals. The criticism does apply to some newcomers who have fluked stardom, made it on their looks rather than on their skill, training and experience.

20. BECOME A DEDICATED CRAFTSPERSON

There are certain rules, conventions, mechanics and techniques of performance which students of the performing arts must discover and apply if they are to become truly professional craftspersons. The musician must learn to control and best use his or her playing instrument. The dancer must know how to execute basic steps and arm positions. The actor must develop and become master of the voice, body and mind. Understanding the rules makes it easier to play the game.

If your ambition is to achieve stardom, first become a good craftsperson — knowledgeable and skilful. It will not keep you from your goal nor slow your progress. In the long run it will prove the quickest, surest way to acting success.

Master the various techniques of acting and then the mechanics of screen acting. Fine-tune your acting instrument to sensitively respond to your every command. And combine the two approaches to acting — *system* and *technique*. They present an effective method for the achievement of the stage task: representing the author's intent and expressing the humanity of the character.

The actor has two persons involved in his/her creative experience: the personal self and the character of the author's imagination. Both require understanding. The internal and external lives of those two persons must unify to become what is known as the 'I am'. From the fusing of elements comes a more human-like character. Because there is a true inner creative state there is less artificiality in performance. The playing instrument begins to function efficiently. The actor 'feels' the role and is able to believe in the given circumstances and events. Theatrical effect gives way to expressiveness which is convincing and seemingly real.

Dedication requires the stripping of mental and physical laziness. It requires discipline and loyalty to the goal to be achieved. The basic craftsmanship of the actor — proper use of the playing instrument — is not learned in short order. It is not to be shirked if success is desired.

SUMMARY OF IDEAS TO REVIEW

1: Bringing a stage character to life requires acting knowledge (theory) in addition to practical experience. Study the theory of acting. Know *what* to do and *how* to do it.

2: Apply the four points on acting theory: (1) *CONTEMPLATE:* know the meaning of the story, the author's intent. (2) *MENTAL PLAN:* discover the purpose and objectives of the character's actions. Know how you will *construct* the character, express the *feelings* of the character. (3) *PRINCIPLES:* apply acting principles in a systematic and subtle way. (4) *RELA-TIONSHIPS:* formulate in your mind apparent relationships between your character and other characters.

3: Aristotle reasoned that stage characters must be motivated by goals and personality traits. They must seem to be real with hearts and minds and be played believably. Read Aristotle's *Poetics*.

4: Shakespeare was the best drama instructor of all time. Hamlet's speech to the players should be memorized and followed to the letter. Shakespeare pinpoints common faults and advises how to correct them.

5: Read *Hamlet* (111,2.) aloud. Speak the speech trippingly on the tongue.

6: Study the theories of Stanislavski. Don't misinterpret and thus misrepresent his system of acting.

7: Try to *feel* the emotions of the characters you play. Don't use tricks such as false gestures, facial animation to convey feelings. Avoid stage posturing.

8: Train the voice and the body. Understand the basics of acting.

9: Stanislavski's system stresses internal techniques. Classic technique teaches discipline of voice, body and mind. Both systems use *internal* and *external* techniques but the *approach* to acting is different.

10: Become a reliable, expert craftsperson.

THE *MIND* OF THE
ACTOR'S INSTRUMENT

SCENE 7

Practical Ideas In This Chapter . . .

- The Instrument of The Actor
- The Actor's Instrument (Chart)
- Early Greek Arts Training
- The *Mind* of The Actor: The *Instrument* Part 1
- Know What You Are Doing And Why
- The Actor And The *Conscious* Mind
- The Actor And The *Subconscious* Mind
- Free The Subconscious And Experience Creativity
- Live The Role of Your Dreams
- Support Your Desires With Faith Advised William James
- Overcoming Stage Nerves And Performance Fears
- Fear Was Star's Greatest Enemy
- Actors Should Know This Truth
- Television Producer Lost His First Job Through Fear
- Film Depicted Fear-Ridden Producer
- Fear Is False Belief
- Seven Words Programmed Subconsciously Overcame Camera Fear
- Isolate Your Thoughts From Fear During Performance
- Role Preparation Brings Confidence And Security
- What Reason Is There To Be Nervous?
- Other Professionals Perform Confidently — Why Not Actors?
- Why Directors Shy Away From Insecure Actors
- Inhibitions Create Acting Havoc
- Michael Parkinson's Mental Anesthetic Technique For Nerves
- Use Your Mind To Fulfill Performance Goals
- Summary of Ideas To Review

SCENE 7

★ ★

1. THE INSTRUMENT OF THE ACTOR

Our next objective is to establish an understanding of the mechanism with which the actor works. Every acting aspirant carries within the essential ingredients to approach the art of acting. There are three basic tools of trade used to carry out the stage task. Collectively they are called the *instrument*. The actor's instrument is the mechanism through which he/she performs the intentions of the author relative to a specific stage character. The three aspects of the actor's instrument are:

(1) THE MIND
(2) THE VOICE
(3) THE BODY

The actor is both instrument and instrumentalist. The instrumentalist must be master of the instrument not slave to it, especially during performances before audience or camera. He/she must remain master of the 'self', be in total control mentally, emotionally and physically, even during moments of crew or audience distraction and particularly during crisis situations. Like the concert violinist, an actor needs to be a supreme technician using the instrument to express creativity. It is the function, the *obligation* of the careerist actor to gain a thorough knowledge of how the instrument functions and how best to use it to achieve the stage task.

THE ACTOR'S INSTRUMENT CHART

THE MIND

(CONSCIOUS)   (SUBCONSCIOUS)

THOUGHT   RATIONALIZATION   MEMORY   IMAGES   FEELING
DECISION

THE VOICE

TONE	POWER	PITCH	RHYTHM	TEMPO	EMPHASIS
QUALITY	ENERGY	INFLECTION	PAUSE	PACE	SUBORDINATIC

THE BODY

MOVEMENT   GESTURE

SITTING, STANDING, WALKING,   HEAD POSITION, BROW POSITION,
RUNNING, CLIMBING, FALLING,   EYE MOVEMENT, JAW POSITION,
BENDING, KNEELING, ROLLING,   MOUTH POSITION, ARM MOVEMEN
JUMPING, LIFTING, LYING.   HAND AND FINGER MOVEMENT.

THE BODY CONVEYS

HEAD:	TRUNK:	LIMBS:
THOUGHT	**FEELING**	**ACTION**

2. EARLY GREEK ARTS TRAINING

Education of the whole personality was the objective of early Greek education, which resulted in outstanding achievements in all areas of the arts. Students were taught to use the will to discipline the mind, voice and body in rigorous daily training in order to fully develop and exploit creative potential in the area of their choosing.

Drama, being a medium of interpretation and a means of communication, requires its exponents to use their entire being in the most effective and creative way. Drama and oratory students must develop the mind, the voice and the body and keep them tuned to perfection, was the advice offered by Greek philosophers and teachers.

3. THE *MIND* OF THE ACTOR: THE *INSTRUMENT* PART 1

The voice and the body are under the direct influence of the mind. The mind is the instrument through which all humans think, feel, believe and act. Thought precedes action. Thought and feeling determine human action: *if you want to cry, first you must grieve.*

Intelligent use of the mind produces truth in acting. No stage action should be carried out without justification. A good rule for actors to follow is: *think first, then act.*

Chapter three reveals that there are two distinct areas of the mind: conscious and subconscious. The conscious mind thinks and decides. The subconscious mind stores information and controls bodily functions. The conscious mind makes us aware of all voluntary or objective actions. The subconscious produces, without conscious awareness, all subjective or involuntary actions. The involuntary actions carried out by the subconscious include: heart beat, pulse rate, breathing, etc. the subconscious is the builder of your body and maintains all the vital functions of your body. It never sleeps. More than 90 percent of your mental existence is governed by the subconscious mind. It speaks to you as impulses, ideas, intuition. Once a skill has been learned it is registered in the 'memory' of the subconscious and can be repeated as often as desired in an involuntary way. Learnt skills such as driving an automobile, riding a bicycle, playing the piano, dancing, playing a sport, writing and speaking, do not need to be re-learnt each time they are performed. Upon command of the conscious mind, the subconscious produces the knowledge and skill to complete a desired action.

4. KNOW WHAT YOU ARE DOING AND WHY

Accepting the premise that thought precedes action, it is logical to accept that, as actors portraying characters, we should first *think* then speak and act with conscious awareness — in a voluntary way — prior to the subconscious taking over to perform its task of involuntary action. Before sprouting memorized dialogue, know what is *meant* by what is to be said. Prior to gesturing or moving, know the *purpose* of the gesture or move. Establish a reason, a *motivation* for everything that is said and done on the stage. A performance that is carried out in an involuntary way because of nervousness, resulting in an inability to control the instrument, will appear mechanical, uninspired and without feeling — the antithesis of truth in acting.

5. THE ACTOR AND THE *CONSCIOUS* MIND

The conscious mind is the analytical, decision-making mind. The interaction of the conscious and subconscious requires a similar interaction between the corresponding system of nerves. The *cerebrospinal* system is the organ of the conscious mind. It is the channel through which humans receive conscious perception via the five senses and exercise control over the movement of the body. This system has its nerves in the brain and it is the channel of volitional and conscious mental action.

The conscious mind is used by the actor to:

(a) Analyse story and dialogue script content.
(b) Decide upon attitudes and actions to be played.
(c) Program the five senses to produce images and feelings (conscious awareness, perception) of people, places and things.
(d) Command the instrument to respond as directed.

6. THE ACTOR AND THE *SUBCONSCIOUS* MIND

The *sympathetic* system is the organ of the subconscious mind. It is sometimes referred to as the involuntary nervous system. It has its center in a ganglionic mass at the rear of the stomach known as the solar plexus. This area is also referred to as the abdominal brain, that channel of mental action which unconsciously supports the functions of the body. The subconscious processes are always lifeward.

The cerebrospinal and sympathetic systems may work synchronously or separately, the important thing is that they work harmoniously. When the conscious mind *thinks* correctly — deposits thoughts and ideas in the subconscious which are purposeful, uplifting and harmonious — the power of the subconscious responds in like manner to bring about purposeful, uplifting and harmonious conditions and circumstances. It is the world within (thoughts, feelings, images) which creates the world without.

All human expression — creativity — is formed within the conscious and subconscious mind of man. Positive inspirations, visions, impulses, intuitions and ideas for a nobler life come from the subconscious. Great musicians, artists, dancers, actors, writers, sculptors, poets, composers, speakers and inventors *tap* their subconscious powers and become illumined and inspired, thus able to bring about highly imaginative and ingenious works and performances. A knowledge of the interaction of the conscious and subconscious will enable you to change your life, to overcome fear, frustration, limitation and lack. It will open up channels of creativity, allowing you to express all that you desire to express in a wonderful way.

The subconscious mind is used by the actor to:

(a) File acquired knowledge.
(b) Retain script text for use as required.
(c) Experience various emotions.
(d) Bring forth ideas, solve problems, release creativity.

7. FREE THE SUBCONSCIOUS AND EXPERIENCE CREATIVITY

When you oppose the subconscious, create obstacles, delays and impediments, you are blocking its intelligence, denying it free expression of creativity. This amounts to mental and emotional disharmony. You are holding yourself back, blocking your own good, thereby attracting fear, frustration, limitation and lack into your inner and outer worlds.

As an actor, you seek free expression of ideas, emotions and acting techniques. You do not want to be hampered by insecure thoughts and feelings which produce stage fright and loss of concentration. It is your desire to be serene, poised and confident as you perform before an audience or the camera. You can release yourself from mental and emotional bondage by feeding into your subconscious affirmative suggestions which inspire, bless, illumine and elevate you in all activities. Whatever you claim mentally and believe to be true, your subconscious mind accepts and brings forth into your experience.

If you desire to take charge of your acting instrument, to use acting techniques to perform in a confident, inspired and creative way, then convey these affirmative desires to your subconscious and it will respond accordingly.

8. LIVE THE ROLE OF YOUR DREAMS

Stanislavski advised students to 'live the role'. *Act as though I am and I will be.* Put yourself wholeheartedly into the role you desire to play in life. Place yourself in the picture of your dreams. Your thought and mental imagery are highly creative. Use the power of sustained imagination to attract the things in life you desire, to express your talents creatively, majestically and beneficially. Be optimistic about your future, about your ability to become a fine performer. There is no block to your future success save in your own thought life and mental imagery.

Your mental attitude, if it is affirmative, will see you through the slumps, the hardships, the problems associated with establishing a career in acting. 'You can use the forces within you to change the material things about you,' said Stanislavski. He knew the secret of subconscious power and revealed it to his followers.

The awesome power of your subconscious can work miracles in your life if you do not block it by habitually entertaining negative thoughts and beliefs. Identify yourself mentally and emotionally with what you desire and your subconscious will bring it to pass. You are the only thinker in your universe. *How* do you think and *what* do you entertain in your mind?

9. SUPPORT YOUR DESIRES WITH FAITH ADVISED WILLIAM JAMES

William James, the father of American psychology, believed that the greatest discovery of the 19th century was the power of the subconscious mind touched by faith. He believed that people attach faith to the wrong concepts and that's the reason they experience a negative existence. 'Make faith in your own good a habit,' he suggested.

Have faith in the ability of your subconscious to attract all the things in life which bless and prosper you. Be faithful to the idea that you are going to be a success in all undertakings. Have faith in your ability as an actor. Have faith in your ability to remember lines, to understand the meaning of the play and to overcome fear and stage nerves.

10. OVERCOMING STAGE NERVES AND PERFORMANCE FEARS

Self-confidence is a state of mind. Within every actor is that limitless power which can overcome fear of performance failure and stage nerves. Self-assurance and calmness during performance will arrive the moment you realize that your subconscious can solve your problems and prosper you if your thought life and mental imagery are affirmative. Fear is a thought in your mind. A quivering voice, knocking knees, moist hands and brow, loss of concentration are fear symptoms. They are indicative of a negative consciousness. They represent a person who has little faith in his or her own ability to take charge. Believe in yourself. Have faith in your mental powers if you want to become a self-assured performer.

Immobilize the attention. Be quiet, still, at ease and release physical tension. This peaceful mental and physical state allows deep mental absorption of your desires, ideas and images. With deep conviction and faith, repeat as often as possible throughout the day the following meditation:

> *Peace, harmony and confidence govern my mind at all times.*
> *I am in control of my life. My work as an actor is creative,*
> *inspired, worthy and highly respected.*

Your affirmation works best when it is specific, when there is no conflict, doubt or argument in your conscious mind. Your subconscious accepts what you feel to be true, what you *believe* in, not idle words, hollow statements or conflicting ideas. Cease saying 'I am nervous, forgetful, timid, unsure of myself.' They are negative affirmations. The *dominant* idea is the one the subconscious acts upon. Make your dominant idea one of command, control and right action.

11. FEAR WAS STAR'S GREATEST ENEMY

A famous Hollywood screen actress told me that fear had played havoc with her work early in her career until she discovered a way to master it. 'I would be quite ill before a performance, worrying that I would forget my lines. At times I would be so panic-stricken, I'd have to excuse myself from the set, rush to my dressing room where I would retch my stomach up,' she said.

Knowing that fear was her problem and that fear has no reality other than in the imagination, she took positive steps to overcome her phantom intruder. 'A friend gave me a copy of your book, *How To Succeed*. After reading it and particularly about the subconscious mind, I composed an affirmation and repeated it until my subconscious mind responded as I desired it to,' she said.

She overcame her fear of acting failure by *autosuggestion*. She mentally clung to the idea that she controlled her acting instrument. For six weeks she followed a routine of sitting quietly in an armchair for ten minutes each night and repeating the following affirmation:

> *I am in charge of my mind and body. I am at ease, serene and confident. I can and will remember my lines. I am truly inspired. I give thanks in advance for my returning strength, power and control.*

12. ACTORS SHOULD KNOW THIS TRUTH

The subconscious mind is amenable to suggestion. It is controlled by suggestion. Actors ought to know this truth. It is helpful during times of auditions and performances. Proper programming of the conscious and subconscious mind can eliminate stage nerves entirely. Stage fright is an idea held in the conscious mind and acted upon by the subconscious.

Stage fright is a phantom. No person has touched stage fright. Millions have felt it and witnessed the results of it. Most fears have no reality. They are sinister shadows hovering in your imagination. Tell yourself that you are going to master your fears.

Eliminate camera shyness, stage nerves, audience fright and fear from your consciousness. Mentally concentrate on what you want. Stop concentrating on what you don't want. Supplant all negative concepts for affirmative ones. Take charge of your acting instrument. Perform as you desire to perform. Unite with the desire to be successful in every acting assignment you undertake. Feel that you are strong, bold, confident and in total command of every situation, event and circumstance in which you are involved.

13. TELEVISION PRODUCER LOST HIS FIRST JOB THROUGH FEAR

A New York television producer I worked with told me that when he landed his first producing job he feared he would lose it. 'I kept imagining myself being fired,' he said. His vivid imagination dramatized the loss of his job until he became nervous and insecure. He was asked to resign.

'I dismissed myself by acting in a foolish way,' he admitted. His constant negative suggestions to his subconscious mind caused it to respond and react accordingly. He has since learned to use the power of his deeper mind in an affirmative way.

14. FILM DEPICTED FEAR-RIDDEN PRODUCER

Gene Wilder starred in *Thursday's Game*, a film comedy about the ups and downs of married life. Wilder, a television producer, harbors an obsession about being fired. His nervous and neurotic behavior catch up with him and he is granted his subconscious wish.

Whether the producers of the film know it or not, there is an inbuilt lesson to be learned from this story. Any person who indulges his/her fears and expects the worst to happen is courting career disaster. Abnormal fear occurs when man allows the imagination to run riot. A runaway imagination spiked with negative concepts attracts failure. *The thing I feared has come upon me*, said Job.

15. FEAR IS FALSE BELIEF

Fear is identification with wrong concepts. It is false belief. Stop believing in the wrong things. Believe in your ability to be creative, personable, healthy, strong, self-assured and successful. Fear is the unseen boogyman. There is no such person save as an idea in your mind. When you're ignorant of the truth, superstitious, gullible, weak-minded, steeped in false beliefs, you are opening the door to anxiety, frustration and ultimate failure. Learn the laws of mind and use them.

16. SEVEN WORDS PROGRAMMED SUBCONSCIOUSLY OVERCAME CAMERA FEAR

A veteran stage actor I coached for his first screen appearance, told me that he had a mortal fear of the film camera. 'It will be my first and last screen role,' he said. 'Not if you gain control over your thoughts and mental imagery,' I told him.

I advised him to use his imagination to mentally see and feel with his whole being a successful screen debut. I wrote for him a seven word affirmation — *I am poised, serene, calm and confident* — and instructed him to repeat it over and over throughout the day and night until he had psychologically firmed it as true in his deeper mind.

He impregnated his subconscious with a desire to be in total control of his acting instrument. He pictured on the screen of his mind the director congratulating him on a fine screen performance. As the scheduled day of filming approached, he grew more and more confident. I was sure he would succeed.

When the film was completed, he told me that his subconscious had responded to his requests and beliefs. 'My first day on the set was a wonderful experience. I had no fear of the camera at all. I was relaxed and in command. The director made a point of complimenting me on my performance,' he told me.

This actor discovered the key to an inspired, zestful, confident, creative performance without fear, by living in his heart the feeling that *he* is the person who decides whether there will be defeat or victory over his problems. Through belief in his ability, he chose to succeed. His subconscious mind, touched by faith, responded to his belief. Remember: *there is no impediment to your acting success save in your own thought life and mental imagery.*

17. ISOLATE YOUR THOUGHTS FROM FEAR DURING PERFORMANCE

In addition to teaching his students how to control their mental processes, Stanislavski taught them to overcome stage fright by isolating their thoughts and feelings against fear. *Concentrate on the stage task. Give your thought and feeling over to the character you are playing,* was his advice.

Dominion over stage nerves is the desire of every actor. Therefore, it is an aspect of learning that is vital if a relaxed, controlled performance is to be experienced. Mental discipline is the key. Focus the attention on how the *character* should feel, not on how you the actor may end up feeling through audience or camera fright. Bring the attention to the stage task. Concentrate on what you are saying, what you are doing. Listen to your fellow actors as they deliver their lines and respond in character. When your mind is centered on playing your role — speaking, moving, listening — it has no time to give to audience fright.

Through mental discipline, you will learn to totally concentrate on what is going on in the soul of the character you are playing. Your thoughts and feelings will be isolated from anything other than satisfying the stage task. You will have no tangled web of fear thoughts. You will cease to be intimidated by stage nerves and your performances will be enhanced and creatively fulfilling.

18. ROLE PREPARATION BRINGS CONFIDENCE AND SECURITY

One reason some actors experience stage nerves is because too little preparation time is spent on the roles they are to play. Preparation includes not only security in lines, moves, stage business and in a thorough understanding of the meaning of the play, but in the use of the voice and body. Good diction and expressive movement require preparation that is often tiresome, boring and time consuming. Long stretches of study and preparation of the instrument are hard work. It is because of this hard work, this meticulous preparation that performance security comes about. Self-confidence dissolves fear. It allows no room for feelings of insecurity. It generates enthusiasm and thwarts memory lapse.

Actors who get themselves into a high state of nervousness are apt to forget their lines, make wrong stage moves and perform poorly. Actors who are well-prepared for their roles and confident about their work perform freely and easily.

When the director calls 'action' this is not the time to go into a mental and physical spasm. Channel nervous energy into the performance and it becomes concentrated energy, *effective* energy, instead of dissipated and destructive energy.

19. WHAT REASON IS THERE TO BE NERVOUS?

Why actors should become paralyzed with fear prior to performance is not an easy question to answer. Perhaps it is because of 'ego' or perhaps it is the basic psychological makeup of people in the performing arts or perhaps it can be put down to inhibition from social conditioning. Also, actors are aware that with each performance a degree of risk is involved. A performance receiving excellent reviews is likely to bring more roles. A poor performance coupled to negative reviews could mean an end to a career in acting. There's no doubt that acting is an insecure business to be in and this factor alone isn't conducive to breeding career security. Whatever the reason or reasons, actors ought to analyse their personal fears and try to eliminate them.

20. OTHER PROFESSIONALS PERFORM CONFIDENTLY – WHY NOT ACTORS?

I've watched surgeons perform delicate heart surgery. I've experienced the steady hands of dentists carrying out work on my teeth. I've listened to and watched musicians play intricate passages of music on expensive instruments. None showed signs of shaky hands, perspiration-soaked brows, quivering bodies. All performed with a great deal at stake. All appeared relaxed. All appeared in control of the instruments they used. All appeared self-assured.

What makes free expression of emotion before an audience or the camera such a traumatic experience for so many actors? In addition to the reasons already mentioned, the following explanations may prove helpful to those who suffer stage nerves:

(a) Insufficient knowledge of the interaction of the conscious and subconscious mind.
(b) Lack of mind discipline. Negative thinking.
(c) Lack of adequate self-esteem. A devalued self-image.
(d) Improper valuation of abilities.
(e) Insufficient training in acting.

160

(f) Improper knowledge of the role to be played.
(g) Insufficient rehearsal time.
(h) Inhibitions and psychological hangups.
(i) Perfectionism.
(j) Poor health.
(k) Lack of finances.
(l) Excessive self awareness.

21. WHY DIRECTORS SHY AWAY FROM INSECURE ACTORS

Directors like to work with actors who can be counted upon to work with the utmost professionalism. Insecure actors often cause production delays. Budget-conscious directors have enough on their minds without having to put up with energy-sapping, time and money-wasting, conflict-ridden, inhibited actors.

Would you retain the services of a lawyer who lacked confidence, broke into a cold sweat, trembled, stammered and fumbled his/her way through a court appearance on your behalf? Would you allow a surgeon to operate on you knowing that he/she lacked the confidence to carry out a successful operation because of nerves? Would you allow a dentist to drill your teeth who came at you with trembling hands? I think not. Why then should directors engage actors who, for whatever reasons, tremble with fear during performance?

Celebrated actors are paid thousands of dollars to perform before an audience or the camera. There is a reason: ability, personality *and* secure, professional performance. This does not mean to say that there aren't nervous actors working in the industry. Some get by and have a reasonably successful career. Others give up along the way when the pressures become too great. They are overtaken by the true professionals who are secure in their work.

22. INHIBITIONS CREATE ACTING HAVOC

Some of the most natural acting comes from children and animals. Children, for the most part, are free of emotion-stifling inhibitions. They appear to 'live' their roles with complete free expression of feeling.

Animals often make very good actors, particularly with training. Watch any Walt Disney production and you'll see splendid performances from dogs, cats, bears, racoons, horses and others. They act without self-conscious awareness — free of inhibitions and in a very human way.

Children moving into adulthood almost always lose their uninhibited naturalness of performance. Social conditioning produces a certain reserve, a holding back of the personality. Anglo-Saxon races are brought up to suppress their emotions. Acting in a manner that is other than conventional is frowned upon. Little wonder that actors feel inhibited when asked to perform before onlookers in a non-conventional way and sometimes as non-conventional types in non-conventional situations.

Usually, inexperienced players have difficulty in conveying to an audience specific emotions they have not experienced or observed in others. This, in itself, can be inhibiting and frustrating to actors. Therefore, personal inhibitions need to be studied, understood and eliminated. Self-knowledge, a deep insight into the human psyche and an understanding of human emotions generally, all help to ground personal inhibitions and free the emotions allowing a free-flow of creativity, thus heightening the work of the instrument and the instrumentalist.

23. MICHAEL PARKINSON'S MENTAL ANESTHETIC TECHNIQUE FOR NERVES

Television interviewer, Michael Parkinson, is renowned for his easy-going interviews of famous people. Talking to stars of the performing arts and world luminaries doesn't phase him at all. He doesn't suffer from stage or camera nerves because he never allows his pre-show thoughts to drift from the job he has to do. 'I cut myself off from others and anything not related to what I have to say and do. I apply a mental anesthetic to stage nerves before they have a chance to take hold. When I walk in front of the cameras, I'm nerveless,' he stated.

Parkinson's technique of mental discipline and total concentration on the job at hand, keeps jittery, jumpy nerves at bay. The breeding ground for camera shyness, stage fright and audience fear is within an undisciplined mind. Thoughts that jump from one thing to the next in quick succession create mental panic which leads to fear, mental conflict and if left unchecked, inevitable performance failure. Be *nerveless* by eliminating all but what you have to say and do from your consciousness prior to performance.

24. USE YOUR MIND TO FULFILL PERFORMANCE GOALS

When you are acting in a production you are creating a character and the power of your mind is working with you. Embrace the power of your subconscious mind — the center of creativity — and use it for performance confidence and control. Concentrate your energies on what you are doing. Apply the principles of acting you have studied in order to reach performance goals and the stage task. Acting techniques supply clues to performance truth. Mind principles give you the means to succeed with the knowledge you have acquired.

Engage your mind in creative sustained imagining. Mentally see yourself in the stage and personal roles you desire. Your talent, training, knowledge, coupled with a sensible application of mind principles, will guide and sustain you in the career you have chosen.

SUMMARY OF IDEAS TO REVIEW

1: The instrument of the actor is the *mind,* the *voice* the *body.* The actor is both instrument and instrumentalist.

2: Learn to discipline the instrument and control it. The voice and body are under the influence of the mind. Thought precedes action. Know *what* you are saying and doing and *why.*

3: The *cerebrospinal* system is the organ of the conscious mind. Humans receive conscious perception through the five senses. The *sympathetic* system is the organ of the subconscious. Also referred to as the involuntary nervous system. Its center is at the back of the stomach (solar plexus). It is the seat of our emotions and creativity.

4: Free the subconscious from negative concepts and you will experience free expression of creativity.

5: Live the role of your dreams. Use sustained creative imagining.

6: Confidence is a state of mind. Overcome stage fright by eliminating fear. Claim boldly: *Peace, harmony and confidence govern my mind at all times.*

7: Concentrate on the job at hand. Isolate your thoughts during performance. Don't allow them to run riot.

8: What reason is there to be fearful? Is it ego, conceit, lack of preparation, poor self-concept or inhibitions? Study your fears, camera shyness and audience nerves. Discover *why* you buckle at the knees at auditions.

9: Directors like to work with secure actors. Would you engage a fear-striken lawyer or surgeon? Become a true professional: secure and relaxed.

10: Embrace the power of your subconscious mind — the center of creativity. Use it for performance confidence. Your talent, training, knowledge, coupled with a sensible application of mind principles will guide and sustain you in your career.

THE *VOICE* OF THE ACTOR'S INSTRUMENT

SCENE 8

Practical Ideas In This Chapter . . .

- The Voice of The Actor: The *Instrument* Part 2
- Specific Training Required
- The Traditional Rules of Acting Begin With Speech
- Develop The Voice To Work In All Acting Mediums
- Drama Critic Condemns Speech Laziness of Actors
- Avoid Criticism By Obeying The Rules of Acting
- Follow Aristotle's Advice on Speaking
- The Mechanics of Voice And Speech
- How Sounds Are Made
- Attaining Correct Voice Production
- Understanding The Four Elements of Voice
- Voice Quality
- Voice Pitch
- Voice Power
- Tempo
- Using The Voice As An Instrument of Dramatic Expression
- Natural-Sounding Speech And Dialogue Realism
- Aspects of Dialogue Delivery
- Reading Punctuation Vs Acting Punctuation
- Effective Use of The Pause
- The Use of Emphasis And Subordination
- Discover Operative Words
- Dialogue Rhythm
- Training The Ear To Hear Correct Sounds
- Do Justice To The Melody of Speech Advises Helen Hayes
- The Focus of Study For Actors
- Using Television To Improve Your Voice And Speech
- Sidney Poitier Overcame Speech Problems By Studying Others
- English Language Is Superb Instrument For Actors
- Summary of Ideas To Review

SCENE 8

★★

1. THE *VOICE* OF THE ACTOR: THE *INSTRUMENT* PART 2

The mind controls vocal communication: voice and speech quality and delivery. One of the foremost performance skills of the actor is expressive use of the voice through speech. Development of the voice and speech (under discipline of the mind) is essential to good acting. No actor can afford to overlook this aspect of training. Lack of knowledge of dialogue interpretation and projection reveal themselves immediately an actor speaks lines. It is an area of acting that cannot be faked.

It isn't possible to give a full treatment of voice training in one small section of a book. The basic techniques offered here will bring improvement providing they are followed as given and put into practice on a regular and systematic basis. However, it is advisable to take lessons from a competent speech trainer. Development of the voice takes time. Proficiency comes through regular *daily* practice.

2. SPECIFIC TRAINING REQUIRED

Concentrate on developing and expanding the range and quality of your voice, knowing the correct breathing functions, recognizing the various qualities in a good speaking voice and learning techniques of reading for clarity of meaning. These aspects involve training in: voice production, articulation, pronunciation and dialogue presentation.

3. THE TRADITIONAL RULES OF ACTING BEGIN WITH SPEECH

From the beginning of theatre history to the present time, the voice of the actor has been emphasized by teachers and drama critics. Two inflexible rules of acting are sometimes put aside by the trendy television actor in a desire to appear 'natural'. Two traditional acting rules to obey are:

(1) TO BE HEARD.
(2) TO BE UNDERSTOOD.

4. DEVELOP THE VOICE TO WORK IN ALL ACTING MEDIUMS

The grandiose style of oratory practiced by the noble Grecians and Romans has given way to a quieter more naturalistic speaking and acting style. In the transition something has been lost — voice power and clear diction. Far too many actors mumble, allow key words to straggle in the back of the throat, lack proper breath control to sustain long sentences, pronounce words incorrectly.

Many screen actors avoid the stage. Live theatre is not for them. Generally speaking, it is because they do not have sufficient voice power to sustain a performance night after night. The ability to project the voice for theatre is one aspect of training that is overlooked by many screen actors. It shouldn't be so. Actors calling themselves professionals should be equipped to work in *all* acting mediums in order to gain complete enjoyment and all-round acting experience. Therefore, train and adjust the power of the voice to the mediums of: theatre, radio, television and motion picture work. Good diction, varied inflection, correct interpretation as well as voice power are basic skills every actor must develop.

5. DRAMA CRITIC CONDEMNS SPEECH LAZINESS OF ACTORS

Drama critic Harry Robinson, feels that too many actors are 'speech lazy' because they 'simply do not understand the power of sound.' The situation has not been helped by the 'low voice techniques' of television. In his review of a professional stage production at Sydney's Nimrod Theatre, Robinson strongly condemned the cast for their failure to project their voices and to speak clearly. In part, he wrote: 'The cast includes nine good names. Why then does the production fail? The whole thing falls down on the voices. Nobody in the cast projects with any power, none manages a consistently clear diction and nobody — absolutely nobody — has a notion of how to deliver poetry with music and sense intact. The great Australian speech laziness and the low voice techniques of television have come together to provide a generation of players who simply do not understand the power of sound.'

6. AVOID CRITICISM BY OBEYING THE RULES OF ACTING

There is much faultfinding from the general public as well as drama critics concerning the lack of voice power and clear diction on the part of actors. American actors tend to overlook the correct speech procedures in favor of speech naturalism, which often produces slovenliness of diction. Some British actors are guilty of artificial stage diction unsuited to modern screen drama, others of garbled speech, plum-in-the-mouth affectation, even incorrect pronunciation.

Obey the traditional rules of acting. Speak up and speak well. There is nothing complicated about developing an effective speaking voice. It is a matter of practice. It is the duty of professional actors to speak clearly without faltering, stuttering and stumbling over words. It is the obligation of an audience to *listen* but not to *decode* what the actors are saying.

7. FOLLOW ARISTOTLE'S ADVICE ON SPEAKING

Aristotle urged his students of oratory and those desiring to be actors to regulate the volume of sound according to the size and distance of the audience from the stage or speaker. He advised them to modulate the pitch of the voice and to speak clearly. No audience, he reasoned, should be forced to strain to hear and understand a speaker. A timely message from the past.

8. THE MECHANICS OF VOICE AND SPEECH

The English language is made up of words that comprise sounds and letters. When we speak we say sounds and when we listen we hear sounds. When writing, letters are used to represent sounds. When reading, we pronounce sounds representing the letters in words. Words are made of sounds and we say sounds for letters.

The voice has four elements:

(1) QUALITY
(2) PITCH
(3) POWER
(4) TEMPO

Variety and contrast in interpretation are brought about when the four elements of voice are utilized in an intelligent way. Development of the four elements constitutes voice training.

9. HOW SOUNDS ARE MADE

It is useful to know how sounds are made. When we use the voice we create sounds produced by vibrations or waves in the air. The sounds are formed by forceful actions of the muscles controlling the ribs and by the diaphragm. The diaphragm is a flat muscle separating the chest from the abdominal cavity. As air is expelled it is modified by the various organs of

169

speech: vocal cords, cavities of upper throat, mouth, nose, tongue, jaw, lips, cheeks, hard and soft palates. Precise enunciation, correct pronunciation and good resonance are brought about by proper use of these organs of speech.

10. ATTAINING CORRECT VOICE PRODUCTION

Correct voice production requires good central breathing, a relaxed throat, flexible tongue and lips and a loose, relaxed lower jaw. The body should be free of rigidness, the mind free of anxiety. When tension takes charge the jaw becomes rigid, throat muscles tighten, the tongue and lips lose their flexibility and breathing is restricted. It is difficult to produce beauty of voice and speech under such adverse conditions.

11. UNDERSTANDING THE FOUR ELEMENTS OF VOICE

Speech is one aspect of thought and feeling expression. It is one of the ways in which personality is established. There is a close relationship between the voice, the emotions and the body. The voice responds to a person's mental and physical state of health. A person who is tired, nervous, fearful and of ill-health reflects these mental and physical states through the voice which sounds weak and colorless. A person who is confident, happy and physically well is likely to express these feelings through the voice which is strong and pleasant-sounding. Developing an effective speaking voice depends very much on good health, good posture, correct breathing and relaxation. The quality, pitch, power and tempo of voice respond accordingly.

12. VOICE QUALITY

A person is often judged by his/her *tone* of voice. Voice tonal quality often expresses an individual's personality: kindly, loving, compassionate, understanding, friendly *or* hurtful, distant, gruff, resentful, jealous, arrogant, intolerant, etc. The response of one person to another is dictated by the tone of voice the speaker uses. A friendly-sounding voice supported by a warm smile is apt to bring a different response to a voice tone that sounds like a snarling dog. Emotions can be projected more effectively by voice tone than by words. The emotions of anger, fear, frustration, happiness, surprise and love, come to life through *feeling* which creates a specific tone of voice.

RESONANCE: good timbre or resonance, such as many actors and announcers possess, has a ring of authority about it in addition to being pleasant to listen to. Voice quality concerns itself with beauty or *richness* of tone. When voice production is good, resonance is rich. An actor with a properly-trained voice can channel the timbre of the voice at will, using both the upper and lower registers, the various voice placements and directing the voice into a particular resonance chamber or against particular resonaters.

RESONATORS: these are the bones, the teeth and the cartilages in the face and head. The resonance chambers are the mouth, the larynx, the nasal passages and the sinuses. But for the resonance chambers and the resonators, the human voice would be a mere squeak. The actor seeking to develop a rich, full-sounding voice must make full use of the resonance chambers and resonators, which means combining use of the bone structure of the head, producing head resonance (upper register) and the chest area, producing chest tones (lower register). The lower register is like a baffle which gives the voice a larger sound in the lower frequencies. Head tones are higher frequency sounds which ring through the channels of the head.

PLACEMENT FOR RESONANCE: the most desirable placement for good resonance is *front* placement, throwing the voice forward and out through the mouth. Front placement enables full use of the lips and tongue which helps to produce clear diction. *Middle* placement gives the voice more room to bounce which produces a fuller, richer tone. *Back* placement produces a raspy, hoarse sound which, if used incorrectly, can bring throat soreness. In attempting to develop greater resonance do not force or strain the vocal cords. The moment any strain is felt, stop using the voice, relax a while before speaking again. There should be no strain if the voice is being naturally channelled into the various resonance areas and if the breath support is coming from the diaphragm.

13. VOICE PITCH

Pitch is closely allied to tone because both are concerned with emotion. The three elements of pitch are: *key, range* and *inflection.*

KEY: is the tonal level of the voice. There is *high* key (pitch), *medium* key and *low* key. A *high*-pitched voice is often the result of tension, emotional upset or illness. In dramatic use, it may be used to indicate anger, frustration, excitement. *Medium* key is the optimum speaking pitch for most voices. Its use in drama is valuable for indicating poise, confidence and control. *Low* key can be used to express despair, pathos, tragedy. A change in mood can be expressed by a change of key — raising or lowering the tone level (the pitch) of the voice.

RANGE: is another element of pitch. It is the distance between the highest and lowest pitch a voice may have. The three aspects of range are: *small, wide* and *neutral.* A *small* range expresses sorrow, moroseness, disinterest, boredom, unhappiness, etc. A *wide* range expresses enthusiasm, energy, excitement, interest. A *neutral* range refers to a single tone without range — a monotone.

INFLECTION: is the rise and fall in pitch of the voice. Because of inflection, the voice shows shades of feeling and meaning. The three types of inflection are: *rising, falling* and *circumflex. Rising* inflection is used whenever a question is to be asked or when expressing doubt. *Falling* inflection denotes finality, an expression of determination. It is used in answer to a question to indicate a definite reaction. *Circumflex* movement is a combination of both rising and falling inflection and is used to express sarcasm, doubt and innuendo. Inflection is best described as a slide from one tone level to another.

14. VOICE POWER

Power relates to volume, the force of air that determines how loudly or softly a person speaks. An increase in volume or intensity is used to indicate anger, determination. A decrease in volume indicates acceptance, futility, weakness. Power also refers to attack and force. It is possible to alter the meaning of a sentence by the forceful emphasis of different words. *Voice projection* — using power to extend the throw of the voice — has nothing to do with shouting. A properly-placed voice will project without strain or without any need to resort to shouting. A good stage voice requires vitality and strength. Expert management of breathing and good health assist in the development of a powerful voice. To speak loudly enough to be heard in a large auditorium without straining the voice, breathe deeply, open the mouth slightly wider than normal, speak slowly and enunciate clearly. When using a microphone, no greater volume of voice is required than is used in normal conversation. There is no necessity to bellow into a microphone.

15. TEMPO

Tempo relates to rate, speed or time used to convey something. The pace of dialogue delivery varies according to the emotional attitude of the character. Thus, tempo, rate, speed and pace are terms used to decide how quickly or slowly a passage is to be delivered relative to the character's feelings and actions. A rapid pace is often associated with nervous, high-energy types. It may be used to express anger, frustration, hate, envy, fear or excitement. Slow pace often denotes a deep thinker, a person who is ill, lonely, depressed, sad or a person who is undecided about some course of action to take. Evenly-paced speech conveys an impression of self-confidence, control and poise. Key phrases are often given a slower rate of delivery. Less important phrases are often spoken more rapidly.

16. USING THE VOICE AS AN INSTRUMENT OF DRAMATIC EXPRESSION

A person speaks in order to express thoughts and feelings. A listener responds in direct relationship to *what* is said, *why* it is said and the *tone* of voice used by the speaker. When speaking, ideas must be conveyed so that the listener hears and understands them. This requires the speaker to voice sounds clearly and to intelligently phrase dialogue.

Voice tone is colored by the amount of *feeling* expressed through words. The greater the feeling, the more colorful or dramatic is the tone. A skilful actor changes his/her tone to suit the meaning, varying the voice in many ways to express joy, surprise, anger, disappointment, etc. Drama requires a flexible voice quality with good tone. Voice intonation is something that cannot be taught, other than elementary principles, for it is a personal expression of an individual's thoughts and feelings.

In part, an actor uses dialogue to convey to an audience the ideas and emotions of a stage character. In order to receive an appropriate response from an audience, the actor must cleverly phrase the character's dialogue, emotionalize it in order to produce proper voice tone and then speak in a natural-sounding way.

The secret of using the voice as an instrument of dramatic expression is to recognize an idea, cast it into mental images, emotionalize it, then communicate it, giving the audience an opportunity to do the same thing.

17. NATURAL-SOUNDING SPEECH AND DIALOGUE REALISM

In normal conversation, a speaker has little difficulty separating thought groups, making sense of what is being said and projecting his/her speech in a realistic and natural-sounding way. Most people when they speak, use dramatic pauses and highlight meaning by emphasizing particular key words. This is carried out unconsciously, without undue conscious awareness or inhibition, which helps to bring a natural speech presentation. It is much harder to accomplish speech naturalness and realism on the stage and before the camera using someone else's words and ideas. From speech delivered *without* studied or conscious awareness to an author's words delivered *with* conscious awareness, a sense of spontaneity, vitality, naturalness and realism are often lost.

Actors unskilled in the technique of natural and realistic dialogue delivery, find it difficult to speak their lines with naturalism. Monotony of speech is also a mark of the unpracticed, inexperienced actor. Success comes quickly when the actor has complete control of the technique of dialogue delivery. In order to bring about dialogue naturalness before the camera, grasp a firm understanding of *what* it is you are saying and *why* you are saying it. Separate logical thought groupings with dramatic pauses. Use emphasis to underscore key words. Don't speak too quickly, stumble over words or the meaning of the author's work will be adversely affected. Do not try to 'act out' words. Speak naturally. Do not allow inflections to become sing-song. 'Lift' words and express appropriate feelings through them.

18. ASPECTS OF DIALOGUE DELIVERY

The various aspects of dialogue delivery comprise: phrasing, pause, emphasis, intonation, rhythm.

PHRASING: is determined by meaning. If the actor is clear as to the author's intent, arranges and presents words according to their proper sequence, speaks clearly, then his/her phrasing will be easy to follow and sound correct. An actor's comprehension of lines to be delivered is essential to effective phrasing. To make the meaning of the text clear, it is often necessary to insert a momentary pause at the end of short phrases. Sometimes short phrases can be run together without pausing, especially where two or more phrases are part of the same idea. Proper phrasing of dialogue allows the listener to comprehend the ideas of the speaker without listening strain.

THE USE OF PUNCTUATION: phrasing according to punctuation — pausing at every comma and period mark — is not advisable for the actor. It can make dialogue sound artificial and stilted. Punctuation is for the benefit of the reader and should be used only as a guide to meaning for the actor. Script writers assemble words to be *spoken* and therefore, punctuate them to assist actors to speak them in an easy, natural-sounding way. Sentence construction is aimed at simplicity of meaning. Sentences are short and punctuated accordingly, thus helping the actor to easily convey the writer's ideas.

PERIOD: this punctuation mark indicates the end of a sentence but not necessarily the end of an idea. Read to the end of *one* complete idea then insert a pause. Where one idea takes in two or more sentences, run them together without a pause, providing there is no distortion of meaning.

COMMA: helps to break up a sentence for meaning for the eye but may not require a pause for the speaker. Riding-through commas can sometimes bring better understanding for the listener and a more natural-sounding delivery by the speaker.

QUESTION MARK: as a general rule, a *rising* inflection is used when delivering a line framed as a question.

EXCLAMATION MARK: used to denote a short, sharp retort, perhaps in answer to a question or when a point is established, a demand made or a critical statement made. Usually delivered using a *falling* inflection to denote finality.

DASH SERIES: (--) when used *within* a sentence, a pause is required. The speaker hesitates, ponders over what to say next or *searches* for the right words to speak. When used at the *end* of a speech the dash series indicates that the speaker's line is a broken speech and therefore to be 'cut across' by the next speaker. One speaker *interrupts* another speaker mid-sentence or before the original speaker can complete what he/she wants to say. Use a rising inflection on a cut speech, clearly indicating that you haven't finished your speech and establish in your mind the missing words of the speech so that you can complete them if your partner doesn't interrupt you.

THREE DOT SERIES: (. . .) used to indicate a pause by the speaker as he/she ponders over something, has a change of thought, has a thought which isn't expressed via words. Some writers use the dot series to indicate a broken speech. That is, the speaker's sentence isn't completed but left hanging. Dot series may fall within a sentence or at the end of it. Does not imply a speech interruption when carried at the end of a sentence.

COLON AND SEMI-COLON: not used by screenplay writers for punctuating dialogue. Appears *within* general action description.

174

19. READING PUNCTUATION VS. ACTING PUNCTUATION

Novels and news stories are punctuated for the benefit of the reader. Scripts are punctuated for the benefit of the *speaker*. The speaker delivers dialogue for the *ear* of the audience. Sentence construction of the novel tends to be much longer than sentence construction of script dialogue. It is more detailed, involved and formal. Dialogue and scene description are combined. Whereas script dialogue writing is concise. Rambling sentence construction gives way to conciseness.

An actor uses script punctuation as a reliable guide to meaning, especially when sight reading at auditions. It indicates where to take breath stops and to insert pauses of varying lengths for dramatic effect. The way in which a writer punctuates dialogue can help or hinder an actor when sight reading or when an actor prepares for performance. Good writers, ever mindful that lines after being read, have to be spoken, punctuate dialogue for the benefit of the *speaker* rather than the reader.

20. EFFECTIVE USE OF THE PAUSE

The pause is used to emphasize an idea, to indicate divisions of thought, to allow for the taking in of air and to help the listener to quickly grasp the meaning of what is said. Pauses also help to bring pace, tempo and rhythm to dialogue delivery. However, best use of the pause is for easy comprehension on the part of the listener.

The pause corresponds to the rest in music. Suspense can be heightened by the timing and length of a pause. A slight pause *prior* to speaking a key word gives prominence to the idea behind the word. A pause used *after* a key word helps to reinforce the idea suggested by the word. Dramatic use of the pause demands understanding of the writer's lines and a 'feeling' for dialogue presentation. Keep in mind that pausing too often can create choppy speech, making it difficult to understand the speaker.

Careful use of the pause is required when playing comedy lines. It is necessary to know when and for how long to 'hold' for audience laughs. The length of time given to a pause is determined by the situation it serves to point. The placing and timing of the pause is a skill which cannot be taught. It is achieved through practice and plenty of experience.

21. THE USE OF EMPHASIS AND SUBORDINATION

Emphasis and subordination are the light and shade of interpretation. Emphasis of key words not only helps to clarify meaning, it helps to dramatize a writer's ideas. Emphasis is the *stress* placed upon a syllable, word or group of words.

Ideas can be made to 'stand out' in the following ways: deliver a word or words with greater force, hold words for a longer period by stretching the vowel sounds, lift or lower them in pitch, separate them with a pause before and or after delivering the key word. Don't pound key words. Gently *lean* on them to draw attention to their meaning.

Words and phrases that are less meaningful or important can be subordinated by delivering them more rapidly — throwing them away — or by lowering the pitch and volume of the voice and deliberately glossing' over them. Bridging words such as: *and, to, if, an, by, as, is, but*, along with the phrases, *in point of fact, on the other hand, but then of course*, carry little weight. Where this is the case, they should be subordinated. Highly-emotive sounding words such as: *kill, thief, murder, liar, dead, death, cheat*, etc, are sometimes more effectively delivered if they are de-emphasized — spoken softly — rather than pounded.

Skill in interpretation of dialogue is necessary to bring about natural delivery. Practice reading aloud and cultivate a sense of the dramatic values of emphasis and subordination.

22. DISCOVER OPERATIVE WORDS

Seek to discover 'operative' or 'key' words which convey important ideas and reveal meaning. If an actor delivers every word and phrase in exactly the same way, then a monotonous and uninteresting mode of delivery is the result. In all scripts, some words are operative, others are simply bridging, which means that key words require more attention than bridging words. Remember: not all words have equal value. Therefore, not all words are given the same intensity or rate of delivery.

In comedy situations, 'throw-away' words or lines appear to be 'tossed aside', but actually carry underlying emotional content and are played in a subtle way so that the audience easily catches the point. Noel Coward was a masterful exponent of the throw-away line. It is a way of *de-emphasizing* a point to draw attention to its meaning.

It is an actor's job to decide the relative importance of words, phrases and sentences and to make sure that his/her audience clearly understands what is being said. The meaning and implication of a line may be completely changed by the use of emphasis to different words. False emphasis, that is, choosing incorrectly operative words and stressing them, distorts the author's intent, thereby confusing an audience.

23. DIALOGUE RHYTHM

Dramatic rhythm is the pattern of different beats, pauses or actions in a play. *Dialogue rhythm* is the integration of phrasing, pace and emphasis. It is the swing of thought and feeling expressed through words.

Dialogue rhythm is best described as a vertical quality representing changes in intensity rather than as a horizontal quality representing changes in speed along a straight line. Monotone speech patterns are horizontal. They lack emphasis or rise and fall. Vertical speech patterns are more interesting as they have a variation of pace and emphasis, a magic key to successful dialogue delivery.

Don't confuse rhythm with tempo, although the two work in harmony. Tempo is speed — the fast or slow pace of speaking. Rhythm concerns itself with the regularity of the recurring beats. Pause is an element in rhythm. The length and number of pauses used when delivering a dramatic piece helps to produce a rhythmic pattern underscoring both the meaning and its emotional implication.

The ear of the actor must be trained to be sensitive to speech rhythm, to detect the presence or absence of it when delivering dialogue. Practice in speaking aloud the rhythms of poetry and prose assists in developing an appreciation of the expressive power of rhythm. It is an in-built quality, readily recognized in music, but present in all the arts.

24. TRAINING THE EAR TO HEAR CORRECT SOUNDS

Intonation is the variation of the pitch of the voice when we speak. (Refer to *voice pitch* covered earlier in this chapter.) Actors who have a problem of monotony in speech should practice intonation by reading aloud material which requires emotional variation in tone. Variety of tone makes the voice musical, more interesting and enjoyable to listen to. Monotony of tone, resulting either from speaking every sentence on one tonal level, or from giving every sentence precisely the same inflection, is due to lack of enthusiasm in thought and feeling or due to a person's inability to hear the melody of speech.

Like singers, actors must learn to train the ear to get the tune right. Neither performer can afford to possess a 'tin ear' — untrained, unable to hear pitch changes. There is no pleasure in listening to a flat-sounding singer or a monotonous, flat-sounding speaker.

A tape recorder is of great value in helping to train the ear to detect incorrect sounds. Record the voice. Read a long passage, pitching the tone as high then as low as possible without straining the voice. Record several passages using your normal speaking voice. Notice the changes of pitch or lack of them. Listen critically to the tones (tunes) produced and use the ear to detect the degree of tone variation in order to control pitch changes and eliminate tone deafness.

25. DO JUSTICE TO THE MELODY OF SPEECH ADVISES HELEN HAYES

During a television interview I conducted with Helen Hayes, first lady of the American theatre, she told me that she 'absolutely cringes' when hearing young actors murder the beautiful English language. 'They do not have musical ears to hear the correct sounds. I've cringed when I've heard actors mumbling and stumbling through important dialogue leaving us ignorant of what the text means. Speech-lazy actors must understand the melody of speech. They must learn to get the sounds right. Inaudibility is a symptom. The cause is an untrained ear. How I wish every actor would study the English language and know how to speak it correctly,' said one of the world's most respected actresses.

26. THE FOCUS OF STUDY FOR ACTORS

Because the English language is made up of words that are written with letters and spoken with sounds, words should be the focus of the study of speech by actors desiring to do justice to the English language. It is important to grasp the meaning of all words used, to know the correct pronunciation of them, as well as the best way to deliver them.

The simplest way in which a word can be read is to give one sound to each letter. The way to pronounce a word correctly is to split the word into syllables, speaking each syllable slowly, allowing the ear to detect the sounds.

Correct pronunciation, text comprehension along with sparkling-clear diction, are the cornerstones of good vocal presentation. Slow, careful practice is necessary during the early stages of training to make sure that you fully recognize the sounds you hear and speak.

27. USING TELEVISION TO IMPROVE YOUR VOICE AND SPEECH

Television offers an opportunity to study diction, dialogue presentation and the use of dialects. In the various new reports, panel discussions, documentary programs, conversational expressions of people from all parts of the world are heard. Television brings into your home the various speech patterns of the world's finest actors, speaking as themselves in interviews or as characters in drama programs.

The documentary series *The World at War* is a valuable study program, not only for its historical content but for superb narrative by Laurence Olivier. The voice is superb — melodic, rhythmic, controlled. The masterful speaker uses voice technique to 'lift' the narrative into great significance. It is a virtuoso performance — clear, crisp and meaningful.

Make it a regular part of your training to watch and *listen* to the best speakers and performers on television.

28. SIDNEY POITIER OVERCAME SPEECH PROBLEMS BY STUDYING OTHERS

Sidney Poitier was ridiculed for his manner of dress and for his West Indian accent when he auditioned for the American Negro Theatre in New York when he decided to become an actor. He was given a script and told to read. It was a disaster. His accent was thick and he stumbled over his lines. Other actors mocked his accent and laughed at his effort.

At the time, Poitier was out of work and broke. He shared a small room in a boarding house in Harlem with a friend. Humiliated at his failure, he decided to rid himself of his accent. He bought an inexpensive radio and spent time every night listening to news broadcasts, interview shows and drama programs. He copied the pronunciation and speaking styles of newscasters and actors. He devoted time each day to reading newspapers and magazines. Study became an obsession. He was determined to rectify his incorrect speech and poor reading ability. He was going to make something of himself.

When he felt he was ready, he attended another A.N.T. audition. Terribly nervous, he somehow struggled through a prepared audition piece. A short time later, he was offered a trial run with the group. Study, determination and persistence rewarded Sidney Poitier with screen stardom. In 1964, his peers selected him for an Oscar for his performance in *Lilies of the Field*. The once shy, inarticulate, inexperienced, would-be actor, is today a most articulate and respected performer.

29. ENGLISH LANGUAGE IS SUPERB INSTRUMENT FOR ACTORS

Approximately 250 million people speak English as their native tongue and nearly 500 million people in almost every part of the world speak English to some degree. Chinese is the only language spoken by more people.

People who speak a number of languages find English easy to learn. Many English words resemble words in other languages and there are relatively few inflections in English. While remaining basically Germanic in structure, English borrows from French, Italian, Spanish, Greek and other languages. Many words came into English through Latin.

The English language is a wonderful instrument for actors because of the range of its vocabulary and its subtlety of use. Much can be made of words through volume of sound, variation of inflection, tonal quality, pace of delivery, timing, rhythm, emphasis and subordination, in addition to clarity of speech. The general vitality given to text presentation can lift it from the meaningless to the meaningful. A thorough knowledge of the English language coupled with techniques on how best to speak it, will bring greater confidence and control in performance and enhanced lyrical beauty and *glamor* of sound when speaking.

SUMMARY OF IDEAS TO REVIEW

1: The mind controls vocal communication. Development of voice and speech (under discipline of the mind) is essential to good acting. Training is required in: voice production, articulation, pronunciation, delivery.

2: The traditional rules of acting begin with speech: to be *heard* and to be *understood*. Speak up and speak well.

3: Develop the voice to work in all acting mediums. Don't be speech lazy. Learn the mechanics of voice and speech. The four elements are: *quality, pitch, power* and *tempo*.

4: Precise enunciation and good pronunciation are brought about by proper use of the various organs of speech: vocal cords, cavities of upper throat, mouth, nose, tongue, jaw, cheeks, hard and soft palates. Correct voice production also requires good central breathing.

5: Resonance is developed via use of the resonance chambers and the resonators and by pitching the voice forward and out through the mouth. Front placement helps produce clear diction.

6: Don't shout. Project the voice with energy. Use the voice as an instrument of dramatic expression. Tonal value is important. Voice tone is *colored* by the amount of *feeling* expressed.

7: Dialogue delivery comprises: phrasing, pause, emphasis, intonation and rhythm. Punctuation is used as a guide for the actor. Scripts are written to be *spoken* by actors, not *read* by audiences.

8: Emphasis and subordination are the light and shadow of interpretation. Key words require gentle stress to point up meaning.

9: Dialogue rhythm is the integration of phrasing, pace and emphasis. The ear of the actor must be trained to hear the melody of speech.

10: Make good use of the English language. Words should be the focus of study.

EXERCISES
TO IMPROVE
THE VOICE
AND SPEECH

SCENE 9

Practical Ideas In This Chapter . . .

- Good Voice Production Requires Energy
- Understanding The Breathing Process
- The Breathing Process Chart
- Gable Overcame Weak Voice By Learning Correct Breathing Process
- Developing Proper Breath Control
- Exercises For Proper Breath Control
- Improving Diction
- Forward Placement Is Best For Voice Projection
- Pronunciation
- The Two Classes of Speech Sounds
- Placing The Accent on Stressed Syllables
- Learning Pronunciation
- Exercises For The Pronunciation of Vowel Sounds
- Exercises For Consonant Sounds
- Exercises In Dialogue Rhythm
- Getting Results In The Shortest Possible Time
- Voice and Speech Definitions
- Summary of Ideas To Review

SCENE 9

★ ★

1. GOOD VOICE PRODUCTION REQUIRES ENERGY

Using the voice in a continuous, effective and powerful way takes enormous amounts of energy. If an actor is in poor health, isn't getting enough sleep, isn't eating properly, smokes, drinks alcohol, takes drugs, medications, doesn't exercise regularly, then he/she simply won't have the necessary energy to speak with vitality and control.

Fatigue (both mental and physical) reveals itself through the voice. The voice becomes toneless, weak-sounding and without expression. Because it lacks energy, the voice cannot produce full, vibrant sounds. Placement and diction suffer. Actors ought to take positive steps to keep themselves in good physical condition.

Oxygen is an important source of energy. Plenty of fresh air through regular deep-breathing exercises will pour oxygen into the blood stream providing a reserve of energy. Daily exercises, including tennis, swimming, jogging and bicycling are valuable in this regard. Keep the body adequately exercised, adequately rested and adequately fed and you will greatly enhance your general well-being.

I've coached hundreds of actors in script reading, dialogue interpretation and speech development. A great many of them I've found to be lazy when it comes to working at speech improvement. They expect a teacher to be a magician and miraculously dissolve problems which only hard work on their part can cure. A good voice quality and the ability to use the voice effectively require diligent practice. Speech exercises and correct breathing, along with good health, are the necessary ingredients and *magic* keys to speaking well.

2. UNDERSTANDING THE BREATHING PROCESS

The first step in voice development involves learning to breathe diaphragmatically. The diaphragm is a muscle located between the abdomen and the bottom of the rib cage. When inhaling, the diaphragm contracts and flattens, enlarging the chest cavity. Air rushes into a partial vacuum through the nose and mouth passing down the air tubes and into the lungs.

When exhaling, the abdominal muscles contract, forcing the diaphragm upward and pulling the ribs in. This reduces the size of the chest cavity, compressing the lungs and driving the air up through the air tubes past the larynx and out through the nose and mouth. Speech is produced as the breath is *exhaled.*

Focus the breathing process in the *center* of the body. This central breathing, with practice, will gradually become an habitual mode of breathing. Make the diaphragm work. Strength of the diaphragm gives support to tone, allows for deeper breathing and enables better control of the voice.

The two spongy masses called the lungs, in themselves, have no power to take in or to expel air. But the chest cavity in which they lie — the thorax — can be enlarged or contracted from the *top*, by lifting the shoulder blade, from the *sides*, by expanding and contracting the rib muscles and from the *bottom*, by the expansion and contraction of the diaphragm.

In taking air in and expelling it, the rib muscles and the diaphragm should work in tandem, with the diaphragm doing most of the work. With most people, the diaphragm is allowed to be lazy. When breathing, the chest is lifted allowing the lungs to be filled only at the top. This is a most inefficient way of breathing and not conducive to good health.

3. GABLE OVERCAME WEAK VOICE BY LEARNING CORRECT BREATHING PROCESS

Clark Gable's rapid ascent to stardom in the early 'thirties was due to his dynamic screen personality. He had a different way of speaking, of presenting himself and a visible advantage was his virile physique. The half-raised brow, the ribbed forehead, the half-shut eyes, the roguish grin and overall look of self-reliance combined to produce a powerful screen presence. Gable was a true screen hero. His peers dubbed him 'The King' — and rightly so. It's doubtful we'll discover another quite like him.

Gable's unique personality shone through every part he played and especially as Rhett Butler in *Gone With The Wind.* Few could forget his strong resonant voice barking that now famous line, 'Frankly, my dear, I don't give a damn!' He had a special way of using his voice that was a distinct advantage to him as an actor. But it wasn't always so. When he was looking for film work in the late 'twenties, his voice was thin, squeaky and

THE BREATHING PROCESS CHART

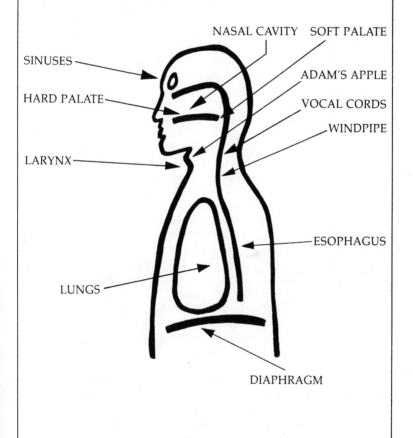

NASAL CAVITY   SOFT PALATE

SINUSES

HARD PALATE

ADAM'S APPLE

VOCAL CORDS

WINDPIPE

LARYNX

ESOPHAGUS

LUNGS

DIAPHRAGM

monotonous-sounding.

Josephine Dillon was Gable's first wife. She was also his drama coach. She taught him to project his personality. She groomed him socially. Perhaps, most importantly, she taught him how to overcome his voice and speech problems.

I interviewed Josephine Dillon in Hollywood in 1957. She told me that Gable's voice lacked vitality because he breathed incorrectly and didn't know how to use chest tones. Nor was his diction clear. 'I taught him to develop his voice by correct breathing and proper voice placement. His thin, reedy vocal sounds eventually gave way to a robust, resonant quality. His voice and manner of delivering dialogue were distinctive and helped make a star of him,' Miss Dillon told me.

4. DEVELOPING PROPER BREATH CONTROL

During speech, inhalation is through the mouth, which allows for a quicker intake of air than does inhalation through the nose. An intelligent, easy-to-understand delivery of dialogue combined into idea groups requires proper breath control. Insufficient air intake results in an uneven flow of speech.

Breath control determines the projection or carrying power of the voice. Insufficient air intake and incorrect placement reduce voice throw and strength. Controlled breathing is more important than deep breathing. Good voice tone is produced by consciously-controlled breathing.

Regular breathing differs to breathing for speech. In the former, inhalation and exhalation periods are equal. Breathing for speech requires limited inhalation and a gradual, controlled period of exhalation. The actor, like the singer, must be able to control breathing, to use the breath like a bellows in order to produce a variety of tones and complete lengthy sentences without gasping for air. The secret is to take in as much air as is required, then regulate its outflow, avoiding gasping and spluttering.

Many voice and speech difficulties stem from improper breathing habits. To check whether you are correctly or incorrectly breathing, place the hands on your sides at the base of the rib cage, thumbs to the rear, fingers facing the front. Take a deep breath. The abdomen must press *outward* as the rib cage expands. If the abdomen caves inward and the chest and shoulders rise, then you are breathing incorrectly.

5. EXERCISES FOR PROPER BREATH CONTROL

The following exercises should be practiced each day for a minimum period of fifteen minutes to develop both lung capacity and breath control.

1: Place the hands on your sides at the base of the ribs, thumbs pointing to the rear, the fingers just touching in front. As you inhale, the chest wall will expand, the abdomen will press out. The greater the expansion, the farther apart the fingers will be. As you exhale, the fingers will meet as the chest wall and abdomen contract.

2: Inhale slowly. Feel the rib cage expand. Hold the breath for a *silent* count of ten, then exhale slowly, evenly for a count of fifteen.

3: Inhale slowly and hold the breath for a count of fifteen. Slowly exhale counting *aloud* until all air expires from the lungs.

4: Take a deep breath. Explode the breath saying: *ha, ha, ha, ha, ha,* until air is expired. Repeat and explode on: *No! Help! Stop! Go! Run!*

5: Inhale and hold for a silent count of five. Break into a hearty laugh as you exhale until air is expired.

6: Inhale, hold for a silent count of five. As you exhale, whistle until air is expired.

7: Inhale deeply. As you exhale, read a selected speech. See how far you can read before taking in more air. *Relax* after each effort.

8: Inhale and hold for a silent count of ten. Exhale, humming the sound *mmmmmm* for a silent count of ten, then open the mouth and merge the sound into *ahhhhh* for an additional count of ten closing the mouth and finishing with the humming of *mmmmmm*. Hold until air is expired.

9: Inhale and hold for a silent count of ten. As you exhale, sing the word *hum*, until air is expired.

10: Inhale deeply. As you exhale, say the words: *going, throwing, sowing, blowing, mowing,* until air is expired. S-t-r-e-t-c-h the vowel sounds.

6. IMPROVING DICTION

Technically, diction involves the proper *articulation* of *sounds* resulting in the correct formation of words. Specific *enunciation* of *syllables* helps to bring distinct speech. Good enunciation requires the training of the organs of speech in precision, flexibility and agility. The vocal cords, the throat, the mouth, jaw, tongue, lips, cheeks and the palates, all contribute in the forming of speech sounds. Exercises to improve the agility of the lips, tongue and jaw help to overcome slovenly speech habits such as mumbling, cutting off vowels and consonants, slurring of words, stammering, etc.

From the standpoint of articulation, speech is primarily a muscular habit. Careless articulation results in poor speech — difficult to understand and defective in one or more ways. The *quality* of the articulation determines good or bad speech. The term 'articulation' refers specifically to the production of the *consonants*.

EXERCISES FOR THE LIPS:

(a) Open the mouth, spread the lips in a smile and say *eeeeee*. Close the lips, round them and say *oooooo*.

(b) Practice blowing out an imaginary candle. Focus the breath at the lips, round them. Expand the cheeks as you blow.

(c) Explode the letter *p* repeatedly and quickly making the sound *puh*.

EXERCISES FOR THE TONGUE:

(a) Say aloud the following words: *lacks, lazy, lily, loo, longly, lastly, lovingly, legalistic, legality, lowly, languishing, silly, salary, Sue, Sid, singing, softly.*

(b) Push the tongue beyond the lips as far as it will stretch. Pull it back into the mouth and repeatedly and quickly touch each cheek.

(c) Press the tongue into the bottom area of the mouth and say *ah* without the tongue lifting.

(d) Flip tip of tongue up and down quickly, saying: *li, li, li, li.*

EXERCISES FOR THE JAW (Perform with care):

(a) Place hands on either side of the upper jaw just below the ears. Move lower jaw from side-to-side *slowly* and *gently.*

(b) Retain hands on either side of upper jaw, open the mouth and stretch upper and lower jaws in a wide yawn. Close the mouth, relax and repeat. Do not *strain* or open mouth too widely. Perform exercise with caution.

(c) Retain hands on either side of upper jaw, open the mouth and roll the lower jaw in a circle (as if chewing), first clockwise ten times then counter-clockwise ten times. Keep the jaw *loose*, move it *slowly* and *gently* to avoid *locking* of jaw.

7. FORWARD PLACEMENT IS BEST FOR VOICE PRODUCTION

The voice carries better if tones flow through the lips without obstruction. Pitch the voice forward. Don't allow sounds to straggle in the back of the throat. Excessive back placement can produce strain on the vocal chords. Talk *through* the throat.

Good voice projection requires tones to be pitched off the tongue and outward through the lips. Mumbling is simply poor projection, caused by tones staying in the throat and mouth and not escaping through the mouth. The throat is constricted, the jaw tight and the tongue and lips inflexible. It is difficult to project back placement of the voice. The most efficient and strain-free way of projecting the voice is via front placement — free-flowing tones directed out through the lips. Voice projection does not mean shouting which can damage the vocal chords. Proper projection is strain-free.

8. PRONUNCIATION

Be ever mindful that enunciation and pronunciation are essential elements of diction. Correct pronunciation depends upon the correct production of *all* the speech sounds, the accurate division of words into syllables and the correct placing of accents. Attention must be given to the use of correct vowel and consonant sounds in words. *Enunciation* is the degree of distinctness in pronunciation.

Correct pronunciation is based upon certain accepted standards. The source of standard pronunciation is the dictionary, although even dictionaries differ somewhat as to pronunciation and spelling of some words. Generally, dictionaries record those pronunciations used by the greatest number of cultivated speakers within their region. Diacritical markings are used above letters to indicate pronunciation. It is beneficial to learn the diacritical markings so that the dictionary can be easily used. For those students studying foreign languages, familiarization with the phonetic symbols of the *International Phonetic Alphabet* (I.P.A.) is recommended. Guidance on how to use the dictionary is generally to be found in its front section. A reliable source for standard diction is the *Daniel Jones English Pronouncing Dictionary* and the *Concise Oxford Dictionary* or *Webster's New World Dictionary* and the *Holt Dictionary of American English.*

Students of acting are advised to become familiar with both *Received Standard* (British English) and *Standard American* (American English) diction. The international screen necessitates actors on both sides of the Atlantic and the Pacific regions to modify regional accents. The terms *mid-Atlantic* and *mid-Pacific* are used to describe neutral accents which do not specifically identify performers with a particular region.

9. THE TWO CLASSES OF SPEECH SOUNDS

Speech sounds are separated into two classes: *vowels* and *consonants.* A *diphthong* is a combination of two pure vowels.

VOWELS: these are classified as *front, middle* and *back* vowels. There are vowel *sounds* in every word and vowels in *nearly* all words. The number of syllables in a word is the same as the number of vowel sounds in the word. In English, each vowel letter has two different sounds: *Long Vowel Sound* (LVS) and *Short Vowel Sound* (SVS). A vowel is an *open* voiced sound made by allowing the breath stream to pass through the mouth without obstruction but modified by the shape of the mouth and the placement of the tongue. The *five* vowels are: *a e i o u.*

FRONT VOWELS	MIDDLE VOWELS	BACK VOWELS
ē as in ēven	ŭ as in ŭpper	ä as in äh
ĭ as in it	à as in àlone	ŏ as in ŏdd
ĕ as in ĕnd	û as in ûrn	ô as in lôrd
ă as in căt	ê as in êarth	ō as in ōld
		o͝o as in ho͝od
		o͞o as in bo͞ot

LVS	SVS
m*a*te	m*a*t
m*e*te	m*e*t
h*i*de	h*i*d
h*o*pe	h*o*p
c*u*te	c*u*t

(NOTE: dictionaries use various diacritical marks to show pronunciation of vowel sounds. The system used here is the *simplified* one.)

CONSONANTS: all letters other than vowels are consonants. Most consonants come in pairs. The consonants are divided into *five* classes: *plosives, nasals, laterals, fricatives, affricatives.* A consonant is made by obstructing the breath stream in the mouth. If there is no vibration of the *vocal folds,* the consonant is said to be *voiceless.* Where there is vibration it is said to be *voiced.* In order to tell whether a consonant sound is voiced or voiceless, place the fingers gently on the throat and feel whether there is any vibration as you speak. Most consonant sounds are formed by bringing together two parts of the mouth and then separating them. Where there is no separation the consonant sound (especially the *final* consonant sound) is not clearly made. Consonant sounds *inside* and at the *end* of words need to be completed for clear diction. For example, the word *little* often ends up sounding like *lil.* The word *cat* sometimes sound like *ca* when the final consonant is not said. Each vowel and consonant sound should be distinct never garbled, smothered or cut off. And remember, a vowel is an *open* sound with free breath. A consonant is a *closed* sound made with the breath wholly or partly checked.

PLOSIVES: a speech sound produced by the complete stoppage and sudden release of the breath. Also called *stop* consonants, they are: *p, b, t, d, k, g.*

NASALS: produced by stopping part or all of the breath in the mouth and permitting it to pass through the nose, as the sounds of *m, n, ng.*

LATERAL: there is only one lateral consonant in English, formed in such a manner that the breath can escape along the side or sides of the tongue. The lateral consonant is *l.*

FRICATIVES: formed and pronounced by forcing the breath through a narrow opening between the teeth and lips, as in the consonants *f, s, v, z.*

AFFRICATIVES: the slow release of stop consonants followed by forcing the breath through a narrow opening between the teeth and lips (fricative) at the point of articulation, as in the words: *judge, latch, wedge, kids, cats.*

SILENT CONSONANTS: in some words one consonant is not pronounced. Single consonant words include: bom*b*, crum*b*, dam*n*, deb*t*, *g*nash, *h*eir, hym*n*, *k*nee, of*t*en, sub*t*lety, solem*n*, *w*rap, *w*hom, etc.

SPOKEN (VOICED) CONSONANTS	WHISPERED (VOICELESS) CONSONANTS
b as in bob	*p* as in pop (plosive)
d as in dot	*t* as in tame
g as in game	*k* as in king (nasal)
v as in vet	*f* as in fed (fricative)
th as in that	*th* as in thin
z as in zone	*s* as in set
zh as in vision	*sh* as in shut
j as in judge (affricative)	*ch* as in chap

10. PLACING THE ACCENT ON STRESSED SYLLABLES

The following groups of words are a few of those in common use which are often mispronounced.

1: Place the accent on the *first* syllable.

ab' so lutely	*in'* flu ence
ad' mi ra ble	*lam'* en ta ble
des' pot ism	*mis'* chie vous
ex' qui site	*pos'* i tive ly
in' ter est ing	*req'* ui site

2: Place the accent on the *second* syllable.

a *dult'*	en *tire'*
ad *dress'*	en *clasp'*
a *dapt'*	ho *tel'*
a *ly'*	in *quir'* y
bac *te'* ri a	sub *mit'*

3: Place the accent on the *first* and *third* syllables.

am' phi *the'* a tre	*ev'* o *lu'* tion
an' a *lyt'* ic	*in'* fes *ta'* tion
cy' clo *ra'* ma	*pho'* to *gen'* ic
cor' o *nar'* y	*sec'* ond *ar'* y
com' men *tar'* y	*tem'* po *rar'* y

11. LEARNING PRONUNCIATION

The learning process starts with syllables, the natural divisions of a word according to pronunciation. A new syllable is formed around each new vowel sound. Each syllable stands by itself in pronunciation.

Where two vowels are separated by a consonant, the consonant is generally pronounced with the second vowel. Thus, apostate is separated as *a pos' tate*, the *p*, joining the second syllable. The consonant is pronounced with the first vowel when that vowel is short but stressed. Genuine is separated as *gen'u ine*, the *n* joining the first syllable.

Two consonants that come together are pronounced separately and belong in separate syllables. The word gesture is separated as *ges' ture*. Consonants that aren't separated are: *ch, ph, sh, th*, as in *watching, philosopher, wishing, thought*, etc, as well as those consonants pronounced as a single sound as in *most, learn, task*, etc.

English words follow no set pronunciation rule as the language has borrowed so much from other languages. Over a period of years, ideas have altered about so-called 'correct' pronunciation of certain English words. Pronunciation of American English is becoming more unified, especially since the introduction of radio, motion pictures and television. Announcers and performers are gradually standardizing the pronunciation of English words.

12. EXERCISES FOR THE PRONUNCIATION OF VOWEL SOUNDS

Read the following exercises slowly, evenly and distinctly, pronouncing the vowel sounds by s-t-r-e-t-c-h-i-n-g them to produce better resonance and clear speech. IE: b*aaaa*y, b*aaaa*by, etc.

a   bay, bray, baby, baker, back, bathing, basic, cap, cat, cake, candle, cancellate, candidate, cannon, capability, capitulate, daisy, date, day, dab, daffy, daddy, debate, evasion, eliminate, engage, fat, fan, faith, fading, failure, famous, gaily, gate, game, gale, gad, gasp, hale, hay, inane, jail, Jane, lame, lately, maid, man, nay, nat, opaque, rain, raid, stain, stay, say, way, wade, Wayne, Vain, vat.

e   Aileen, bean, bed, bet, belief, beginning, breach, deem, deep, den, demure, eat, even, flea, fleet, fleecy, grease, greed, green, heed, heaving, indeed, jeep, keeper, keen, lean, leaving, lead, led, met, meet, needy, plead, please, queen, queasy, reed, set, wet, wed, weak, wean, weekly, wheat, weep, wheeling, yielding, zeal, zeppelin.

i   aside, assign, bide, bind, bride, cider, die, dining, dial, did, define, decide, fine, gliding, hiding, highly, highway, I'll, ill, icon, idle, isolate, jibe, kindly, light, life, liar, lid, lit, might, mile, Nile, nigh, pile, prize, ride, Rhine, rise, size, time, tile, tigress, tithe, vine, vile, write, white, zion.

o   abode, alone, bone, bozo, code, cone, cove, cogent, doze, doan, dope, elbow, groan, go, hope, home, hosting, joking, lone, lower, moan, moe, ohm Ohio, ozone, phone, road, rose, stone, stove, toad, tone, won't, afoot, boom, doom, gloom, Hoover, loom, moon, soon, too, typhoon.

u   assume, argue, beauty, Butte, cute, cube, dupe, due, durable, duty, duration, eventual, euphemism, euphoria, evacuate, execute, fume, fuse, fusion, future, human, impugn, jute, nude, nuance, opportunity, pure, purely, putrid, tube, tune, unify, utility, you, youth, Zulu.

SENTENCES FOR PRACTICE:

a   Athol is ageing admirably. Aileen's graceful ways. The baker's baby is brainy. Daisy May is eighteen today. Say it again this way, Jay. The candidate is berating the opposition. At last, a baby for Jane and Jack.

e   Better bet on eating even though you've seen Jean. Those green lean leaves are leaving an uneven trail. I conceive he's mean. The lean coyote leaped and loped along then crossed the field and stream. The leader eats beans and meat. My friend is meeting the keeper today.

i   The bride is biding her time, Brian. Life is highly exciting, Ida. I'm tidy, although it's tiring and time-consuming, Ivan. The pile is a mile high and almost reaching the sky. Isolate the idle. The high-rising tide.

o   Go home alone, Joe. It's a stones throw to Rio. Ten below zero is cold. The moon rises over the tomb and the wind blows and blows. High noon brings a gloom and throws darkness over Ohio. There is mobility as we tow the old boat.

u   I assume the account is due Tuesday. It's humid, June. Don't fret and fume. Unify the tune. It's a putrid tube. I'm immune. I can't be duped. Humans are beautiful and cute.

EXTRACTS FOR PRACTICE OF VOWELS:

Song from Aglaura by Sir John Suckling (1609-1642)

Why so pale and wan, fond lover?
Prethee why so pale?
Will, when looking well can't move her,
Looking ill prevail?
Prethee why so pale?

Why so dull and mute young Sinner?
Prethee why so mute?
Will, when speaking well can't win her,
Say nothing do't:
Prethee why so mute?

Quit, quit for shame, this will not move,
This cannot take her;
If of her selfe she will not love,
Nothing can make her:
The Devil take her.

From: Letters And Social Aims by Ralph Waldo Emerson. (1803-1882)

A good voice has a charm in speech as in song; sometimes of itself enchains attention, and indicates a rare sensibility, especially when trained to wield all its powers. The voice, like the face, betrays the nature and disposition, and soon indicates what is the range of the speaker's mind. Many people have no ear for music, but every one has an ear for skilful reading. Every one of us has at some time been the victim of a well-toned and cunning voice, and perhaps been repelled once for all by a harsh, mechanical speaker. The voice, indeed, is a delicate index of the state of mind . . .

What character, what infinite variety belong to the voice! Sometimes it is a flute, sometimes a trip-hammer; what range of force! In moments of clearer thought or deeper sympathy, the voice will attain a music and penetration which surprises the speaker as much as the auditor; he also is a sharer of the higher winds that blow over his strings.

From: *Pickwick Papers* **by Charles Dickens (1812-1870)**

He was traversing the scorching sands of a mighty desert, barefoot and alone. The sand choked and blinded him; its fine thin grains entered the very pores of his skin, and irritated him almost to madness. Gigantic masses of the same material, carried forward by the wind, and shone through, by the burning sun, stalked in the distance like the pillars of living fire. The bones of men, who had perished in the dreary waste, lay scattered at his feet; a fearful light fell on everything around; so far as the eye could reach, nothing but objects of dread and horror presented themselves. Vainly striving to utter a cry of terror, with his tongue cleaving to his mouth, he rushed madly forward. Armed with supernatural strength he waded through the sand, until exhausted with fatigue and thirst, he fell senseless on the earth. What fragrant coolness revived him; what gushing sound was that? Water! It was indeed a well; and the clear fresh stream was running at his feet. He drank deeply of it, and throwing his aching limbs upon the bank, sunk into a delicious trance.

13. EXERCISES FOR CONSONANT SOUNDS

The consonants which give difficulty include: *th, wh, w, l, r*. Practice the exercises slowly. Distinguish between *voiced* and *voiceless* consonants. Letters *th* may represent a whispered or spoken sound in a word.

VOICED: *b, d, g, j, th, v, z, zh,* as in the words:
bob, bat, batch, battery, do, Dan, Dane, don't, danger, gun, gas, gaiter, gallop, jump, jamb, Jane, January, June, that, thank, than, vat, van, vaporize, variant, vampire, vacant, vision, vitalizing.

VOICELESS: *b, ch, f, k, p, s, sh, t, th, wh* as in the words:
bus, breath, church, chip, fat, fan, kite, king, pat, pop, sure, sat, shut, hall, sun, think, thin, tame, tea, which, what, whip.

PLOSIVES: *p, b, t, d, k, g,* as in the words:

p   ape, apish, happy, hop, hope, Japan, jeep, keep, lap, lip, loop, lope, pap, pip, pop, popping, rap, ripe, rope, shop, soup, trap, troop, up, warp, weep, wipe, vapor, vaporisity, zip, zap, zeppelin.

b   babe, bad, bat, bate, bobbing, bottle, busy, buzzing, cab, cob, dab, dob, ebb, flab, jab, job, lab, lob, mob, nab, obituary, pebble, rebel, rib, robe, sob, sub, tab, tub, tube, web, vibe, yob, Zambia, zebra.

t   at, ate, bat, bate, battle, bet, better, bottle, cat, cattle, cot, daft, deft, dot, eat, fat, fit, fought, got, hat, hit, hot, it, kite, let, letter, mat, matter, met, pat, pet, pot, put, rant, rest, rot, sat, set, sit, sot, utter, wart, wattle, what, wet, yacht, yet.

d   aid, aiding, bad, bade, cad, Eddy, fad, fed, food, glad, had, head, hod, lad, land, lend, lid, load, loud, mad, mend, mod, Ned, nod, odd, quad, rod, red, sad, send, sud, wand, would, yard, yield, yodel, Zend.

k   ask, back, Buick, chalk, choke, desk, Eskimo, dusk, fake, hawk, hook, ilk, kick, lack, like, look, make, pack, rack, rock, sake, seek, soak, socks, tack, talk, tank, tick, tuck, weak, wick, wok, woke, work.

g   agape, bag, beg, clog, dog, egg, fog, gage, gaggle, goggle, gossip, haggle, hog, jig, jug, lag, leg, log, mug, nag, ogle, rogue, rug, stag, tag, toggle, wag, Wagga, yoga, yogurt, zeugma, zig-zag.

SENTENCES: plosives

(The lips should articulate together with muscular pressure for *p* and *b*.)

p   People present popular presentations probably quite proudly, Peter.
Replenish the poppies and put the pansies on the platform, Patty.
Step up and put the portfolio on Paul's part of the platform promptly.

b   Billows of black smoke broke over the bleak, blustery boundary.
The babbling brook breaks the banks but balks at the pebbles.
The biology books bring better bonds between Bob and Ben.

(The point of the tongue articulates with muscular pressure upon the teeth ridge for *t* and *d*.)

t   What's the matter with the waiter? He's neater but full of chatter.
Travel to the terminus, take a turn to the top then to the right.
Don't be too late, Tom. I don't want to tell Ted to down tools.

d   Ned, in the middle of the day a sudden fear invaded my mind.
Did Don read the ode prescribed for Monday by Dan Donald Dalton?
The depth of meaning is hidden and difficult to understand, Desley.

(The back of the tongue is pressed hard against the soft palate. Articulate the *k* and *g* when they occur at the end of a word or before another consonant.)

k   Tackle this task with skill and check all work correctly, Kenny Kelso.
Don't awaken the sick and weak, Kate but use kindness when talking and working.
Take away the toggle switch and tackle the job carefully to keep calm, Kal.

g   The girls forgot Gordon's gallantry as he graciously ignored Sylvia.
Don't gag the rogue, Geoff, give the beggar a belting and get him going.
Gather grapes girls in jugs, guarding against haggled thistles and thorns.

EXTRACTS FOR PRACTICE OF CONSONANTS:

From: *Fancy* by John Keats (1795-1821)

Sit thee there, and send abroad,
With a mind self-overawed,
Fancy, a high-commission'd: – send her!
She has vassals to attend her:
She will bring, in spite of frost,
Beauties that the earth hath lost;
She will bring thee, all together,
All delights of summer weather;
All the buds and bells of May,
From Dewy sward or thorny spray;
All the heaped Autumn's wealth,
With a still, mysterious stealth:
She will mix these pleasures up
Like three fit wines in a cup,
And thou shall quaff it: – thou shalt hear
Distant harvest-carols clear:
Rustle of the reapèd corn;
Sweet birds antheming in the morn.

From: *Julius Caesar* by William Shakespeare (1564-1616)

(First performed in 1599. A classic example of circumflex accent to give
words a double meaning is Mark Antony's play upon the word *honourable*,
using changing intonations, first to placate Brutus and the other plotters,
then to inflame the mob against them. A pause before that last *honourable*
gives it added punch.)

That noble Brutus
Hath told you Caesar was ambitious;
If it were so, it was a grievous fault,
And grievously hath Caesar answer'd it.
Here, under leave of Brutus, and the rest —
For Brutus is an honourable man:
So are they all, all honourable men —
Come I to speak in Caesar's funeral.
He was my friend, faithful and just to me;
But Brutus says he was ambitious,
And Brutus is an honourable man.
He hath brought many captives home to Rome,
Whose ransoms did the general coffers fill;
Did this in Caesar seem ambitious?
When that the poor have cried, Caesar hath wept;

Ambition should be made of sterner stuff;
Yet Brutus says he was ambitious,
And Brutus is an honourable man.
You all did see that on the Lupercal
I thrice presented him a kingly crown,
Which he did thrice refuse. Was this ambition?
Yet Brutus says he was ambitious,
And, sure, he is an honourable man.
I speak not to disprove what Brutus spoke,
But here I am to speak what I do know.
You all did love him once, not without cause;
What cause withholds you then to mourn for him?
O judgement! thou art fled to brutish beasts,
And men have lost their reason. Bear with me;
My heart is in the coffin there with Caesar,
And I must pause, till it come back to me.

From: *Guy Mannering* by Sir Walter Scott (1771-1832)

The alehouse, for it was no better, was situated in the bottom of a little dell, through which trilled a small rivulet. It was shaded by a large ash tree, against which the clay-built shed, that served the purpose of a stable, was erected, and upon which it seemed partly to recline. In this shed stood a saddled horse, employed in eating his corn. The cottages in this part of Cumberland partake of the rudeness which characterises those of Scotland. The outside of the house promised little for the interior, notwithstanding the vaunt of sign, where a tankard of ale voluntarily decanted itself into a tumbler, and a hieroglyphical scrawl below attempted to express a promise of 'good entertainment for a man and horse.' Brown was no fastidious traveller — he stopped and entered the cabaret.

DIFFICULT CONSONANT SOUND: *th, wh, w, l, r,* as in the words:

th bathe, bath, both, deathly, earth, faith, gather, hearth, loath, mother, mathematical, nothing, other, path, rather, seethe, soothe, thaw, thatch, thank, thesis, thief, thigh, thick, thin, these, they, them, though, thus, thou, then, that, thud, those, with, weather, writhe, youth.

wh awhile, herewith, whale, wharf, whatever, whatsoever, what, wheat, wheedle, wheel, wheeling, wheeze, when, where, whether, which, while, whimper, whimsical, whine, whip, whirl, whish, whistle, white, who, wholesale, whoop, whosoever, whopper.

w awake, awareness, award, away, awash, dwell, herewith, unwary, unworn, unwitty, unwrap, wad, wade, wafer, wage, wagon, waif, waist, waive, walk, wall, wander, want, warn, warp, washed, waste,

.ι, water, war, wave, wind, wine, wood, work, world, worse, ϳrry, worth, would, wounded, woven, wow, worshipper.

l
apple, anvil, available, alone, aloof, all, alike, alert, alibi, bill, billiard, billion, billow, black, blue, bland, bodily, chill, child, disillusion, emptily, eminently, feel, fellow, file, film, final, forlorn, handling, idol, ill, lull, little, legality, letter, library, liberal, libel, lifeless, liken, lingering, lively, loathsome, local, looseness, looking, lotto, louvre, loveliness, lovely, mole, melt, overall, pale, rail, stall, stale, tall, tale, tell, vainly, vegetable, wall, yale.

r
arise, arrest, arrange, barber, barrage, coral, corollary, correction, correlate, correspond, corrode, corrugate, far, gather, heather, law-yer, marsh, marsupial, patterns, rain, rag, rest, rack, radiant, radio, recall, receive, recording, reptile, republican, reservation, reserved, retirement, retrograde, returned, revealed, revelation, rhetoric, rhap-sodize, rhino, rhythm, rhyme, rhubarb, riddle, rip, rock, run, under, war.

From: *Areopagitica* by John Milton (1608-1674)

Behold now this vast city: a city of refuge, the mansion house of liberty, encompassed and surrounded with his protection; the shop of war hath not there more anvils and hammers working, to fashion out the plates and instruments of armed Justice in defence of beleaguered Truth, than there be pens and heads there, sitting by their studious lamps, musing, searching, revolving new notions and ideas wherewith to present as with their homage and their fealty the approaching Reformation, others as fast reading, trying all things, assenting to the force of reason and convincement. What could a man require more from a Nation so pliant and so prone to seek after knowledge? What wants there to such a towardly and pregnant soil but wise and faithful labourers, to make a knowing people, a Nation of Prophets, of Sages, and of Worthies?

From: *Idylls of the King* by Alfred Lord Tennyson (1809-1892)

Dry clashed his harness in the icy caves
And barren chasms, and all to left and right
The bare black cliffs clanges round him, as he based
His feet on juts of slippery crag that rang
Sharp-smitten with the dint of armed heels —
And on a sudden, lo! the level lake
And the long glories of the winter moon.

From: *Tales of Mystery and Imagination* by Edgar Allan Poe (1809-1849)

Suddenly there shot along the path a wild light, and I turned to see whence a gleam so unusual could have issued, for the vast house and its shadows were alone behind me. The radiance was that of the full, setting, and blood-red moon, which now shone vividly through that once barely-discernible fissure, of which I have before spoken as extending from the roof of the building in a zigzag direction to the base. While I gazed, this fissure rapidly widened: there came a fierce breath of whirlwind; the entire orb of the satellite burst at once upon my sight; my brain reeled as I saw the mighty walls rushing asunder; there was a long tumultuous shouting sound like the voice of a thousand waters, and the deep and dark tarn at my feet closed sullenly and silently over the fragments of the 'House of Usher.'

14. EXERCISES IN DIALOGUE RHYTHM

As you read the following phrases aloud, be conscious of the differences between weak and strong syllables:

1: The young girl is great in philosophy.
2: Psychology is your best study in university.
3: A red horse won the race for the first prize.
4: Block that kick and block that tackle.
5: A tall man stands silently in the shadows.

Stress the capitalized words in the following sentences. Be conscious of the different meanings conveyed by the change of rhythms:

1: The YOUNG girl is GREAT in philosophy.
2: The young GIRL is great in PHILOSOPHY.
3: PSYCHOLOGY is YOUR best study in university.
4: Psychology IS your BEST study in university.
5: Psychology is your best STUDY in UNIVERSITY.

Sense the rhythm in the passage from Lincoln's *Gettysburg Address* (1), the emphasis, pause and rhythm in the poems *Out Upon It* by Sir John Suckling (2) and the extract by Sir Walter Raleigh (3).

(1) That government of the people
    By the people
    For the people
    Shall not perish from the earth!

(2) Out upon it, I have lov'd
    Three whole days together;
    And am like to love three more,
    If it prove fair weather.

    Time shall moult away his wings
    Ere he shall discover
    In the whole wide world agen
    Such a constant lover.

(3) O eloquent, just, and mighty death! Whom none could advise, thou hast persuaded; what none hath dared, thou hast done; and whom all the world hath flattered, thou only hast cast out of the world and despised. Thou hast drawn together all the far-sighted greatness, all the pride, cruelty and ambition of man; and covered it all over with those two narrow words: Hic jacet.

15. GETTING RESULTS IN THE SHORTEST POSSIBLE TIME

However much an actor may bring to a role in terms of creative imagination and technique, good vocal sounds and delivery are required: sustained tone, correct emphasis and inflections, proper pace, tempo and rhythm. Governing delivery is text understanding — thorough knowledge of the author's work. The finest voice quickly loses appeal if text meaning is distorted.

The quality of an actor's vocal presentation is marred by an inability to 'hear' the correct sounds he/she produces. Practice material in this chapter is a positive aid to 'awareness' of speech faults. Keep in mind that old habits are slow to die. Some 'ears' fight against changes in well-ingrained sounds they've become comfortable with. Others will accept changes almost immediately. Worth quoting is the axiom: *the quicker the start, the faster the finish.*

Become your own voice and speech coach. Be conscious of your speech habits. Take immediate steps to break bad habits of speech. Pronounce words correctly and clearly. Don't use "f" when the correct sound is 'th'. Don't say dea*f* for dea*th*. Don't place an 'a' sound at the end of words ending in 'er, as in great*a* which should be pronounced great*er*. Pronounce all syllables in words. Don't say *goen* to represent *going*. Think, listen, change and improve your speech.

VOICE AND SPEECH DEFINITIONS

ARTICULATION: precise production of the consonants.

BREATH CONTROL: governs vocal strength, depth of tone, endurance.

CENTRAL BREATHING: focusing breathing in the center of the body.

CONSONANT: all letters except vowels are consonants: *b c d f g h j k l m n p q r s t v w x y z*. Any sound made by stopping and releasing the air stream or stopping at one point while it escapes at another.

DELIVERY: orderly arrangement of text ideas expressively spoken. Encompasses: phrasing, pace, emphasis, intonation.

DIAPHRAGM: partition of the muscles and tendons between the chest cavity and the abdominal cavity.

DICTION: manner of expression of words. Clear enunciation, correct pronunciation. Good production of consonants and vowels and voicing all syllables.

DIPHTHONG: two vowel sounds said together as one continuous sound.

EMPHASIS: stress placed on a syllable or word to denote meaning.

ENUNCIATION: to pronounce words distinctly, especially syllables.

FLEXIBILITY: to vary the voice in pitch, rate, inflection, pauses, emphasis.

INFLECTION: the rise and fall of the voice showing feeling.

INTENSITY: rising from attitude and feeling of the speaker.

KEY: tonal level of the voice: high key, medium key, low key.

PHRASING: grouping ideas and separating each with a pause for meaning.

PITCH: allied to tone as both are concerned with emotion. Three aspects of pitch are: key, range, inflection.

PRONUNCIATION: correct utterance of words so that vowels and consonants are given their correct sounds and syllables their proper accents.

RANGE: the distance between the lowest and the highest pitch of a comfortable speaking voice.

RATE: the speed of speaking. How quickly or slowly speech is paced.

RESONANCE: beauty and richness of the tone of voice.

RHYTHM: accenting syllables and use of the pause. Pattern of different beats.

VOWEL: letters are *a e i o u*. A voiced speech sound.

SUMMARY OF IDEAS TO REVIEW

1: Good voice production requires energy. Get yourself in good shape. Fatigue reveals itself through the voice. Rest is essential. Eat the right foods. Stop smoking, taking drugs, drinking to excess.

2: Understand the correct breathing process. Breathe diaphragmatically. Insufficient air intake results in an uneven flow of speech. Don't heave the shoulders and chest upward when taking air in. The abdomen must press *out* as the rib cage expands.

3: Diction involves proper articulation of sounds resulting in the correct formation of words. Specific enunciation of syllables brings distinct speech.

4: Forward placement is best for voice projection. The voice carries better if tones flow through the lips without obstruction.

5: Correct pronunciation depends upon the proper production of all speech sounds, the accurate division of words into syllables and the correct placing of accents. Use a dictionary as a reference.

6: Speech sounds are separated into two classes: *vowels* and *consonants*. There are vowel *sounds* in every word: *a, e, i, o, u*. All letters other than vowels are consonants. A diphthong is a combination of two pure vowels.

7: A new syllable is formed around each new vowel sound. Each syllable stands by itself in pronunciation.

8: Consonants which give the most difficulty are: *th, wh, w, l, r*.

9: The quality of an actor's vocal presentation is marred by an inability to hear mistakes. Become aware of mistakes and correct them.

10: Be conscious of everything you say as you read practice material aloud.

THE *BODY*
OF THE
ACTOR'S
INSTRUMENT

SCENE 10

Practical Ideas In This Chapter . . .

- The Body As An Instrument of Dramatic Expression
- Posture Reveals A Great Deal About You
- The Effects of Incorrect Posture
- Pointers To Develop Good Posture
- Correct Posture When Standing And Sitting (Chart)
- Rhythmic Movement
- Standing Correctly
- Sitting Correctly
- Rising Correctly
- Walking Correctly
- Turning Correctly
- Kneeling Correctly
- Lifting Correctly
- Falling Correctly
- Entrances And Exits
- Justify All Stage Actions
- Expressing Emotions Through Controlled Actions
- Using The Three Aspects of The Body With Economy
- Setting The Pace of Movement
- Don't *Creep* On Stage
- Body Positions
- The Actor's Body Positions (Chart)
- Sound Stage And Theatre Stage Acting Positions And Areas
- Stage Areas And Positions (Chart)
- Screen Acting Doesn't Always Follow Traditional Stage Rules
- Study The Rules of Acting Before Breaking Them
- Bending The Rules
- Camera Terminology Relative To Movement
- Blocking Differences Between Stage And Screen
- Enticing The Audience To The Screen
- Helpful Pointers To Achieve Meaningful Playing Actions
- Gesture
- Use The Hands To Reveal Character And Ideas
- The Timing of Gestures
- Question Your Actions To Reveal Their Validity
- Effecting Dramatic Rhythm To Enhance Actions
- Motivated Sequence
- The Eyes In Close-Up
- Nonverbal Expression Requires Analysis of Verbal Content
- Relax As You Carry Out Stage Actions
- Keep The Mind Alert And You'll Keep The Body Alert
- Gielgud And Relaxation
- Relaxation Exercises (Chart)
- Summary of Ideas To Review

SCENE 10

★★

1. THE BODY AS AN INSTRUMENT OF DRAMATIC EXPRESSION

An actor in performance is required to show evidence of 'feelings'. They must be revealed and projected in a visible and audible way so that an audience easily comprehends them. Some actors are capable of expressing character emotions easily and spontaneously. Others find it a difficult proposition and often, what is expressed, is not representative of the character's words and actions.

Good movement is the art of using the body correctly and expressively to clearly indicate feelings — with or without dialogue. More times than not, the actor is seen before being heard. Therefore, body expression is a vital aspect of interpretive training.

The actor's body needs to be healthy, flexible of movement and perfectly controlled in order to be an effective instrument of dramatic expression. Body training can accomplish this. Physical exercise and sport playing are beneficial in developing muscle strength, agility, energy and overall physical fitness.

A well-trained, disciplined body is capable of enduring long hours of labor without depleting its store of energy. A well-exercised body is an alert, co-ordinated, flexible and strong body. It moves with a minimum of effort and responds immediately and specifically to the demands of any situation. Every professional actor needs this kind of *responsive* body.

2. POSTURE REVEALS A GREAT DEAL ABOUT YOU

Since an actor's personal appearance is important, both on and off the screen, good posture should be given priority in body improvement. Good posture can make you appear taller and slimmer and it promotes graceful, balanced and rhythmic movement.

Whether you are tall or short, fat or thin, the way you carry yourself reveals so much about how you *feel*. Sitting, standing or walking, your body attitudes unmask your degree of energy, your moods and your level of self-assurance.

3. THE EFFECTS OF INCORRECT POSTURE

Body alignment affects your health as well as your appearance. Wilted posture — hunched and drooping shoulders — cramps the chest and restricts breathing. Slouching shoulders bring backache and fatigue, causing you to look tired, depressed and beaten. Poor posture affects the digestive system.

Good body alignment is a vital factor in maintaining good health. When you stand, sit and walk correctly, less energy is sapped, the voice is free and more pleasant-sounding and you maintain a feeling of well-being. Good posture wards-off fatigue, allows you to work longer and more comfortably. The body moves more efficiently and dynamically. Good posture makes you appear at ease, in control, energetic and physically attractive.

4. POINTERS TO DEVELOP GOOD POSTURE

Good posture requires the body to be properly aligned and balanced. The pelvis, torso and head should be lined up one directly above another. The spine is made up of vertebrae, one above the other and padded between with cartilage. If the head is thrust forward, the chest and hips pushed forward, then the body sags into an 'S' shape.

As you stand, think of yourself as tall. Keep the chest high and the back straight. Tighten the muscles of the abdomen and hips causing the abdomen to flatten and the buttocks to tuck in. This helps to keep the body in proper alignment, eliminating a sad-sack look. Check your posture in a full-length mirror and straighten any section which sags-out from the center line.

5. RHYTHMIC MOVEMENT

The secret of fluid, rhythmic movement is the *ease* with which you move your weight. Placing the weight of the body on the heels causes the feet to drag, the shoulders to swing in an ungainly way. It also causes the hips to pivot which throws the body off-balance. Swinging shoulders and pivoting hips indicate that the legs are not functioning efficiently. Movement should be graceful, easy and comfortable, the length of stride not too long or too short. The weight of the body should be balanced on the balls of the feet allowing the body to move without undue effort and always in perfect balance.

CORRECT POSTURE WHEN STANDING AND SITTING CHART

CORRECT

INCORRECT

STANDING: body weight should be evenly distributed between the ball and the fore part of the foot. Stand 'tall' with the lower abdomen flattened, the shoulders down and back.

POOR POSTURE: silhouette (above) depicts the wrong way to stand. Poor posture is often the cause of actor fatigue. Don't allow the body line to get out of balance with the line of gravity.

SITTING: the hips should be back far enough in the chair to allow the thighs to support the body weight. Feet should be placed flat on the floor, one foot slightly forward of the other. The lower part of the back is supported by the chair back. Don't allow the head to droop when seated.

POOR SITTING POSITION: Don't drop into a chair allowing the body to slump, the spine to curve. Don't allow the legs to sprawl too far forward. If seated on a sofa, keep the body straight, sit as close to the edge as possible to allow a comfortable, easy rise.

6. STANDING CORRECTLY

Pull yourself up to your full height as if an invisible string were attached from the top of your head to the ceiling. Tighten the string, stretching all your muscles. Hold the chest and ribs high, flatten the tummy and tuck the buttocks in. Keep the head level and straight, don't let it pitch forward. The body weight should be evenly distributed between the ball and the forepart of the forward foot. Don't stand stiffly, as if to attention. Relax and look comfortable. Position the upstage foot slightly forward of the downstage foot.

7. SITTING CORRECTLY

When you arrive at the place you are to sit, turn and unobtrusively feel the edge of the chair with the calf of one leg, then gently *ease* into the chair as if between two vertical lines. Don't poke your seat into the chair and flop down. Descend into the chair gracefully. In sitting, maintain an erect position, keeping the base of the spine at a 90-degree angle to the seat. Gently lean against the back of the chair without letting the body slouch. Keep the tummy tucked in. The weight of your body should be supported by your sitting bones, not your thighs. Keep the legs together with the upstage foot slightly forward of the downstage foot. Crossing the legs restricts circulation and puts an unnecessary strain on the spine. Females may find it appropriate to cross the ankles. Hands will ordinarily rest on the arms of the chair or on the lap. Crossing the arms on the chest restricts breathing.

8. RISING CORRECTLY

Allow the chest to lead, not the head. Body weight should be balanced on the balls of the feet. With the upstage foot slightly forward of the other (body angled to camera/audience), rise, using the downstage foot to take the weight and to act as a lever to push yourself up. Take a deep breath as you rise. Never try to rise when deeply seated in a softly-cushioned sofa. Ease the body to the sofa edge, then begin you rise. Sofa seats are wide, soft and difficult to rise from without seeming awkward.

9. WALKING CORRECTLY

Modify the length of your stride for the screen and theatre stage. Your body should swing easily from the hips, not the knees, the arms in free and easy opposition to your legs. Keep the head level and straight. Avoid looking down as you walk. Keep the body straight but not stiff. The weight of the body should be carried along the center and outer side of the foot with the feet being used in parallel position so that the toes point straight ahead. Keep the body weight forward on the balls of the feet, not back on the heels. Energetic movement gives an impression of mental alertness. Where practical, step off with the upstage foot, the weight being taken by the downstage foot as you take your first step. In a stationary position, the upstage foot will be slightly forward of the downstage foot which opens the body to the camera/audience.

10. TURNING CORRECTLY

Turns on the stage and before the camera must be accomplished with a minimum of movement and without awkwardness. Fluid turns occur when there is perfect balance and an easy transfer of weight from one foot to the other. Normally and where practical in stage work, all turns are made to the front. But this is not a set rule for camera acting. Flexibility of camera positioning in motion picture work and the use of multi cameras for television drama, allows the audience the luxury of viewing performances from the best-possible positions. The safe rule to follow is to make the shortest, easiest and most natural-looking turn possible. In making stage turns, rotate on the balls of the feet, not the heels.

11. KNEELING CORRECTLY

Come to a standstill, feet together. Now take one step forward with the *up stage* foot, sink to the kneeling position on the *down stage* knee. The up stage leg may now be brought into a kneeling position also. When rising, place the weight on the *down stage* knee.

12. LIFTING CORRECTLY

In stooping to lift a light object, bend both knees, lean from the hips keeping the trunk straight. To lift a heavy object, bring the feet as close as possible to the object, squat and begin to lift, easing the body backwards. Don't bend the body, using the back to take the brunt of the weight. Keep the trunk as straight as possible. To lift and carry a person, kneel beside the body, place one arm under the knees, the other under the back, now gently lift the legs and back until the body is in a sitting position with the seat still on the ground taking the weight. With the main weight close to your chest and the head resting on your shoulder, lift the body as you get to your feet. This lift takes practice to avoid damage to your spine. *The rule*: lift with care.

13. FALLING CORRECTLY

A stage fall must be carried out with precision with the body as relaxed as possible to avoid being hurt. Inebriated persons and babies are seldom hurt by short falls because they are relaxed.

SIDEWAYS FALL: rise slightly onto the toes. Relax and drop the shoulders, let the knees sag, lean them in the direction of the fall. Push both arms forward to the side opposite that to which you have directed the knees. This helps to counter-balance your weight which is dropping in the direction taken by the knees. Fall from the ankles, rolling sideways onto the knees, then onto the hip, then to your shoulder to cushion the fall. Execute the fall with reasonable speed. Don't pitch the body forwards or backwards as you fall, but to the side, with your weight on the opposite leg from the side on which you will fall.

FAINTING FALL: relax all muscles. Allow the body to crumble under its own weight. The head waggles. The shoulders, arms, hands and legs go limp. The body buckles and falls in a completely relaxed manner. Follow the *sideways* fall method to cushion the fall.

BULLET FALL: being hit by a bullet has a sudden sledge-hammer effect. The body staggers, then drops quickly. To cushion the fall, drop to the side then pitch the body in the direction the bullet is travelling.

KNIFE-WOUND FALL: the body lurches, staggers, the face registers pain, then slowly and awkwardly the body crumples. Follow the *sideways* fall method to cushion the fall.

BODY-PUNCH FALL: a blow to the head or to the body generally, causes it to stiffen, then the body drops in a completely relaxed fall as if fainting. Pitch the body sideways, drop to the knees, then to the hip and shoulder. As an alternative, drop to the knees and cushion the fall by extending the arms and pitching forwards if the punch is to the torso. A punch to the head snaps it back, then the body can pitch sideways as it falls to the knees and forwards or backwards from that point.

FORWARD AND BACKWARD FALLS: these are not done directly forwards or backwards but sideways onto the knees, then the body pitches to the front or to the back.

14. ENTRANCES AND EXITS

Begin an entrance or an exit by stepping off with the *up stage* foot where this is practical. If you are making an entrance with another player, it is customary for the player speaking the first line of dialogue to enter *first*. When making an exit, the player speaking the final line of dialogue leaves *last*. When entering or exiting through a door which has to be opened and closed, open the door with the *up stage* hand (opening the body up to the camera) and without turning back to face the door, reach back and close it with the *down stage* hand. The speed of an entrance or an exit is determined by the event taking place and the mood of the character. When you make an entrance, know in your mind where you've just come from and the reason for your presence at this point in the story.

15. JUSTIFY ALL STAGE ACTIONS

The theoretical explanation of movement as applied to acting is: *an action of a person or group moving specifically and in a particular manner.* An action is a physical expression of a desire or need. Actions are governed by attitudes. Therefore, to move 'specifically' and in a 'particular manner' establish a reason to do so.

All movement before the camera must be justified, it must tell a story. It must have a beginning, a middle and an end. No action should be undertaken unless it has a bearing on what the character is saying and feeling. The character's actions must represent attitudes and emotions, then they'll be justified.

Vague, unmotivated actions distort the projection of a characterization and help to confuse an audience. Even though physical expression is nonverbal in nature, it must be communicated in the simplest and clearest way. Apply the rule of movement: unless an action can be justified, refrain from taking it. Let all stage actions be controlled, motivated, symbolistic and natural and they'll be believable.

16. EXPRESSING EMOTIONS THROUGH CONTROLLED ACTIONS

Mime and pantomime are familiar terms to actors. Moving and gesturing without words are basic acting skills. Pantomime is the basis of characterization and characterization is the basis of acting. Serious-minded actors will want to develop their ability to express ideas and emotions through posture, gesture, facial expression and movement.

It is true to say that all people use some form of pantomime or body language to express themselves, but not always are they aware of what their physical expressions are communicating. More often than not, bodily stance, gesture and facial expression are subconscious reactions — carried out without conscious awareness. It isn't difficult to detect in others whether they are tired, sad, happy or excited. The body readily exposes attitudes and feelings. It can communicate to others very specific information.

Body expression is primarily concerned with the communication of thought and feeling. Therefore, body movements must be shaped and directed to reveal specific ideas in unison with the author's intent. Actors, like good poker players, must learn to control and direct their physical expressions to reveal only those things they need to reveal. Undisciplined emotions can create havoc. They produce runaway actions capable of confusing an audience. Disciplined body expression increases your potential for creative characterization. Concentration plus conscious awareness of what needs to be expressed in a non-verbal way puts you in command of your stage actions and allows your audience to 'read' you correctly.

17. USING THE THREE ASPECTS OF THE BODY WITH ECONOMY

Each part of the body — head, trunk, limbs — must be seen to be an expressive part of the whole instrument conveying thought, feeling and meaningful action in a natural and spontaneous way. Movement should be unobtrusive. An actor must be able to sit, to rise, to walk upstairs or downstairs, to run, to carry objects, to turn easily and to gesture without being awkward, self-conscious or *mechanical* and without distracting attention from the main interest of the scene. The mechanics of movement require constant practice if they are to be carried out in a smooth and effortless way for the camera.

211

One of the hardest things for actors to do is to be still when talking and listening. Actors must learn to be *still* for the camera. They must learn to move and gesture only when it is essential to do so. If a move has to be made on another player's lines, move unobtrusively, unless the move requires the attention of the audience. Otherwise, don't upstage yourself or your fellow player.

There should be an economy of movement when playing in tightly-framed shots. Keep the hands clear of the face and close to the body. Move the body with slightly *less* speed than you would normally move. This applies to filming generally. Film is shot and projected at 24 frames per second. It has a tendency to make normal actions appear hurried. Take your time, but without loss of performance energy.

18. SETTING THE PACE OF MOVEMENT

Dancing and marching have a rhythmic flow, a pace and tempo set to a beat which can be pleasant to watch. Movement in acting requires a particular rhythm, pace and tempo, a physical plasticity which enables the performer to give an immediate and free-flowing response to an imaginary situation. Graceful, co-ordinated actor movement is also a pleasing thing to watch.

The pace of movement is determined by the state of mind as well as the age and weight of a character. Loneliness often creates a particular mood which is not conducive to brisk movement and flamboyant gesture. Dramatically, an elderly person cannot move in the same manner as a young person, a fat person cannot move as easily as a thin person, a sick person cannot move with the same agility as a well person and a happy person moves with greater energy than a depressed person. Therefore, it is necessary to allow the character's state of mind, personality, age, weight and well-being, coupled to the story conditions to dictate the pace, tempo and rhythm of the character's movement.

19. DON'T *CREEP* ON STAGE

All movements on stage and before the camera appear stronger than they actually are. One small step, the slightest gesture, can appear to be deliberate actions which, if unmotivated, can confuse an audience, 'upstage' fellow players and imbalance the scene.

Nervous actors are prone to stage-creeping. They edge away from their marks (positions), creep an inch or two every time they speak, gesture unnecessarily and in general, lack discipline, confidence and control over their work.

It's particularly important when acting before the camera to accurately hit marks given to you by the director. An inch camera left or right can be critical in regard to camera framing, lighting and the throwing of shadows on fellow players. A slight turn of the body, a hand gesture can mask a fellow player. Don't creep, move the body, gesture without cause when the director calls 'action' or when it is your turn to deliver lines. Hold your position and direct your energy into speaking, listening and moving in character.

20. BODY POSITIONS

There are five basic body positions relative to facing the camera or an audience. The one-quarter front, the profile and the three-quarter back positions can be made with the body angled either to the left of stage or to the right of stage. The positions are then designated as: one-quarter left or right, left or right profile and three-quarter left or right.

FULL FRONT: the actor faces the camera or the audience. Considered to be the strongest of the body positions. The full front and the one-quarter front position (facing slightly to the left or right) are called the *open* positions. The others are called the *closed* positions.

FULL BACK: the actor stands with the back to the camera or the audience, usually for a brief period. Used for dramatic effect. A strong body position.

ONE-QUARTER FRONT POSITION: the body is positioned so that it is a quarter-turn away from the camera or the audience either facing slightly to the left or to the right (one-quarter front left, one-quarter front right). Also referred to as three-quarter front. Being an open (strong) position, it is the one most frequently used.

PROFILE: the actor stands or sits facing either to the left or to the right in profile allowing the camera or the audience to see only one side of the face and body. When two actors face one another in profile they are said to be 'sharing' the scene. Sometimes profile is referred to as the half-position. It is not particularly strong. The theatre actor looking to the right is said to be in *right profile*, the left side of the face and body open to the audience. The camera actor facing to the right is said to be in *camera left profile*, as all positions for the screen actor are designated according to the camera's point of view.

THREE-QUARTER BACK POSITION: the actor turns the body nearly full back to the camera or the audience angling it either to the right or to the left so that less than one side of the head and shoulder are visible. A decidedly weak position.

21. SOUND STAGE AND THEATRE STAGE ACTING POSITIONS AND AREAS

It is important to know the key terms and symbols used to describe the various actor positions and acting areas of a traditional theatre stage, a motion picture sound stage and a television studio floor. Actors are given specific positions (marks) and particular moves (blocking) within the designated staging areas.

The traditional theatre stage has fifteen areas for big musical productions played on a large stage, nine areas for drama productions played on a large stage and in recent times, a modified six area division favored by

— THE ACTOR'S BODY POSITIONS —

1: FULL FRONT POSITION

2: FULL BACK POSITION

3: ONE-QUARTER FRONT POSITION

4: PROFILE POSITION

5: THREE-QUARTER BACK POSITION

contemporary directors working smaller theatres. The six area plan should be familiarized by the screen actor as it is used for television and film production stagings.

Theatre stage positions, with the exception of center stage, up stage and down stage, are the *reverse* of screen stage positions. Stage left and stage right positions to the theatre actor mean left and right from his/her point of view *facing* the audience. The camera actor's stage positions are taken from the *camera's* point of view facing the actor. Thus, stage left becomes camera right and stage right becomes camera left.

The traditional theatre stage areas and their symbols (bracketed) for the fifteen area plan are:

> Center Stage (CS)
> Left Center (LC)
> Left (L)
> Up Center (UC)
> Up Center Left (UCL)
> Up Left (UL)
> Down Center (DC)
> Down Left Center (DLC)
> Down Left (DL)
> Right Center (RC)
> Right (R)
> Up Right Center (URC)
> Up Right (UR)
> Down Right Center (DRC)
> Down Right (DR)

Because the modified six area system is the one most frequently used by both stage and screen directors, it is the system we shall use in this text. Its universal appeal, no doubt, is due to its simplicity. The six basic stage areas of this plan are:

> Up Center
> Down Center
> Up Right
> Down Right
> Up Left
> Down Left

22. SCREEN ACTING DOESN'T ALWAYS FOLLOW TRADITIONAL STAGE RULES

There are numerous rules and traditions which have been passed down to actors through the long history of the theatre. Many of them are valid today, some aren't. There are actors who feel that conventional theatre

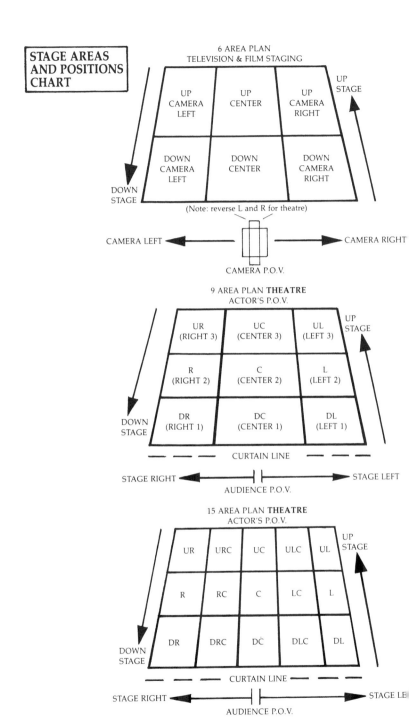

STAGE AREAS AND POSITIONS CHART

6 AREA PLAN
TELEVISION & FILM STAGING

| UP CAMERA LEFT | UP CENTER | UP CAMERA RIGHT |
| DOWN CAMERA LEFT | DOWN CENTER | DOWN CAMERA RIGHT |

UP STAGE

DOWN STAGE

(Note: reverse L and R for theatre)

CAMERA LEFT ◄——— ———► CAMERA RIGHT

CAMERA P.O.V.

9 AREA PLAN **THEATRE**
ACTOR'S P.O.V.

UR (RIGHT 3)	UC (CENTER 3)	UL (LEFT 3)
R (RIGHT 2)	C (CENTER 2)	L (LEFT 2)
DR (RIGHT 1)	DC (CENTER 1)	DL (LEFT 1)

UP STAGE

DOWN STAGE

— — — CURTAIN LINE — — —

STAGE RIGHT ◄——— ———► STAGE LEFT

AUDIENCE P.O.V.

15 AREA PLAN **THEATRE**
ACTOR'S P.O.V.

UR	URC	UC	ULC	UL
R	RC	C	LC	L
DR	DRC	DC	DLC	DL

UP STAGE

DOWN STAGE

— — — CURTAIN LINE — — —

STAGE RIGHT ◄——— ———► STAGE LE

AUDIENCE P.O.V.

acting rules are outmoded and so they ignore them. Many of the elder statesmen of the theatre argue that every art must have its rules which provide discipline and so they strictly adhere to them.

Because screen acting imposes its own set of rules and conventions, traditional stage rules, by necessity, are subject to regular infraction. This does not please the traditionalists — in some cases, rightly so. Stage deportment has to do with the way an actor speaks, moves and, in general, to the way in which an actor conducts himself/herself relative to the director and fellow actors. The basic rules of professional behavior in this regard will never become outmoded. Nor will the two elementary rules of acting (so often broken) which require the actor to be *heard* and to be *understood*.

In recent years, acting has undergone a transformation. It is now more natural and less stylized. Emphasis is placed on ease of body movement, natural-sounding text delivery. Screen acting, in particular, requires performance understatement rather than overstatement — as in the theatre. The screen actor requires far less audio dynamics, scaled-down gesture and facial expression. One of the keys to good performance is to apply the rule of self-discipline. The most important rule for the screen actor is to speak and move *naturally*.

23. STUDY THE RULES OF ACTING BEFORE BREAKING THEM

As this book is concerned primarily with screen acting techniques, it is not possible to devote very much space to the traditions of theatre craft. There are many excellent books on the subject and I strongly urge beginning actors to seek them out and study them.

Actors should be well-schooled in the fundamentals of theatre acting. Being fully conversant with the methods, rules and conventions of stage acting will help to bring about a better understanding of acting generally.

Actors must be careful not to defy convention by ignoring the traditions of acting which date back to early Greek theatre. There are basic rules *all* actors should learn before undertaking professional assignments. The screen actor will find that many of the conventional rules of stage acting are inappropriate for television and film work. Nonetheless, they should be studied and evaluated before being discarded. When you know the rules, you've earned the right to break them.

24. BENDING THE RULES

You will want to rid yourself of poor posture and sloppy movement habits as quickly as you can. However, there will be times when a character's bodily attitude requires you to break the rules of good posture and graceful movement. If a particular character you have been chosen to play is afflicted with hunched shoulders, out-of-rhythm movement and a physical awkwardness, those afflications should be *assumed*, as opposed to permanent afflictions of your own making.

217

After completing your role, dispose of the character's physical flaws. Check your posture in a full-length mirror. Get back to the rules of good physical appearance.

25. CAMERA TERMINOLOGY RELATIVE TO MOVEMENT

It is necessary for actors who wish to work in television and film drama productions to familiarize themselves with the key expressions used by directors. The following terminology is applicable to both television and motion picture work.

ACTION: call by the director for the actors to begin the scene. On the call of 'action' silently count *two* beats then begin.

BACKGROUND ACTION: the activity of extras and minor players in the background of the scene to add atmosphere. Background action should not be too busy, but unobtrusive or the principal players in the foreground will be upstaged.

BLOCKING ACTION: actor positioning and moves on the set given by the director.

BUSINESS: a specific action such as putting on a jacket, pouring a drink, opening a window, packing a suitcase, etc.

CHEAT: ease into a more favorable position for the camera. The head or body is adjusted only slightly, particularly when 'cheating' for a close up.

CLEAR: when your scene is finished and you have no further scenes for the day, the assistant director gives you 'clearance' to leave the studio or location. The term is 'you're clear.'

CUT: command of the director to stop camera, sound and the action of the actors. *Also* refers to line cuts and scene cuts in the script.

DIALOGUE CROSS: when two players cross during an exchange of dialogue, the more important player walks slightly ahead and up stage of the other player. Refers to any cross when speaking dialogue.

DOWN STAGE CROSS: crossing down toward the camera or a cross below other players. Crossing in front of other players is a strong move.

EXIT FRAME: walking out of scene either to the left or to the right of camera. If exiting the *short* side of frame, exit slowly.

FIRST POSITION: call by assistant director or floor manager to take up beginning positions. First, second, third, etc, positions are moves as they come in sequence as blocked.

FREEZE POSITION: don't alter position in any way until told to move.

LONG SIDE EXIT: side of frame which has the greater distance to travel to 'lose frame'. In two-shot, player usually exists long side of frame, camera then centers on remaining player.

OVER-THE-TOP: performance too big for camera, requires reducing.

PARALLEL MOVES: two different actions occurring simultaneously.

PANTOMIME ACTION: expressed without dialogue using gestures and lip movement to avoid upstaging foreground action.

PHYSICAL CUE: hand signal by assistant director or floor manager who stands in sight-line of player so signal can be seen.

PICK UP: continue with uncompleted scene from point where it went wrong.

POP FROM FRAME: exiting too quickly or sitting or rising too fast.

POSITION CENTER OF INTEREST: actor is *favored* in scene positioning.

POSITION MARKS: tape or chalk marks on floor to indicate players' positions. 'Hitting marks' is essential for camera framing. Actors must hit marks without searching for them.

P.O.V.: point-of-view of camera, audience or actor.

SHORT SIDE EXIT: shortest exit point. Should be made slowly to avoid 'popping' from frame too quickly.

SILENT CROSS: a cross without dialogue. Also called an *action* cross.

TAKE AND PRINT: scene filmed is successful and is to be sent to laboratory to be printed.

UP STAGE CAMERA CROSS: a cross **above** other players. A cross made at furthest point from camera.

WALK INTO FRAME: entering scene from an off-camera position.

26. BLOCKING DIFFERENCES BETWEEN STAGE AND SCREEN

A marked difference between performing on a theatre stage and before the camera is the method of blocking actors. The theatre director will attempt to make the most of the *width* of the stage. The stage picture is spread out to give good balance and composition. Actors working on a proscenium stage are used to making horizontal crosses more so than vertical ones. Usually, the theatre actor will play at least an arm's length from the partner. Crosses, as a general rule, are made on a slight curve or in a straight line. Players favor the 'open' body positions rather than the 'closed' ones. This allows an audience to see the faces of the players.

Blocking for the stage must always take into consideration the audience and its ability to see the stage action from the auditorium. A stage director must be an artist who utilizes the principles of unity, balance, rhythm and proportion in the grouping and spacing of characters and furniture on the stage. Informal stage balance is generally better than symmetrical balance. The two halves of the stage picture must draw the same amount of interest to avoid audience restlessness.

In blocking for the camera, the director must think in terms of *depth* rather than width. The screen picture must be kept 'tight' for better compositional balance. Actors must play closer together, especially for tight two-shots. They tend to make more vertical and diagonal crosses than horizontal ones. Action is tightly blocked to allow the camera to capture important action rather than a lot of empty space and unimportant backgrounds. On the screen, depth is suggested through the use of *planes*. One actor is positioned closer to the camera than another, each on a different plane which adds depth to the picture. The stage actor is required to *extend* moves and gestures to reach the last row of spectators. The screen actor reduces body actions, understates his/her performance, allowing the *camera* to carry the performance to viewers. Providing the screen actor 'feels' something, the camera will capture it.

27. ENTICING THE AUDIENCE TO THE SCREEN

In the theatre, an audience is a 'captive' one. The stage actor is required to reach out to the audience. In screen acting, the audience comes to the actor.

Falseness of performance is more apparent in screen acting than it is in theatre acting. The big-screen closeup reveals performance insincerity. The essence of good screen performance is sincerity and naturalness, tempered with restraint — an ability to scale things down without energy loss.

28. HELPFUL POINTERS TO ACHIEVE MEANINGFUL PLAYING ACTIONS

PLAYING DEATH SCENES: the body should be kept immobile. A character in great pain does not show much vitality. Restrain movement and gesture. The voice of someone near death is barely audible. When death does come, the head relaxes and drops slightly to one side. In order to create the illusion of dying, analyse the cause of death of your character. Dying from a massive heart attack, from a lengthy illness or after being stabbed are quite different actions and each requires an appropriate playing action effected in a believable way.

PLAYING LOVE SCENES: the director will decide whose face is to be featured at the moment of the embrace and kiss. Don't end a kiss abruptly. Hold the embrace, then slowly withdraw from the kiss. Stand close to your partner and predetermine the position of feet to avoid stepping on one another's toes. A collision of noses can be avoided by one player tilting the head slightly in the direction of down stage, the partner tilting the head slightly in the direction of up stage. The male's down stage arm slips under the female's down stage arm with the hand resting slightly above her waist. His up stage hand rests on her shoulder blade. Her down stage hand rests on his down stage elbow, shoulder or chest, whichever is comfortable and appropriate. Her up stage hand rests on his up stage arm or on his chest. Now slip the arms further around each other. These are basic *stage* positions for practice. Camera acting requires *all* stage actions to be executed in a natural-looking way.

AFFECTING INSANITY: not all insane people scream their heads off or act in a totally irrational or violent way. Insanity has many variations. Some individuals are silent types, withdrawn and shy. Others are nervous, hyperactive, quick to fly into a rage, even violent when provoked. There are insane people who have moments of insanity only when they are nervous and fearful, otherwise they appear to be normal. Discover the logic of the insanity. Look for its origin and play the physical actions that indicate the particular insanity of the character.

Actress Frances Farmer was in and out of mental institutions during her unfortunate and traumatic life for reasons vividly depicted in the film *Frances*. The 'thirties actress was excellently portrayed by Jessica Lange, particularly those scenes where Frances is seen in a rebellious and hysterical state of mind. The film *The Snake Pit*, is another example of how insanity can be portrayed. This film depicted insane women incarcerated in a deplorable way. For some, the insanity exploded through their appearance, looks and uncontrolled actions. For others, through their somber and withdrawn personalities. As another example, *One Flew Over The Cuckoo's Nest* graphically displayed the fears, frustrations, anxieties, obsessions and insecurities of the patients. The actors, in particular Jack Nicholson and Louise Fletcher, gave outstanding performances. It was the first film since *It Happened One Night* to win all five top Oscars.

In Alfred Hitchcock's *Psycho*, we see a mentally unbalanced character, well played by Anthony Perkins. He appears to be a nice, friendly young man, if not a little awkward and nervous in his speech and actions, but seemingly normal. Change comes about when he steps into the personality of his dead mother. Here is a person who appears to be sane one moment, insane the next.

Hitchcock presented a different sort of personality in Mrs. Danvers, in *Rebecca*. Judith Anderson gave a strong portrayal of the psychologically-unbalanced housekeeper. We see her gazing at her hand through Rebecca's transparent underclothes, stroking the sleeve of Rebecca's fur coat against her face and admiring the bed in which Rebecca slept before her puzzling death. Mrs. Danvers isn't insane, but surely she can't be far from insanity. Her behavior isn't normal. Yet Judith Anderson plays the character's actions as if they are perfectly normal and acceptable. Mrs. Danvers lives within her imagination. It's a world of past memories which she is obsessed with preserving at all costs.

Humphrey Bogart presented a well-orchestrated psychologically-unbalanced character in *The Caine Mutiny Court-Martial*. Captain Queeg, commander of the U.S.S. Caine, is an old-fashioned martinet whose rigid dictatorial methods have pushed his crew into mutiny. Queeg isn't insane. He's a sadist, a psychotic, whose personality is very seriously disorganized. Bogart nervously rolls steel balls in his hand during courtroom questioning and this action, along with his neurotic ramblings, condemns him.

AFFECTING DRUNKENNESS: this is one of the most difficult conditions for an actor to simulate. There are many kinds of drunks: shy ones, silent ones, aggressive ones, violent ones. Observation of actual persons in a drunken state, in addition to understanding *why* the character you are to play drinks to excess, will help to overcome stereotyped actions such as rubbery legs and slurred speech. Perhaps the key to playing a person who is drunk is to know that nearly all inebriated persons or alcoholics attempt to hide the fact that they are intoxicated. An attempt is made to look and sound sober.

Several actors have perfected the simulation of drunkenness on the screen. In the 40's and 50's Jack Norton portrayed comic-drunks in a host of pictures. Audiences responded immediately Norton entered a scene. In 1945, Ray Milland received an Oscar for his outstanding portrayal of an alcoholic in *Lost Weekend*. The film and its director, Billy Wilder, received Oscars. Jack Lemmon and Lee Remick have to be singled out for their convincing portrayals of drunks in *Days of Wine and Roses*. Screen stars James Mason and Susan Hayward have given emotionally-moving performances as alcoholics. And Humphrey Bogart won an Oscar for his comic-drunk in *The African Queen*.

STAGE SLAPS: these must be carried out with precision and with care so that they are convincing without being harmful to fellow players. Cup the hand and strike the person in the area of the jawbone, well clear of the ear and the neck. Cupping the hand with the fingers drawn together creates the correct sound and doesn't leave finger marks on the person slapped. Actresses sporting long finger-nails should be careful not to scratch the faces of those they slap. When receiving a slap, turn the head away from the slap at the moment of impact.

LAUGHTER: it can be produced mechanically by expelling air from the lungs in quick bursts or by beginning to cough, slowly at first, then rapidly until you are out of breath. Anticipate the end of a gag line by beginning the laugh with a smile then breaking into laughter at the completion of the speaker's line. Genuine laughter is the result of something or someone amusing you. It is a motivated response. It requires a discovery of the *reason* for laughing in order to produce natural laughter sounds, rather than mechanical ones.

TEARS: shedding tears at the drop of a hat is difficult, particularly for inexperienced actors. Desperately trying to shed tears frequently results in no tears. It is necessary to express sorrow in a *truthful* way but not necessarily in a real way because we are interested in creating *illusions* before the camera. Crying is the result of giving in to feelings, a physical release of built-up tension. It will help to focus on a sorrowful event from your past which evoked tears at the time. Recall how you felt, what sparked the tears and how hard you cried. Perhaps the eyes were moist without flowing tears. Concentrate on the cause of your character's grief and try to relate to it in some way. And in real life, one usually tries to *stop* crying or to hide it from others.

Sorrow and grief do not always bring tears. It is not always necessary for a character to shed tears while under emotional stress. There are a variety of ways to indicate unhappiness. For example, staring at an object such as a picture of a loved one while concentrating on the cause of the emotion, or clinging to someone or something very tightly can produce the emotional impact that is desired.

To project the illusion of crying, inhale in little gasping sobs, increasing the tempo and the volume of the sobbing until the desired result is achieved. Do not cry on spoken words or it will be difficult to be understood. Speak on a gasping breath between sobs. Use the abdominal muscles to make the sobs more explosive.

In order to project a *truthful* emotion on stage, experience an internal physical response to someone or something. 'Give in' to some situation or circumstance, allowing some kind of physical response to indicate your feelings. Without the physical sensations, an audience is unable to share in the emotions of the performer. When a performer identifies with the character's emotional state of mind, the audience will empathize and feel the same emotional response.

EMOTIONS AND BREATHING: an important physical condition for projecting an emotion is proper breathing. When you are excited, worried, fretful, anxious and angry, your breathing will be quicker than when you are relaxed, confident and calm. Your emotions correspond to a particular breathing pattern, creating different rhythms. Take note of your personal breathing patterns when you are experiencing an emotional *high* or an emotional *low* period.

CONSUMING FOOD AND DRINK: the rule is to eat small portions of food and sip fluids. Eat and drink slowly, unless of course it's part of the character's personality to do things in a hurried way. Avoid eating meat, particularly if you have lines to speak. Avoid taking in air through the mouth as you eat. It could cause you to choke Vegetables are easier to chew and digest and there is less chance of them lodging in the throat. A mouthful of food or fluid makes speaking difficult.

SMOKING: this is another acting hazard, not only for the smoker but for those around the smoker. Director Edward Dmytryk, commenting on working with Humphrey Bogart, an inveterate smoker, said that he would have to wait for ten minutes or so before each of Bogart's scenes so that the actor could 'cough his lungs out' to avoid coughing during his scenes. The late James Mason told me that he always avoided smoking during a scene where possible because smoking dries the throat and causes the eyes to weep and squint. Smoking is a health *and* an actor hazard.

TAKING A .45 SLUG: a bullet taken at close range smashes into the body with force and can knock a person six feet in the direction it is traveling. To create a dynamic visual effect a special harness is fitted so that the actor can be thrown in the direction the bullet is moving at the moment of impact. Whatever the effect desired by the director, clearly register shock following the bullet's impact. The effects of western slugs were never more graphic on the screen than were seen in the bloody death scenes in Sam Peckinpah's, *The Wild Bunch.*

FIGHTS: fist fights require expert planning and rehearsal if actors are to avoid being hurt. The sequence of blows needs to be well-timed and as well-choreographed as a dance routine. It is best to practice fist fights in slow motion until the routine is perfected, then bring them to the proper tempo. Barroom brawls and wild street fights — beautifully staged in so many of the John Wayne westerns — require a stunt co-ordinator and experienced stuntmen to make them seem real. A stunt co-ordinator choreographs action scenes to avoid actor confusion, mayhem and people getting hurt.

USING A TELEPHONE: as a stage prop, hold the telephone receiver with the up stage hand and keep the mouthpiece below the chin to avoid masking the face. Don't forget to make seven revolutions when dialing if using a rotary dial phone. During the breaks in conversation, give the impression that you are really listening. Create dialogue for the other speaker in your mind. Cut that conversation by half and the timing for speaking your own lines will seem to be correct.

HANDLING STAGE PROPS: stage business usually involves the use of stage props. *Hand props* are small objects such as: a book, newspaper, glass. *Stage props* are items or objects which relate to the set, such as: chair, lamp, telephone, radio. *Personal props* are items of a personal nature, such as: watch, pen, eye glasses, wallet, money. *Costume props* are dress accessories, such as: gloves, hat, pocket hankerchief, belt, tie or any special attire that isn't normally worn. A props man/woman is responsible for all hand props used in a production. A wardrobe master/mistress is responsible for costumes and costume props.

OTHER ACTIVITIES: dancing, singing, playing a musical instrument, driving a car, playing a sport, all require practice and skill to effect them convincingly. If you are expected to ride a horse, drive a car, dance, swim, play tennis, sail, sing or perform something of a specialized nature, then train for it under professional guidance. If you try to fake your way through a specific action you will feel uncomfortable and appear awkward in its execution.

29. GESTURE

Gestures can be used to intensify a feeling or an action as well as to reveal a specific state of mind. A person displaying anger may clench the fists or wave the arms about in a menacing way. A person displaying affection is apt to express his/her feelings with graceful, small gestures. Bodily movement of a relaxed person is slower, more controlled than a person who is under great stress.

Gesture is the movement of any part of the body which assists in expressing an idea or conveying a feeling. It may be a toss of the head, movement of the eyes, the lift of an eyebrow, movement of the lips or movement of the arms and hands. Every gesture should have a purpose and not be wasteful, since the idea behind a gesture is to emphasize or clarify a thought or feeling.

30. USE THE HANDS TO REVEAL CHARACTER AND IDEAS

An actor can impart to an audience a great deal of information simply by the way in which he/she uses the hands: hands in the pockets, hands on the hips, hands at the forehead, hands outstretched, hands tightly clasped. All tell a story. Handshakes, too, can be revealing. A firm, forceful handshake, a weak, hesitant handshake, a hearty pumping up and down handshake can alert an audience as to a character's feelings toward another in addition to revealing something of his/her personality.

Bring the hands to 'life' and use them expressively but also use them sparingly and without upstaging fellow players or masking your face. Combine *expressive* use of the hands with *controlled* use of the hands.

The control of gesture comes from the muscles behind the shoulders. It is the shoulder muscles that give the impetus for the movement of the arms, wrists and hands. Playing golf, tennis and swimming and playing the piano are excellent exercises for developing shoulder muscles and for co-ordinating movement of the arms, wrists, hands and fingers.

31. THE TIMING OF GESTURES

Gesture must spring from thought and feeling. Sometimes it precedes speech, sometimes it accompanies speech and sometimes it follows speech. Whether to gesture prior to a line, during a line or after a line is left to the discretion of the actor. Timing is a subtle quality of acting which becomes intuitive after a while. An actor should select and time gestures so that they appear natural to the character and seem spontaneous, then by practice make them appear natural to him/herself. The emotion of a character will impose a particular gesture on an actor and the gesture should last only as long as the emotion lasts — or perhaps end sooner if it is appropriate and natural to do so.

Gesture, whether it be movement of the arms and hands, the eyes or the head, must communicate its intention to an audience and not confuse them. A frown or a smile are two facial gestures which indicate two different states of mind. A raised arm with clenched fist or an extended arm with an open hand tell two very different stories. Consider the state of mind of the character you are to portray, the purpose of the dialogue that is spoken and then create appropriate gestures which enhance the characterization.

32. QUESTION YOUR ACTIONS TO REVEAL THEIR VALIDITY

Every actor in a play is responsible for his/her playing actions, which means that every actor should take the time to evaluate them in order to discover their validity.

In an analysis of your stage actions, ask the following questions:

1: Are they necessary and pertinent to the words spoken?
2: Do they clearly indicate the character's feelings?
3: Do they indicate the character's desires?

Character actions need to reveal the thoughts, feelings and desires of the character in a positive way. An audience should not be misled by them or confused as to what a character is doing and why. Movement and gesture need to be integrated with dialogue in a skilfull way. You will have to solve for yourself your stage actions — how much, how little, when, where — and then drill yourself until they become a rhythmic part of your stage personality.

33. EFFECTING DRAMATIC RHYTHM TO ENHANCE ACTIONS

Dramatic rhythm refers to the patterns of different beats in a play. It is denoted by changes of action and by heightened or lessened intensity or emotional variety of action by players. Dramatic rhythm provides emphasis by contrast in the form of accented beats of action — a certain timing between one movement and the next.

Throughout nature there is evidence of rhythm in the ebb and flow of tides, the change of seasons, the beat of the surf, etc. Man, too, expresses rhythm through speech, movement and a bodily rhythm expressed through breathing. There is a characteristic rhythm to each sport man plays, evidenced by the actions of tennis players, footballers, cricketers, swimmers, baseball and basketball players, etc. In the arts, there is rhythm expressed through music, drama, prose and poetry, etc.

Feel the swing of rhythm when walking, jogging, dancing, singing, playing tennis, golf or swimming. During performance, try to bring about a harmony of speech and movement which produces a pleasing rhythmic flow.

34. MOTIVATED SEQUENCE

Movement helps to keep a play interesting. Players in fixed positions become uninteresting to watch. Action creates interest. However, movement won't bring a 'dead' play to life on its own. Stage actions need justification. They must be motivated by a purpose consistent with characters and plot. And they must appear in appropriate sequence.

In dramatic work on the stage or before the camera, the *response* sequence is: *listen, think, see, feel, move.* Begin with your eyes. Let them respond first, then your face, then your head and then the rest of your body. This reaction process is called a *motivated sequence.* Your reactions are attached to your feelings and are being motivated by them. It is an excellent way to gain control of your actions, eliminating free, unmotivated movements and gestures which appear regardless of what the words and emotions are suggesting.

35. THE EYES IN CLOSE-UP

The eyes, it is said, are the windows of the soul. Through the eyes can be seen a person's true feelings. The eyes are an important factor in screen acting. An actor's playing falseness and personal insecurity reveal themselves in screen closeups. Nothing is as effective in screen acting as an actor's sincerity of feeling expressed through the eyes.

Keep the eyes relatively still. Don't allow them to shift too quickly. Move the eyes slowly. Blink normally, not excessively because of nervousness. Normal blinking, rather than allowing the eyes to become fixed, prevents them watering or taking on a glazed look. Be conscious of the importance of the eyes in projecting emotions, particularly in nonverbal reaction shots.

36. NONVERBAL EXPRESSION REQUIRES ANALYSIS OF VERBAL CONTENT

Once you have a script in your hands it is your job to discover what the character must think, feel, say and do *and* why. When you understand your character's goals you are in a position to justify your character's actions and to establish appropriate feelings. A complete analysis of the verbal content brings accurate, revealing and believable nonverbal expression.

Read *between* the lines your character has been assigned. Grasp the author's intent. This will overcome text insecurity, help to avoid wrong characterization and shallow performance.

37. RELAX AS YOU CARRY OUT STAGE ACTIONS

Release the body of tension as you perform. Cease worrying about performance failure which promotes tenseness. The body needs to be alert to carry out stage actions. The body needs to be under the total command of the mind, responsive to any stimulus which may come along. A relaxed, *controlled* body allows you to carry out well-executed, fluid, graceful moves and gestures. A tense body produces stiff, awkward movement, zombie-like actions which indicate that you are not in control of your acting instrument. A relaxed but alert body creates an environment for spontaneous and expressive facial expression, hand movement and general body performance.

38. KEEP THE MIND ALERT AND YOU'LL KEEP THE BODY ALERT

Lack of concentration tends to destroy body relaxation. As the mind drifts from one thought to the next, energy is diverted to the extraneous thoughts and your bodily reflexes become slower. Focus your attention on your role. Don't allow your thoughts to be side-tracked from role playing. An undisciplined mind creates uneasiness, tenseness and insecurity. It makes you self-aware and self-consciousness displays itself in nervousness, awkwardness of movement, memory lapse and hesitant speech.

Keep the mind alert. Fix your thoughts on the positive aspects of role playing during performance: speaking in character, listening in character, moving in character. You will be amazed at the personal role-playing security a relaxed, *disciplined* mind can bring.

39. GIELGUD AND RELAXATION

Sir John Gielgud, for so long a respected actor, director and producer, expert Shakespearean player and equally expert screen actor, has always given the appearance of a totally relaxed performer. His laid-back characterization of the man-servant in the film *Arthur*, is a study in total performance control. In all of his work, Gielgud's self-assurance makes his acting seem effortless.

Perhaps the key to this great artist's acting prowess lies within the advice he has given to beginning performers: 'I believe relaxation is the secret to good acting. Keep the body free of energy-draining tension. Relax. It has helped me greatly.'

40. RELAXATION EXERCISES

Before attempting voice and movement exercises and prior to performance, relaxation exercises should be carried out. Bending, stretching, shoulder rolling, head and neck rolling and limb shaking are excellent ways to become relaxed but alert. Relaxation means freedom from tension, aches, fatigue and tight muscles. Tension is responsible for voice fatigue, poor posture, nervousness and the suppression of creativity.

The mental and physical exercises which follow will prove beneficial if used by those who find it difficult to relax at will. They are aimed at reducing tension, anxiety, muscle tightness and fatigue.

MENTAL RELAXATION EXERCISES:

1: Sit in a comfortáble position or lie down. Darken the room. Close the eyes. Concentrate on relaxing the body. Commence with the toes. Wriggle them, command them to relax. Proceed to the legs and thighs. Feel the tension releasing. Now move to the trunk of the body and stretch. Next center attention on the neck, the head and the eyes. Quiet the mind. Picture on the screen of your mind black velvet drapes. Hold this picture and rest as long as desired.

2: Sit or lie down. Close the eyes. Picture a cat stretching. Mentally stretch your body, imitating the stretching movements of the cat.

3: Sit or lie down. Close the eyes. Picture a tranquil country setting. Mentally paint the setting onto a canvas. 'See' and paint on your canvas snow-capped mountains, green meadows, cows grazing, a stream, smoke trailing into a blue sky from the chimney of a cabin.

4: Sit or lie down. Close the eyes. Breathe deeply, evenly and slowly. Silently repeat the affirmation: 'I am relaxed, at peace, still, poised, serene and happy.'

5: Sit or lie down. Close the eyes. Mentally picture a group of people seated in a single row of chairs. In unison they repeatedly yawn. Mentally join them.

PHYSICAL RELAXATION EXERCISES:

1: **THE BUTTERFLY SWING:** stand with the feet about eight inches apart, one foot slightly forward of the other. Lift the left heel slightly, bend the left knee and swing the trunk of the body as far to the right as possible, then as far to the left as possible raising the right heel and bending the right knee on the swing back. Continue the side-to-side movement allowing the arms to swing loosely as they follow the movement of the body. Hold the head upright as it moves in unison with the body. Don't let the eyes dart from side-to-side. Follow an imaginary line (at eye level) around the room. Repeat this exercise for five minutes.

2: **THE RAG DOLL:** position the body as above. Take a deep breath. As you exhale, allow the body to flop forward from the waist, the arms dangling limply. Try to touch the floor with the fingers without straining the back. Slowly ease the trunk of the body upright, swaying from side to side as you rise. Don't attempt to lift the back in a straight line or rise quickly. When upright, drop the head back, stretch the neck, clasp the hands behind the back and pull back the shoulders. Hold for a count of ten, then release the hands and repeat the exercise.

3: **THE HEAD RELEASE:** gently drop the head to the chest, raise it and drop it back as far as is comfortable. Bring the head to a level position and drop it to one shoulder. Bring it level and drop it to the other shoulder. Repeat the exercise ten times, gently and slowly.

4: **THE SHOULDER RELEASE:** take a deep breath and lift the shoulders as high as possible. Hold this position for ten seconds, then exhale and relax. Breathe out vigorously and audibly. Allow the arms and hands to throw-off tension by shaking them for several seconds. Repeat several times.

5: **THE JAW ROLL:** mimic a cow chewing. Open the mouth and without strain roll the jaw in a circular motion, first ten times from right to left, then ten times from left to right. Practice this exercise slowly. Make sure the jaw is *relaxed* to prevent it locking. Keep the face as still as possible.

6: **THE CAT STRETCH:** raise the arms above the head and stretch the trunk of the body. Then raise up onto the toes and stretch again. Drop the arms to the sides, the heels to the floor and relax. Repeat several times.

7: **THE RUNNING ENERGIZER:** run on the spot for a count of one hundred, then relax. Lift the knees as high as possible.

8: **THE WINDMILL:** swing both arms in a clockwise circle ten times, then in an anti-clockwise circle ten times. Don't stiffen the body or swing the arms too vigorously, but slowly, gently and evenly.

9: **THE ARM RELEASE:** laying flat on your back, as relaxed as possible, raise your right arm as high as you can manage and stretch to your finger tips. Relax the arm allowing it to fall gently and limply to the side. Repeat with the left arm.

10: **THE LEG RELEASE:** lying flat on your back, raise your right leg at right angles to your body. Shake your foot, release tension, then let the leg drop gently and limply to the floor. Repeat with the left leg.

— RELAXATION EXERCISES CHART —

1: Butterfly Swing

2: Rag Doll

3: Head Release

4: Shoulder Release

5: Jaw Roll

6: Cat Stretch

7: Running Energizer

8: Windmill

9: Arm Release

10: Leg Release

SUMMARY OF IDEAS TO REVIEW

1: Expressive movement is an acting requirement. It is an ability to project thoughts and feelings using the body — aided or not by dialogue. Body expression is an important aspect of interpretive training.

2: Good posture requires the body to be correctly aligned when sitting, walking, running, standing. Keep the chest high, the back straight, the abdomen flat and the buttocks tucked in.

3: Learn to walk, sit, rise, turn, lift and fall 'theatrically'. This means easily, naturally and comfortably. Begin an entrance, an exit, a stage cross by stepping off with the *up stage* foot.

4: Justify all stage actions. Move and gesture because there is *reason* to do so.

5: The theatre actor reaches out to the audience. The audience comes to the screen performance. Reduce performance dynamics for the screen — without loss of energy.

6: Dramatic rhythm refers to the patterns of different beats in a play. Balance and harmonize movement and speech to produce a rhythmic flow, a natural-looking performance.

7: Thought precedes action. *Listen, think, see, feel* and *move* in motivated sequence.

8: Nonverbal expression requires understanding of verbal *content*. Be aware of what you are communicating and why. Be clear as to stage actions.

9: Relax as you speak and move. John Gielgud discovered *relaxation* to be the key to creative acting.

10: Spend time on mental and physical relaxation exercises. They reduce tension.

Large numbers of extras were required for this scene from the film *Phar Lap*. Two cameras are readied for race-action shots as the assistant director checks riders and bystanders. Scene represents Agua Caliente race track of the 'thirties. Preparation for films of this kind is lengthy and actors require patience and stamina while crew prepares camera, sound and lighting equipment and wardrobe and makeup checks are made in readiness for a take. Screenplay was written by *David Williamson*. Director of Photography was *Russell Boyd*. (Photo John Sexton Productions — Michael Edgley International)

3:
PERFORMANCE

★★

COMMENT . . .

The more naturally a screen action is executed, the easier it is for an audience to accept its reality. A competent screen actor makes acting appear effortless and natural, even though a great deal of time may have been spent in careful preparation and rehearsal.

This third section on screen acting focuses on the relationship of the actor to the screenplay and the use of techniques to perform truthfully and with *naturalism*. The following concepts are also aimed at broadening interpretive ability to bring greater dimension and force to characterization.

ROLE
PREPARATION:
A STUDY OF THE
SCREENPLAY

SCENE **11**

Practical Ideas In This Chapter . . .

- Understanding The Work of The Screen Writer
- The Mark of A Good Screenplay
- Assessing The Screenplay
- Identifying The Screenplay Form
- Screenplay Subject Matter
- Structure of The Screenplay
- Screenplay Structure Terminology
- Screenplay Format
- From Synopsis To Shooting Script
- Screenplay Abbreviations
- Script Playing Time
- The Screenplay Division of Units
- Dialogue Length
- Dialogue Interpretive Directions
- Script Preparation Time Is Limited
- Script Changes Upset Bogart-Bergman Making Casablanca
- Analysing The Screenplay
- Story Analysis
- Diligent Story Analysis Influences Character Portrayal
- Text Analysis
- Role Preparation Is Vital Says Award-Winning Director
- Don't Expect Acting Lessons From The Director
- Olivier's Preparation Is A Director's Delight Says Wyler
- Line Retention
- Screenplay Example: *Day of The Phoenix*
- Marking The Script
- An Example of Script Marking
- Summary of Ideas To Review

236

SCENE 11

★★★

1. UNDERSTANDING THE WORK OF THE SCREEN WRITER

The foundation of a screen drama is its story — the work of the screen writer. The structure to this foundation is provided by the efforts of the director and the actors. All must perform as a *unit* to bring a satisfactory result. All must plan, research, study and execute *craftsmanship.*

Some motion pictures and television dramas are marred by poor acting, others by poor directing. A screen drama has little chance of success unless it has a strong, well-written screenplay. Because screenplay writing is the basis of a successful screen-story presentation, actors, by necessity, must gain a workable understanding of a script's content: form, structure, dramatic intent, etc.

The actor's first duty upon receiving a script is to arrive at a correct character interpretation. This can be achieved with relative ease providing the actor knows what to look for when studying the text. It is in this regard that a knowledge of screenplay writing is most advantageous.

The terms, *plot, subplot, formal text, subtext, exposition, transition, point of attack, theme, premise, resolve,* etc, need to be understood in order to grasp the intentions of the writer. This chapter, hopefully, will motivate the reader to explore beyond this work, the art of screenplay writing.

2. THE MARK OF A GOOD SCREENPLAY

A superior screen story takes its audience below surface emotions. It makes an impact, both intellectually and emotionally, from the first scene to the final fade out. A good screenplay provides entertainment, enlightenment and self-revelation.

A poorly-written screen story is one which fails to involve, challenge or move its audience. It leaves them with vague, indifferent and unsatisfied

237

feelings. Far too many insubstantial, synthetic works reach the screen. Those which lack artistic truth, fail to say anything, waste the time of an audience, can never be considered works of screen art.

A screenplay writer expresses concepts in words that are descriptive and appropriate to the story he/she desires to tell via the actions of the characters. From the standpoint of the actor and the director, a good screenplay doesn't necessarily have to *read* well, but it must *adequately* present scenes to be photographed, actions to be viewed and dialogue to be heard. When the finished work is screened, its audience should feel involved, intellectually and emotionally stimulated and left with the feeling that here is a story truly representing life.

3. ASSESSING THE SCREENPLAY

It is important that an actor be able to *objectively* assess the merits of a screenplay. This is particularly essential when featured-player status or stardom arrives, for in conjunction with his/her agent, roles will be accepted or rejected primarily on the *quality* of the story and its characters. Actor-director Clint Eastwood has a staunch opinion about stardom. He says: 'Most of the success a motion picture actor enjoys belongs to the material he chooses. That's what makes or breaks him.'

When studying a screenplay, assess its strengths and weaknesses. What are your immediate impressions? Does the story provide entertainment, enlightenment and self-revelations? Are the characters one-dimensional or are they true-to-life with complex backgrounds? Are you left with unsatisfied feelings or are your mind and emotions stimulated from reading the story? Your answers to these questions will be the measurement of the screenplay's *impact* on you.

4. IDENTIFYING THE SCREENPLAY FORM

A screenplay appears in a different written form to a stage play. However, both share the same general classifications. The main story forms or categories come under two chief divisions: tragedy and comedy.

COMEDY: deals with human problems in an amusing way. The characters are often amusing because of their idiosyncrasies, inept way of dealing with others or because of their personal shortcomings. In situation comedy, the audience is able to identify with the circumstances, events and misfortunes of the central characters, which end successfully.

TRAGEDY: is the assertion of human nobility in the face of negative forces that can be resisted but not overcome. The hero or heroine plods on despite personal sacrifice and suffering. Ideals are held sacred and worthy of selfless dedication, but end in defeat.

TRAGICOMEDY: some stories mix the elements of tragedy and comedy, just as every-day life involves humans in serious and amusing situations and events. A threatened disaster is averted, bringing a happy ending to things.

FARCE: exaggerated comedy showing characters in ludicrous but funny circumstances and actions. The characters act in an absurd way and the situations are beyond belief. However, the characters take it all in stride. Not to be confused with *slapstick* which involves comic-violent acts.

MELODRAMA: the extreme exaggeration of tragedy, but with a positive ending. The good win over the evil. The characters are cast either entirely honest and principled or entirely dishonest and wicked.

5. SCREENPLAY SUBJECT MATTER

Screenplay subject matter can be classified under the following headings:

ACTION-ADVENTURE STORY	ROMANTIC-COMEDY
CRIME STORY	SITUATION COMEDY
DETECTIVE-MURDER MYSTERY	MUSICAL-COMEDY
PSYCHOLOGICAL-MYSTERY	WESTERN-COMEDY
THRILLER	FANTASY-COMEDY
SUSPENSE-CHASE STORY	FANTASY-MUSICAL
PRISON DRAMA	COMEDY-ADVENTURE
SPY-POLITICAL INTRIGUE	FARCE-MURDER MYSTERY
PSYCHOLOGICAL-HORROR	BIOGRAPHICAL STORY
STORY	HISTORICAL RE-ENACTMENT
HUMAN SOCIAL CONFLICT	SEMI-DOCUMENTARY
WAR THEME	WESTERN DRAMA
RELIGIOUS THEME	CHILDREN'S MELODRAMA
PHILOSOPHICAL THEME	STRAIGHT MUSICAL
POLITICAL THEME	SERIAL DRAMA/MELODRAMA
LOVE STORY	TRAVELOGUE

6. STRUCTURE OF THE SCREENPLAY

It is beneficial to know the various elements which make up the structure of a screenplay. This knowledge allows the actor a greater appreciation of the writer's work and makes it easier for the actor to grasp the intent of the writer.

Although the screenplay writer, the playwright and the novelist use different techniques, all are concerned with artistic truth — explaining man to himself via thought, feeling and action.

Unlike the stage play, a screen story must 'get up and move'. It must avoid being sedentary. The screen writer deals primarily with things in motion — dynamic movement of story and characters. Good screen story technique dictates that the camera be allowed to speak *visually*. A screenplay, where possible, lets the *camera* comment rather than the actors via dialogue. When something cannot be told visually, then the actors express it through their dialogue.

Moving pictures have their own way of expressing things quite differently to the stage play and the novel. A screenplay is a *blueprint* for the makers of the story rather than a piece for reading. It is aided by interior and exterior location settings, music, sound effects visual effects, lighting and graphic photography. The camera, through its various points-of-view, makes comment in *visual* terms. It records what people say and do.

The script may go through many *draft* stages until the producer and the director are satisfied that they have a story ready for the camera. The final draft is known as a *shooting script* and from it a shooting schedule is planned. This is a day-by-day timetable for the filming, with the scenes grouped so that as far as practical those scenes with the same set or location or the same group of actors can be filmed together.

A screen story is structured around a theme, premise, plot and characters. A breakdown of these and other screenplay elements, follows.

7. SCREENPLAY STRUCTURE TERMINOLOGY

The following descriptions will help to bring a better understanding of the various elements incorporated within the structure of a screenplay.

SHOOTING SCRIPT: a written composition which serves as a work diagram for the producer, director, crew members and the actors. A final draft screenplay contains dialogue and action sequences ready for the camera.

THEME: is what the story is about. It may have secondary themes but these are generally linked to the central theme. The theme must be clearly defined. The theme of Shakespeare's play *Romeo and Juliet* concerns two young lovers trapped by the prejudices of their elders. The theme of the motion picture *The Inn of the Sixth Happiness* concerns a young English missionary leading a hundred Chinese orphans to the safety of a mission compound after the Japanese invasion of North China. Her aim is the protection of life and the saving of souls.

PREMISE: sometimes confused with theme. Although closely related, they are different. Premise is the *moral* the story points up, the proposition or the hypothesis on which the argument of the story is based. It is the point which the play proves or disproves. It is a specific idea that gives unity and purpose to everything that happens in the story. The premise is sometimes stated by a line of dialogue or worked into the story's title. Often it is left to the imagination of the audience to interpret. Some examples of premise are: *honesty is the best policy, love conquers all, brutality leads to self-destruction, man's indolence leads to failure, crime doesn't pay, conceit leads to humiliation, confusion leads to frustration, poverty encourages crime, faith overcomes diversity.*

PLOT: the story line, concerning what happens to whom, at what time, where and how. Plots incorporate premise, character and conflict. The central plot involves the actions of the main characters. Subplots branch out from the main story and characters to secondary events and characters. All plots have a climax, resulting from the solving or from the not solving of the conflicts. Also called *narrative*.

SUBPLOT: in dramatic form, subplots are foils for the main plot. The attention is momentarily diverted by secondary characters whose actions are tied in with the central players and main story.

CONFLICT: contributing factors which give rise to action. A collision of opposing forces because of their sharp disagreement.

TRANSITION: leading from one point to the next. There are two main poles in every life and in between there is transition: birth and death, youth and manhood, middle age and old age, anger and assault, failure and success, depression and happiness, ill health and well-being. Transition shows the events *leading* to the change.

EXPOSITION: an exposing of vital information about the story and its characters. *Story* exposition reveals the premise, plot, subplots, scenery and the mood of the play. *Character* exposition reveals necessary information about the characters, such as: age, marital status, occupation, goals, health, social background, etc.

AUTHOR'S INTENT: becomes known via the dialogue and actions of the characters. It expresses the author's ideas, points-of-view, general feelings, moral, social and philosophic concepts in strongly-worded statements and actions spoken and taken by the characters. It is the responsibility of the director to see that the actors remain true to the author's intent.

POINT OF ATTACK: the starting point of a chain of events which leads to a crisis. A character's decision which precipitates conflict which leads to a crisis point.

FORMAL TEXT: a grouping of words revealing necessary information about the characters: who they are, what they want, what they are doing and their intentions as to future actions. Screenplay dialogue contains short sentences, suspended lines, interrupted speeches, questions and statements indicating how characters feel.

SUBTEXT: what the character says is not necessarily what the character thinks, feels and intends to do. Subtext is the *true* attitude, feeling and intention of the character rather than that which is expressed verbally. It is hidden meaning, a covering up not readily apparent to other characters. However, an audience must be made aware of subtext material if it is to follow a story without confusion.

SPECIFIC INCIDENT: the earliest event exposing the basic conflict and affecting the major characters. It is related to *point of attack* and sometimes referred to as *initial conflict*.

ANTECEDENT EVENTS: the important events which have occurred prior to the opening scene.

LOCALE: settings where the story takes place.

MOOD: the overall quality of the story and its effect: happy, gloomy, sentimental, cruel, funny, tragic, etc.

ATMOSPHERE: relates to the quality of a particular *scene* as opposed to the overall mood of the entire story.

OBLIGATORY SCENE: those scenes which lead to the main crisis, thereby proving the premise — the hypothesis on which the argument of the play is based.

CHARACTERS: a variety of 'types' whose personalities are easily discoverable via their dialogue and actions. Major and minor characters must appear to be real people not one-dimensional caricatures. They may be simple people or complex people but they must possess human qualities — needs, wants, attitudes, feelings — to bring three-dimensional realism.

PROTAGONIST: a central character who creates conflict and moves the story forward. A pivotal character around whom the story centers. A person who fights for a cause, takes the lead, is strong, even ruthless. The protagonist may be positive or negative in regard to his/her character but must be an uncompromising type.

ANTAGONIST: any person or group of people who oppose the protagonist. They are enemies. The antagonist is as strong, as ruthless and as uncompromising as the protagonist.

DIALOGUE: lines spoken by the players which contribute to character and story exposition to warrant use. The essence of good dialogue writing is its simplicity of understanding, its brevity, its ring of conversation and its use of words which create clear images in the minds of those listening.

CRISIS: the *high* point of the suspense leading to the climax.

CLIMAX: each scene carries its own climax which leads to the *major* climax which is the final answer to the conflict drawing the story to a close.

RESOLVE: the fate of the characters and the action which takes place following the climax — a resolve to all that has occurred.

8. SCREENPLAY FORMAT

The printed format of a screenplay can differ from country-to-country. In the US, screenplays are printed on American quarto-size sheets, as are television drama scripts, then bound within soft covers. In some countries, Australia, for example, television drama scripts are nearly always printed on foolscap-size sheets and seldom are they bound within covers.

The standard screenplay format of the 'forties and through to the 'sixties, included lengthy character descriptions, camera directions and actor playing directions. Today, the trend is to eliminate all character descriptions, camera references and actor playing suggestions. Where writers include them, directors usually ignore them.

Once a script has been issued to cast and crew, all revisions, scene changes and dialogue cuts are printed on paper of a different color to the original. This clearly indicates to all concerned that changes to the script have been made.

9. FROM SYNOPSIS TO SHOOTING SCRIPT

A finished script, sometimes referred to as a final-draft screenplay, evolves from an original story idea, a short story, an adaptation of a novel or from a produced or unproduced stage play. It is the result of much preparatory work on the part of one or more writers.

The writer's first task is to prepare a ten-page story and character outline called a *synopsis*. A screen *treatment* of some fifty pages is then developed from the synopsis and it includes a detailed plot outline and sample dialogue.

The third stage is the preparation of a *master-scene* script which includes scene description, character action and dialogue but minus any reference to camera positioning or angles. The writer then shapes this into a *first-draft* screenplay which will go through many revisions until a *shooting* script is completed.

10. SCREENPLAY ABBREVIATIONS

The following abbreviations apply to both motion picture *screenplays* and television *teleplays*.

B.G.: background.
C.C.U.: choker close-up.
C.U.: close-up.
E.C.U.: extreme close-up.
E.L.S.: extreme long shot.
EST.: establishing.
EXT.: exterior
F.S.: full shot.
INT.: interior.
L.S.: long shot.
M.C.U.: medium close-up.
M.L.S.: medium long shot.
M.S.: medium shot.
O.T.S.: over-the-shoulder.
V.O.: voice over, an actor's off-screen dialogue.

11. SCRIPT PLAYING TIME

A script's playing time can be approximated by its number of pages. Each quarto-size page of character action, dialogue and scene description approximates one minute of screen time. A 120-page screenplay, depending upon its editing and the length of its opening titles and closing credits, would play *approximately* 120-minutes.

A television drama to fill a one-hour time slot, would require a script of approximately fifty-pages. The playing time would be about fifty-minutes which would then be edited, titles and end credits added bringing its total running time to no more than 48-minutes to allow for station commercials (approximately twelve minutes each hour).

12. THE SCREENPLAY DIVISION OF UNITS

A movie or television drama script is a record of what people say and do. In order to bring to the screen clearly-defined character actions, the story

and its characters are filmed in a specific way — referred to as a *division o*
units. These specific units are: *shot, scene, sequence.*

SHOT: a separate component of a scene. A continuous view filmed
without interruption.

SCENE: a succession of shots, although a scene can be composed of a
single shot. Technically speaking, a scene is a place or setting. However, fo
practical purposes, shot and scene are generally interchangeable terms.

SEQUENCE: a series of shots complete in itself in which there is no lapse
of time. May occur in a single setting or several settings. A sequence may
begin as an exterior and continue as an interior.

13. DIALOGUE LENGTH

It is generally accepted by screen writers that there is little place in
modern screen writing for long-winded speeches which impede action
Because movement is the major requisite of picture making, short speeche
are usually adhered to by experienced writers of screen drama.

Where long speeches are used, they seldom describe events which can b
presented in action. They are used to describe thoughts and feelings which
cannot be portrayed successfully by action.

The tempo of a screen story can be regulated by the length of it
speeches. Up-tempo scenes use short, sharp speeches and interruptions o
cut lines. Slower scenes incorporate longer speeches, more leisurely
spoken dialogue passages.

14. DIALOGUE INTERPRETIVE DIRECTIONS

Many screen writers cannot resist attaching interpretive suggestions to
script dialogue, particularly where they feel there could be doubt in an
actor's mind as to interpretation. Some actors are quite insulted by this
practice. Tagging the statement 'I could kill you!' with an (angrily) i
unwarranted. The meaning is explicit. No competent actor would require
suggestion as to its delivery.

There are times when an actor is in a quandary as to interpretation and
line delivery. Where the meaning is obscure or in doubt, confusion and
insecurity can lead to incorrect interpretation and wrong delivery. A
writer's direction would overcome the problem.

Prominent writers have told me that while experienced actors seldom
require interpretive suggestions, inexperienced ones nearly always do need
them. 'I often agonize over an incompetent actor butchering my lines,'
screen writer told me. 'I make them as clear as possible, but where there
could be some doubt, I add signposts for the benefit of the actor,' he said

15. SCRIPT PREPARATION TIME IS LIMITED

Unlike the theatre, screen work seldom allows the luxury of many week
of actor rehearsal and preparation time. Some film directors, like Alan
Pakula, insist on adequate rehearsals prior to the shoot. Television dram

series and low-budget feature films, in the main, do not allow the actor sufficient breathing space from the time a script is received until the commencement of production.

Somehow, actors are expected to create performance miracles. Instant characterization is the requirement. In my own experience, I've been sent scripts a day or two prior to scheduled calls. And once, I was handed a script when I arrived on the set because the writer hadn't completed the final draft. 'We'll get to your scene in about an hour,' the first assistant director told me. 'But, it's five pages,' I protested. 'I'm sure you'll manage it,' he replied, dashing off to give another unsuspecting actor his script.

Because rehearsal time is limited or non-existent, read and analyse the script immediately you receive it. Comprehend what the role is about *prior* to committing lines.

16. SCRIPT CHANGES UPSET BOGART-BERGMAN MAKING CASABLANCA

Script alterations often occur after a final draft has been handed out. Occasionally, a script is still being written or re-written after production commences. During the making of *Casablanca*, the script was still in the writing stage which caused production delays and much cast annoyance. According to Ingrid Bergman, the writers, Julius and Phillip Epstein, seemed quite vague as to how they would end their story.

'We didn't know from one day to the next what we were going to do. All of us, especially Bogart and the director Michael Curtiz, were most upset. I didn't know whether I was to go off with Rick or Lazlo. It was hard to know how to play the character's emotions in this regard. I was told to "play it down the middle". It was very hard and very confusing,' Miss Bergman recalled in an interview she gave just prior to her sad passing in 1982.

Today, few producers risk plunging into shooting without a completed script. However, script changes during shooting are commonplace. Even if an actor receives a script well prior to a shoot, alterations to scenes during production require role reappraisal. It is the best insurance against incorrect interpretation should dialogue changes and scene cuts alter character relationships and objectives.

17. ANALYSING THE SCREENPLAY

When an actor has been contracted to play a role, the director expects the actor to thoroughly analyse the script so that he/she can establish the role *prior* to attending the first rehearsal (if there is one) and be word perfect each time there is a camera appearance.

Approach script analysis in the following two ways:

(1) STORY ANALYSIS — its form and meaning.
(2) TEXT ANALYSIS — its meaning, inference, interpretation and presentation.

245

18. STORY ANALYSIS

Read the script from beginning to end in *one* reading. Discover th
author's intent — what he/she says via 'messages' presented in the stor
Establish the form and subject matter. Gain a deep insight into the them
and premise. Understand the central plot and subplots.

It is important to note all pertinent information supplied by the writ
concerning *environments* in which the characters live and the location
where the actions take place. It is also important to pay close attention
the time of year (specific season) and to the prevailing social, economic ar
political influences of the period in which the story unfolds. All of the
aspects will have some bearing on the attitudes and moods of the variou
characters in the story.

Separate the script into the following components and study each
subsequent readings:

PLOT AND SUBPLOTS: how does your character fit into the centr
plot and or subplots? What *reason* is there to appear in each designate
scene? Write down the central plot and the subplots. Establish a ment
image of the story locations.

ANTECEDENT EVENTS: what important events have taken pla
prior to the opening of the story and do they concern your character? Wri
them down.

POINT OF ATTACK: what is the *first* incident which occurs exposi
the basic conflict? Make a note of it.

ATMOSPHERE-MOOD: what is the prevailing atmosphere of ea
scene and the overall mood of the story? Make a note of each.

CHARACTERS: who are they and what do they seek? *Visualize* the

PROTAGONIST-ANTAGONIST: which are you or which *side* do y
support? What are the motivations behind your actions?

TRANSITION: at what point on the emotional scale, success scale, li
scale, marital scale, etc, is your character?

CRISIS POINT-CLIMAX: pinpoint the obligatory scenes leading to t
main crisis and tag the high point of the suspense leading to the climax

RESOLVE: how does it all end? What is the fate of the central characte

AUTHOR'S INTENT: write down the theme and premise.

19. DILIGENT STORY ANALYSIS INFLUENCES CHARACTE
PORTRAYAL

Because the script is a bare outline consisting of speeches and acti
directions, the actor needs to approach the story content with mu
deliberation. The goals of the writer and those of the character need to
set, in order to arrive at a playing method to bring the character to 'lif
Story evaluation and analysis greatly assist in this regard.

Understand the play first of all as a structure. How well it is put togeth
and whether it says what it means. The theme should be evident throug

progression of dramatic action affecting the characters. It should conclusively prove its premise. Come to a conclusion as to the quality of the writing. Is the play strong in plot, rich in character development and dramatically expressive through dialogue?

The analysis of the screenplay the actor makes prior to performance, will influence the final acting result. Whenever possible, a script should be 'nursed' for as long as possible in advance of performance. The more time there is to study a script, the better the formulation of ideas concerning the author's intent, the character's objectives and the structure of a role personality. I believe that the longer one has to explore, research, decode, meditate on the work of the writer, the more *truth* one may draw from his/her work.

20. TEXT ANALYSIS

Because the text or speeches are to be acted, consideration needs to be given to the *way* they are to be acted relative to their meaning. Good writers choose the words they assign to story characters with great care. Words impart meaning, reveal ideas and intentions, but only when they are assembled and spoken in a logical and coherent way. The proper speaking of dialogue for clarification of meaning deserves special consideration during text analysis. It is essential that formal text be separated from subtext. And the final step in studying the text comes when the actor pinpoints the idiosyncrasies of the character and attempts to work them into physical actions.

FORMAL TEXT ANALYSIS: characters speaking formal text leave no doubt as to what they are saying and why. Formal text quite openly reveals story and character information. It sheds light on the person speaking, the person spoken to and those spoken about. It reveals character relationships, supplies information about locales, antecedent events and future happenings. It imparts information in a straightforward way. Formal text needs analysis to extract as complete an understanding of the author's work as possible, prior to line memorization and character construction.

SUBTEXT ANALYSIS: as explained earlier in this chapter, subtext is *camouflaged meaning* within certain lines. It represents a character's *true* thoughts, feelings and intentions rather than those expressed verbally. Subtext does not necessarily have to be grasped by those the character is speaking to, but generally, it must be understood by an audience if it is to make sense of what is going on.

Modern plays contain much subtext material and the actor must discover it and know how to express it. Inner meaning of a speech can be implied by tone of voice, by manner of delivery of a particular line and via body language — hesitant movement, awkward gesture, lack of eye contact with another player, etc. In some instances, subtext material is purposely hidden from the audience to confuse them at a particular point in the story. The writer casts 'red-herrings' to intrigue and mystify the audience or to place doubts in an audience's mind as to the real intentions of a character. It is necessary to discover which subtext material is to be revealed to an audience and which is to be masked from it.

Understanding formal and subtext material boils down to 'delving between the text layers' — discovering in precise terms what the author desires to be expressed and *how* it is to be expressed. Text analysis in this regard brings the required information to construct a three-dimensional character and to perform that characterization with confidence, skill and according to the desires of the writer.

TEXT ANALYSIS FOR TECHNICAL DELIVERY: during a performance an audience receives *one* opportunity to hear and to comprehend players' lines. Clear diction, adequate projection and clarity of text expression are essential components of professional performance. An audience expects no less, yet, often it is treated to less by actors who have not learned their craft. It is not the duty of an audience to strain to hear actors speak nor to be forced to try and unravel what actors mean when they deliver lines. An audience has a responsibility to listen, to feel and to respond in an appropriate way. The play is for the benefit of its audience, not its actors — although there is benefit to the actors. A play's actors have a responsibility to enrich the texture of the words they speak and to make the meaning of those words easily understandable.

An expedient way to 'hear' the melody, rhythm and meaning of dialogue is to read lines aloud as you study the script. As you read, mental pictures will form of the physical look and personality of each character. Formulate ideas — *methods* — of how best to deliver your lines and to impart their meaning with the utmost clarity, thereby removing any confusion or misunderstanding when they are spoken.

21. ROLE PREPARATION IS VITAL SAYS AWARD-WINNING DIRECTOR

Alan J. Pakula has created several film masterpieces. Among them, *All The President's Men, The Sterile Cuckoo, Klute* and *Sophie's Choice.* His films are best remembered for their subjects and their stars. He has established a reputation as an actor's director.

Pakula says he never gives an actor direction until he's seen the actor do something which reveals how much time has been spent on preparation. 'An actor must know what each scene is about and how to approach it. If an actor hasn't a clue it will be impossible to give full vent to emotions. Preparation is vital to competent performance,' Pakula maintains.

22. DON'T EXPECT ACTING LESSONS FROM THE DIRECTOR

An actor must not shirk his/her acting responsibility. An actor must not expect a director to give lessons in character development, line delivery and movement. It is not the responsibility of a play's director to teach the cast how to act. Some actors lean on a director, expecting an easy performance ride. Role preparation for them is out because it requires time and effort. Good actor-director relationships arise from mutual respect, trust and confidence in each other's ability to perform professionally.

Acting is not mere reciting of words coupled to movement. It's far more complex. Every actor who accepts a part in a professional production has a responsibility to know what he/she is doing and to have the acting expertise to carry it out. Adequate preparation — study, planning, practice — prior to stepping before the camera will help to meet this requirement.

23. OLIVIER'S PREPARATION IS A DIRECTOR'S DELIGHT SAYS WYLER

Laurence Olivier established early in his career a reputation as a craftsman who gives attention to character detail prior to filming. He prepares step-by-step how he will speak, move, handle props. He knows his lines in advance of rehearsal which allows him to come to the set totally prepared, knowing precisely what he intends to do with his role.

William Wyler, who directed Olivier in *Wuthering Heights* and *Carrie*, said, 'Olivier is an absolute delight to work with, he prepares so thoroughly. Because his part is so well conceived, a near-perfect performance is assured and little directing is required, except for technical things.' Wyler said that actors should follow Olivier's example and spend as much time as possible on script analysis and role preparation.

24. LINE RETENTION

Memorization of lines should not be the initial part of preparation but the near-end of it. It is pointless to commit dialogue before you have an opportunity to comprehend its meaning. It's dangerous, too. Imperfect interpretation often leads to incorrect line delivery. Once you've impregnated the subconscious mind with words practiced in a set way (a particular rhythmic pattern through emphasis and use of the pause), it's hard to remove that pattern later, should it be necessary to do so.

Memorize your speeches *after* you understand the underlying intent of your actions. Don't panic because of limited time. Memorization will be easier once you're familiar with the story, its characters and what they say and do. In this way, you'll be memorizing something you are knowledgeable about, comfortable with and confident of playing. As a bonus, you'll save time.

The problem is how best to memorize lines isn't easy to solve. Some actors find line memorization a tedious, boring, time-consuming exercise. Others find it easy. For a time in the 'sixties, I lived at the Park Sheraton Hotel (since renamed) on Seventh Avenue in New York. Jackie Gleason occupied the entire top floor. Production meetings and run-throughs of his television show were held there. 'When does he get time to memorize his lines,' I enquired of a friend who was wardrobe mistress on the show. 'Jackie reads through his script once or twice and he's word perfect. He doesn't need to spend much time on such mundane things,' she told me.

Actor John Carradine never worried about committing scripts to memory — one reading and the words were set. Having a photographic memory is a decided asset.

Actors have told me of their special 'sure-fire' ways of learning lines quickly. I am yet to discover a 'quick' method. For most actors, learning lines by rote — slowly impregnating them into the subconscious — is the time-tested way. Most actors find that the brain is clearest in the early morning and learning lines is best done then. When you're young, late at night could prove suitable. Olivier admitted to finding it difficult to learn lines. 'Problems come with age to the faculty of memorizing. The difficulty has to be faced and allowances and provisions made for it,' he said. Four suggestions are offered which may prove helpful:

(1) Memorize by *context* or *meaning.* As the role is analysed and your understanding of the part grows, commit each speech via comprehension of its exact meaning. By studying your character's personality, attitudes, feelings and actions, the text begins to formulate in the mind's eye and then gradually becomes set in the subconscious mind. While this is a slow-study method, it is a practical one.

(2) Memorize by *rote.* This is a fixed, mechanical, hard-slogging way of memorization, but a successful one. Lines are repeated until committed to memory.

(3) *Cueing* method. Another person reads *all* parts slowly and mechanically. Close the eyes and form images in your mind of what the words represent. Repeat the lines of your character *after* they are read. A tape recorder may be substituted if you cannot find a partner willing to help you. Record your part and the speeches of others. As a *straight* cueing method, record the parts of others and leave blank spaces for your own lines. Drop them in 'live' as you play the tape.

(4) Develop an 'actor's memory' — memorize *thoughts* and *images* more than words.

A terror for any actor is the possibility of 'drying' during performance. Actors who are fearful of making mistakes usually do encounter drying problems. The only counter measure to drying is to know your part completely and then to instill confidence in yourself that you will perform perfectly.

25. SCREENPLAY EXAMPLE

The following scenes are taken from *Day of The Phoenix,* written by the author in collaboration with Robert Frederick. This excerpt is an illustration of *standard* screenplay format. It is a murder-mystery. A pattern of action taken by a group of unscrupulous characters who, because of their greed and corruptness, destroy themselves and the lives of others. The theme and premise reveal themselves as the story unfolds, is brought to a climax and then resolves.

The opening scenes are action-oriented and expressed visually. No dialogue passes between the intruder and the security guard. The low camera angles and point-of-view shots strengthen the dramatic effect of the film's opening, prior to titles.

The protagonist is Slade, caught in a situation which appears hopeless. When brought into conflict with the antagonists, he is forced into crisis situations which eventually reach a climax and then resolve to his satisfaction.

The killings are not witnessed by the audience but imagined by means of indirection — we *hear* a shot, *see* a bright flash *and* two shots blast into camera — enough to *suggest* that persons have been mortally wounded.

The scene between Slade and Flagg is direct confrontation. Two equally strong characters lock horns. Each has a goal. Each strives to achieve his goal. One wins and at the close of the scene is exuberant. The other loses and becomes bitter at his momentary defeat.

The scene between Slade, Da Silva and Laura is character and story revealing. We learn something of the characters and what they are up to. Slade 'discovers'. Da Silva and Laura 'cover-up'.

The conflict and action in this story grow out of the characters — their goals, their environment. Laura seeks money, a less-constrictive lifestyle. Da Silva seeks affluence and power. Slade becomes the 'fall-guy'. He's honest, incorruptible As you study this script, discover the goals of each character. Establish each character's personality. Pinpoint the theme and premise.

DAY OF THE PHOENIX

FADE IN

1. EXT. STREET – HIGH ANGLE   RAIN – NIGHT
   A deserted, well-heeled suburban street, under heavy rain.

2. EXT. STREET – LOW ANGLE   RAIN – NIGHT
   The beam of a car's headlights flashes into frame. It turns into a driveway, stops at closed entry gates. WE ESTABLISH a Rolls Royce.

3. INT. ROLLS – DRIVER'S P.O.V.   RAIN – NIGHT
   A security guard emerges from his car parked within the grounds, heads towards the Rolls.

4. EXT. ENTRY GATES – ROLLS   RAIN – NIGHT
   The guard swings open the gates, says a few words to the driver. The Rolls heads up the drive.

5. EXT. FLEMING HOUSE   RAIN – NIGHT
   The Rolls stops. The driver emerges from the car, moves to the front door of the house.

6. EXT. INTRUDER – CLOSE   RAIN – NIGHT
   He draws a Browning automatic from his raincoat, inserts a key into the doorlock, turns the knob, silently pushes the door open. He

disappears from FRAME. A shaft of light highlights a visible section of the hallway. WE HEAR a shot . . . SEE a bright flash. The door swings open wider and the intruder brushes by CAMERA.

7. EXT. ROLLS   RAIN – HEAVY
    It screeches away towards the gates. The guard emerges from his car. He's heard the shot. He stands in front of the gates, arms raised, challenging the driver to stop.

8. EXT. GUARD'S P.O.V.   RAIN – NIGHT
    The Rolls stops. The driver's electric window glides down.

9. INT. ROLLS – DRIVER'S P.O.V.   RAIN – NIGHT
    The guard moves to the driver's window. The Browning automatic comes into FRAME.

10. EXTREME CLOSE SHOT – BROWNING MUZZLE
    It fills the SCREEN. Two shots blast into CAMERA. The barrel emits a short trail of smoke, fuses with the muzzle forming a grotesque shape which

                                              FADES OUT OF FOCUS

    FADE IN TITLES

11. EXT. INTERNATIONAL AIRPORT   DAY
    A 747 touches down, taxi's towards the terminal building.

12. INT. IMMIGRATION DESK   DAY
    CLOSE on Egyptian passport – hands enter FRAME, open to photo of ARAM SHARIF. The hands leaf through several pages and a myriad of visa stamps. A blank page is found and stamped. CAMERA PULLS BACK reveals immigration agent handing passport to Sharif. He is dressed in a sporty check suit. A snappy suede hat sits at a rakish angle. He carries a rapier-thin rolled-umbrella and an attache case. He's tall, dark, sinister looking. He smiles, nods as he collects his passport.

13. INT. DETECTIVES OFFICE   DAY
    The interrogation is in progress. FLAGG, a burly senior, hard-line detective sits on the edge of his desk confronting MATHEW SLADE, confident, sombre, a 'special agent' who's 'been there', 'seen it all'. Slade is seated.

                            FLAGG
        You can beat this, Mister. Who you working for? I
        need a name.

                            SLADE
        I can't do that. You've no grounds for holding me.

FLAGG
(bellowing)
I can rig a dozen things. I'm going to bust you,
Mister. You aren't going to con me. You're a prime
suspect.

SLADE
I bet you hate this kind of work.

FLAGG
(raps his knuckles on desk)
I mean it. I'll see you get five to ten in the cooler.
You won't be so fancy there.

SLADE
If you think I killed them, book me. But you'd
better know you can make it stick.

Sgt. Donelli enters. He hands Flagg a folder, moves to his desk, sits.
He's younger than Flagg, less aggressive.

DONELLI
Lab report . . . Getting anywhere?

FLAGG
(puts on spectacles, reads)
Both shot from close range. Fleming once through
the pump, the guard twice in the face. Nasty. The
gun was a Browning automatic.
(Looks up, to Donelli)
He needs sweating. A little muscle might loosen
him up.

DONELLI
You knew Mrs. Fleming well, didn't you? Like,
really well.

SLADE
Fairly well. But I get what you mean.

DONELLI
For how long?

SLADE
(impatiently)
You've got all that.

FLAGG
So we have. Less than a year. Social or otherwise?
Or aren't you the type who says?

                    SLADE
Not to a voyeur. Look, Fleming was a friend. I
knew his wife — *socially.*

                    DONELLI
Where is Mrs. Fleming at the moment, Slade?

                    SLADE
Sorry, I can't tell you that. Unless I get it in writing
from the Commissioner that she gets protection.

                    FLAGG
Book him on suspicion of accessory after the fact.
Get his prints. Throw him in the lock up.

                    SLADE
Who are you trying to fool? You'd have to prove I
assisted the murderer. Who is he? Where is he?
And what was the motive?

The phone rings. Donelli picks it up, listens, screws up his face, nods
several times.

                    DONELLI
He's right here. Best you tell him. You'd better
hear this.
                 (Passing phone to Flagg)

                    FLAGG
                   (into phone)
Yeah? . . . Is that so? . . . That's it then . . . Allright.
                 (hangs up phone)
You can beat it. Somebody likes you. But you
aren't off the hook, smart guy. We've got a real
interest in you. We'll be calling again — *soon.*

                    SLADE
You have a nice routine. You had me going there
for a while. So long, boys.

119. INT. HALLWAY COLONY CLUB   NIGHT
     Slade passes along a hall leading to Da Silva's office at the rear of the
     club. WE HEAR the music of a quintet. WE SEE a door marked
     'Private' and HEAR muffled voices raised in anger, sudden
     successive slaps then a woman's muted scream. Slade tries the door.
     It is locked. He stands back, kicks it open.

120. INT. DA SILVA'S OFFICE – SLADE'S P.O.V.   NIGHT
     Da Silva has a tight hold on Laura Fleming's wrist. She tears at his
     face with her other hand. He lets out a grunt. Blood trickles down his

face. He slaps her again, hard. SLADE MOVES INTO FRAME, slams Da Silva against the wall, jabs him in the stomach. Da Silva buckles, clutches at his stomach, coughs.

SLADE

Fearless stuff, Eddie. Are you the bad guy?

DA SILVA
(taking breath)

This is a private affair, friend. I don't like your jokes.

SLADE

So don't laugh. What am I supposed to do when a two-bit shyster starts beating up my client?

DA SILVA
(hedging)

With the events of last night, we're a little nervous. We've had a small . . . disagreement. Yeah, a falling out over a matter that . . well —

SLADE
(abruptly)

Come to the point.

LAURA

We're in disagreement over a gambling debt —

DA SILVA

Yeah. Gambling debt, friend. It's no big deal.

SLADE

Bulldust. I've walked into a frame. Two potbellied cops picked me up this morning and tried to stretch my neck. Someone tipped them I'm involved with the murders. I've got a gut feeling one or both of you set me up.

LAURA

He's trying to get rid of both of us. He called me here to kill me. I'm sure of it.

DA SILVA

Why the rotten, little tramp. She came in here with a pistol, said she'd blast my head off unless I gave her the Phoenix. She's got the idea I knocked it off, killed her husband.

LAURA
(shrilly)

He's a liar. Make him tell the truth. Beat it out of him.

She flays into Da Silva, slaps him across the face, bangs her hands against his chest. Da Silva yelps, staggers back, recovers his footing and lunges at her with a closed fist. She lets out a muffled scream as the fist glances across her left shoulder. Slade moves between them.

SLADE

Come on you two, behave.

LAURA

He's such a liar. If I had a gun I *would* shoot him.

SLADE

(exasperation)

Look, I'm in a jam. Pretty soon we'll all be in the slammer unless the police get a plausible story. Two people have been murdered. The Phoenix has been stolen. You two know more about this than you're letting on.

DA SILVA

Don't get so excited, old friend. You're jumping to conclusions. The police will come to see you aren't involved . . . unless, of course, you are —

SLADE

(angrily)

Ah, this is hopeless. Well, I'm not your guardian. You'll do your talking to them soon enough.

DA SILVA

I'm clean, Slade. She's dangerous. It's my guess, she's had someone heist the Phoenix and there's been a double cross.

LAURA

You tried to buy the Phoenix from Richard. When he wouldn't sell, you used my gambling debt to try and blackmail me into stealing it.

DA SILVA

(laughs)

The dame's got an imagination that doesn't stop. I'm no small-time black-mailer. It's not my game.

SLADE

What would your game be?

DA SILVA

This club. A little gambling. The occasional antique sale. All honest.

SLADE

Strictly top drawer. Who are you kidding? You've made a career out of shaking down people.

A pre-production storyboard still from *Day of The Phoenix*.

DA SILVA

You've got some nerve, friend. You bust in here
and assault me, make crazy accusations. How do I
know you aren't in this up to your neck, with her?

SLADE

(angrily)

You can sort out your own stories. I'm not sticking
my neck out for either one of you. It's not going to
take the police long to get around to both of you.
The way I see it, you'll both end up in the can.
Think it over.

Slade exits. They exchange worried looks. Da Silva indicates to Laura
to follow Slade. She goes after him. Da Silva moves to his desk
presses an intercom button.

122. EXT COLONY CLUB   NIGHT

A couple enters. Slade emerges. An attendant moves to Slade's car
parked near the entrance. Laura emerges.

LAURA

Mind dropping me off?
The car arrives.

SLADE

Get in.

The attendant opens the door for her. Slade tips him, moves behind the
wheel. The car moves into the night traffic, disappears from FRAME.

26. MARKING THE SCRIPT

When the director blocks your scenes and gives you specific moves and
positions, record these positions in the margins of your script. Notations
and comments on characterization should be recorded on the *blank* side of
script pages. It is helpful to underline operative words and to *flagg* and *bridge* speeches to separate key ideas. Use a red or blue lead pencil to mark your
script, never a pen as ink is difficult to erase should alterations to original
markings be necessary. The following are some of the commonly used
notations:

CHARACTER'S NAME: underline your character's name at the head of
each assigned speech. If desired, dialogue lines may also be underlined.

KEY WORDS: underline operative words which require special emphasis. Avoid excessive underlining of words.

KEY IDEA SEQUENCES: insert slanted lines between thoughts (/)
This is called *flagging*. It helps to separate key ideas and allows for the taking on of additional air supply during each brief pause. An idea sequence

may contain several sentences which all relate to a complete thought. A single flagg indicates a *one*-beat pause. Two flaggs (//) indicate a *two*-beat pause.

INTERRELATED IDEA SEQUENCES: where several sentences relate to a single idea, *bridging* may be necessary to briefly separate them for the ear of the audience and to take on additional air supply. A bridge is a sub-pause representing a *half*-beat pause. A bridge is used to connect interrelating thoughts — what has gone before is bridged to what is to follow with the *suggestion* of a pause. The symbol used is a slanted line topped by a curved line (7). Correct bridging of interrelated ideas helps to produce a rhythmic flow during delivery and assists in clarifying the meaning of lengthy passages of dialogue.

SITTING AND RISING: a downward arrow may indicate 'sit' (↓) and an upward arrow 'rise' (↑).

CROSSING: to note a stage cross use the symbol *XCR* (cross center right), *XCL* (cross center left), *XUR* (cross up right), *XUL* (cross up left), *XDR* (cross down right), *XDL* (cross down left).

27. AN EXAMPLE OF SCRIPT MARKING

The following example of marking a script is a guide only as most actors prefer to devise their own marking method. However, the fewer the markings the better, to avoid confusion. Marking example is given for the role of *Wendy*.

JOHN

Sorry, Wendy. I can't be there Monday. It's too short notice.

WENDY

Stares at him a moment, rises, walks to window. She's visibly upset.

I'm disappointed./*Hurt.*/You *promised.*/By the way, Dad will be home tomorrow.

JOHN

I'm glad. Heard from your brother?

WENDY

No./Best we forget him./He's a lost soul./Not reliable./Too aggressive./Abusive./The family *resents* him.

↑ Despises his way of life. // Are you *sure* you can't make it on Monday?/It's *important.*(XDR to chair)

JOHN

Yes, I know. Perhaps next time.

WENDY

↓ If there *is* a next time. ↓ You don't seem to understand./I'm — well — it's *hard* to put into words — you've *changed.*/↑ (X to John.) You're *different.*

SUMMARY OF IDEAS TO REVIEW

1. The foundation of the screen drama is its story. The structure to this foundation is provided by the works of the director and actors. All must perform as a unit.

2. Gain an understanding of the form and structure of a screenplay — how a writer assembles a story. It will help to develop your acting ability.

3. Study your script. Assess its story and character values. A good screenplay takes its audience below surface emotions, makes an impact on its audience, both intellectually and emotionally. A good screenplay provides: *entertainment, enlightenment, self-revelation.*

4. Identify the elements of a screenplay: theme, premise, plot, subplot, conflict, transition, exposition, author's intent, etc. Learn the various abbreviations used.

5. Script preparation time is limited. Read your script immediately you receive it. Script changes may necessitate re-thinking the part.

6. A director expects that you will come to rehearsal and first day's filming knowing *how* you are going to play the role *and* be word-perfect with your lines.

7. Script analysis should be approached in two ways: analysis of the story and analysis of the dialogue.

8. Know how your character fits into the plot and subplots. Visualize the main characters. Discover important events which have taken place prior to the opening of the story. Discover the prevailing atmosphere of each scene.

9. Consider how dialogue should be presented for meaning and effect. Separate formal text from subtext material.

10. Don't expect acting lessons from the director. Prepare every aspect of your part. Once you are familiar with the story, memorize lines.

CHARACTER
ANALYSIS
AND
PORTRAYAL

SCENE 12

Practical Ideas In This Chapter . . .

- Creating Illusions
- The Game of Pretends
- Characters Must Reveal People Not Actors Voiced Hitchcock
- The Actor As Impersonator
- Actors Bring Something of Themselves To Role Playing
- Self-Extension And Character Projection Require Explanation
- Measure of Performance Is Whether You See Actor or Character
- Brando's Style Is The Same But Characters Different
- Harrison Ford On Characterization
- Cary Grant A Master of Character Projection
- Locked Into Rocky Image For All Time Says Stallone
- Self And Illusion Mold Characters Said Sir Ralph Richardson
- Characterization Is An Extension of Dreaming Says Mel Gibson
- Audience Attraction To A Character Is Due To Actor's Skill
- Get As Close To The Character As Possible Says De Niro
- Understand The Requirements of The Part Is Cagney's Advice
- Characterization Comes From Wearing Thoughts And Feelings of Those You Play Says Kirk Douglas
- Find Character's Basic Goal Says Helen Morse
- Enter The Character's Soul Says Jack Lemmon
- An Actor Must Draw Me Into His Character's Life Says Film Critic
- Secret of Stardom Is Character Believability Said Warner
- Don't Rubber Stamp Characters Says Persoff
- Drama Is Concerned With The Thoughts And Feelings of Characters
- Establish An Angle of Vision
- Angle of Vision Includes A Character Profile
- The *Inner* Profile
- The *Outer* Profile
- Ascertaining Personality Characteristics Via Astrology
- Character Profile (Chart)
- Character Conflicts Derive From Objectives Fulfillment
- Drive Motives
- Character Interpretation
- A Character Has No Soul Until Playing Concept Set
- Remaining In Character
- The Two Categories of Role Playing
- Playing Small Roles And Cameo Parts
- Originality Is Valued Higher Than Imitation
- The Play's The Thing
- Summary of Ideas To Review

262

SCENE 12

★★★

1. CREATING ILLUSIONS

> *Acting is honesty. If you*
> *can fake that, you've got*
> *it made.*
> — George Burns.

Actors sometimes misinterpret the term 'acting reality'. It means actions that *seem* real. Very little that occurs on the screen, in terms of character action, is real. Actors, through characters, create *illusions* of reality. The situations and events which take place appear real. And as George Burns amusingly points out, acting is about faking honesty.

Stanislavski's reference to 'acting truth' is quite clear as to its meaning. The reference is to something that is not actually in existence but which *could* happen. The actor believes in the *possibility* of actions originating on the plane of imaginative fiction. And he/she produces feelings that 'seem to be true'.

It was Charlie Chaplin who said: *inspirational acting breeds communion and oneness with the artist and his audience*. An audience is supportive of an actor's action deceptions. An audience wants, above all else, to *believe* in the circumstances and events as they unfold on the screen. The more convincing the performances, the more pleased and involved the audience becomes. An audience expects players to share 'feelings' with them and feels cheated if this does not occur.

2. THE GAME OF PRETENDS

Laurence Olivier, in his autobiography, *Confessions of an Actor*,* refers to acting as 'a game of pretends'. He in no way denigrates acting as a vocation or as an art form by this statement, but points up the very nature, the essential character of acting. He adds, 'For what is acting but lying, and what is good acting but convincing lying?'

The operative word in Olivier's statement is *convincing*. There are actors who are far too theatrical and mechanical of technique to be convincing in their performances. There are those who are in control of their acting instrument and are subtle in their approach to dialogue delivery, movement and character impersonation, resulting in convincing performances.

It is easy for the novice actor to be misled into thinking that the game of pretends is an easy game, a push-over, one without prescribed skill. Good actors certainly make it *look* easy. But as any serious student of drama knows, convincing character portrayal can take years of study, practice and experience to master.

3. CHARACTERS MUST REVEAL PEOPLE NOT ACTORS VOICED HITCHCOCK

Alfred Hitchcock, a director who knew the extraordinary power of the screen camera to make or break an actor, maintained that the performer must display human qualities appropriate to the character being portrayed rather than expose inappropriate personal qualities. 'We must see people, not actors in the roles they play,' he said.

The camera *records* what it sees — often more than imagined. It can reach below surface emotions displayed by an actor to reveal sincerity or falseness. Artificial performance is quickly exposed by the camera's recording powers. It 'reads' an actor's personal subtext.

4. THE ACTOR AS IMPERSONATOR

No human being can become anything other than him/herself. No actor can become another person, but he/she can become *like* another person. An actor is an impersonator. A great actor is a great impersonator who, through use of the imagination, believes in the possibility of character circumstances, events and actions. An actor is akin to the magician — an illusionist in the profession of making things *look* real.

5. ACTORS BRING SOMETHING OF THEMSELVES TO ROLE PLAYING

Some aspect of an actor's personality is brought to every role he/she plays and this is a desirable thing. Firstly, an actor draws from within to construct a stage character, taking what is beneficial from personal knowledge and experience. Then an outer search begins to fill in the missing elements to construct a 'living' character.

*Confessions of an actor, Weidenfeld and Nicolson

An actor may take a little of the personal self or a lot and inject it into a characterization. The degree of personal extension is determined by the similarity of his/her own thoughts, feelings, beliefs, knowledge and experience to those of the character to be played.

It is necessary for an actor to have empathy for and love of the character to be performed if there is to be depth of characterization. This does not mean that the actor has to agree with the ideas and actions assigned to his/her character by the writer, but there must be an *understanding* of them.

6. SELF-EXTENSION AND CHARACTER PROJECTION REQUIRE EXPLANATION

Many television and motion picture stars are accused of too much self-extension rather than character projection in the roles they play. Their critics are quick to point out that stars seem to be the same in everything they do and only 'play themselves' instead of extending themselves into true characterizations. In the main, I feel that this criticism is unfair.

Actors are type cast according to their personality, general manner of presentation and physical look. Seldom are they cast in roles that are outside their type and playing range. Type casting often limits actors to portraying characters which *seem* to have a sameness about them. Playing similar character types can, in some instances, give the impression of total self-extension — playing the self — rather than projecting a character — blending the self with the personality of the character. Where an actor does not need to greatly submerge personal qualities and appearance, he/she is said to be playing a *straight* role.

It isn't often that actors are called upon to completely alter their manner of speech and appearance. Occasionally it happens, as in the film *The List of Adrian Messenger*. The physical and vocal alterations, brilliantly executed by the actors, aided by the makeup and wardrobe people, make it difficult to identify which star portrays which character.

The film *Gandhi*, saw Ben Kingsley make extensive physical, vocal and personality changes to suit the role of Gandhi. Kingsley received a well-deserved Oscar for his role playing.

Dustin Hoffman's double characterization in the film *Tootsie*, required him to make major physical and vocal alterations each time he donned wig, dress and makeup to impersonate the female character and he brought it off brilliantly. Another of Hoffman's convincing characterizations is Ratso, in the film *Midnight Cowboy*.

In each of the aforementioned films, the stars used their own personalities as the *spines* upon which to construct their characters. These kinds of parts are called *character* roles.

Because stars become familiar faces on the screen in straight roles, audiences tend to see them as familiar characters — each performance seems to be like the one before. To be fair, actors' performances need to be compared and analysed before criticism is passed. It isn't every day that parts such as Gandhi, Tootsie and Ratso come along allowing an actor the opportunity to widen the playing range in a showy character role. However, in the main, a screen actor is given parts which require him/her to act through the medium of his/her *own* personality.

7. MEASURE OF PERFORMANCE IS WHETHER YOU SEE ACTOR OR CHARACTER

I am in agreement with Hitchcock's view that an audience must see *people* on the screen, not actors posing as people. And this is the measure of a good screen performance, whether or not an audience gets beyond the personal identities of the actors and becomes involved with seemingly real characters.

When an audience is consciously aware of an actor 'acting', it can be disturbing to them. The performance is seen to be artificial rather than real. In order to overcome this, an actor needs to submerge his/her personal identity or with skill blend it into the stage character's personality. An inability to do this will spoil an actor's chance to attain lasting screen stardom.

8. BRANDO'S STYLE IS THE SAME BUT CHARACTERS DIFFERENT

Marlon Brando has played many similar types of characters. In some, there has been a sameness of acting style: *A Streetcar Named Desire, The Wild One, On The Waterfront, The Fugitive Kind, The Chase.* He brings a brooding, heavy-muscled, inarticulate, brutal quality to the roles in these films. While the characterizations have a similar ring to them, they are not totally identical. All are played with genuine artistry, albeit with less than satisfactory diction. The groping for words, half-sentences ended by body shrugs and multitude of sullen looks, are Brando, but each characterization fits and one becomes completely engrossed in what Brando does with each character.

In the films *The Young Lions* and *Mutiny on the Bounty*, gone are Stanley Kowalski and Terry Malloy. In their place we see characters that are charming instead of brutal, different in accent and more dandy than lout. In Francis Ford Coppola's *The Godfather*, Brando creates a character of marvellous proportion. It is the key to the film and to the contributions of the cast. Archer Winsten in his New York Post review, said: *The measure of this performance is the way you think of him as Don Corleone, not Brando.*

9. HARRISON FORD ON CHARACTERIZATION

A major studio boss once told Harrison Ford he didn't have what it takes to become a star. The actor went on to make one of the most exciting films I've seen, *Raiders of the Lost Ark*. He's been in many very good films. *Raiders* and his Indiana Jones characterization in *Temple of Doom*, have brought him world-wide audience recognition.

'I alter the way I think and look to blend into each film. I create behavior that tells a story. If it's not appropriate, it's out. I try to put something different into each different character I play.' That's sound advice from an excellent screen actor.

10. CARY GRANT A MASTER OF CHARACTER PROJECTION

Cary Grant became identified as the source of a *type*: handsome, sophisticated, well-groomed, witty, man-of-the-world. Analysing his screen performances, one becomes impressed with his versatility as an actor. The characters he played in *Notorious, To Catch A Thief, North by Northwest* and *Charade*, have a similarity about them, but Grant managed to inject something different into each one of them.

'As a youngster, I tried to develop an acting style, a composite of several famous people of my day. I tried to become that sort of character in American pictures. The actor and the character became welded together. I've always tried to think and act like the character should, even when it departed from my own screen image,' Grant said. The crude and intolerant character the star created for the film *Father Goose*, attests to his characterization skill.

11. LOCKED INTO ROCKY IMAGE FOR ALL TIME SAYS STALLONE

'I'm battling typecasting. I'm locked into this image of a lamebrain. I'll always be Rocky,' complains Sylvester Stallone. *Rocky, F.I.S.T., Paradise Alley* and *First Blood*, are films where the screen characters display very much the same personality. The same playing approach and manner of dialogue delivery crept into *Nighthawks* and *Escape to Victory*. In Stallone's case, his audiences aren't turned-off, they want more. They've taken his Rocky character to heart. They feel a *real* character. For them Rocky lives. I suspect Mr. Stallone's acting career will continue to prosper, even though he's locked into playing one type of character. The public has type cast him and made him a multi-millionaire in the process. Carbon-copy acting does have its rewards.

Warner Baxter, best remembered for his starring roles in the Columbia Pictures Crime Doctor films of the 'forties, had this to say about type casting: 'Actors often object to studio typing, but I don't. It is the public who types an actor not the studio. If an actor is good in a particular characterization, he can afford to submerge his desire to play many different roles in favor of a welcome financial return and public acclaim.' Baxter's comments are worthy of consideration, for while there is no mention of creative satisfaction, financial rewards and public adulation may well be sufficient incentives to remain *typed* for many actors.

12. SELF AND ILLUSION MOLD CHARACTERS SAID SIR RALPH RICHARDSON

British stage and screen star, Sir Ralph Richardson, died in October 1983. An actor who once confessed that he suffered dreadfully from stage fright, his 50 years before audiences brought many memorable performances. His characterizations were real and varied. His approach to acting was exemplary.

'You have to take as much of the self as is required and add illusion when developing a character. Acting is an illusion, as much an illusion as magic. It's the ability to dream on cue. Actors have to dream to order. Nothing is really true. Even when you say to a woman that you love her, it's not wholly true. Part of it is. If actors want to create living characters they must use their imagination and be good dreamers.' Excellent advice from an all-time great actor, one who will linger in the minds of his peers.

13. CHARACTERIZATION IS AN EXTENSION OF DREAMING SAYS MEL GIBSON

Mel Gibson launched his screen career in the Australian Films *Gallipoli*, *Mad Max*, *The Road Warrior* and *The Year of Living Dangerously*. Gibson says that every part he plays he actually develops from various units of himself. 'It's like a dream, a fantasy. What you have to do is to stop those things that are prominent in your personality, then bring to the forefront some of those recessive qualities you may have and alter the balances a little so you become a different type of person. Acting is a way of dreaming. My acting is an extension of my dreaming. I have a vivid imagination so I cast myself into the role of my fantasies.' The ability to *dream on cue* has brought screen stardom to Mel Gibson.

14. AUDIENCE ATTRACTION TO A CHARACTER IS DUE TO ACTOR'S SKILL

I have made it a practice to study older classic films as well as contemporary ones. Some of my favorite motion pictures include: *Casablanca*, *The Maltese Falcon*, *Mildred Pearce*, *Alfie* and *Chinatown*. They are wonderful examples of the screen art. Directing, writing and acting magically come together to bring about colorful and controversial characters involved in seemingly real situations.

I'm drawn to Mildred Pearce the screen character, rather than to Joan Crawford the actress. Even though I've watched this film a dozen or so times, the illusion of reality remains intact. As I watch *Casablanca*, I am taken in by the lives and troubles of Rick, Ilsa and Lazlo. Sam Spade and Kaspar Gutman intrigue me, mesmerize and shock me as I watch them clash in *The Maltese Falcon*. The character Alfie disturbs me. I am distressed by his callous treatment of those who love him. And Robert Towne's first-rate screenplay *Chinatown*, succeeds because he knows that audiences want to escape into a story with a strong narrative line. J.J. Gittes is a beautifully-orchestrated characterization by Jack Nicholson. These films take me into another world where the situations and the characters hold my attention and stir my emotions. I am drawn to the characters via the skill of the actors.

15. GET AS CLOSE TO THE CHARACTER AS POSSIBLE SAYS DE NIRO

Robert De Niro digs deeply to discover the truth of his character. He spends time analysing each role because he feels that an actor must know what drives a character to a particular course of action.

'I want my acting to be as truthful as I can make it and I want to get as close to the character as possible,' De Niro says. And he feels that the quickest way to accomplish this is through story and character analysis.

16. UNDERSTAND THE REQUIREMENTS OF THE PART IS CAGNEY'S ADVICE

I'd not been afforded the pleasure of meeting Jimmy Cagney. But I knew his brother, William, when I worked in Hollywood. We went to the same barber on Hollywood Boulevard. Bill, a friendly, good-humored man, talked openly about his brother and his remarkable ability to get inside a character and bring it to life. Bill produced many of Jimmy's films, among them the one which brought Jimmy an Oscar, *Yankee Doodle Dandy*.

'Understand the requirements of the part. Get an insight into the background of the character, then go after it with all you've got,' Cagney told a Hollywood columnist after he won his Oscar. 'That was his secret,' Bill told me. 'Jimmy had to play a lot of thinly-written characters in many of his films. He was a professional who knew how to add several dimensions to characters who were basically one-dimensional.'

Cagney's portrayal of Martin Snyder in *Love Me or Leave Me* is a beautifully-conceived piece of screen acting. The critics enthused over it and he was nominated for another Oscar. He lost to Ernest Borgnine for his role in *Marty*. Doris Day said of her *Love Me or Leave Me* co-star: 'The most professional actor I've known. He made me feel it was all real. He made the part "real" and in some scenes I forgot we were making a film.' Cagney understood film acting. He spent time researching his parts so that his characterizations would not only have *appeal* but *realism* about them.

17. CHARACTERIZATION COMES FROM WEARING THOUGHTS AND FEELINGS OF THOSE YOU PLAY SAYS KIRK DOUGLAS

Kirk Douglas told me that he blends the chore of studying lines with studying the character — what the character thinks and feels and why. 'I wear the character's attitudes, try them on for size in order to take on the mood, the feeling and the working of a scene.'

The star advises students of acting to 'study people' and 'draw on yourself' when developing a character. 'Think about what you must do before you enter the world of illusion. Be disciplined. Characterization needs to be controlled. I don't lose myself. The audience loses itself in my acting out an illusion of character actions,' says one of the true stars of the screen.

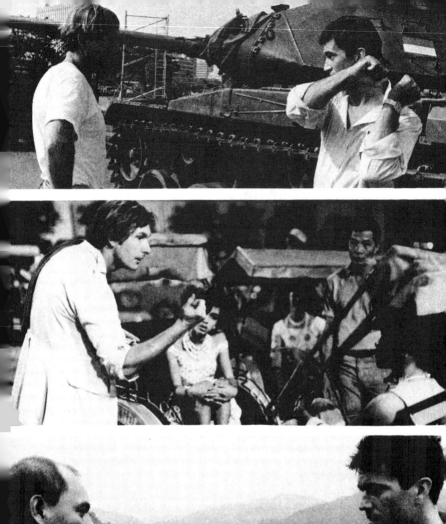

(*Top*) Director *Peter Weir* studies *Mel Gibson's* threatening stance for scene in the McElroy & McElroy production *Year of Living Dangerously*, released by MGM.
(*Center*) *Peter Weir* describes action he requires of players for location night scene.
(*Bottom*) Actors *Bembol Roco* and *Mel Gibson* share location shot, helping Gibson to 'dream on cue'.
(*Year of Living Dangerously* photographs supplied by Metro Goldwyn Mayer and reproduced with their permission.)

18. FIND CHARACTER'S BASIC GOAL SAYS HELEN MORSE

In an interview with Lee Tulloch of *Vogue Australia*, screen star Helen Morse, when asked how she approached the portrayal of a character, said: 'I dissect it and analyse it. I usually try to have an overall picture of the character — I think "This person is like somebody I know or met once" — and then I usually find something in the script that is her basic goal.'

Helen's initial training as an actress was in the theatre. She firmly established herself as a screen actress with excellent portrayals in *Caddie*, *Agatha* and *A Town Like Alice*.

19. ENTER THE CHARACTER'S SOUL SAYS JACK LEMMON

Director Billy Wilder claimed audiences have greater rapport with Jack Lemmon than with any other performer since Charlie Chaplin. And perhaps audience-character rapport is the secret of Lemmon's screen success. He's been nominated for seven academy awards, winning Oscars for his work in *Mr. Roberts* and *Save the Tiger*.

'I cannot feel I've got a character set until I'm in his skin. I possess the character. It's like entering his soul,' Lemmon says. While making *Days of Wine and Roses*, the actor regularly attended meetings of Alcoholics Anonymous to identify with the character's tragic drinking problem. He has that rare ability to make an audience feel that they are part of the story and totally involved with the character's life.

20. AN ACTOR MUST DRAW ME INTO HIS CHARACTER'S LIFE SAYS FILM CRITIC

Australian film critic, film historian and television host Bill Collins, feels that an actor must have the ability to draw an audience into the life of a character, become involved, moved and concerned by his/her ideas, feelings and actions. 'An actor must get me so involved with what's taking place on the screen I forget it's an actor and see a true-to-life character. When I watch actors work, I respond if I'm convinced that I'm watching someone's life experiences,' Bill told me.

I arranged a private screening for Bill of a film I released in Australia, *The Execution*. After seeing it, he said to me: 'As I watched Jason Robards, Hardy Kruger and Gila Almagor, I felt as though I was up there on the screen with them, suffering with them, being happy with them. I was involved with their lives. When actors can do that through their characterizations, they're good.'

21. SECRET OF STARDOM IS CHARACTER BELIEVABILITY SAID WARNER

The late Jack L. Warner was an aggressive, abrasive, feisty, showy vulgarian studio head who upset many of the people he met and particularly many of the stars who worked for him.

I liked Warner's sense of humor and his directness. He said what he felt.

Very few of his stars had much to say in his favor, but they recognized his ability to spot a potential star and to make good movies. I asked him, during a social meeting at the Ambassador Hotel in Los Angeles just prior to his retirement, what makes a screen star. 'An ability to lean in any direction, look like many people but still project a personal charisma through each characterization. You've got to feel like you know the people you see on the screen. You've got to love them, hate them, feel for them and with them. An actor has to be able to make an audience forget where it is and take them along with him as the story unfolds. If he can't do that, he'd better go back to pumping gas.'

22. DON'T RUBBER STAMP CHARACTERS SAYS PERSOFF

Nehemiah Persoff, who's played so many characters on film, television and stage that he's forgotten how many, feels he has to be on guard to avoid trotting out stereotypes. He maintains each characterization requires a specific direction relevant to the direction of the story and characters. He attempts to discover 'an involvement with life' and to find 'the human side' of the various characters he portrays, otherwise they are likely to turn out one-dimensional, a rubber stamp of the one before. He feels that good characterizations require lots of preparation and analysis to grasp the inner and outer life of each role. 'It is necessary to know a character's thoughts and feelings in order to justify his actions,' Persoff says.

23. DRAMA IS CONCERNED WITH THE THOUGHTS AND FEELINGS OF CHARACTERS

A writer reveals the thoughts and feelings of a play's characters via the dialogue and actions assigned to them. Words on their own have little significance. What counts is how words are strung together and expressed — what they represent and reveal. Each speech is an expression of a particular character's ideas, emotions and often, intended actions toward the person, place or object of his/her attention. As words are spoken to reveal the 'mind' of the character, an actor's aim should be to create the illusion that the words spring from personal thoughts — spontaneously and naturally.

24. ESTABLISH AN ANGLE OF VISION

In order to be in full contact with a role, an actor needs to give much thought to the inner and outer life of the character to be played. Draft a biographical sketch of the character's past, present and dreams of the future. It is an excellent way to gain an in-depth view of the life to be constructed. By searching the character's history an *angle of vision* and deep insight into the soul of the character is established. And this helps to 'lift' the character from the pages of fiction into the world of reality.

Information required to establish an angle of vision includes:

Hardy Kruger and *Gila Almagor* in scene from *The Execution*, which also starred *Jason Robards*. Film was directed by *Reza S. Badiyi*, produced by *Delta Commerz*.

- What circumstances, conditions and events from the past are responsible for the present life of the character?
- Does the character have strong ideas, opinions and feelings about the things he/she does? How easily swayed from these convictions is the character?
- Are the character's goals worthy or are they dishonest?
- What is the nature of your character's past failures and successes?
- Has your character been greatly affected by the losing or winning of past goals?
- How have other characters been affected by the losing or winning of your character's goals?
- Establish your character's attitudes toward others and things in each scene.
- What feelings do you wish the audience to experience as they view your character's actions?
- How does your character feel about those who stand in his/her way?
- What interrelationships need to be established?
- What do you like or dislike about your character's personality?
- Are there strong motivations for what the character says and does?
- What moods need to be established as the character becomes embroiled in conflicts with others?
- Can you easily establish in your mind's eye and ear the way your character speaks, moves and looks?
- After detecting your character's primary objectives, draft a list of secondary objectives and establish as to whether they are won or lost.

25. ANGLE OF VISION INCLUDES A CHARACTER PROFILE

As Helen Morse points out, perhaps the character is like someone you already know or met once. This makes it easier to *profile* the character because you have something tangible to go on. Where this is not the case, a fresh character profile will have to be established. You will need to construct a personality for your character and a physical 'look'. You must get close to your character to understand impelling motives behind actions taken. Prepare a character profile chart. It should comprise as much information as you can discover re your character's *physiology, sociology* and *psychology*.

26. THE *INNER* PROFILE

Every human being has both inner and outer personality factors. The inner aspects are *mental, emotional* and *spiritual*. The outer aspects are *physical* and highly visible. Often a character's personality factors are easily identifiable because some individuals are straightforward, friendly, open types with few emotional problems. Others are complex, difficult to understand and their personalities need time to identify and thoroughly establish. Generally speaking, individuals fall into 'types' reflecting upbringing, education, social status, well-being, etc.

Establish the type of personality your character represents. This can be accomplished by studying the writer's description of the character, by analysing the character's dialogue and reactions to other characters, in addition to the things other characters say about your character. Add to this information your personal observations and gut feelings about people you know or have known and how *you* would think, feel and act in circumstances similar to those of your character.

MENTAL CHARACTERISTICS: is the character bright, intelligent, quick-witted, optimistic, generous, decisive, meticulous, discriminating *or* slow-thinking, dull, boring, pessimistic, mean, indecisive, indifferent, stupid?

EMOTIONAL CHARACTERISTICS: is the character self-confident, poised, happy, of good humor, courageous, compassionate, sensitive, creative, of even disposition, affectionate, tolerant, *or* insecure, timid, shy, morose, bad tempered, cowardly, highly reactionary, unfeeling, intolerant, lacking self-respect, noncreative, insensitive, highly volatile?

SPIRITUAL CHARACTERISTICS: is the character an idealist, attached to a particular religious group, ethical, of high morals, honest *or* an atheist, unethical, of low morals, dishonest?

27. THE *OUTER* PROFILE

Having ascertained the inner characteristics of your character – ways of thinking, feeling and responding to people and circumstances – the next step is to construct the outer expression – general appearance, ways of moving and speaking. If the character were an animal what would he/she be in appearance and temperament? Would the physical mannerisms be like those of an elephant, bear, cat, dog, goat, tiger, lion, horse, cow or bull? If the character were a reptile would he/she be a snake, alligator, lizard, turtle? Whatever you can do to assist in the establishing of vivid mental pictures of your character will prove advantageous when it comes time to speak and move as the character in performance.

PHYSICAL CHARACTERISTICS: age, coloring, posture, mannerisms, facial expression, quality of health, energy level, walk, gesture pattern, tense, relaxed, quick-moving, slow-moving, tired-looking, dress sense, grooming. *Visualize* your character.

ORAL IMAGE: quality of voice, diction, inflection, pitch, volume, projection and what is indicated by general manner of speaking. If the character were a musical instrument, what would he/she be? Are speech sounds like a violin, double bass, trumpet, trombone, piccolo, tuba, snare drum, piano or organ? Determine the character's speech pattern. *Hear* it in your mind's ear.

28. ASCERTAINING PERSONALITY CHARACTERISTICS VIA ASTROLOGY

Actors who have knowledge of graphology, phrenology, palmistry and astrology, will know that it is possible to 'tag' an individual's personality, general character and aptitude through a careful analysis of handwriting, shape and protuberances of the head, the lines and marks on palms and the relative positions of the moon, sun and stars at the time, place and date of his/her birth.

Humans do conform to particular personality and character structures which influence the way in which they speak and act. Quite often we hear others using the phrase, 'he's the type who ...'. Type casting is commonplace in society, not just in the acting profession.

An actor who has knowledge of astrology, might find it worthwhile, if not a pleasant exercise, to give each character to be played a specific astrological birth sign. This can, with reasonable accuracy, be achieved by analysing the character's profile chart, carefully noting the plus and minus personality factors supplied by the writer and coming to a conclusion as to which sign the character might have been born under.

A strong, ambitious, aggressive type might prove to be a *Leo*. A creative, sensitive, impatient, perfectionist, leader, could possibly be an *Aries*. Once a basic 'type' has been established, tag him or her with an astrological sign and then add additional characteristics associated with that sign. Be careful to stay within the character perimeters set by the writer. Do not create an entirely separate character to the one devised by the writer.

29. CHARACTER CONFLICTS DERIVE FROM OBJECTIVES FULFILLMENT

Every human being has basic wants, needs and objectives in life and will make compromises, sacrifices and often, indulge in personal risk to fulfill them. Fictional characters, to reflect *humanness*, also have objectives to achieve. When an actor studies a role, he/she must pinpoint the character's scene objectives — what the character seeks, needs and is striving to achieve. It is important to discover the *motivating* factors supporting each of the character's wants.

Fulfillment of personal objectives — from the inconsequential to the complex — is a game all humans play. It is an *achievement* game, designed to bring some form of gain or to retain things already won — power, prestige, possessions. Basically, humans share a desire for the same things. Therefore, they share the same basic *drive motives* — reasons and forces stimulating their desire to be, to do and to have.

While humans share the same basic wants, approaches to achieving them differ. Not all persons who seek wealth rush out and rob a bank or steal from their fellow man. But some do. Not all persons desiring power, influence and control become army generals, police officers or politicians. But some do. Not all persons seeking creative fulfillment become actors,

CHARACTER PROFILE CHART

CHARACTER NAME

PHYSIOLOGY

Sex
Age
Height
Weight
Coloring of hair, skin, eyes
Posture
General appearance
Physical defects
Manner of dress
Grooming habits

SOCIOLOGY

Marital status
Social status
Occupation and income
Education
Religion
Nationality
Political affiliation
Union affiliation
Club or organization
Hobbies
Sports
Achievements
Interest in the arts

PSYCHOLOGY

Standard of morals
Temperament
Attitude toward life
Intelligence level
Prejudices
Type of personality — introvert, extrovert
Personal ambition
Failures and frustrations
Obsessions
Personal qualities — strengths
Personal qualities — weaknesses
Special creative abilities

Languages spoken
Major and minor goals

dancers, musicians, painters or writers. But some do. Not all persons desiring 'things' persist with goals striving. But some do.

When translating a character's objectives into stage actions, be sure to define the drive motives. Don't play actions without understanding them or being able to justify them. Formulate apparent relationships to people, places and things and establish how and why those relationships affect the character's wants, needs and objectives.

Having discovered your character's objectives, pinpoint the *obstacles* the character encounters in the pursuit of them. Sometimes referred to as *counter-movements*, they are the strivings of other characters who are in opposition or 'elements' the character comes up against or is in conflict with.

30. DRIVE MOTIVES

It has already been pointed out in chapter four that every human being has four basic *needs* which he/she strives to fulfill: *physiological* needs, *social* needs, *psychological* needs, *creative* needs. Linked to these needs are five basic drive motives — reasons and forces supporting goals striving. They bring the mind into conflict with itself and into conflict with various elements and other humans. The five drive motives are:

(1) **GAIN** — a desire for recognition, power, security, possessions, etc.
(2) **PRIDE** — brought about by material possessions, appearance, creative achievement, judgement social status, family relationships, associations, etc.
(3) **FEAR** — created by loss of position, social status, loved ones, loss of possessions, inability to achieve, loss of beauty, physical activity, etc.
(4) **IMITATION** — a desire to be as good as the next person, to go one better than the next person, to set personal standards higher than normal to satisfy ego demands, to conform to general surroundings and feel in-step with associates, friends and family.
(5) **PLEASURE** — to acquire an easier existence, greater happiness, creative fulfillment, enhance well-being, bring added comforts, enjoy new experiences, establish new friendships, experience love relationships, reduce tension, fatigue, fear and frustration.

31. CHARACTER INTERPRETATION

Interpretation means the *expression* of a person's conception of a work of art through acting, playing, writing, criticizing, etc. Character interpretation is the expression of an actor's conception of a writer's story character. An actor's conception of a role and the performance of it are not always true to the intent of the author. There is danger of this happening where the training, skill and experience of an actor are suspect.

As a director, I have always made it a practice to tell my casts at the onset

278

of rehearsals, the dangers of too many interpretations floating through a production. Writer, director and actors need to *unify* their ideas on story and character interpretation or there will be a hodge-podge production of little creative and technical merit.

The basic source of enquiry is the writer's script. The clues to interpretation are to be found *within* the text. It is permissible and sometimes necessary to venture beyond the writer's work in order to gain a broader understanding of a character's personality and to crystallize the playing of a part. But an actor, while free from restraint to create his/her dream, must not stray from the writer's premise, theme and character concept.

The *approach* to playing a character may differ from one actor to another. This is because no two actors share the same personality, the same experiences of life, the same thoughts and feelings. The *depth* of an actor's performance is determined by his/her role analysis, playing experience, skill as an actor and personal background.

Because the performance approach differs from actor to actor, the conception — interpretation — of a role must be in line with that of the writer. An actor is expected to *develop* an assigned part. There is no authorized right to *change* it, resulting in a character different to the one designed by the author. An actor who is guilty of destroying an author's intent, is undeserving of the part he/she has been entrusted with. Remember: there are countless ways to *approach* a characterization, but all approaches must lead to the one *true* interpretation — the circumstances proposed by the writer through his/her text.

32. A CHARACTER HAS NO SOUL UNTIL PLAYING CONCEPT SET

A stage character is brought to life — given a soul — only after a player has determined the meaning of the lines, discovered the motivations underlying them and has found a means of identifying with the character to be portrayed. A visual and vocal image begins to take form as the character's speeches are understood. The life of the character and the life of the actor begin to merge as the actor 'feels' the reality of the character's circumstances. At this point the actor ceases to be an observer. He/she becomes an active participant in the affairs of the character. There is an entering of the character's soul, a communion with a living spirit devised by the writer and expanded through the mind and heart of the actor.

33. REMAINING IN CHARACTER

An actor's performance requires a *consistency* about it or there won't be an harmonious blend of thought, feeling and action. A role needs to have a 'continuous being'. From fade in to fade out, an actor is required to stay in character, remain married to the part, form a chain of unbroken links which represent the character's past which has flowed to the present and continues on into the future. Every speech, every move, every gesture must be in keeping with the *mood* of the story and the *personality* of the character.

An actor must not allow the mind to wander from the stage task. Should this occur, the actor separates from the character, breaks the staged atmosphere, the creative mood of the other players and the audience's illusion of the reality of the staged events.

Don't allow the mind to dwell upon personal thoughts. Remain true to the thoughts and feelings of your character. Concentrate on your role playing. Speak when it is your turn to speak and listen when it is your turn to listen. When your mind is disciplined in this way you will remain in character and thus benefit your own performance as well as benefitting the performances of your fellow players.

Robert Redford maintains that a lot of what acting is 'is paying attention'. He feels an actor must submit to what is going on and be able to do that fully without losing concentration.

34. THE TWO CATEGORIES OF ROLE PLAYING

Basically, there are two categories of role playing. The first is called a *straight role* and the second a *character role*. Within each category there are *straight comedic* or *straight dramatic* situations and *character roles* involving comedic or dramatic situations.

(1) **STRAIGHT ROLE:** defined as a part well-suited to a particular actor because of age, ethnic origin, personality, physical characteristics that are similar to the character to be portrayed. Straight roles as a general rule are normal, attractive people of any age.

(2) **CHARACTER ROLE:** defined as a part which necessitates the altering in some way of an actor's physical and sometimes psychological makeup. Character roles embody some degree of eccentricity. These roles seldom resemble their actors in either look or personality. Mostly, these parts deal with interesting characteristics such as age, ethnic origin, erratic or controversial behavior, a particular manner of dress, posture, movement and speech. Most actors prefer good character roles to straight roles because they offer an opportunity to reveal an actor's technique and artistry. Charles Laughton was a masterful character role player. Anthony Quinn, Judith Anderson, Vincent Price, Wendy Hiller, Bill Kerr, Laurence Olivier, among others, are examples of character role players who have the technique and range to play a variety of interesting parts.

35. PLAYING SMALL ROLES AND CAMEO PARTS

There are no minor roles, it has been said, just minor actors — those who grumble when offered small parts. Should you be cast in a small role because of your inexperience or in a cameo role if you are a professional, well-established actor, give the part all you've got. Small roles, especially cameos, demand suitable preparation time to discover character relationships, line meanings and characterization correctness. A screen drama

Three stills from the feature film *Razorback*, directed by *Russell Mulcahy* for the producers McElroy & McElroy. *Bill Kerr* played Jake Cullen a character role which offered a chance to display his strengths as an actor. Character roles usually embody some form of eccentricity, controversial behavior, special manner of dress and speech.

(Photographs reprinted with permission of McElroy & McElroy)

Alex Cord is dramatically framed in low-angle shot from *Inn of The Damned*, which co-starred *Judith Anderson* and *Michael Craig*. Film had plenty of good straight and character roles. Cord's straight role was as a bounty hunter investigating the disappearance of tourists visiting a run-down inn operated by a seemingly senile old couple (Anderson and Joseph Furst).

Fast-moving stagecoach was used to shoot title sequences for the suspense-thriller written and directed by *Terry Bourke* who also co-produced with *Rod Hay*. *Graham Ware* and *Reg Gorman* played the stage drivers.

Terry Bourke (seated behind camera) watches actors *Lionel Long* (on horse), *Alex Cord* and *Michael Craig* (right), as scene is slated. On far right, a cameraman covers the making of the film using a 16mm, Arriflex camera.

requires as near-to-perfect acting as a director can coax from the cast — even those in non-speaking roles.

The $25 million television mini-series Marco Polo, brought together a number of distinguished actors playing what amounted to *cameos* — small but important roles. Ann Bancroft, John Houseman, Leonard Nimoy, John Gielgud, David Warner, Sada Thompson and Burt Lancaster were among those who accepted cameo roles in the production.

'It did not concern me that my role was a small one. It's the quality of the role that is important,' was Lancaster's comment. Actors need to consider the *depth* of characterization a part offers rather than how many lines it contains. A few strong lines well played can have dramatic impact and bring creative and career rewards. Supporting roles are often more interesting to work with and more demanding of ability than some leading roles. The challenge lies within the *type* and *dimension* of the character to be portrayed, regardless of how small or large the role may be.

36. ORIGINALITY IS VALUED HIGHER THAN IMITATION

The original Mona Lisa painting is worth millions of dollars. I've seen Mona Lisa prints costing five dollars a copy. Every art gallery in the world would love to hang the original Mona Lisa. No art gallery of any merit would hang a five dollar copy. There is always greater value and prestige attached to something *original* over that which is an imitation of an original.

Be original. Don't copy the acting styles of others. Develop your own *unique* style, basing your characterizations on the author's intent not on how others have or might approach them. Carbon-copy acting is superficial acting, an imitation lacking originality.

Burt Lancaster's fine portrayal of Robert Stroud in *The Birdman of Alcatraz*, made a deep impression on me. Robert Vaughan's portrayal of Frank Flaherty in the TV series *Washington Behind Closed Doors*, is a characterization I shall long remember because of its strength and depth. I was impressed with Vaughan's acting style and professionalism when I worked with him in the television mini-series *The Last Bastion*. Here is an actor who practices his craft. And I am in awe each time I watch Humphrey Bogart play the tough, snarling, greedy gold prospector, Fred C. Dobbs in *The Treasure of the Sierra Madre*, a frightening representation of civilised man in a terminal stage. Sir Ralph Richardson's brilliant portrayal of James Tyrone in *Long Day's Journey Into Night*, will always be, for me, one of the best of screen performances by an actor. I loved Ingrid Bergman's charm, beauty and naturalness as Ilsa Lund in *Casablanca* and marvel at the many and varied screen portrayals devised by Meryl Streep and Bette Davis. The work of these talented actors is of great dimension and feeling.

Imagination and invention are required to lift a screen characterization above the ordinary. The complete assimilation of a character's background, with meticulous attention given to personality detail, supported by creative imagining, will bring impressive and impeccable truth of characterization.

37. THE PLAY'S THE THING

With regard to character interpretation, an actor may feel that he/she knows better than the writer or director and want to perform in a manner contrary to the author's intent. No actor should attempt to radically alter a writer's concepts — whatever the reason. The play's the thing, not an actor desiring to build-up or restructure a part. Don't tamper with the objectives and personality assigned to your character — develop them, *yes*. Change them, *no*. Unify with other characters. Follow the guidance of your director and conform to the author's character and story plan. Become a member of the acting team, not separate from it.

SUMMARY OF IDEAS TO REVIEW

1: Actors are in the business of creating *illusions* of reality. An audience wants to believe everything it sees on the screen. Actors can help them to do this via convincing performances.

2: Acting is a 'game of pretends'. Acting is lying and good acting is convincing lying. Good actors make acting look easy. Technique is the key to *ease* of performance.

3: The camera reveals acting insincerity. You can't fake emotions when playing before the camera. *Think* and *feel* your way through performance.

4: Actors bring something of themselves to every performance. Discover what you can use from your own experience and personality to bring greater 'life' to your characterizations.

5: Actors are type cast according to personality, manner of presentation, physical look and age. If you are continually cast to play the same *types* of characters it does not mean that you should play every part the same way. Bring different aspects of *personality* into play. Make each part different in some way.

6: Spend sufficient time analysing your roles. Script analysis helps you to comprehend the author's intent.

7: Establish an *angle of vision*, an in-depth look at the life of the character. The more information you possess, the easier it is to construct a believable characterization.

8: Construct a character *profile* — inner and outer aspects — to create a picture of *who* the character is, *what* the character looks like, *how* the character sounds, *where* the character is from. Chart the character's *physiology, sociology* and *psychology*.

9: Establish the major and minor objectives of the character.

10: *Remember*: the play's the thing. Become a member of the acting team.

SCREEN
ACTING
REALISM

SCENE 13

Practical Ideas In This Chapter . . .

• Screen Magnetism Is Personality Plus Talent And Naturalness
• Anthony Perkins And Screen Naturalism
• Personality Appeal *And* Acting Talent Count At The Box Office
• Acting Realism
• Extended Playing Stopped Many Stage Actors Becoming Screen Stars
• Why It's Difficult To Act Naturally
• Resist Flirting With The Audience
• Bring Only What Is Needed To The Mind of The Character
• Draw An Imaginary Circle Around The Acting Perimeter
• Don't Get Lost In Role Playing
• On The Screen It's The Appearance of Things That Counts
• The Key To Naturalism Is Seeming Unawareness
• Fix The Point of Attention Where It Belongs
• Carry The Point of Attention Through Entire Performance
• Style And Naturalism
• Creating Realism Through Sincerity And Belief
• Gary Cooper Was One of Screen's Most Natural Players
• Bergman's Style Was Simple And Unaffected
• Bogart Added Mystery To His Naturalness
• Acquiring Naturalism Through Technique
• Believability And Naturalness Ultimate Goals of Screen Acting
• Summary of Ideas To Review

SCENE 13

★★

1. SCREEN MAGNETISM IS PERSONALITY PLUS TALENT AND NATURALNESS

The most valuable asset of a screen actor is screen presence, that magical 'something' which instantly commands the attention of an audience and propels an actor to screen stardom. Presence is a particular quality of personality, an unusual way of self-presentation, a personal power and a charisma which hypnotizes audiences and makes them feel something of themselves is attached to the actor.

The list of screen stars with personal magnetism is lengthy. Each year the list expands, as new, young and talented actors make their mark. These fortunate people are truly endowed with a special quality. It's deeply embedded in their being, showing itself in the way in which they speak, move and act. It is a magnetism which lifts what is said and done above the ordinary.

Richard Harris speaking about Richard Burton, said: 'A remarkable man. He had that gift, that aura, that charisma. I don't know why he was so great, but he was. He really was the prince of players. He could stand with a dozen naked women on his left and a dozen naked men on his right and you would watch Richard Burton. He was a star, a truly great star.'

The *quality* an actor exudes as a person will be the base upon which to construct his/her screen characterizations. The more appealing is that quality, the more acceptable will be the playing. Directors have told me that the quality of an actor's personality can sometimes be more important than his/her acting skills.

It is my own view that personality *and* acting skill go hand-in-hand, particularly if an actor desires a lasting screen career. I know of several actors who exhibit wonderful personalities but lack acting skill. All have starred in television or film dramas. After a short career, all have fallen by the wayside.

2. ANTHONY PERKINS AND SCREEN NATURALISM

When he was 19, Tony Perkins hitch-hiked across the US to Hollywood, where he landed a juvenile lead in an MGM film. Since the age of 14, he'd been gaining acting experience in summer stock theatre.

'I watched myself on the screen in that first role and saw I wasn't ready. I wasn't an interesting screen character. I had no technique, no range, little presence and no confidence. I packed my bag and took the train back east. If I had stayed in Hollywood, I'd have been a small-part actor all my life,' he maintains.

Perkins developed his ability in live television and on the Broadway stage. Five years after returning east, William Wyler cast him in *Friendly Persuasion*. His performance bought him screen success and won him an Oscar nomination.

Tony Perkins is not on my personal list of all-time great actors, but his professionally-competent performances are convincing, appealing and powerful, especially in roles which suit his distinctively-different, rather hypertonic personality. He projects screen naturalism, a boyish charm which, added to his solid acting background, assure him continuing screen stardom.

3. PERSONALITY APPEAL *AND* ACTING TALENT COUNT AT THE BOX OFFICE

Personality and physical appearance play a dominant part in determining the *type* of actor any person may become. Good looks and bright personality are two ingredients favorable to screen success, although they are no guarantee of it. Personality appeal — charisma — in the screen sense, is not necessarily derived from excellent acting. Not all screen idols have been nor are now, first-class actors. The screen stars of the 'twenties, 'thirties and 'forties, had beauty of feature and figure. It was important, it was thought, to sell beauty and glamor to audiences. Better acting would come with training at studio schools and with experience. Screen 'glamor' was the thing. Good acting was a bonus.

Studio talent scouts and agents searched for attractive young men and women with well-marked facial bone structure, eyes set well apart, well-shaped mouth, nice teeth, finely-proportioned forehead and nose and attractively-shaped head. Good figure, straight posture, ease of movement, pleasant voice tone, good height and bright personality rounded out the picture of a potential screen star. If an individual had acting talent, the opportunity for success was enhanced.

While few screen stars of today can claim all the attributes mentioned, many do possess these to some degree. Physical beauty and 'glamor' are not as important as they once were. Screen *appeal* plus acting *talent* are the present requirements. Audiences now demand more realistic screen stories and characters, which in turn, require a high standard of acting.

If the student of acting has an ability to project 'realism' through characterization, can act and presents well on the screen, chances are audiences will 'discover' him or her and want to see more. Beauty, *minus* talent, even though supported by Hollywood publicity, will be meaningless if the public fails to respond to a performer where it counts — at the box office.

4. ACTING REALISM

The meaning of realism in art and literature is: *the attempted picturing of people and things as they really are.* Acting realism is the playing of people as audiences expect them to look and sound. An actor creates an illusion of real people involved in real situations, playing his/her various characterizations in a natural way.

It should now be evident that the screen stage requires a different style of acting than does the theatre stage. Screen acting is more laid-back, more reined-in, more intimate and controlled than theatre acting. The subtle expressions required in close-up would be lost if duplicated for a theatre audience. Extended stage technique filmed in close-up would cause mild amusement to a screen audience. Screen acting realism cannot be attained by overplaying a role — extended movement, bigness of voice. Its expression is via the eyes and subtle use of body language. The screen actor must be seen to be truthfully experiencing all that he/she says and does. And, as in all acting mediums, the secret lies in *timing.*

The intimate nature of screen acting allows the player personal contact with each viewer. The screen actor talks to you, not the masses. In the theatre, this intimacy is not possible to the same degree. Visual dynamics and audio dynamics employed by the stage actor — even in the smallest theatre — require extension so that the audience can see and hear everything. The projected voice, sweeping gesture, valid for stage work, can destroy screen intimacy.

The screen actor is required to speak lines as though he/she has just thought of them and must move with purpose and ease. The screen actor must really listen to fellow players and react in a natural way befitting the character. This is not to say that the stage actor does not act in the same way, but it is the *degree* to which these actions are carried out that separates the two approaches to acting.

In Olivier's autobiography *Confessions of an Actor*, he discusses the difference between screen and stage acting, pointing out that at one time it was thought that they were two separate professions, two entirely different crafts. Not the case, he says. 'They call for the same ingredients but in different proportions.' It took Olivier many years to learn to film-act, to incorporate 'the truth demanded by the cinema' and to reduce the 'measure of theatricality'.

5. EXTENDED PLAYING STOPPED MANY STAGE ACTORS BECOMING SCREEN STARS

The established Broadway technique of the 'twenties and 'thirties was more showing off than acting realism. The stars of that period played full front and in high-profile, pounded their lines, tried to kill other actors' lines with extended gestures, moves and stage tricks. When the new, young English actors invaded Broadway, their American counterparts realised how poor their own work was. Noel Coward, Lynn Fontanne, Roland Young, Leslie Howard, Laurence Olivier, Gertrude Lawrence and others, moved about the stage with ease, spoke their lines in a subdued and subtle way. They actually paid attention to what fellow actors were saying. They were articulate, technically-proficient professionals.

From 1921 to the end of 1930, about 2000 plays were produced in New York, employing approximately 2000 American actors. Only five of the many who were invited to work in Hollywood became major screen stars: Clark Gable, James Cagney, Humphrey Bogart, Spencer Tracy and Fredric March. Others of course did rise from the ranks of musicals and from vaudeville. The ingrained acting habits of the New York stage actors were not suitable for the screen. Unable or reluctant to change, many stage actors missed a golden opportunity to become moving picture stars.

6. WHY IT'S DIFFICULT TO ACT NATURALLY

Carrying out normal every-day actions in a 'natural' way is a difficult task for most humans, for we spend much of our waking day 'in performance'. That is, in communicating with and attempting to impress others. Very few individuals are completely at ease, able to feel totally comfortable and relaxed when socializing or working closely with others. The tendency is to *perform*, rather than to *be*.

Generally speaking, we humans have a deep need to be liked. We desire to be respected, praised and acclaimed. In order to achieve our personal desires we feel it necessary to impress others. Strengths are displayed and weaknesses masked. A personal subtext is devised. We say we are happy, healthy, pleased, successful, when often, we are not. We say 'yes' when we feel like saying 'no'. We perform actions when we'd rather not because we do not wish to offend others. Whether we recognize it or not, all humans are actors playing out their lives on the stage of life.

What we do when we are unobserved, at ease, not under pressure, can be classified as 'natural' action. But, putting up a 'front', attempting to impress others is 'acting' rather than at-ease behavior. About the only time we do not *act* is when we are alone, without need to impress or when we are with close friends or family members.

What then, for the actor, is the meaning of so-called natural acting? It is, simply stated, being true to the personality of the character, speaking and acting as the character should, without affectation or falseness and without trying to impress an audience with 'look how good I am'. Truth in acting

a captures energetic playing of
n the John Patrick play *The Hasty*
Extended performance required
atre acting becomes too 'heavy' for
een. When the play was produced
motion picture, Ronald Reagan
and Richard Todd (Lachland) per-
with the right amount of energy
pression for the camera.

from the Los Angeles stage pro-
of *The Hasty Heart* shows the
(Digger) about to swat *Chuck*
(Tommy) as the two characters
ge friendly insults. Show was
d by *Walter Mills.*   ▶

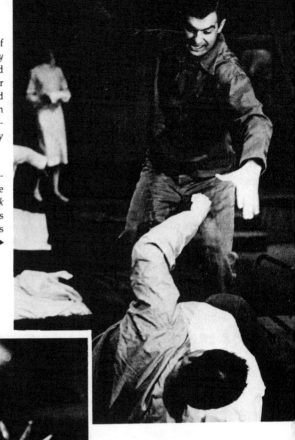

The stage production of Ira Levin's
Deathtrap requires energetic and powerful acting from the cast. The play transferred well to the screen. Michael Caine,
Dyan Cannon and Christopher Reeve
gave highly-spirited performances without going over-the-top for the camera.
Their playing is a good example of performance control for the screen.

Still from the Michael Edgley — J.C.
Williamson (Australian) stage production
of *Deathtrap*, directed by *Michael
Blakemore*, shows the author (Porter
Milgrim) sizing-up victim.
◀

prevails when an actor performs without self-conscious awareness, eliminating any desire to impress the spectators.

An actor's forces must not be wasted on unnatural efforts. He/she must give the 'self' completely to communing with the soul of the character to bring about a living image of the writer's invention. At this point, *natural* performance will come about.

7. RESIST FLIRTING WITH THE AUDIENCE

> *All acts in human life are natural until placed behind the footlights on the stage of life. There they become forced and artificial in an attempt to please and impress.*

The actor must resist the urge to 'show-off' during performance. Efforts designed to impress an audience produce acting artificialty. The actor must submit to rigid mental and physical discipline, concentrating his/her efforts on fitting comfortably into the character's surroundings. No time should be given to 'flirting' with an audience — this is exhibitionism. *Impression* playing kills-off inspiration. *Forced* acting smothers creativity. *Artificiality* devours realism. All three result in an amateurish style of overplaying.

8. BRING ONLY WHAT IS NEEDED TO THE MIND OF THE CHARACTER

Even the most professional of actors have difficulty evicting unwanted thoughts from their performances. Worries, problems to solve, unwell feelings require the strongest will to blot out during performance. When personal feelings intrude, attention divides itself between things on stage and things off stage. Divided attention dissipates energy, makes concentration difficult and creates performance uncertainty. When concentration shifts from the soul of the character to the soul of the actor, lines and moves become mechanical and devoid of inspiration.

Reject all thoughts extraneous to the life of the character. Center the attention where it belongs. Acting realism ceases the moment concentration of attention is lost to things outside the acting perimeter.

9. DRAW AN IMAGINARY CIRCLE AROUND THE ACTING PERIMETER

Stanislavski's *circle of attention* technique is a workable one, for it helps the actor to focus the attention on persons or objects within the performance area. The eye of the actor may pass from one point to another, but it must not go beyond the limit of the circle of attention. The area within the circle is lighted, the area beyond it is in darkness or invisible. All objects and persons within the circle draw the actor's attention, there is no attraction outside the circle.

Draw an imaginary circle around the acting perimeter, place yourself within the circle and isolate your attention to the actions occuring within it.

Your circle can be narrowed to include yourself and objects such as a chair, table, lamp or to include another person. The circle can be enlarged as you desire. As it expands, the attention stretches, taking in more objects and persons. By confining your attention to the actions within the imaginary circle, concentration is enhanced because your mind focuses on the *character's* feelings rather than on your personal worries and anxieties.

10. DON'T GET LOST IN ROLE PLAYING

Edmund Kean, considered one of the greatest poetic actors of the nineteenth century, became psychologically unbalanced because he could not distinguish between his acting roles and his own personality. In 1814, he made his first dramatic triumph as Shylock in *The Merchant of Venice*. He was a leading Shakespearean actor of his time, one who put great effort into trying to 'become' the characters he portrayed.

Actress Sarah Bernhardt, one of the greatest of her time, was admired because of her richness of voice tone, exquisite diction and grace of stage movement. Born in Paris in 1844, she toured the world scoring triumph after triumph. In 1912, she appeared in the film *Queen Elizabeth*. Bernhardt had similar problems to Kean in that she wanted to 'experience' all that her stage characters were supposed to experience. 'I must be the character, not just act the character,' she once told one of her tour promoters.

Submerging *too* much of the personal self into a characterization can result in loss of objectivity and control. An actor must retain some of his/her identity and all possible objectivity if there is to be command over the performance. Distinguish between your acting roles and your own personality. Remember, you cannot *be* anyone other than yourself, but you can become *like* another person, merge into the *image* of another person. Your stage task is to create an *illusion* of carrying out certain actions. When you control your work, creativity is enhanced, which in turn helps to sustain performance realism.

11. ON THE SCREEN IT'S THE APPEARANCE OF THINGS THAT COUNTS

The beginning of screen acting realism also brought a refinement in screenplay writing and directing. Writers fashioned their stories and characters in more realistic ways and directors showed greater insight into the presentation of life — more as it really is, rather than as it had been depicted in early films. From the late 'thirties on, actors, writers and directors refined their approach to the screen arts. Actors developed characterizations with understanding and feeling and *underplayed* rather than overplayed their roles.

The drastic changes in screen acting style meant that actors didn't strive to behave in a natural way, they strived to *appear* to be behaving naturally. Voices took on a conversational tone, faces became still rather than animated and gestures were restrained. The likes of Alan Ladd, Ronald Colman, John Garfield, Robert Taylor, Ida Lupino, Joan Fontaine, Ann

Sheridan, Loretta Young, etc portrayed their screen characters in a subtle and natural way. *Subdued* acting was the new method, the standard that potential stars were required to reach.

12. THE KEY TO NATURALISM IS SEEMING UNAWARENESS

One of the most important attributes a screen actor can obtain is the ability to perform with seeming *unawareness* of the spectator. Maintaining this illusion gives an audience the feeling that it is eavesdropping on the screen events. The technique requires mental concentration.

Actor Lloyd Nolan told me that seeming unawareness of an audience is vital to relaxed, natural acting. It's important to think about only what is happening in the scene. 'It's necessary to mask what's going on beyond the camera. My memory is a bit shaky, so I need to hold my attention to what the character is saying and doing. It's mental isolation. It helps to bring a better performance and create the illusion that what's going on is really taking place,' Lloyd told me.

I asked Shirley Jones how she managed to appear so natural in her screen roles and she replied: 'I take on the atmosphere of the scene. I allow the mood created by the other players, the set, the costumes and the lighting to create a reality of the events taking place. I close my mind to everything that is not related to the scene. I'm only aware of what's taking place in the scene and this helps me to feel the part.'

13. FIX THE POINT OF ATTENTION WHERE IT BELONGS

Give conscious thought to those things associated with the character's scene objectives. Don't admire yourself or become upset with yourself during a performance. Arrest runaway thoughts to prevent mental anarchy, incoherent speech actions and playing insecurity. Keep your attention *within* the acting perimeter.

Don't be half-in and half-out of the part. Transfer yourself from outside observer to inside participant. Put your imagination to work and involve yourself in role playing. This will help you to 'exist' in your imagined life. You will be in communion with your character's thoughts and look believable as you carry out his/her actions.

14. CARRY THE POINT OF ATTENTION THROUGH ENTIRE PERFORMANCE

When directing, I'm appalled whenever I discover an actor who identifies with the life of his/her character only when speaking assigned lines. I call it start-and-stop acting. As soon as the actor stops speaking and is required to listen, there is an immediate retreat into his/her private sanctum.

Start-and-stop acting deforms the life of a character. It throws out-of-kilter other actors' performances and is disturbing to those viewing the performance. The antidote is to fix the point of attention on the stage action.

15. STYLE AND NATURALISM

Style is a personal way of doing things, a characteristic manner of self-expression. It is a particular way of putting thoughts into words, an appropriateness of gesture and deportment. Style should not be confused with affected mannerisms, pretentiousness and unsubtle presentation of the self due to ego-tripping.

Most actors possess characteristics by which their work may be recognized. They display individual styles in their methods of acting. These characteristics transcend the techniques acquired through study, practice and experience. Style and naturalism are difficult qualities to capture. In simple terms, *style* is that personal stamp actors put on their work to make it unique and memorable.

16. CREATING REALISM THROUGH SINCERITY AND BELIEF

Acting requires an illusion of realism in its execution or an audience will quickly lose interest in the events and conflicts involving the characters. No amount of acquired 'technique' can make a performance interesting and 'alive' unless it is supported by an actor's *performance sincerity* and *belief* in the imaginary circumstances taking place.

An actor is said to be 'performance sincere' when there is *truthful* rendering of an author's work. This means that the actor *understands* the role to be portrayed and performs it in accord with the author's intent. It also means that the actor is able to *believe* in the given circumstances and carries them out with a sense of *realism*. When this does not occur, an actor is said to be 'faking performance' and displaying 'performance insincerity'.

Director George Cukor, watched his actors carefully to spot performance faking. 'Many times an actor will try to get away with faking a scene, will make a big show of trying to "look" the part. I can see through it and so can the camera, particularly when it's right up close. A lot of stage actors need to learn to act for the camera. They can't fling themselves around, suffering pretentiously. That's sham acting. Sincere acting is devoid of tricks. It doesn't try to bluff and that's the key to screen acting realism,' the celebrated director told a Los Angeles student group.

Cukor had little patience for 'those actors who fail to examine their lines' and especially for those who demanded to alter their dialogue. 'If actors don't keep to the author's words, things get fuzzy. There's got to be belief behind what an actor says. The text has to be delivered with meaning intact, which means an understanding of it and belief in it.' And Cukor's advice to aspiring actors: 'Learn your craft. Don't be an eternal amateur. Become a professional.'

17. GARY COOPER WAS ONE OF SCREEN'S MOST NATURAL PLAYERS

The late Gary Cooper began his acting career in silent movies. His first talkie, *The Virginian*, launched him as a major screen star. His performances caused many film writers to tag him, 'the actor who least seems to act'. His stiff mannerisms, awkward way of delivering lines but natural warmth, were appealing qualities which endeared him to audiences. His unique acting style won him Oscars for his roles in *Sergeant York* (1941) and *High Noon* (1952).

D.W. Griffith held the view that Gary Cooper was one of the very few Hollywood actors who could perform in a perfectly natural way. 'His was an unusual style, laid-back, hesitant, stripped of affectation. He spoke his lines as if he'd just thought of them,' said Griffith.

Ingrid Bergman, who worked with Cooper in *For Whom The Bell Tolls* and *Saratoga Trunk*, felt he was the most natural actor she ever worked with. 'When he went into his dialogue, I thought he was still talking to me. He didn't change his voice or move a muscle. He was exactly the same off the set as he was when acting. I thought our work would be a disaster until I saw the rushes. His personality on the screen was overpowering, his manner so natural,' she said.

18. BERGMAN'S STYLE WAS SIMPLE AND UNAFFECTED

Ingrid Bergman's naturalness and unaffected charm, combined with her beauty and acting ability, made an immediate impact on Hollywood when producer David O. Selznick brought her from Sweden to star in the English version of *Intermezzo: A Love Story*. She won two Oscars, *Gaslight* in 1944 and *Anastasia* in 1956. Many of her fans felt she should have won in 1943 for her exceptional characterization as Ilsa Lund in *Casablanca*.

Perhaps the secret of acting success for both Ingrid Bergman and Gary Cooper is that their acting remained simple, uncluttered and natural throughout their careers. They were actors who perfected the art of screen performance realism.

19. BOGART ADDED MYSTERY TO HIS NATURALNESS

It has been said that, to become a screen star, it is necessary to add mystery and eccentricity to naturalness and talent, so that audiences can admire or puzzle over the things that are different and unique.

Humphrey Bogart had an unusual twitching of his upper lip when he spoke and he 'colored' his dialogue by stretching the vowel sounds in key words. He portrayed unusual, mysterious characters. Some of them possessed qualities and capacities most people find highly charismatic. Within a world of fantasy, Bogart created seemingly real screen characters. His acting talent won him an Oscar in 1951 for his role as the whiskey-soaked boatman in *The African Queen*.

Legions of fans still line up at the box office to see his films. *The Maltese Falcon* (1941), *Casablanca* (1943), *The Treasure of the Sierra Madre* (1948), *The Caine Mutiny* (1954) and *The Harder They Fall* (1956), are among his best and most popular films. The Bogey cinematic cult lives on.

Bogart first appeared on Broadway in *Drifting* in 1921. A year later, he

From 1930 to 1956 *Humphrey Bogart* made 75 films. And on his own admission, some of them were 'stinkers'. He felt that *John Huston* qualified as 'the best director around.' Bogart asked actor *Holbrook Blinn* how he could build a reputation. Blinn replied: 'Keep working. If people keep seeing you they'll think you're pretty good and producers will hire you.'

made two films, *A Devil With Women* and *Up The River*. His early film career was unspectacular. When he made *The Petrified Forest* in 1936, he became one of the three resident actors who specialized in gangster roles on the Warner Brothers lot. His career surged after the release of *The Maltese Falcon* and was consolidated as King of the Warner lot when he was nominated for an Academy Award for *Casablanca*. Audiences were delighted when he was paired with Lauren Bacall in *To Have and Have Not, The Big Sleep, Dark Passage* and *Key Largo*.

Bogart thought of himself as a *technique* actor. He loathed having to work with 'those pseudo-method actors who think they're Stanislavski.' Questioned by a reporter as to his success as an actor, Bogart replied: 'I think my way into a role. If you think it, you'll look it. If you feel upset, you'll look upset. You've got to know the ropes. Confidence comes from knowing your trade, it has nothing to do with vanity.'

Bogart knew how to abuse people on and off the screen. He was a nonconformist, an individualist, perhaps more individual than any other actor in Hollywood history. Above all, he was a first-rate screen actor who knew his trade, knew how to appear natural, mysterious and effective in performance. Bogart was and still is, a hero to millions. And let Ingrid Bergman have the last word on the talent of Bogart: 'He was a natural actor who had no complications getting into the mood. He was always in the mood. He worked hard and was concerned about his scenes. In Casablanca, you realize what an enormous talent he had with that tough way, yet he brings out so much love. I greatly admired him as an actor.'

20. ACQUIRING NATURALISM THROUGH TECHNIQUE

All great actors possess a particular 'quality' that is inherent, but no performer can adequately present that quality until there is mastery of the acting instrument and then control over the material to be performed. With control comes confidence and as Bogart once remarked, 'confidence comes from knowing your trade'. Knowing your trade means to apply what has been learned through study, training and experience. Acting naturalism cannot be taught. It has to be acquired via personal observation and practice, then nurtured through experience and the application of technique.

The purpose of this chapter has been to focus the reader's attention on the essential ingredients which help to produce an 'ease' of acting. Character realism cannot be achieved by trick acting. It must surface through technique, an applied skill which is personal to each actor. Mere behavior — walking through a role — is not substantial enough to bring interesting and captivating screen performance. Therefore, it is necessary to discover your own 'special' way to be effective in performance.

21. BELIEVABILITY AND NATURALNESS ULTIMATE GOALS OF SCREEN ACTING

Technique depends upon dynamics of vocalization and expressive movement. Both speech and body dynamics convey the image of the character as he/she is seen in your mind's eye and ear. The deeper the acquaintance of acting technique, the easier it is to 'feel' the inner life of your role.

Believability and naturalness of performance are screen actors' basic goals. Characterization as expressed through speech, gesture and body movement, must be born from the play itself, from the thoughts, feelings and desires of the character. Providing you believe in the truth of your character's actions, rather than in their reality, you will be well on your way to the achievement of believable and natural performance.

Arthur Rubinstein said, 'You've got to possess talent. But you can learn a basic attitude toward your craft.' His statement just about sums up what professional screen performance is all about.

SUMMARY OF IDEAS TO REVIEW

1: The quality an actor exudes as a person will be the *basis* of his/her characterizations. The quality of personality, attached to acting skill, helps to produce screen magnetism — essential for stardom. Presence *and* talent count at the box office.

2: Acting realism is the portrayal of persons as audiences expect them to sound and look. Actors are in the business of creating *illusions* of reality.

3: The screen actor talks to *you*, not to the masses. This requires subtle performance, not overplaying. Accommodate the closeness of the camera and microphone. Realize the closeness of the audience to the screen action.

4: Resist flirting with an audience. Keep your mind on role playing, not on impressing the audience with your acting.

5: Draw an imaginary circle around the acting perimeter. Place yourself within the circle and isolate your attention to the action within it.

6: Do not lose control of your acting instrument by submerging *too* much of yourself in the role. You cannot *be* another person but you can become *like* another person. Retain objectivity.

7: Seeming unawareness is the essence of acting naturalism. The viewer should feel as though he/she is 'eavesdropping' on private conversations and actions.

8: Fix the point of attention on the stage action and don't release it until the performance is over. Do not break the ebb-and-flow of stage life.

9: Create your own acting 'style' — a personal way of speaking and moving.

10: Work toward believability and acting naturalness, the ultimate goals of screen performance. Believe in your character's actions.

CREATIVE
PERFORMANCE
TECHNIQUES

SCENE **14**

Practical Ideas In This Chapter . . .

- Technique Brings Acting Competence
- Develop Technique Through Discovery Advises Hollywood Coach
- Creative Expression Finds Its Outlet Through Technique
- Understand What You Are To Do Before Attempting To Do It
- *Who-What-When-Where-Why-How* Theory
- The Nature of Human Actions
- The Reality of Human Actions
- Actions of Fictional Characters
- Study Human *Attitude* Action Playing
- The Technique of Justifiable *Attitude* Action Playing
- Naming Actions
- *Attitude* Action Playing Example
- 9/10ths Analysis To Establish Feelings And Justify Actions
- Don't Learn Lines Says Kirk Douglas Study Them
- Image Recall And Subconscious Impression Playing
- Catalogue Past Events Impressions And Feelings
- Externals Stimulate Feelings
- Dormant Feelings Which Relate To Externals
- Understanding The Sensory Receptors
- Attitudes-Feelings-Actions (Chart)
- Sight And Sound Most Important of Senses
- Use The Senses For All They Are Worth
- Exercises To Enhance Sensory Awareness
- The Nervous System Controls Thought, Feeling And Movement
- Perception And Awareness
- Points of Reference
- Inner And Outer Scenic Environment Adjustment
- Kybernetic Attack
- An Actor Must Control Energy Said Burton
- Inject Life Into A Part By Energizing It
- Drive Personal Magnetism Through Characterization
- Create An Inner Flame To Illuminate Emotions And Actions
- Sing Inside To Create Life In Art Said Rubenstein
- Technique And Emotion Key To Torvill And Dean Artistry
- Repressed Physical Acting
- Avoiding Audience Communication Lag Where Possible
- Communicate On The Same Wavelength With Fellow Players
- The Seriousness of Playing Comedy
- Techniques For Playing Comedy
- The Comedy Genius of The Marx Brothers
- An Insight Into Comedy
- Suggestions On Acting From Dame Sybil Thorndike
- The Actor's Dual Personality
- Controlled Personality Identification
- Search The Interior World
- Approach The Art of Acting With Intelligence
- Summary of Ideas To Review

SCENE 14

★★

1. TECHNIQUE BRINGS ACTING COMPETENCE

Many persons have a keen interest in becoming professional actors. But interest alone is not enough. Interest needs to be coupled to knowledge and skill in order to enhance performance success.

As a teacher of drama and screen directing, I am concerned that so many drama students fail to recognize the necessity of acquiring a sound technique, a means to making them flexible enough to play many different roles.

More and more directors are calling for actors with trained voices and bodies, professionals who have learned their trade. Personality-veneer and an attractive face are insufficient to win roles which demand technical skill and a deep understanding of the means to bring about correct characterization.

The screen actor must be seen, heard and understood. The skill to be so in a *convincing* and *realistic* way is what acquired technique can accomplish. Technique is an actor's passport to competent performance.

One of the many benefits of acting is the increase in personal joy and creative satisfaction as skill is acquired. It is not an overnight jump from inexperience to experience. Skill is gained from extensive knowledge, study, practice, perseverance underscored by patience and lots of it. Studying the principles of acting, both classic *technique* and Stanislavski's *system*, will occupy a great deal of time, but the serious-minded student will work hard and long to produce a *personal* technique upon which to construct the many characterizations he/she may be required to play.

2. DEVELOP TECHNIQUE THROUGH DISCOVERY ADVISES HOLLYWOOD COACH

One of the most sincere, dedicated and knowledgeable drama teachers I've known is Sondra Rodgers. An excellent actress with experience in radio, stage, television and films, she is perhaps best remembered for her strong portrayal of Shellie, in the Universal film *Tap Roots*.

Until recently, Miss Rodgers devoted much of her time and energy to private drama coaching in Hollywood. Her students were given intensive training in speech and interpretation and taught discipline and professionalism. She advised them to acquire as deep an awareness of life as possible and to be more sensitive to people, places and things. She put them on life's road to discovery.

She feels that actors must open their minds and hearts to new experiences if they want to be effective and creative as actors recreating human existence. 'Remove the blinkers and open the five senses,' she says. 'Far too many actors, even seasoned professionals, stay too long with old thoughts because of their tendency to be isolationists. No actor can afford to mentally and emotionally stagnate. Acting is a lifelong study of piling knowledge-upon-knowledge and experience-upon-experience. Discovery advances technique,' she says.

Miss Rodgers made a regular practice of escorting her students on field trips to broaden their knowledge. Art galleries, music recitals, the zoo, botanical gardens, introductions to interesting people, even lawn cemeteries were visited. 'Everything in life has a value if proper attention is given to it. Whatever you see and hear, wherever you go, whomever you meet, try to discover something worthwhile which can be used in developing technique and applied to role playing,' she once instructed me during an enlightening trip to the Japanese Gardens in Pasadena, California.

I shall be eternally grateful for all that Sondra Rodgers taught me. She is a person of compassion, wisdom and of selfless dedication to the service of others. As a former student, I have great respect for her training method. I only wish that there were more like her.

3. CREATIVE EXPRESSION FINDS ITS OUTLET THROUGH TECHNIQUE

Sometimes an actor will become severely critical of personal performance efforts. His/her characterization concepts fail to find suitable expression in performance. The harder the effort, the less is achieved. Unable to find creative satisfaction, the actor becomes tense, anxious and insecure about future acting assignments. It's frustrating not being able to 'put across' what is 'felt' and intended. And to the dedicated artist, an idea conceived but unable to find expression is sheer torment.

A well-known actor I dialogue-coached for an important film role, told me that his ideas for the part were clear in his mind but weren't finding expression at rehearsals. 'I cannot put across the effects I want and it's exasperating,' he said. I explained that his main problem lay in his lack of

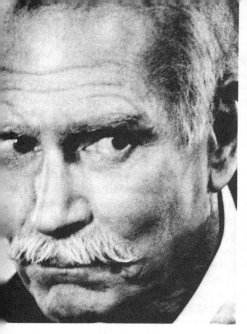

Laurence Olivier, recognized as one of the best exponents of classic technique acting. He began his screen career in 1930 in *The Temporary Widow*.

Screen star, *Cary Grant*, knew secret of ▲ camera technique. His first film was *This Is The Night*, made in 1932.

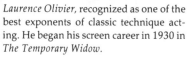

Sondra Rodgers in medium three-shot with *Whitfield Connor* and *Susan Hayward* in scene from Universal International's *Tap Roots*. Miss Rodgers ranked as one of Hollywood's best drama coaches.

technique. He was unable to direct his instrument to perform effectively due to his lack of knowledge and practice in this area.

Technique is the means by which an actor is able to express his/her character conceptions in a clear, truthful and meaningful way. It is the ability to render artistic work with a high degree of expertness. Therefore, it requires a mastery of the acting instrument. In this regard, self and formal training are a must. Study, observation, awareness and as Sondra Rodgers suggests, 'removing the blinkers and opening the five senses', are ways to develop personal technique. When you broaden your knowledge generally, you stretch your interpretive ability and advance your acting skill. It is not a difficult undertaking, but it does require time and effort. The actor who is desirous of becoming a respected craftsperson can, with patience and perseverance, teach him/herself sufficient technique to improve the clarity and style of personal performance.

4. UNDERSTAND WHAT YOU ARE TO DO BEFORE ATTEMPTING TO DO IT

Every actor of experience consciously or unconsciously takes apart an assigned role *prior* to line memorization. Pre-characterization analysis is insurance against doing injustice to the author's intent, taking a role for granted or ending up with a single-dimension character.

Gain an understanding of the motives behind the character's actions. Examine the circumstances of the character's past and present life and what hopes the character has for the future. When you fully comprehend your part, the playing is easier because you have put yourself 'in contact' with the author's wishes for the character you have been assigned.

5. WHO-WHAT-WHEN-WHERE-WHY-HOW THEORY

Proper role research — appraising the facts as revealed by the writer — helps to determine underlying dialogue intent and to relate that intent to the meaning of the play. The key to a character's inner existence is secreted within the text and often requires patient research to reveal it. The more story and character background information at your disposal, the more coherent and exacting will be your performance. The *who-what-when-where-why-how* theory is a method of discovering *extra* information to assist you to better relate your character to other characters and to the circumstances and events as they unfold.

WHO is the character — protagonist or antagonist? Good person or bad person? Helpful person or obstructionist? Intelligent person or not-too-bright person?

WHAT emotional transitions must the character make within and between scenes? Identify their nature as to whether they are positive or negative.

WHEN does the character first reveal his/her major objective(s)? At what point in the story does your character encounter objectives success or failure?

WHERE does the central action take place? Does the scenic environment influence your character's actions?

WHY does the character behave as he/she does?

HOW does the conflict between your character and others resolve? And what feelings are harbored by your character toward others throughout the story and particularly at its close?

6. THE NATURE OF HUMAN ACTIONS

All life is an expression of action. Human life consists of the attainment of an uninterrupted series of objectives. In the course of reaching personal objectives, humans carry out specific actions — all day, every day. External actions are motivated by *internal* impulses and desires. Things 'felt' and 'desired' become objectives (goals) to achieve.

True action — normal, natural human behavior — has a sense of purpose, a certain logic about it. True action has *inner* justification. An idea becomes an act only when *motivated* to do so. When it is acted upon it leaves the imagination and enters the world of actuality. A justifiable inner objective sets the scene for justifiable outer action.

7. THE REALITY OF HUMAN ACTIONS

Normal human actions begin as 'ideas' in the conscious mind. They are 'visualized' and 'experienced' internally before taking shape externally. Visual images have the power to arouse emotions which in turn stimulate actions. Consciously-conceived objectives require consciously-conceived actions to bring them to reality.

Things we desire to experience externally can be experienced internally via our imagination. We can play the game of pretends by throwing up onto the screen of our imagination the actions of buying a new car, taking an overseas vacation, purchasing a new wardrobe, winning stardom, etc. However, for most of us, pretending to be, to do and to have is unsatisfactory. We desire to experience the *reality* of things hoped for. We seek to turn the unreal into the real, to experience things on the physical plane as well as the mental plane.

Pretending to be, to do and to have ceases the moment we begin external action playing. Internal plans become external acts in a desire to reach objectives. Somewhere along the way a personal technique surfaces and it is used in action playing to enhance the achievement of objectives. It comes in the form of *attitudes* which reveal desires, opinions, prejudices and general disposition. Attitudes produce a *manner* of acting. They reveal our innermost thoughts and feelings.

8. ACTIONS OF FICTIONAL CHARACTERS

A writer's fictional characters are assigned personal objectives and these are supported by justifiable reasons for their fulfillment. It is the job of the actor to perform the character's actions in a clearly definable way so that an audience may easily comprehend them.

In the pursuit of objectives, a character's attitudes and actions — what the character says and does — must appear to be logical, justifiable and sometimes predictable. Illogical attitudes and actions, due to actor incompetence, poor writing or both, will not receive audience acceptance. Therefore, the actor must develop a workable technique to perform actions in a seemingly realistic way — with justification — rather than in a staged and mechanical or uncommunicative way.

9. STUDY HUMAN *ATTITUDE* ACTION PLAYING

Actors are advised to make an in-depth study of their own attitudes and actions taken in pursuit of personal objectives. Analyse *what* is thought about, spoken and then carried through as a physical action. Understand *how* and *why* actions are taken. Also, observe the attitudes and actions of others in their quest to do, to be and to have. Are their motives and objectives linked to and clearly revealed in their actions? An analysis of human *action playing* will assist in discovering a workable technique for *character* action playing.

10. THE TECHNIQUE OF JUSTIFIABLE *ATTITUDE* ACTION PLAYING

The key to playing stage actions is to understand the character's *attitudes* — what he/she thinks and feels and *why*. As already mentioned, information of this kind is to be found within the character's assigned lines. Keep in mind that fictional characters, like real people, strike *attitudes* which motivate *actions* to fulfill objectives. Normal behavior, as a rule, has a sense of purpose about it. It can be justified in some way. Link attitudes and actions to the character's objectives. Justify in your own mind *why* the character speaks and acts as he/she does.

Playing an action is doing something of a specific nature to reach an objective. The technique of justifiable *attitude* action playing encompasses the following three aspects:

(1) The *pinpointing* of the character's minor and major *objectives* in every scene in which he/she appears.
(2) The *clarifying* of the *actions* to be undertaken in the pursuit of objectives.
(3) The *practice* of using an *active verb* to name attitudes/actions in order to play lines with the correct intent.

Because a character's objectives are 'suggested' or 'revealed' in assigned dialogue, a study of the text — speech-by-speech — is necessary to uncover *inner* meanings which, in turn, suggest ways of delivering the lines and playing suitable physical actions in the pursuit of objectives.

Simply stated, *dialogue* action playing is a specific manner of stating something which clearly reveals the speaker's attitude relative to the objective he/she seeks to achieve. *Physical* action playing is expressed via body language and it may or may not be accompanied by dialogue.

310

After pinpointing the character's objectives and comprehending the intent of the lines to be delivered, go back to the text and 'tag' the attitude(s) each speech expresses. A character's attitude emerges out of the statements made or the questions he/she asks. The character desires something to occur or not to occur, so speaks and acts in the pursuit of or the defence of personal objectives. All human action is an expression of attitude: thoughts, beliefs, feelings, needs, wants.

A character's attitudes are not fixed. They are flexible and change according to how he/she sees and feels about things at a particular point in time. A character's attitudes are often directly or indirectly influenced by others. Each speech assigned to a character will contain one or more attitudes to be expressed. Each attitude, generally speaking, requires a different playing action. When one action has been played it can be forgotten, allowing the next one to be expressed. In this regard, it is essential to know when each objective is achieved or attempted and rejected. If, for example, the first objective is to quench your thirst, then your physical action is to drink a glass of water. When you have fulfilled this objective and your thirst has been satisfied, your playing action is complete and you move on to the next one.

Dialogue actions need not accompany *physical* actions. In this instance they become verbal and emotional actions played on another character to bring about a specific response. If, for example, the playing action is to *emotionally* hurt another character, then the dialogue is delivered with that intent in mind. Hurtfulness is expressed via the attitude struck and the manner in which the dialogue is spoken. The action is played *through* the lines. The 'attack' is a verbal one, not a physical one and is fulfilled at the completion of the speech. The objective is won or lost according to the *reaction* of the other character. If the character has a change of heart and apologizes for the remarks, then the action changes as a new attitude is struck.

11. NAMING ACTIONS

Naming or 'tagging' actions is a relatively simple process. The rule is to avoid words that are too general in their description of attitudes to strike. Be specific by using an active verb which itself will suggest the objective and allow the action to be performed at once. Pin down the attitude. Does it represent what the character desires to achieve? An attitude is a reflection of a mood, an emotion, a desire, a belief. Decide upon the attitude each line suggests. When you strike the correct attitude, you automatically play the correct action — your dialogue sounds right and your actions seem right.

As an additional aid to action playing, preface the active verb with the words, 'I desire to . . .' or simply, 'to . . .'. Examples of active verbs which describe and link attitudes and objectives and are immediately 'actable' through the expression of dialogue, include:

| To *threaten* | To *vilify* | To *compliment* |
| To *berate* | To *charm* | To *reveal* |

311

To *organize*	To *protest*	To *applaud*
To *thank*	To *challenge*	To *laugh-off*
To *insinuate*	To *dismiss*	To *defend*
To *relax*	To *justify*	To *stir*
To *persist*	To *stall*	To *attack*
To *provoke*	To *goad*	To *oppose*
To *coax*	To *pacify*	To *confront*
To *escape*	To *probe*	To *rescue*
To *appraise*	To *prompt*	To *chastise*

12. *ATTITUDE* ACTION PLAYING EXAMPLE

In the example which follows, George has two minor objectives to achieve in his meeting with Helen which, if successful, pave the way for the achievement of his major objective — to marry her. George, as his first goal, needs Helen's confidence before he can win his second objective — to take her to dinner. Write in the blank space what you think George's attitudes/actions should be.

GEORGE

To _____ Helen, you're the kind of girl every man would like to marry.

HELEN

George, you're a flatterer.

GEORGE

To _____ Would you have dinner with me?

HELEN

I don't know you.

GEORGE

To _____ I'll tell you about myself over dinner.

HELEN

Sorry. I don't know anything about you.

GEORGE

To _____ I'm a lawyer. I work for the State Department.

To _____ Your brother's a lawyer. He knows me.

HELEN

Lawyers can be scoundrels.

GEORGE

To _____ Not this one. My reputation means everything.

To _____ The Attorney General hired me.

That's a recommendation, isn't it?

To _____ Please, give us both a chance. One dinner.

HELEN

Allright. One dinner. And we'll see.

13. 9/10THS ANALYSIS TO ESTABLISH FEELINGS AND JUSTIFY ACTIONS

During the late winter period of 1954, I made an Atlantic crossing from Liverpool to Boston on a rather small passenger-cargo ship. For most of the journey, the ship rolled and pitched its way in heavy seas. The days were windy, wet and gray. Because of the intense cold most passengers remained below-decks. One particularly bleak morning, I decided to brave the elements and take a brisk walk on deck to stave off sea sickness. I noticed a ship's officer taking photographs of small, white formations protruding from the water.

'Icebergs and mighty dangerous,' he told me. There were a lot of them and the ship's captain had reduced speed as a precautionary measure. 'They seem small and rather harmless,' I said. 'They may look that way, but nine-tenths of their substance lies beneath the waterline. It's what can't be seen, what isn't obvious that one has to look for,' he replied.

Whenever I prepare for a part I think about those icebergs in the Atlantic. It's what lies *below* the surface that counts. Nine-tenths of a character's personality is often secreted within the lines spoken by other characters or indicated not so much by what the character *says* but by what he/she *does*. Clues to a character's thoughts and feelings are found not by accident but by an in-depth analysis of the entire script.

All humans have private thoughts and feelings which influence their behavior. The subconscious is the storehouse of these concepts and emotion memories. The subconscious represents nine-tenths of an individual's existence because it holds *keys* to life itself — knowledge, awareness, perception, intuition and control over bodily function. The subconscious is the seat of our emotions. It is the *activator* of our actions.

An actor must learn to penetrate the 'subconscious' of his/her character in order to successfully understand the thoughts, feelings and physical actions. The 9/10th analysis method helps to discover a character's underlying thoughts and feelings which motivate physical actions. Through script analysis and other research, it is possible to create a personality, a *soul* for a character, in addition to a scenic truth in which the actor can believe while he/she is in performance.

The 9/10ths analysis method seeks what is below the surface of seemingly ordinary lines. It decodes subtext material, discovers the character's prejudices, peculiarities, desires and intentions. It is a deep penetration of the author's work coupled to internal and external research which provides a solid base upon which to construct a true-to-life character. This method of study deals in specifics, not generalities. It supplies the actor with action motives so that everything the character says and does is logical. It helps the actor to deduce from the assigned dialogue and other sources of inquiry, the character's physiology, sociology and psychology. It encourages the use of imagination and intuition.

The 9/10ths analysis method is an intellectual approach to discovering the author's intent. It proceeds beyond standard line study and memorization, encouraging the actor to penetrate the subconscious to stir memories and recall specific incidents and feelings. It is painstaking research which results in story and character revelation leading to in-depth playing. The information gained forms the nucleus of a fictional character's body and soul.

14. DON'T LEARN LINES SAYS KIRK DOUGLAS STUDY THEM

I attended a private screening of a film starring Kirk Douglas at the home of actress and television personality Pamela Mason. Mr. Douglas was in attendance. I asked him how he managed to bring such realism to his screen roles. 'Lines have to become familiar. I dig into them. I don't learn lines. I study them, get to know what the writer wants his character to be. It has nothing to do with learning lines. Any fool can do that. I have to know what a character thinks and feels before I can speak his lines. I have to construct attitudes for him, wear his moods, understand his goals. Research, not just reading lines is the key. I commit myself to research,' Kirk Douglas told me.

Kirk Douglas came to films via Broadway. Hal Wallis signed him to his first screen role in *The Strange Love of Martha Ivers*, produced in 1946. Three years later he was propelled to stardom in *The Champion*, a boxing drama. Some of his best work has been with frequent co-star, Burt Lancaster. Both actors have a dynamic screen presence and work extremely well together. In 1983, Douglas played a dual role in the Australian art film *The Man From Snowy River*. Worth study are five of the star's most interesting characterizations: *Out of The Past* (1947), *Detective Story* (1951), *Lust For Life* (1956), *Paths of Glory* (1958) and *Seven Days In May* (1964).

15. IMAGE RECALL AND SUBCONSCIOUS IMPRESSION PLAYING

Laurence Olivier stated he's a scavenger. He scavenges human life to help prepare for a role, taking anything needed to expand his character and make him real. 'You pick up small bits of things like people crossing a street, making a telephone call, eating in a restaurant, buying something in a store, giving someone directions and you store it in your mind for later use. When it needs to be brought back it appears as an image, a mental impression which the subconscious has kept,' he said.

It has already been stated that nine-tenths of a person's life is tucked away within that person's subconcious mind. Millions of bits of information, both small and large, along with impressions, lie dormant in the memory ready to surface on demand. The nature of these 'memories' and the impressions created at the time of discovery, determine how vividly one may recall them at some future time as inner images and feelings.

Image recall and subconscious impression playing is a technique actors can use to bring to characterization and performance, personal feelings, memories and images of past events which correspond to the emotions and events taking place in the life of the character. If sadness, due to the loss of a loved one is the character's emotion, then the actor searches his/her background to recall a similar event which caused sadness. By *associating* circumstances and events and remembering the feelings which were aroused at the time, emotional truth is injected into performance. *Image recall* throws onto the screen of the mind *pictures* of events, people, places and things. *Subconscious impressions* associated with these mental pictures return to be 're-lived' as *feelings* in the stage character's life.

16. CATALOGUE PAST EVENTS IMPRESSIONS AND FEELINGS

It is a good idea to catalogue the major and minor events which have occurred in your life and to carefully note the impressions and feelings they engendered. Write them down in a notebook. List them according to their positive or negative aspects — whether they represented successes or failures, brought happiness or sadness. Recall your reactions to others who were involved in each event or situation and how they acted toward you.

Catalogue past and present relationships with family members, close friends and casual acquaintances. What kinds of people attract you? How do others influence you? Have your friends helped or hindered you? Do you find it easy to get along with others? How do you act when meeting others for the first time? Can you recognize insecurity or insincerity in others?

When preparing for a role, discover if your own personality and lifestyle match the character's in any way. Do you share the character's moral stance, religious and political persuasion, general approach to life? Is there anything from your past that can be used to enhance your understanding and playing of the character's actions? *Persist* — search your past to resurrect images, impressions and feelings that are helpful to performance. If you cannot generate appropriate feelings, you will never play a part well. Your performances will be mechanical, devoid of creativity because they lack understanding and 'heart'. Remember: in art it's the *feeling* that counts.

17. EXTERNALS STIMULATE FEELINGS

Emotions are not manifested at random. They lie dormant, waiting to 'flare-up' when stimulated, motivated or provoked. They are part of every human's life. They reside in the subconscious — always present. Life would be meaningless without them. Feelings bring purpose and meaning to life. Actors are well advised to come to grips with their feelings, to get to know them, to awaken them and to know how to motivate them during performance.

All emotions have a common characteristic: they are internal effects related to external causes which in turn become motivators of actions. They are responses to information derived from the senses. Humans are affected by and respond to the things they see, hear, taste, touch and smell. The sensory receptors are human guideposts, constant informants to the brain. It would be difficult, if not impossible, to live without them.

18. DORMANT FEELINGS WHICH RELATE TO EXTERNALS

Our feelings are aroused when we see, hear, taste, touch or smell things of a positive or negative nature. A bad road smash, if seen and heard, can produce unpleasant feelings. It could also arouse a feeling of sympathy for those injured. Witnessing two friends being united in marriage can arouse a feeling of goodwill for the couple's future and bring personal joy. To hear of the death of a friend or loved one can bring feelings of sadness, loneliness and remorse. To hear of a deserving person's good fortune can bring feelings of satisfaction, pride and happiness. The *impressions* we form of people, places and things stimulate our emotions and our emotions motivate us to take specific courses of action.

Feelings which lie dormant in the deeper mind awaiting arousal, include: fear, anger, inferiority, envy, jealousy, hate, boredom, loneliness, unhappiness, remorse, happiness, pride, sympathy, confidence, love, compassion. (Refer to the Attitudes/Feelings/Actions Chart.)

19. UNDERSTANDING THE SENSORY RECEPTORS

Senses are the means by which we humans can *tune-in* to life, to understand what is happening in our environment. Scientists have discovered that humans have more than five senses. These additional senses give information about body needs such as, hunger, pain and thirst. Senses are divided into two groups:

(1) **INTERNAL SENSES:** these detect internal body changes. They send messages about body changes to the brain for action. They respond to chemical and physical stimuli in the circulatory, digestive, respiratory, excretory and central nervous systems. They control such feelings as pain, fatigue, hunger and thirst. They also respond to the position and movement of the joints, to tension in the muscles and to the position of the head. Internal senses maintain order within the body.

(2) **EXTERNAL SENSES:** some of these senses detect things far from the body and other things which come in contact with it. We detect things in the external environment with our senses of sight, hearing and heat. These are called *distance receiving senses*, requiring a minimum of stimulus to respond. The senses of taste, touch and smell involve contact with the body and are called *contact external senses*, requiring a large stimulus to respond. Intense pressure needs to be applied to the skin to feel an object and many thousands of molecules of a substance need to be present for something to be tasted.

ATTITUDES
STIMULATE *FEELINGS* WHICH MOTIVATE
ACTIONS

NEGATIVE ATTITUDES-FEELINGS

HATE
ENVY
GREED
PREJUDICE
JEALOUSY
BOREDOM
DISAPPOINTMENT
UNHAPPINESS
FRUSTRATION
ANXIETY
FEAR

MOTIVATE **NEGATIVE**
ACTS OF . . .

HOSTILITY
SELFISHNESS
AGGRESSION
VIOLENCE

POSITIVE ATTITUDES-FEELINGS

LOVE
KINDNESS
SYMPATHY
HAPPINESS
SELF-CONFIDENCE
GOOD HUMOR
FORGIVENESS
ENTHUSIASM
HUMILITY
CONTENTMENT
TRANQUILITY

MOTIVATE **POSITIVE**
ACTS OF . . .

FRIENDLINESS
HELPFULNESS
CO-OPERATIVENESS
GENEROSITY

317

20. SIGHT AND SOUND MOST IMPORTANT OF SENSES

Sight and sound are the most receptive of impressions of our five senses. Impressions are readily made through our eyes and ears. In addition to outer vision and outer sound, humans have the ability to create *inner* images and sounds. The sights we see on the external plane can be created on the internal plane — projected onto the screen of the mind. External sounds can be reconstructed and heard in the inner ear of the mind. Our senses of taste, touch and smell play an auxiliary role in acting but are most helpful in influencing our emotion memory.

21. USE THE SENSES FOR ALL THEY ARE WORTH

The word *feeling* conjures up many ideas as to what life is, how it can affect us, give to us, take from us. All of our life-long experiences come out of our feelings. Our relationships with others, with places and things create feelings, *experiences* of life both pleasant and unpleasant. And through our sensory receptors, the things we *see*, the sounds we *hear*, the things we *taste*, the objects we *touch* and the aromas we *smell*, all stimulate and motivate particular feelings which in turn bring about specific courses of action. In *Confessions of an Actor*, Olivier mentions how once he stopped for a meal in Orange (France) and it being so delicious 'it caused me to weep.'

Most of us take for granted the extraordinary work carried out on our behalf by the sensory receptors. Thought should be given to how our life might alter if one or more of these marvellous life-giving instruments were to cease functioning. Without the ability to taste, feel, smell or hear, life would be an obstacle course, void of so many of the pleasures we now enjoy. Loss of sight would bring a dramatic change to the way most of us live. Give thanks — *everyday* — for these precious gifts.

The senses are agents of the brain. They are our links to awareness, perception, imagination and creativity. Put them to work. Be conscious of their value and thus maximize their use generally *and* specifically when performing.

22. EXERCISES TO ENHANCE SENSORY AWARENESS

Develop sensitivity to what you see, hear, taste, touch and smell. Become more aware of people, places and things around you. Perceive your own living sensations. Extend your feelings and stimulate your imagination as you go about daily living. Not only will you enjoy life more, you will become a more creative person. Practice the following exercises to enhance sensory awareness:

(1) Concentrate on *one* of the five senses each day for the next five days. Note how your awareness of things increases each time you give full attention to one of the sensory receptors.

(2) Make a comprehensive study of a member of your family or a close friend. Make a detailed list of things observed: speech habits,

mannerisms, personality traits, dress and grooming habits, state of health, posture, tolerance level, etc.

(3) Take note of your feelings and reactions when using the five senses in the following ways:

    (a) *see* colors, structural forms, human forms.

    (b) *feel* various textures.

    (c) *smell* various aromas: perfumes, flowers, food.

    (d) *taste* various kinds of food and liquid.

    (e) *listen* to various sounds: music, voices, birds, traffic.

23. THE NERVOUS SYSTEM CONTROLS THOUGHT FEELING AND MOVEMENT

Every actor should have a basic understanding of his/her nervous system. It consists of three main parts, the *central* system, the *peripheral* system and the *autonomic* system, which consists of *sympathetic* and *parasympathetic* divisions. The nervous system provides channels along which information passes from a person's surroundings to the brain.

CENTRAL NERVOUS SYSTEM: functions as a central switchboard co-ordinating the activities of the entire nervous system. It consists of the brain and the spinal cord. The nervous system has billions of cells called *neurons*. Cordlike masses of neuron fibers are called *nerves* which form a network of channels that conduct information throughout the body. The brain consists of three parts, the *cerebrum*, the *cerebellum* and the *brain stem*. The cerebrum makes up 85 per cent of the brain. It directs sight, hearing and touch along with the ability to think, speak and feel emotions. It is the center of learning. The cerebellum maintains the body's sense of balance and co-ordinates muscular movements with sensory information. The brain stem is connected to the spinal cord at the base of the skull. It contains neurons that relay information from the sense organs. Neurons that regulate automatic functions such as balance, blood pressure, breathing and heartbeat are also in the brain stem. The spinal cord contains pathways that carry sensory information to the brain.

PERIPHERAL NERVOUS SYSTEM: carries all the messages sent between the central system and the rest of the body. It consists of 12 pairs of nerves originating in the brain and 31 pairs of nerves in the spinal cord. Messages are carried to every *receptor* — located in the eyes and ears and other sense organs of the body — and to every *effector* — muscles and internal organs — which carry out the brain's instructions. Receptors carry nerve messages called *impulses* to the brain which decodes them and sends out instructions to the effectors for action. The sight of an on-coming vehicle is decoded as 'danger'. The brain sends out a message 'move away'.

AUTONOMIC NERVOUS SYSTEM: is a special section of the peripheral system which regulates such automatic bodily processes as breathing and digestion without conscious control by the brain, enabling the body to maintain a stable internal environment. This system has two parts. The *sympathetic* division responds to the body's needs in emergencies and during heavy activity, speeding up the heartbeat, sending additional blood to the muscles and enlarging the pupils of the eyes. The *parasympathetic* division opposes the actions of the sympathetic division. It slows down the heartbeat, diverts blood from the muscles to the stomach and intestines and contracts the pupils of the eyes. The balance of activity between these two divisions is controlled by the central nervous system.

24. PERCEPTION AND AWARENESS

A person's so-called *sixth sense* is a power of perception which seems as strong as any of the five senses which are consciously received through direct stimulation of the bodily organism or of the sense receptors. Also called *intuition*, sixth sense is the immediate knowing of something without conscious use of reasoning. It is instantaneous apprehension.

Kinaesthesia (kin-aes-the-si-a) is the sensation of position, movement, tension of parts of the body perceived through nerve end organs in muscles, tendons and joints. It is a generalized feeling of movement.

25. POINTS OF REFERENCE

Points of reference are people, places and things an actor communicates with or refers to during performance. They may be static or moving, tangible or intangible, real or imagined.

By moving toward or gesturing in the direction of another player or an object, the actor is making a specific point of reference which changes the focus of attention of the audience from one player to another or from a player to an object. A player rising from a chair and crossing to a door, shifts the focus of attention from the first position to the second position. If the player then crosses to a window, the attention changes again. Gesturing toward a painting or other object within the acting perimeter, focuses the attention on the painting or object, giving it significance.

A hand prop such as a letter, book, newspaper, spectacles, gun, knife, glass or item of clothing can be used as an effective point of reference to reveal an important story point or to enhance a characterization. A hand prop can be made the focus of attention in a scene by means of an actor's look or gesture toward it or by the special handling of it. Bogart, as the neurotic Captain Queeg in *The Caine Mutiny*, rolled steel balls in his hand during the interrogation scenes to highlight the character's neurosis.

Tangible points of reference are things of actual form and substance within the sightline of the actor and the audience. They can be seen and the actor can pick them up, use them in some way or refer to them. *Intangible* points of reference are persons, places or things beyond the sightline of the actor and the audience. They cannot be seen, touched or used, only referred to. Intangible points of reference require an audience to use its imagination, to mentally 'see' persons, places, objects and incidents referred to by the actor. Intangible points of reference may also be things which occur within the imagination of the character such as dreams or hallucinatory images and sounds. They are without form and substance, but can be easily referred to.

Point of reference playing must not be forced, obvious or overplayed. It needs to be subtle in its expression. The actor draws attention to a person, place or thing by clever timing of dialogue and appropriate use of look or gesture.

26. INNER AND OUTER SCENIC ENVIRONMENT ADJUSTMENT

There are two environments which involve the actor in role playing. One is external, the other internal. Called *scenic environments*, they influence a character's actions.

EXTERNAL SCENIC ENVIRONMENT: is a location or setting where incidents in the story take place. These may occur indoors or outdoors, in a particular country and city. A character's external scenic environment has the potential to influence his/her ideas, feelings and actions. Some of these influencing factors are: climate and other environmental conditions prevalent in the location, social and political forces of the area and the character's home, employment and social lifestyle and community status.

INTERNAL SCENIC ENVIRONMENT: represents a character's *inner* life of thoughts and feelings. All humans are products of their environment. They are influenced by external conditions, circumstances, events and associations. A person's personality and character are shaped according to his/her background – where and how he/she has been brought up. Even climate can have a bearing on a person's thoughts, feelings and actions. Oppressive heat can affect thinking and acting. It also plays a part in determining mode of dress. Extreme cold has an energizing affect on thinking and acting. A person living under a brutal regime will think and act differently to a person living under a free society. A poorly-educated person, one who has suffered harsh parental treatment and social injustice, is likely to think, feel and act in a different way to a person who has enjoyed a pampered, free-of-hardship existence. Discover the external scenic environment factors likely to have a bearing on the way your stage character thinks, feels and acts.

27. KYBERNETIC ATTACK

Kybernetic attack is a method of controlling the intensity of feelings in performance. Kybernetic is a Greek work meaning *helmsman*. It comes from the word *kybernetes*, which in turn has spawned the modern word *cybernetics*, used to represent that science dealing with the comparative study of complex electronic equipment and the human nervous system in an attempt to explain the nature of the brain.

Kybernetic attack places the actor as helmsman, controller of his/her acting instrument, directing it to function at the required emotional and physical intensity during performance. Kybernetic attack is a programmed thrust of energy which intensifies feelings and stimulates actions with discipline and control. It is beneficial in stemming runaway emotions and actions.

Actors are sometimes guilty of turning scenes into shouting matches, releasing too much energy far too early. A dramatic scene must not begin with a high burst of emotion at its lowest point. It must *build* to its high point. Emotion rises to a high pitch before it explodes. Sudden outbursts without reason shock an audience. Uncontrolled shouting matches cripple creativity, stifle subtlety of meaning and are an assault on the ears of an audience.

When playing scenes which require great intensity of feeling, begin at an emotional level which allows feeling *expansion*, so that the emotions can be maximized at the climax of the scene. Controlled *emotion-expansion* brings a more true-to-life performance than does instant emotion-explosion. The kybernetic attack method determines *when* and by how *much* energy is released to intensify emotions and actions in a scene. It gives the actor control over his/her emotions rather than the emotions controlling the actor.

28. AN ACTOR MUST CONTROL ENERGY SAID BURTON

Richard Burton, referred to by some reviewers as 'an actor of great magnetism', was often criticized by others for being 'too rigid' and 'overly-theatrical'. Burton made several good films, among them, *My Cousin Rachel* (1952), *Alexander the Great* (1956), *Becket* (1964), *The Spy Who Came in from the Cold* (1965), *Who's Afraid of Virginia Woolf?* (1966).

While Burton attained success in films, he was more at home on the stage. This medium best suited his broad, larger-than-life voice projection and performance style. Had alcohol not taken its toll, he could have reached far greater heights as an actor. He was a masterful technician who knew how to effectively use his acting instrument. Prior to his death in 1984, he remarked to a journalist that an actor needs to be able to control performance energy to keep from overplaying and acting in a physical way. 'At first, my acting was purely physical. I charged into parts like a bull. I soon learned to control my energy, to keep it in reserve and let it out gradually and when it was most needed,' he said.

29. INJECT LIFE INTO A PART BY ENERGIZING IT

Actress Madeline Kahn, says she prepares for her scenes by building up an 'appropriate energy level' while waiting to be called to the set. She feels that controlled injections of energy during a performance bring a character to 'life' by intensifying the character's show of emotions and actions. 'Energy is important when playing comedy where fast pace is necessary to generate excitement,' she feels.

Lifeless acting is due to several causes, mostly it's due to lack of vitality in an actor. Performance comes from the neck up. The body is lifeless. In this instance, the mind should be used to generate interest and enthusiasm to produce surges of energy which permeate the whole being. A negative state of mind drains energy. Laziness, disinterest, boredom and depression affect perception and awareness in addition to attracting poor health. Performance suffers when an actor's energy is low. Uplift your mind. Concentrate on the *positiveness* of life. Generate enthusiasm for your role, genuine interest in it. Be conscious of how energized a character must be. Play your part with controlled energy which brings flexibility of voice, enlivened physical actions and greater emotional rage.

30. DRIVE PERSONAL MAGNETISM THROUGH CHARACTERIZATION

Personal magnetism is the power to attract, to charm with personality, to impress with dynamics of voice, movement and presence. Some actors are devoid of personal magnetism, others have it in varying degrees. Gable had it, as did Bogart, Bergman and Crawford. Paul Newman and Marlon Brando have it and so do Hoffman, Streep and Redford.

Producer Aaron Spelling, whom I once met briefly at the wedding of a mutual friend in Hollywood, told me that personal magnetism, which he calls 'stardust', must shine through an actor's role playing if he/she is to be noticed and given an opportunity to become a screen star. A former actor himself, Spelling maintains that an actor must have not only the ability to act but a strong camera personality. 'If the camera doesn't agree with an actor's personality and the way he acts, there is little a director can do to help him,' Spelling told me.

Personal magnetism and camera appeal aren't things one develops after reading a book or taking an acting lesson. Acting ability can be enhanced through expert training but magnetism is an innate quality which one nurtures and refines. In all the years I've been teaching, I've yet to manufacture magnetic screen appeal for a student. If this special quality is there, it can be drawn out and enhanced, but not manufactured.

An absence of screen magnetism does not preclude an actor becoming a good actor, but in most cases, it does preclude an actor becoming an international screen star. I have no workable technique for producing 'stardust', but what I can suggest is that every acting aspirant put controlled energy into characterization, thus preventing lackluster performance. Drive as much of your own personality through the role as will permit and support it with acting technique. Give your very best to what you do and pray that the camera is sympathetic to your personality.

31. CREATE AN INNER FLAME TO ILLUMINATE EMOTIONS AND ACTIONS

During an acting assignment in Hawaii, I visited the Honolulu Academy of Arts to view an exhibit of August Rodin's drawings and sculpture. The mystique and beauty found in his work are truly outstanding. Ranked by many as the greatest sculptor of the 1800's and referred to as 'the father of modern sculpture', Rodin created figures with enormous emotional intensity covering a wide range of human vitality, passion and suffering. His best known works include *The Thinker* and *The Kiss*.

Rodin created an 'inner flame' which appears to shine from 'within' his works, illuminating them, making them life-like with a strong sense of movement to each part. He believed that sculpture should reflect something of emotion. It must not only look life-like, it must give a feeling of 'life'.

I find Rodin's approach to art a key to inspired emotion playing, his work a lesson in acting, easily applied to characterization. A stage character must reveal human qualities, give a feeling of 'life', be a human spirit capable of penetrating the heart of an audience. Think of Rodin's *inner flame* as *energy*, a stimulator of mind and body which overcomes passivity, dullness and mechanical response. The inner flame lights the soul, inspires creative action so there is movement from the soul to the body, an extension of feeling to its physical form.

When there is no inner flame there is no power, just a passive state, energyless mechanical thinking, feeling and acting. Passivism smothers inspiration, creativity and spiritual activity. It deadens the soul. Passive emotions are strangled within. They fail to reach a physical form. When there is no outpouring of emotion there is no force to vitalize movement, gesture and voice tone. A character may look life-like but give no feeling of 'life'

32. SING INSIDE TO CREATE LIFE IN ART SAID RUBENSTEIN

Arthur Rubenstein was one of the world's great piano virtuosos. At the age of 12, he performed as a soloist with the Berlin Symphony Orchestra. A student of the famous Ignace Jan Paderewski for a short time, Rubenstein played not only with technical skill but with verve and intense emotion. Genius shone through his public performances and recordings.

Speaking to a group of students in a televised program shortly prior to his death, Rubenstein told them of a pianist who played a number of Chopin pieces at a concert he had attended. 'I couldn't fault or criticize his playing technically, but he made Chopin sound commonplace because he played technically, but without heart. An artist must sing inside, make beautiful inner music. He must play with feeling if he wishes his audience to respond with feeling,' Rubenstein said.

Technique alone isn't enough to create genuine artistry in acting. Any actor who cannot or will not light an inner spark, 'sing inside', will make a writer's work commonplace. Acting is the projection of feelings. Feeling must come from the heart. Experience inwardly, then combine technique to project true-to-life feelings which will give substance to the writer's words.

33. TECHNIQUE AND EMOTION KEY TO TORVILL AND DEAN ARTISTRY

In February 1984, at the Zetra Stadium in Sarajevo, Yugoslavia, Jane Torvill and Christopher Dean captivated an estimated TV audience of 100 million with a superlative demonstration of classical ice-dancing at the Winter Olympic Games. The audience rose in unison to salute a display of interpretative skating that one dares to say has no precedent. It won the pair a gold medal.

Torvill and Dean 'sing inside'. They display an intensely shared creative brilliance. There can be no question that their skating is drama, theatre, poetry and ballet on ice. They pirouette, glide, swoop their way across the ice in perfect unison. They combine technique with *feeling*. Their Olympic performance was to Ravel's Bolero. They played out the tragic love story to such perfect pitch that the heart sang with them as they swung between the emotions, a gesture of despair here, a loving smile there, before the suicide pact cast them into the volcano. The couple's aesthetic grace, emotion-expression perfection and sheer artistry, scored for them an unprecedented 12 perfect marks. Torvill and Dean, now professional performers, are not only brilliant skaters, they are sensitive artists using their emotions to enhance technically-excellent ice-dance routines.

34. REPRESSED PHYSICAL ACTING

Beginning actors almost always fall into the trap of over-dramatising a part by trying to physically *act-out* the words assigned to them. Dialogue is pounded, rushed, over-emphasized and often, delivered with little meaning intact. More often than not, movement is without justification and poorly co-ordinated with dialogue. Some beginning actors cannot resist the urge to 'act' with all stops out, to take a performance 'over-the-top'. Usually, the results are dismal. Mostly, they are downright embarrassing to watch.

Repress the urge to overpower and strangle a part. Don't approach acting as operation overkill. Restrain exhibitionism. *Think* through dialogue. Understand the *effects* the words are designed to have on other characters. Stir-up feelings relative to the text and to the character's objectives. Genuine expression of feelings will *automatically* produce the appropriate physical responses.

Repressed physical acting is not aimed at tearing down or restricting extended development of characterization. Its aim is to keep performance within acceptable limits. It is insurance against tearing a part to shreds. Place *checks* on performance. Become your own critic. Sense when you are overstating dialogue, playing it too heavily and making unnecessary body movements. A good rule to follow is to cut what you are doing by *half*. But in the process, don't dampen feelings or play without an appropriate energy level. The aim is to repress the urge to show-off, to eliminate *excess* acting.

35. AVOIDING AUDIENCE COMMUNICATION LAG WHERE POSSIBLE

A certain proportion of an actor's stage dialogue is often missed, half-absorbed or purposely not listened to by individuals in an audience. Where some members of an audience mentally 'drop out' — one or a succession of times during a performance — communication lag occurs. Sometimes actors are at fault for allowing an audience's mind to wander from the stage action. This is sometimes due to acting incompetence — inaudibility, distortion of meaning, lackluster performance, uninteresting characterization — which causes an audience to struggle to keep up with or to comprehend what the actors are saying and doing. At times, individuals within an audience are likely to 'tune-out' and center the attention on 'distractions' such as traffic noise, personal discomfort and worries.

Unless an audience is kept absorbed in the stage events, it will quickly lose interest and enthusiasm for the performers and switch its attention to other things. An audience has no wish to suffer mental strain while it is being entertained. It gives time, attention and money in expectation of relaxation and enjoyment. It should not be expected to act as a computer to work out what the performers are doing, to decode their texts and unscramble their actions. Don't make it tough for an audience to comprehend the stage events. Keep your acting simple and perfectly meaningful.

Audience communication lag isn't something that can be entirely eliminated, but it can be minimized. Interesting characterization and performance skill are audience attention-holders. Proper communication of an author's words brings instant understanding. Words spoken as a reflection of genuine feelings generate interest and concern for those speaking them. It is a matter of awakening the *minds* and livening the *responses* of an audience in order to capture and hold its attention.

36. COMMUNICATE ON THE SAME WAVELENGTH WITH FELLOW PLAYERS

Many television shows and motion pictures start shooting without adequate rehearsal, which means actors seldom get to know fellow players. You walk on the set, meet the director and cast who are working that day and shortly thereafter begin performing your scenes. Social contact with cast members and the director is minimal. People who are supposed to work and be creative together don't *know* one another on a personal level and seldom fully understand where each character is headed in the story. It's a dismal situation, often resulting in performers acting *at* one another rather than *with* one another.

Actors must communicate on the same wavelength, must understand who they are, what they are and in which direction to take a scene. Without sufficient discussion and director guidance prior to the shoot, actors are apt to flounder, walk-through a part and sprout lines minus feeling. Well-trained, experienced screen actors stand a chance to make something of their roles, but for the untrained and inexperienced there is little chance of this happening.

A helpful technique to play on the same *wavelength* with others, is to be *less* conscious of speaking and listening to words and *more* conscious of putting across ideas and listening for meaning. In everyday conversations we are not really conscious of the words we use, but conscious of the *thoughts* we wish to communicate. When listening we do not listen to words but listen to discover what the person means *underneath* the words. In order to have an emotional involvement with others on stage, act *with* them — get on the same wavelength — listen for *meaning* and react with *feeling*. Without absorbing from others and giving of yourself — mentally and emotionally — to others there can be no spiritual union on stage.

37. THE SERIOUSNESS OF PLAYING COMEDY

The late Groucho Marx once said: 'Comedy needs to be played with an innocence. What you say and do should take on an importance, a seriousness. You can't think of what you do as funny or try and play it for laughs. If you're laughing, then your audience won't. Play it straight, as if what you're doing is really happening.'

Madeline Kahn feels that comedy is 'a personal statement about life'. She classes herself as an actress rather than a comedienne. 'It is a very individual way of using your voice, body and face. A woman should play comedy straight, not try for laughs or she will be considered too clownish and aggressive,' she says.

Peter Sellers was able to achieve classic comedy characterizations because he played everything absolutely straight without facial mugging, pratfalls or funny hat routines. 'The best lesson on playing comedy an actor can learn is that it is only funny when it is dead-on serious,' he is quoted as saying.

38. TECHNIQUES FOR PLAYING COMEDY

Playing comedy with dead-on seriousness does not imply that it should be played as if it were drama — to do so would kill the humor entirely. Some of the success of comedy playing lies in the comic *mood* established by the cast. Players should appear to be engrossed in their objectives, even enjoying their actions without going over-the-top when pointing-up lines and actions to bring out the humor.

Comedy must move rapidly and be precise as to its intent. Pick up cues swiftly to avoid slowing the action. Speeding up cues does not mean speeding up the delivery of words so that comprehension is difficult due to poor diction. Increase pace and tempo but speak clearly. *Pointing* of lines — placing emphasis on the right word and the timing of pauses — is very much an intuitive thing, as is the 'holding' for laughs. The techniques which apply to playing comedy are learned through practical experience rather than via theory analysis. However, the following suggestions may prove helpful:

- Play laugh lines deadpan. Lift the end of the punch line and leave it hanging or play it 'flat'. Resist the urge to facially mug to get laughs. Clinch the laugh line with a slight body reaction — a look, gesture or turn of the head.
- Develop an air of innocence. Give the appearance of being *unknowledgeable* as to what is about to occur, thus showing surprise at the events as they happen.
- Deliver comic lines as written. Don't try to improve the author's work. Adding or omitting words or lines could affect another player's feed or laugh lines or cues.
- Topping and underplaying is vital to the success of comedy. Where the scene is building to a climax, the actors top one another — increase volume, tempo, emphasis — until one player breaks the topping sequence by suddenly changing pitch and underplaying the laugh line.
- Players having 'cut-in' lines — those following the laugh line — must not cut in too quickly or the laugh will be smothered. Nor should the cut-in line be held back too long or the intensity of the scene will drop. Cut-in lines are usually non-essential lines, their function being to 'silence' an audience before it laughs itself out and becomes too relaxed. Timing is an important factor when playing cut-in lines.

39. THE COMEDY GENIUS OF THE MARX BROTHERS

The Marxes played with an air of innocence but always with deadly seriousness in the pursuit of their objectives. Their beautifully-orchestrated comic-characterizations bear little resemblance to real people — living or dead. Yet, the characters and their wild mischief seem perfectly real and acceptable, often desirable, as when they take pot shots at any pompous oaf who crosses their path.

The Marx Brothers' antics are highly implausible, graceless, even vulgar in words and images, but there is a certain reality and humanness in their work. It is the most fascinating and most rewarding, in a humorous way, of all that done by the various comic teams who made it to the screen.

The Marxes' work moves rapidly, naturally and clearly. They are sure of themselves. We understand what they are about. They play without self-conscious awareness, seemingly unaware that their antics are anything but standard behavior. They 'heave dead cats into sanctuaries' and get away with it. They shoot down in flames those who are pretentious and we applaud them. They take on the world and win and they become our heroes. They were true masters of their art.

As a team, they made thirteen films. *A Night At The Opera, A Day At The Races, Room Service, A Night In Casablanca, The Big Store,* etc, attest to their genius as comedians. Their uninhibited approach to life comes through their screen performances which gives their comic characterizations that extra sense of conviction, naturalness and believability. Their work will live long in the hearts of their many admirers.

40. AN INSIGHT INTO COMEDY

The word comedy comes from the Greek word 'komos' which means revelry. Shakespeare, Moliere and Shaw are said to be the three best writers of stage comedy of all time. One of the best modern-day comedy writers is Neil Simon, whose numerous stage plays have been transferred to the screen.

Comedy written for the screen — situation comedy — usually revolves around light, slightly exaggerated every-day type situations involving amusing characters whose sparkling dialogue and unpredictable reactions to their predicaments, cause us to laugh. Also called sophisticated comedy, it has always been the delight of actors and audiences because of its brilliant use of dialogue between highly-amusing people disparaging socially-accepted standards.

In *situation* comedy, the characters are nearly always 'average' types, but in some instances may be less than average in that they are blunderers, rogues, dreamers, idealists or romanticists locked into situations which seem insurmountable. The protagonist in situation comedy usually overcomes opposing forces and wins his or her objectives. In *farce*, the characters are improbable types involved in improbable situations — everything is done strictly for laughs.

Comedy is built around characters, particular expressions of dialogue and physical actions, situations and events. Some plays incorporate both tragedy and comedy. When we think of comedy we think of funny people in conflict with situations which make us laugh. Examples of excellent screen comedy include: *Plaza Suite, The Odd Couple, The Sunshine Boys, A Shot In The Dark, The Goodbye Girl, A Touch of Class, Play It Again Sam, Being There, Arthur*, etc.

It can be said that nearly all forms of comedy have their basic appeal to the intellect rather than the emotions. An appeal to the heart is made where an audience feels love, compassion, tenderness and pity. In farce we tend to laugh at the grotesque, the unnatural, the horrifying, the exaggerated, the incongruous, anything which brings release from the stress of daily living and aids in placing things in better perspective, allowing us to laugh at our problems and see ourselves as others see us.

41. SUGGESTIONS ON ACTING FROM DAME SYBIL THORNDIKE

Dame Sybil Thorndike, an actress of great range and power, understood the value of technique and used it with ease and effectiveness. The following suggestions are an extract from an interview she gave shortly after completing her screen role in Olivier's production of *The Prince and the Showgirl*.

'Actors ought to accumulate worthwhile techniques. They are essential to good performance. I've always said that acting is a natural thing and any intelligent person can do it and be good at it providing self-consciousness is mastered. Technique must be used without effort and in a subtle way. An actor needs to add to his technique that indefinable thing called personality. That's what makes all the difference. Acting technique by itself isn't enough. Personality gives that added dimension. Young actors need to study their personal tragedies, struggles, worries and attitudes and get to understand them. Relate them to the lives of stage characters then use technique to put across what they have to say and feel. But don't be self-conscious about it. Get to know yourself. You can't play a stage character until you know him and understand him. Knowing yourself helps you to understand the people you may have to play.'

42. THE ACTOR'S DUAL PERSONALITY

Some actors give full attention to external embodiment of a part. Others rely upon internally-inspired emotions in an attempt to 'live the part'. An actor's duty to the author is to create a *whole* personality — one who thinks, feels, speaks and moves in accord with the author's wishes. Therefore, an actor needs to work on the inner instrument, which creates attitudes and feelings and also on the external physical instrument, which produces *styles* of speaking, moving, gesturing. By merging the two aspects of the instrument, a more substantial, more *real* characterization is possible.

An actor is said to have a 'dual personality' when part of his/her personality is married to the personality of the character to be portrayed. The actor's personality is used to interpret the significance of the words to be spoken and the deeds to be carried out. It is also used to inject 'life' and 'style' into the performance. In this regard, the actor must *empathize* with the character. In the theatrical sense, he/she places the *self* in the position of the character in order to *experience* and *participate* in the character's feelings and actions (the imaginary life), while at all times remaining in control of his/her own personality — the instrument of expression.

43. CONTROLLED PERSONALITY IDENTIFICATION

Because an actor identifies both internally and externally with a role and is strongly influenced by the character's words and deeds, the actor must resist giving in to them completely or the risk is run of losing performance control. The technique of *controlled personality identification* permits *identification* with the life of a character without becoming slave to it.

The purpose of this technique is to assist the actor to distinguish between his/her own personality and the personalities of the various characters he/she is likely to play. It also is a limiting factor and guideline on how far one may go in an attempt and desire to 'become' the part. Remember, Edmund Kean became psychologically unbalanced because he couldn't distinguish between his own personality and the personalities of the stage characters he so desperately wanted to become. Performance control is imperative. Therefore, personality extension needs to be governed to keep it within safe performance and psychological limits.

44. SEARCH THE INTERIOR WORLD

The poet Ted Hughes expresses through his works his feelings on man's *inner landscape* — a world to be explored and opened up. And he tells us: 'There is the inner life, which is the world of final reality, the world of memory, emotion, imagination, and which goes on all the time, consciously or unconsciously, like the heartbeat.'

Because acting is an expression of attitudes and feelings, what spurs attitudes and feelings into action requires some degree of understanding. An actor needs to explore and 'open up' his/her interior world in order to gain a fuller comprehension of the 'self' or the mysterious 'I' as Stanislavski called it. To *know thyself* is of course no guarantee of eventual stardom or acting brilliance, but it does offer a deeper insight into life and this must surely be a stimulant to creativity to bring pleasure to acting and at least, to bring acting competence.

45. APPROACH THE ART OF ACTING WITH INTELLIGENCE

An actor needs to be cautious in approaching the art of acting to avoid falling into bad performance habits, to be aware when he/she is receiving the wrong instruction and direction and can distinguish between genuine technique and artificial performance.

It is important to accept the premise that acting *is* an art and therefore needs to be studied as any other art is studied. It needs to be approached with seriousness, a desire to master workable techniques which are then used as a foundation upon which to add experience. Acting skill is acquired through practice and experience of applied technique to which is added personal creativity. The actor should approach the art of acting intelligently, allowing nothing to impede the goal of satisfactory intellectual and artistic expression. The study of acting can be and should be a source of great enlightenment for the serious-minded acting aspirant and, hopefully, he/she will develop in the necessary strengths: bearing, confidence, vocal power, technique and magnetism.

SUMMARY OF IDEAS TO REVIEW

1: *Technique* is a passport to competent performance. A series of acting techniques combine to produce a *personalized* acting system.

2: Apply the *who, what, when, where, why, how* theory when building a character. It will reveal vital information about the character.

3: Life is an expression of *action*. Normal behavior has a sense of purpose about it. In the pursuit of objectives, a character's attitudes and actions must seem logical.

4: *Attitude* action playing is a method of pinning down the character's attitudes and playing actions which match them. *Dialogue* action playing is a way of stating something which reveals the speaker's thoughts. Use an active verb to name each attitude-action to be played.

5: The 9/10ths analysis method looks for what is *below* the surface of seemingly ordinary lines. It encompasses searching out subtext material, discovering everything there is to discover about the character and the story.

6: Image recall and subconscious impression playing bring personal feelings, memories, images of past events back into focus so that the emotions that were once experienced can be recalled and used in the life of the stage character.

7: Use the five senses for all they are worth. Develop 'sensitivity' to things you *see, hear, taste, touch* and *smell*. Understand your nervous system — how the sensory receptors work.

8: *External* scenic environment is a location or setting. *Internal* scenic environment represents the character's thoughts and feelings.

9: Kybernetic attack is a method to control the intensity of feelings during performance. Release energy slowly and *build* intensity.

10: When playing comedy give the appearance of being unknowledgeable as to what is about to occur. Play laugh lines deadpan.

THE TECHNICAL
ASPECTS
OF
SCREEN ACTING

SCENE 15

Practical Ideas In This Chapter . . .

SCENE 15

★★★

1. SCREEN WORK IS A TEAM EFFORT

Television productions and motion pictures, to bring them to the final presentation stage, require the co-operation of a great many craftsmen, craftswomen and technicians working side-by-side as a team. A film production unit, not including actors, comprises forty-six members or more and there are approximately 246 different trades, crafts and professions brought into the making of a single motion picture. It is a costly business which requires *team* work — *time is of the essence.*

Actors are not the be-all and end-all of screen production. But they are an important *part* of it. Their work often requires clever camera positioning, artistic lighting and skilful editing to lift what is said and done above the ordinary. It is important that screen actors place themselves in proper perspective to other screen arts members and maintain an attitude which produces professional conduct. Confrontation with fellow workers due to unwarranted temperament and self-importance does damage to a production. Actors have a duty to bring to the set their best manners and ability. Well-mannered, hard-working actors are a credit to their profession. They make the work of director and crew easier and less traumatic.

2. THE PRODUCER

The manager of a production company is known as a producer, responsible for the efficient running of a production. The producer reports to the executive producer who in turn reports to the board of directors controlling the company's finances. A producer is given a specific amount of money (budget) to spend on producing a screen story (property). A producer is usually a business person sensitive to public tastes in screen entertainment. He/she may or may not have a working knowledge of writing, directing and acting, but will most assuredly have sufficient business acumen to cope with the multitude of problems relating to contract negotiations, legal and insurance requirements, finance and funding, distribution and publicity, etc.

When an original story idea or a proposed adaptation of a novel has been selected, the producer will assign a writer to prepare a screen treatment which will be followed by various screenplay drafts until a final-draft script is ready for production. During this time money is raised, cast and crew are assembled and the necessary pre-production arrangements set in motion. Sometimes specialist writers are called in to 'doctor' the script — re-write dialogue, change or add scenes. When the producer and director are satisfied with the property, pre-production requirements are finalized and a production commencement date is set.

Some producers try their hands at directing. Stanley Kramer, Joseph Mankiewicz and George Pal are imaginative producers/directors. George Pal, whom I interviewed on my Hollywood television show *Adams At Noon*, told me that producing can be a frustrating grind, whereas, 'directing is a highly creative and personally-rewarding job,' which is the reason he does both. Having produced-directed a number of productions for both the stage and screen, I wholeheartedly concur with Mr. Pal's remarks.

3. THE DIRECTOR

A screen director is a hard-working, responsible, technically-knowledge-able and sensitive individual who is usually the first to arrive on the set and the last to leave. The function of the director is to involve him/herself in all phases of a production's preparation and execution. Actors will be given their stage moves (blocking) and rehearsed in their scenes. The director is required to have a working knowledge of acting, writing and photography. In addition, it is important to know something of costume design, music, lighting, sound recording and editing.

As it is the director's responsibility to translate a writer's work and bring it to the screen in a technically-professional and creative manner, a close liaison with the writer is essential, particularly if major dialogue and scene changes are necessary. The director, during pre-production, will work closely with the production manager and the first-assistant director to finalize shooting schedules. The director will have discussions with the wardrobe and makeup departments, with the director of photography, camera operator and sound recordist. He/she will consult with the art director and property master. The director will nearly always have a hand in selecting cast and key crew members.

Most directors have a personal 'style' which is recognizable. John Huston, Alfred Hitchcock, John Ford, William Wyler, Carol Reed, Stanley Kubrick, Steve Spielberg, George Cukor, Michael Curtiz, Akira Kurosawa, Ingmar Bergman and the Australians Peter Weir, Gillian Armstrong, Bruce Beresford, Simon Wincer and Terry Bourke, show in their films a highly-personalized style of directing for the screen.

Orson Welles, seated in director's chair, talks to head cinematographer *Gregg Toland,* on the set for the making of *Citizen Kane.* The pair created exciting advances in filming technique with innovative lighting, staging, wide-field sharp focus and dissolve editing. Welles starred, produced, directed and co-wrote the screenplay in the RKO Radio Pictures classic 1941 production. (Photo Alex Kahle)

Producer *John Sexton* (standing) and director *Simon Wincer* watch crew preparation at race track location for *Phar Lap,* a story about the training and performance of one of the world's greatest horses. Film had excellent action photography and good actor characterizations.
▼

The real test of a director is in how effectively he/she uses the actors and the camera to translate the work of the writer. The use of long shots, medium shots, close-ups, cut-ins, cut-aways, moving shots, various camera angles, the blocking of actors to give variety and dramatic effect to scenes, all reflect how imaginative and talented a screen director is.

Since screen directing deals with human emotions and conflicts as well as the mechanics of staging and photography, the director needs to know something of human nature — *people.* The screen is positively a director's medium and he/she must use the medium to make screen images move in a natural, logical and dramatic manner. The art of the writer and the art of the actor must be fully comprehended by the screen director if there is to be articulate expression of the writing through inspired performance.

It is sincerely hoped that a screen director's worthiness is greater than the value accorded by Noel Coward: 'The real use of a director is to stop actors bumping into each other.' There are some, I'm sure, who fit this category. But there are others, like those previously mentioned, who truly know their craft.

4. THE ASSISTANT DIRECTOR

FIRST-ASSISTANT: in a film production unit, the first-assistant director's job is to relieve the director of as many material worries as possible, to keep tabs on cast and crew, round up extras, give them their positions and moves and call line players and the stars to the set. The assistant director calls for 'quiet' when the director is ready to rehearse and shoot and gives the actors their release at the end of the day or when their scenes have been completed. Other duties include assisting the director to scout locations, liaison with the production manager on production requirements and the preparation of schedules on a day-by-day basis which take into account the number of script pages the director will be able to film in a day. The first-assistant's job is handling *production* matters rather than the creative aspects of film-making.

SECOND-ASSISTANT: virtually an assistant to the assistant director. He/she is engaged where there is plenty of exterior action utilizing large numbers of extras.

FLOOR MANAGER: in a television studio production unit, the FM is the director's link between the control room and the studio floor, where he/she is boss. Instructions to the performers are relayed through the floor manager's headset and they are conveyed via hand signals [see chart] or cards. The FM calls the performers to the studio floor from their dressing rooms or the green room (actors waiting room) and is responsible for 'clearing' them at the conclusion of their performances.

5. THE CONTINUITY PERSON

A professional screen production presents a continuous flow of visual

floor manager gives players their
'e' for camera. Floor manager is
tween director and actors in televi-
udio productions.

manager listens to actors rehears-
es prior to taping of scene for *The
Doctors.* This soapie ran 1,396
es, making it longest-running
in Australian television history.
is seen in more than 30 countries.
ed by *Grundy Television,* it gave
o hundreds of actors and launched
of its stars to careers in films.

or manager gets in on the act for
the last 'live' television drama
General Motors Theatre, produced
Canadian Broadcasting Corpora-
d viewed on its network Sunday
gs during the 'fifties. Scene is from
isode "Face To Remember",
d by *Paul Almond.* Standing
actor *Charles Templeton* (seated) is
hor. (Photo Dale Barnes)

images, supported by sound, showing events in a logical way. Each sequence of scenes, built up from selected shots, must follow each other so that no inconsistencies are apparent. Poor continuity can ruin a production. To guard against this happening, a script or *continuity* person is hired to stay beside the director and make detailed notes of every shot filmed.

In regard to the actor, careful attention is given by the continuity person to wardrobe, makeup, props handling, body positioning, dialogue and direction of looks to avoid errors in continuity. A continuity person requires a good memory and a particularly-sharp eye for detail — a mind like a detective. Shots which follow one another may not always be filmed on the same day. As a general rule, scenes are shot out of sequence because it is neither convenient nor economical to film scenes in the exact order in which they appear in the script. Scenes are grouped so that those with the same location or set, requiring the same actors, can be filmed together, thus saving valuable time and money. A character viewed in a shot wearing a jacket but seen without it in a succeeding shot with no logical explanation for its removal, creates a *wardrobe* continuity problem. Continuity and wardrobe persons take photographs of cast members to avoid errors.

Director, the late Norman Foster, told me that when he worked with Peter Lorre on the *Mr. Moto* pictures, he was surprised to find Lorre an expert at matching scenes. 'He was a master of continuity. When we'd stop filming and then begin again, Lorre knew precisely what he had been doing, how he was holding his body, where he was standing, whether his coat was buttoned or unbuttoned, his direction of look and use of hand props. He was amazing,' Foster said.

Actors can help the director and the continuity person by remembering marks, whether a jacket is on or off, the direction of a look and the position and posture of the body. In addition, it is important to repeat dialogue exactly as written and spoken in each masterscene, close shot, cover shot and retake. All it takes is concentration.

6. THE PROCESS OF PRODUCING A MOTION PICTURE

PRE-PRODUCTION PERIOD: after the producer has selected the story and approved the writer's shooting script for production, he/she will work in close liaison with the director to select a crew and cast. Casting is achieved with the help of a casting director. Actors are read and often screen tested for some major and nearly all supporting roles. The stars, most likely, will have been selected prior to the general cast being contracted and sometimes even before a director is assigned as some stars have the right to approve their director, the script and their co-stars.

During pre-production, wardrobe and makeup tests are conducted, studio sets constructed and dressed, exterior and interior locations selected, the necessary location permits and permissions obtained and schedules prepared. The steady tempo of pre-production organization now turns into a frenzy of production activity.

FLOOR MANAGER'S
HAND SIGNALS CHART
[TELEVISION STUDIO PRODUCTION]

1: Standby — Action.

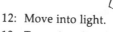

12: Move into light.

13: Turn in direction indicated.

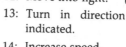

14: Increase speed. (Speed of hand movement indicates by how much.)

2: Cut.

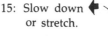

3: Now off camera Can move or stop action.

15: Slow down or stretch.

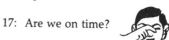

4: Keep volume up.

16: On time. Things are 'spot on'.

5: Volume down.

17: Are we on time?

6: Silence.

18: It's OK, everything is fine.

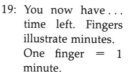

7: Get closer together.

19: You now have ... time left. Fingers illustrate minutes. One finger = 1 minute.

2 min.   or   ½ min.

8: Move further apart.

9: Move upstage.

20: Wind up.

10: Move downstage.

21: Applaud now.

11: Play to this camera.

22: Stop applause or action.

PRODUCTION SHOOTING: the actual number of shooting days varies from film-to-film. It is linked to budget, delays caused by weather and equipment failure, the work patterns of the director and the stars, plus a myriad of other problems which seem to plague every production unit. Some films are shot in a matter of weeks, others over several months. However, each film does have an allotted and hoped-for number of weeks in which interior and exterior filming will be completed.

The filming of a single shot, which may last seconds or a minute or so, can involve a great deal of preparation and time, particularly from the standpoint of lighting. Many adjustments may be necessary before the director of photography is happy with the lighting effect. The recording engineer will seek the best possible position for the microphone to ensure good sound. The set will receive last minute checks to see that props are in place and if there are to be special effects these will be readied. The stars' stand-ins take their positions for camera and lighting tests. When these preparations have been completed the assistant director calls the principal players to the set and under the director's watchful eye, rehearsals for camera and for the actors begin.

When the director is satisfied with rehearsals, the instruction is given to roll sound and camera. A slate is placed in front of the camera lens, the slateholder identifies the production title, the scene and take numbers and then slaps the clapper sticks to make a visual and sound impression to facilitate the editor's 'syncing' of the scene. The information on the slate helps to identify each shot for editing purposes as well as to identify the production unit when the raw stock is sent to the laboratory for processing.

If the director is not satisfied with the performance or if there are technical problems, a *retake* will be ordered and the process is repeated until the director feels that the scene is satisfactory. The director indicates which 'takes' he wants printed. The exposed film of each day's shooting is sent to the lab for processing and a print taken from it. These prints are known as 'dailies' or 'rushes' and are viewed by the director, editor, key crew members and principal cast players the following evening in a viewing theatre. An interior set is not dismantled until the director has approved the rushes. With principal photography completed, post-production work begins.

POST-PRODUCTION: the job of the film cutters and of the film editor now begins. The editorial process is a gigantic one. It includes selection of the best takes and the splicing of them in their proper sequence to form a 'rough-cut'. This is viewed by the producer, the director and the film editor and any additional footage or retakes which may be required are scheduled prior to the dismantling of the studio sets and the loss of cast and crew to other engagements.

When the editing is completed, opticals such as fades, dissolves, wipes, etc, are added at the laboratory. Individually recorded and edited dialogue, music and sound effects tracks are re-recorded onto a single track which is 'married' to the picture negative after it has been cut to match the edited print. The first *answer print* — completely edited, dubbed and scored picture — is generally of unacceptable color quality, so further prints are color-graded until a satisfactory result is achieved and then *release prints* are struck for distribution to theatres.

EXHIBITOR RELEASE: previews are often held prior to the general release of a film to test the reaction of audiences. Publicity and advertising then support the actual launch which may begin with a single premiere or a series of premieres in selected cities around the world. The stars will nearly always attend the major premiere along with industry people and local dignitaries. Press stories, radio and television interviews with the stars and the director help to promote the film's initial release.

As a general rule, a 35mm theatrical feature film will have a revenue-producing life of about seven years. Classic films, such as *Gone With The Wind*, earn extensive revenue far beyond this period. If a film is of any quality, it will be sold to television. Additional income will be earned via a film's release on 16mm and on videotape to organizations, clubs and home viewers. Some films are never released due to legal or financial reasons or due to the fact that distributors don't see them as financially-viable propositions at the box office.

7. THE IMPORTANCE OF CAMERA POSITIONS AND ANGLES

A screen story is presented via a number of continuously-changing images portraying events and character actions from a variety of viewpoints — camera positions and angles. The position and angle of the camera can shift the attention of the audience from one player to another, from one action to another. Screen drama has the advantage of being able to position its audience anywhere the director desires. The audience has a perfect sightline, for it sees what the camera lens captures as it moves from long shot to medium shot to close-up.

A director positions the camera after analysis of the script to determine the story requirements. Properly-selected camera angles can heighten dramatic visualization of the story. Poorly-chosen angles can detract from it and confuse and annoy an audience. A specific camera angle can be used to favor one actor over another, to strengthen or weaken the stature of a character or to impart some psychological meaning to a scene.

Actors can make their work more interesting by understanding basic camera set-ups. Observation on the set is the best teacher. Study camera positions selected by the director. Visualize in your mind the framing and composition of each shot the camera records. Appreciation of the director's function will remove some of the mystery of camera acting.

8. TYPES OF CAMERA ANGLES

There are three types of camera angles: *objective, subjective, point-of-view.*

OBJECTIVE ANGLE: the camera films from a sideline as if an unseen observer. The event is not seen from the viewpoint of any particular person within the scene, therefore it is known as an *impersonal* point-of-view. Actors do not look directly into the camera lens but to either side of it, above or below it or away from it. Nearly all screen dramas are shot from objective camera angles. Also referred to as the audience point-of-view. If an actor inadvertently looks into the lens, he/she breaks the illusion of the scene and it must be retaken.

SUBJECTIVE ANGLE: the audience participates in the screen event as a personal experience. The viewer either trades places with a player, seeing things through the player's eyes or is placed in the scene as an active participant. When a player looks into the lens the viewer and the player establish an eye-to-eye relationship. If the camera acts as the eyes of a viewer, such as shooting through the windscreen of a car as it careens down a twisting road or the camera takes a ride on a roller coaster, then the viewer experiences the event as if actually seated in the driver's seat of the car or seated in the roller coaster. Where the camera changes places with a player and the preceding shot is a close-up of the player looking at an event taking place off-screen the viewer sees what the player is viewing. Upward or downward points-of-view of a player are simulated by similar camera angling.

The MGM film *Lady In The Lake*, used subjective camera treatment throughout the story. The camera traded places with the detective played by Robert Montgomery. He was seen by the audience only when introduced and when reflected in mirror shots. Whenever the cast related to him they looked directly into the lens. Subjective camera is employed only on rare occasions in this manner in dramatic screen stories. Looking into the lens is reserved mostly for newscasters and hosts of television shows or for presenters-narrators of documentary films.

POINT-OF-VIEW ANGLE: records the scene from a particular player's viewpoint. The p.o.v., is an objective angle, but because it falls between the objective and subjective angle, it is given a separate category. The camera is positioned at the *side* of a player and the viewer sees what the player sees but not through his/her eyes. Point-of-view shots often follow over-the-shoulder close-ups, when two players face each other and exchange dialogue. The over-the-shoulder shot establishes the relationship between the two players, then the p.o.v. shot moves the viewer cheek-to-cheek with one player, providing a more intimate view of the other player.

9. SUBJECT ANGLES

A cameraman angles the camera relative to the subject he is shooting to achieve as best as possible an impression of picture *depth*. This is further enhanced by player movement and with lighting effects. By adjusting the height of the camera to the subject, the cameraman is also able to contribute artistic and dramatic values to the story-telling process and to the performances of the actors.

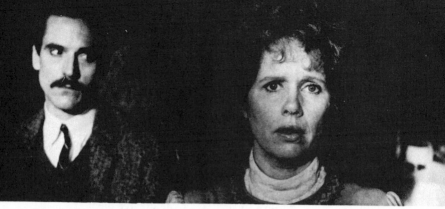

▲ In this informally balanced medium close-up, *Jeremy Irons* directs look to *Liv Ullman* who dominates scene because she is positioned right of frame and favorably angled toward camera.

▲ *Jeremy Irons* and *Lucinda Jones* are seen in profile shot. Player on right is favored because she is in slightly better position and well modeled with light.

Lucinda Jones is given compositionally stronger positioning although placed on left and lower in frame because she is favorably angled to lens showing three-quarters of face. Also aided by *Arthur Dignam's* direction of look. Scenes are from *The Wild Duck*, produced by *Philip Emanuel* and *Basil Appleby*, directed by *Henri Safran* for Tinzu Productions. (Photos Jim Townley)

LEVEL ANGLE: films from the eye-level of a person of average height *or* from the subject's eye-level. A player who is facing toward the camera, centered within the frame and is addressing an off-screen player, should take an eye-line slightly to one side and just above or below the lens depending upon the off-screen player's positioning.

HIGH ANGLE: any shot in which the camera is tilted *downward* to view the subject. High angles are chosen for their psychological, technical or aesthetic advantages. An angle looking down on a subject tends to reduce his/her height as well as indicating a diminishing of prestige and self-image values. The appearance of a person who is lonely, sad, depressed and unhappy is intensified by high-angle camera treatment. If a player is looking *up* to another player, the eye-line should be slightly to one side of the lens and just above it. This eye-line is applicable where a player is seated and looking up to a standing player with the camera positioned to simulate the eye-line of the standing player.

LOW ANGLE: any shot in which the camera is tilted *upward* to view the subject. A low angle helps to increase the height of a subject and to intensify the feelings of an audience, especially where it is desirable to inspire them. An angle looking up on a subject adds stature and dominance to the subject. The angle is particularly effective in filming persons of high office such as a judge, politician, police officer, army general, etc. If a player is looking *down* to another player, the eye-line should be slightly to one side of the lens and just below it. This is applicable where a player is standing and looking down to a seated player with the camera positioned to simulate the eye-line of the seated player.

ANGLE-PLUS-ANGLE: filmed with the camera angled in relation to the subject and tilted either upward or downward. Also referred to as a *double-angle* shot. It is most effective in producing a three-dimensional effect, eliminating 'flat' photography. Used where a dramatic effect is desirable such as a group of horsemen or soldiers approaching their rendezvous. Eye-line of players is determined by positioning in scene and direction of look.

DUTCH TILT: a shot in which the vertical axis of the camera is at an angle to the vertical axis of the subject, resulting in a 'tilting' of the screen image. Used most effectively for sequences where violence, horror or weird effects are required. A dutch tilt works well to indicate a character who is in a highly-emotional state or being terrorized by someone unseen. This shot is used by directors to dramatically show a natural catastrophe such as a tidal wave, an earthquake, a volcanic eruption, etc. Eye-line of player is determined by positioning in scene and direction of look.

Production personnel and writers use many terms to identify the type and content of camera shots. Moving shots, pan and tilt shots, crane or boom shots, helicopter shots, dolly shots, tracking shots, all have their special place in motion picture and television production. An understanding of how various scenes are being photographed not only adds to the enjoyment of acting, but to the performance itself.

346

SUBJECT
ANGLES

EL ANGLE: ▶
Harrison and *Arkie Whiteley* are
ioned in *profile* for this level-angle

ANGLE: ▶
Hayward, David Argue and *Bill Kerr*
amed from camera's effective high
ge point.

ANGLE: ▶
and trees loom up in dramatically-
low camera angle.

by Carolyn Johns from the McElroy &
production *Razorback*)

▲ Camera is set for *high-angle* shot on two players. Actor beside camera is ready to 'feed' lines to on-camera players.

Camera is set for *low-angle* shot of train and players. (Photos from No
▼ Longer Alone – World Wide Pictures)

Director, Robert Wise, feels that actors ought to have an understanding of how a feature film is put together and to be very much aware of screen terminology. 'The more knowledge an actor has of these things, the more assistance he or she can be to the director, thus saving time and performance energy,' he says.

10. SUBJECT IMAGE SIZES

The image size of a subject is relative to the over-all framing of each shot. This is determined by the distance of the subject from the camera and the focal length of the lens used by the cameraman. Image size can vary during a shot due to the subject moving toward or away from the camera or due to the camera itself moving or through the use of a zoom lens. The various image or subject sizes are designated as follows:

EXTREME LONG SHOT (ELS): depicts a vast scenic area from great distance. Valuable to show grandeur of location or to cover extensive action. A city skyline, a mountain range, desert area, armies in battle, stampeding cattle, are some examples of extreme long shot coverage.

LONG SHOT (LS): takes in the entire area of action to acquaint the audience with location, the people and objects involved in the scene. Also referred to as an *establishing shot.* Players are shown full-figure.

MEDIUM LONG SHOT (MLS): covers the players full-figure but does not show the entire setting as in the long shot. Also referred to as a *full shot,* especially when shooting interior scenes.

MEDIUM SHOT (MS): an intermediate shot which falls between a long shot and a close-up. Players are filmed from just above the knees or just below the waist to just above the head. The camera is close enough to capture important facial expression and gesture. Used extensively for motion picture and television dramas, usually with two or three players framed in the shot.

OVER-THE-SHOULDER CLOSE-UPS (OTS): a close-up of a player as viewed over-the-shoulder of another player. Generally filmed in opposing pairs, uniform in image size and similarly angled. Provides an effective transition to a point-of-view close-up. Usually framed from just below the shoulders to just above the head.

MEDIUM CLOSE-UP (MCU): frames player midway between the waist and shoulders to just above the head.

HEAD AND SHOULDER CLOSE-UP (HSCU): framed from just below the shoulders to just above the head. Generally referred to as 'close-up'.

HEAD CLOSE UP (HCU): framed from the top of the shoulders to just above the head.

CHOKER CLOSE-UP (CCU): framed from just below the lips to just above the eyes. A dramatic framing of a character's face to show fear and surprise via the eyes.

EXTREME CLOSE-UP (ECU): used to frame and magnify tiny objects or

SUBJECT ANGLES

ANGLE-PLUS-ANGLE: subject looms up in frame, background falls away for dramatic effect.

DUTCH TILT: effective for violent, weird or impressionistic screen effects.

to show a portion of an object or a player such as the muzzle of a gun, eyes, lips, fingers, etc.

CUT-IN CLOSE-UP: a magnified portion of the preceding larger-framed scene which continues the main action but shows a player or an object from a close view.

CUT-AWAY CLOSE-UP: is related to but not part of the preceding scene. It depicts secondary action occurring at the same time elsewhere.

NOTE: a close-up in regard to exact image size will vary from cameraman-to-cameraman and director-to-director. Unless specified, a close-up usually refers to a subject framed from just below the shoulders to just above the head.

11. PERFORMANCE FOR THE CLOSE-UP

When playing in tight close-up, keep the head and shoulders relatively still to avoid 'popping' in and out of frame. Head stillness is imperative in a choker close-up where a player's thoughts and feelings need to be expressed through the eyes. Don't allow the eyes to dart about or to blink excessively. Move the eyes slowly and blink normally or occasionally. In moments of fear, the eyes widen and become fixed.

Michael Caine, who confesses his screen idol is Humphrey Bogart, maintains an actor when *listening* should refrain from blinking. 'You hold people with your eyes and listen to what they say and you don't blink. Bogart never blinked. Blinking breaks the line, breaks the tension, the rhythm of the moment. It was one of Bogie's techniques,' Caine says.

Keep the head straight rather than angled in a close-up. Keep the body still when an over-the-shoulder shot frames across your shoulder to another player. And don't tense the body or it will be reflected as a strained look through the eyes and around the mouth. Keep the face as still as possible. Avoid distorting the mouth when speaking. Allow feelings to express through the eyes. Stillness does not mean looking and acting zombie-like.

The overstatement of playing which the stage actor must sometimes employ becomes unnecessary when acting for the camera and particularly so when playing in close-up. Because the camera can move in close and capture an intimate viewpoint, understatement of playing is essential. Facial animation in close-up appears unnatural.

12. THE KEY TO PLAYING IN CLOSE-UP IS RESTRAINT SAYS TERRY BOURKE

Terry Bourke, one of Australia's most experienced directors, told me that actors ought to understand the meaning of *restrained playing* if they want to become successful screen actors. 'The chief thing is to allow the camera to do its job. It is capable of picking up feelings providing an actor is experiencing them. Don't force emotion-playing. Just speak the lines as written and when it's time to listen, really listen. Don't give a stage

IMAGE SUBJECT SIZES

EXTREME LONG SHOT: depicts vast area from long distance to establish geography of location and to show players in relation to it.

LONG SHOT: establishes area of action and the positions of players who are show in full-figure.

MEDIUM LONG SHOT: covers the player full length but does not show setting in its entirety. Also referred to as a *full shot* when shooting interiors.

MEDIUM 3 SHOT: three players feature in this intermediate shot filmed from just below the waist to just above the head. Also called a *pyramid shot*. Male is placed in dominant position, females in profile. [Actors l. to r. *Maria Dujany, Tony Partridge, Karen Lennox*].

MEDIUM 2 SHOT: players face one another in this *profile* shot.

OVER-THE-SHOULDER CLOSE UP: filmed in opposing pairs and framed from just below the shoulders to just above the head.

REVERSE OF ABOVE: over-the-shoulder close-ups are an effective transition to point-of-view close-ups.

MEDIUM CLOSE-UP: frames player midway between waist and shoulders to just above the head.

HEAD AND SHOULDER CLOSE-UP: framed from just below the shoulders to just above the head.

HEAD CLOSE-UP: framed from the top of the shoulders to just above the head.

CHOKER CLOSE-UP: framed from just below the lips to just above the eyes.
(*Subject sizes* photographs by Robert Greenberg)

performance for the cameras. Be conscious of the image size the camera is recording and adjust the performance accordingly,' is Terry's excellent advice.

13. MOVING IN AND OUT OF CLOSE-UPS

Players are often required to walk in and out of close-ups or to sit into or rise out of close shots. Move slowly. Keep hands away from the face to avoid masking it. Move with ease and naturalness. Give the cameraman time to follow your move to avoid frame imbalance or disappearing too quickly from frame when making an exit.

14. DELIVERING DIALOGUE DURING CLOSE-UPS

Because close-ups are dropped into master scenes, the actor needs to be conscious of sound editing difficulties which can arise should there be dialogue overlaps during close-ups. The term 'keep dialogue clean' means to leave sufficient 'air space' between cues so that players' lines do not overlap or butt too closely together. This problem does not arise when working before multiple television cameras. Sound and image are recorded simultaneously onto magnetic videotape and the director virtually edits the program during recording, cutting from one camera to another without a break in the performance. In motion picture production, the image is captured onto raw stock — unexposed film negative — and the sound onto magnetic audio tape. While both camera and recorder are in sync — photographing and recording simultaneously — the dialogue sound, after being recorded, is transferred to sprocketed tape for editing purposes. It is then re-recorded in combination with the music and effects tracks onto a final sound track which is then 'married' to the images on film. A print of a completely edited, dubbed and scored motion picture is called a first trial composite print or *answer print*. The process is a complex one. Any assistance actors can give a film editor in regard to clean sound — no *overlaps* during close-ups — is of immeasurable benefit.

15. FEEDING LINES TO ON-SCREEN PLAYERS IN CLOSE-UP

During the filming of close-ups, the actor or actors involved in the master scene who are now *off*-screen, feed their lines to the *on*-screen player from *beside* the camera, not from their original positions. This becomes necessary for technical reasons — shooting in a confined area, positioning of the camera, etc. Therefore, not always will the on-screen player have a direct eye-line to those he/she is addressing or listening to. The on-screen player's eye-line is 'cheated' making it look as though the player is looking directly at the off-screen player(s). Where this is the case, fix your mind on an *image* of the player(s) in your sightline and direct your look to the *original* position of the person you are addressing or listening to. Usually, a director will give a player sufficient instruction and rehearsal in eye-line positioning, particularly if there is off-screen movement to follow.

16. THE MASTER SHOT – PICK-UPS AND RETAKES

A master scene or shot is a *continuous* take of an entire event which occurs in one setting. Theatrical films employ the master scene and inter-cutting of closer shots pattern of shooting because the *action* is staged for a *single* camera and therefore has to be repeated each time the camera is re-positioned. Television's use of studio *multiple* cameras allows inter-cutting of different shots without stopping and re-positioning the cameras.

Some directors insist on perfect-take master shots. If an actor misses a mark or 'fluffs' a line, the director may insist on starting the scene from the beginning. Some directors, knowing that the master scene will be edited and close-ups inserted, will call for a 'pick-up' of the actor's mistake. This means starting the scene from the point where it went wrong. Some experienced actors will pause for a few seconds at the point of the mistake and begin the line again. In a highly-dramatic scene, most actors prefer to start the scene from the beginning in order to build and sustain dramatic intensity.

Some directors, providing the technical aspects are correct, will allow less than perfect acting to pass if they are running behind schedule. To counter this, some actors purposely 'blow' lines to force a director to do a retake. Ralph Bellamy said he learned very early in his career how to ruin a take when a scene wasn't up to scratch. 'When I worked in quickie pictures we would shoot them in ten days or so. Directors didn't like retakes. I learned to ruin a take if I felt my performance needed improvement. If I hadn't, the director would have pressed on to the next scene,' said the veteran actor.

17. INCLUDE THE CAMERA WITHIN YOUR CIRCLE OF ATTENTION

Confidence is needed in handling the technical aspects of screen work. The camera should not be feared. The wise actor learns to use the camera to 'bounce' off, to relate to as if it were another character.

Throw your circle of attention around the camera. Include it in your points of reference without looking directly into the lens. Don't allow the camera to intimidate you. It is a part of the whole production process. Don't fight it. *Unify* with it. Respect its ability to capture intimate acting moments, colorful and exciting images. The more screen performances under your belt, the more self-assurance you will develop, which will help you to work *with* the camera in a beneficial way.

18. SWITCH ON TO OTHER CHARACTERS

Instead of starting a scene thinking about camera fright, switch on to the other characters in the scene immediately you hear the director's command for 'action'. Maintain your concentration on the stage action until you hear the command to 'cut'.

Michael Dokes, former heavyweight boxing champion recalled how he once lost a major bout because he lost concentration. 'When I was knocked out, my attention was on a personal problem which had crept into my mind. I should have been concentrating on fighting my opponent. That's when I lost the fight, at the point of my lost concentration,' he said.

Acting, like boxing, requires perfect timing, concentration and discipline. Success depends on keeping the mind alert, focusing the attention on the stage action and channeling nervous energy into *positive* performance.

19. GET INTO AN EMOTIONAL GROOVE DURING PERFORMANCE

Australian director Carl Schultz once told me that actors need to 'get into an emotional groove' to maintain dramatic rhythm in order to avoid 'falling below playing pitch'. He feels that the theatre actor has an advantage over the screen actor in that he/she can build emotional momentum as the play progresses. The process of making films requires the actor to work in short bursts and therein lies the danger of dropping below pitch. 'The screen actor is really in the hands of the director who must watch to see that there is no drop below pitch. If this occurs, the director simply has to work harder to bring the actor back up to the required performance level,' he said.

20. MODIFYING VOLUME AND PROJECTION FOR THE RECORDER

In 1874, Alexander Graham Bell worked out the principle of transmitting speech electrically. A couple of years later, he demonstrated his new apparatus. Called a telephone, the world was delighted with Bell's ingenious device capable of transmitting recognizable voice sounds along wires. Early users of the telephone shouted into the mouthpiece in order to be heard by their listeners. Today, users of the modern telephone experience no such vocal strain. Advanced technology allows the telephone user to speak in a conversational tone.

Early models of the sound microphone — the first being Bell's transmitter — required considerable voice projection by performers in order to be audibly recorded onto wax discs. Audio recording technology has made great advances over the past quarter century. The super-sensitive shotgun, studio and lavalier condensor microphones, coupled to highly-efficient sound recorders, require clear diction but minimum voice projection.

A solid-sounding, well-projected voice is essential to the stage actor. For the screen actor, it can be a handicap unless modified to suit the sound recorder. In theatre performance, the actor must extend the range of the voice and project it so that it reaches the very last row of seats in the auditorium. Home television viewing audiences have the advantage of being able to adjust the audio level of programs to a comfortable listening level. In a motion picture theatre, a film's sound level is preset (generally far too high) so that all audience members are able to hear without listening strain. Because of highly-sensitive microphones and recorders, screen acting requires a different level of voice projection to theatre acting. It is called *modified delivery*.

21. SPEAK TO ONE PERSON NOT A CAST OF THOUSANDS

In the early days of film production, directors wishing to speak to large groups of players were required to use an instrument called a megaphone. Instructions were shouted into the megaphone's mouthpiece which amplified the sounds to some considerable degree. Watching some actors at work in front of the camera reminds me of the megaphone users. It would appear that they are addressing a cast of thousands, not one or two players close to them.

Speaking too loudly, projecting dialogue too heavily, destroys screen intimacy and realism. The television viewer and the motion picture patron want to be entertained in a way which makes them feel comfortable. They do not wish to be shouted at. Unless a scene calls for strong vocal emphasis, deliver dialogue *conversationally*. Most screen acting calls for modified voice projection. It is accomplished via proper voice placement, precise articulation and varied vocal expression.

22. KEEP IT CASUAL BUT DON'T FORGET ENERGY AS YOU SPEAK

A practical way to develop good microphone technique is to imagine that you are in a restaurant engaged in a private conversation you do not wish others to hear. Your tone of voice is normal, yet casual and easy to hear by your partner. Providing your diction is clear, your partner will not have to ask you to speak up. Remind yourself of this exercise the next time you are in rehearsal or performance. But do not allow the words *casual, intimate, conversational* to mean *unhearable*. Project the voice sufficiently to be heard by your partner and speak clearly.

23. MAKE THE LINES SOUND LIKE YOUR OWN ADVISED JAMES MASON

James Mason was a much-admired screen acting craftsman. He wasn't a flashy actor but he had style. He gave original performances in the more than 100 films he made beginning in 1935. He spoke quietly, effectively, fully understanding the screen acting process. His characterizations were unexcelled in *Odd Man Out* (1947), *The Desert Fox* (1951), *The Pumpkin Eater* (1964), *Voyage of the Damned* (1976) and *The Verdict* (1982). He was nominated for an Oscar for his performance opposite Judy Garland in *A Star is Born* (1954).

Over dinner one evening in Hollywood in 1967, Mason told me that he did his best to make writers' words sound like his own. 'That's the test. Does the dialogue sound like an actor speaking memorized lines or a character speaking his own thoughts? Screen characters can be blown-out a bit, exaggerated somewhat without losing believability. However, the dialogue can't be forced, stilted in delivery, too overdone or it loses appeal and naturalness. Talk it. Don't recite it,' he said.

24. ALAN LADD DELIVERED HIS LINES QUIETLY BUT EFFECTIVELY

Alan Ladd was a very good screen actor. His deep, resonant voice and good looks, coupled to his low-key acting style, ideally suited the camera. I met him on the set of *Boy on a Dolphin*, during its production in Hollywood in 1957. I was in Hollywood as a writer-broadcaster, gathering stories and interviews for my newspaper and radio show in Canada.

Ladd was not very tall, but he looked tall on the screen. As I watched him work, I felt that he was a much under-rated actor. He possessed a controlled energy which he pushed through his characterizations when demanded. He allowed his feelings to extend through his lines and through his eyes. He was a 'still' actor — some say 'wooden'. But his stillness in performance — minus body movement, facial animation and gesture — is a lesson in camera acting.

In checking some of his earlier-made films such as *The Blue Dahlia* (1946), The Great Gatsby (1949), Shane (1953), Ladd delivered his lines quietly, conversationally and realistically. His last film was made in 1964, *The Carpetbaggers*, the same year he died of alcohol and sedatives. A study of his performances shows that Ladd looks less mannered than many of his contemporaries.

25. MAKE DIALOGUE CONVERSATIONAL ADVISED STAR OF TV SERIES

While working on an episode of Hawaii Five-O, I heard the star of the series advising an actor that his lines would work better if he spoke them in a conversational way. The actor was using far too much volume and heaviness which created a sound imbalance. The actor responded to the suggestion and toned down his delivery. His proper audio dynamics for the screen greatly improved his performance and he sounded and looked natural and believable.

26. HOLLYWOOD DIRECTOR ADVISED ACTORS TO TALK NOT ACT

A television series in which I appeared was shot in Canada and utilized a veteran Hollywood director. Many of the actors in the series were inexperienced. The director was patient with their over projection of dialogue. One day he called the cast together during a lunch break and gave advice I've kept in my mind whenever working before the camera. It was short and to the point: 'If you want to sound and look right on the screen, just talk your lines to one another, don't project them. Stop overacting. Confine your personal mannerisms. You don't have to shout or gesture in the way you're doing for the camera. It's all too big. The screen audience is neither deaf nor blind. Let my camera do the heavy work for you.'

Clint Eastwood's subdued voice tone and still manner of acting do not comprise an ideal actor's instrument. However, his 'style' works marvellously well for him on the big screen. His soft, toneless voice is a contrast to the violent behavior of the characters he plays. Eastwood has a screen style well-suited to his personality. His playing is a lesson in discipline and control.

27. ACTOR FRIEND WAS GIVEN GOOD ADVICE FOR CAMERA WORK

Robert Legionaire, a strong, well-articulated actor who has worked in New York and Hollywood for many years, told me that a director gave him worthy advice when he first started acting. 'When I call for action, start but stop acting,' the director said. 'I was confused momentarily, but soon got his message and it's worked well for me,' Bob told me.

On the call of 'action' start but stop acting. It means to play scenes without undue vocal and physical exaggeration. The trick is to reduce playing 'heaviness' without losing vitality which is necessary to keep the performance pitch up.

A quality of *stillness* is one of the prerequisites of screen acting. An actor must let the camera do the work, not get into competition with it or overwhelm it with heavy playing. Reduce overly-mannered acting, tone down strong personal mannerisms. In this regard, assistance from the director is sometimes required.

28. WILD LINES AND WILD TRACKS

Wild lines are unsynchronized words or lines which the actor reads into a microphone either on the sound stage or on location at the time the sound problem arises or at the completion of shooting in a sound studio sans camera. Lines recorded in this manner without the camera are called *wild tracks*.

Wind, traffic noise and other unwanted sound problems can play havoc with recording while shooting on location. Where this occurs, actors are called at a later date to re-record dialogue scenes in a sound studio under controlled conditions. Sometimes on interior scenes, the boom operator is slow in swinging the microphone through part of the shot which results in inferior sound quality. Instead of re-shooting the scene, the director will call for a wild track, which is recorded there and then.

29. SYNC-SOUND DUBBING

Where dialogue has to be lip-synced to the original image, the actor is presented with a far more complex situation than just reading lines into a microphone. Sync-sound requires precise duplication of dialogue to match the screen character's lip movements. Dubbing of lines, to achieve perfect lip-sync, can be time-consuming and energy-draining work.

In the sound studio, the actor reads his/her lines into a microphone while watching a playback of the scene on a screen. Sound and or light cues are given after a screen count down from ten. Each recording 'take' is examined until perfect lip-sync is achieved. Experience is the one and only teacher for sync-sound dubbing.

▲ Actor *Alan Cassell's* dialogue is picked up by highly-sensitive studio microphone placed above camera framing.

▲ Bosch *video* camera shoots exterior scene for a television serial. Shotgun microphone is out of shot but close enough to pick up clear sound of actors.

▲ Boom operator walks ahead of players but out of camera framing to record sound for location setting. Microphone is a Sennheiser shotgun encased in a windshield.

Boom operator positions microphone for pick-up of lines by actors. Wild lines are recorded when unwanted sounds spoil recording of dialogue during filming.

Camera is positioned for high-angle shot ▲ by *Jim Devis* as director *Nick Webster* contemplates scene.

The sound recordist takes a break during lull in shooting. Two Nagra recorders and boom microphone can be seen on table. Camera is readied for tracking shot.

▲ Production shots from the television series *Runaway Island*, a Dickens-style story set during the 1830's — telecast worldwide, produced by Grundy Television. It is recorded on film then transferred to videotape for television transmission. Actors should take an interest in the mechanics of putting a story onto the screen. *Listen* and *observe* the director, director of photography, sound recordist and crew members as they prepare each scene for a take.

▲ Production shot from producer *Paul Lazarus III* film *Capricorn One*. Photographer *Bill Butler* and his team filmed this sequence in Mojave Desert. Bi-plane is piloted by daredevil character played by *Telly Savalas*. Film was written and directed by *Peter Hyams*.

30. WORK WITH EFFICIENCY SAYS GREER GARSON

Shortly after arriving in Hollywood in 1961, this time to settle, a writer friend, Ivy Crane-Wilson, took me to meet actress Greer Garson at her home in Bel Air. I found her to be a knowledgable, charming person with great personal charisma. Part of our conversation centered around actors and acting and I well remember her comments on screen acting. Queen of the MGM lot from 1940 to 1946, Miss Garson was a top box office attraction who acted impeccably in a series of major films which included: *Goodby Mr. Chips* (1939), *Pride and Prejudice* (1940), *Blossoms in the Dust* (1941), *Mrs. Miniver* and *Random Harvest* (1942), *Madame Curie* (1943), *Mrs. Parkington* (1944), *Julius Caesar* (1953), *The Singing Nun* (1966).

'It's important that screen actors know their craft in order to work with efficiency. Directors like acting efficiency. It saves them time, creates fewer production problems, saves money and results in better films being produced. During my time at Metro, it was like working in a factory. We actors worked long and hard, but what wonderful training. Unfortunately it's not available to beginners today. Actors who can get the job done, who have style and talent, they are the ones directors pick. Actors need plenty of ammunition to get themselves started — training, persistence, a good agent, talent and a professional attitude,' Miss Garson said.

31. BE A MIRROR OF HUMAN LIFE SUGGESTS CHARLES PILLEAU

A producer friend of long standing, Charles Pilleau, told me that actors need to develop their characterizations so that they become a 'mirror of human life'. Charles feels that audiences love 'colorful heroes', characters whose lives they can identify with and dream of emulating. 'The mirror of human life as audiences imagine it, is an exaggeration of reality. Screen heroes must appear larger than life. Actors must have the ability to inject style into their performances, as did Flynn and Gable,' he maintains.

Charles Pilleau and Errol Flynn were friends, especially so in their youth in Australia. Charles feels that Flynn's success at Warner Bros. was due to the hero-acting parts he was assigned and his ability to play them with great gusto and style. 'In all of us there is the Walter Mitty, the dreamer. Audiences saw Errol as a self-styled hero. He was the man of their dreams leading a lifestyle they desired,' Charles said.

32. PREPARE FOR THE SAUSAGE FACTORY

The actor working in a television series — taped or filmed — has to learn to work quickly with a minimum of fuss. This means he/she has to know the screen acting process inside out. Every minute of shooting time is precious. The actor who cannot work quickly will find television and film acting frustrating and probably unappealing. Soap operas are like stage plays videotaped in large chunks. Constant line memorization, instantaneous characterization, little preparation time and rehearsal can be soul-destroying to the sensitive, dedicated theatre actor. The television series actor requires stamina, discipline, technique and an ability to commit dialogue to memory quickly, particularly if he/she is to keep up the pace and stay the distance, week-after-week, month-after-month. It's very much like a sausage factory with the actors being ground through the machine as efficiently as possible.

Tony Spinner, television producer of the series *The FBI, Cannon, Dan August* and others, feels that television actors need a strong personality and lots of training so they aren't 'embarrassing' on the screen. 'I'm appalled that some actors presenting themselves for work have no training, no background as actors, can't say the lines right or even sit in a chair correctly. Interviewing them is a waste of time. Using them is a disaster.' Spinner feels that television, because it is a 'factory', can't spent the time to develop new people, particularly because of the cost factor involved. 'Good television actors are able to make adjustments, they're flexible and they work quickly,' he says.

33. PREPARE FOR SEEING YOURSELF ON THE SCREEN

Some actors eagerly await the release of their first film or television show to see how well they look in performance. For some, it's quite a shock, particularly those trained in the theatre. Greta Scacchi, a talented actress, wasn't prepared for seeing herself on the screen for the first time. 'Doing film was frightening. I was shattered the first time I saw myself. I had to keep running out of the auditorium and throwing up. It was such a shock seeing my face on that huge screen, talking and laughing,' she recalled during a media interview.

A leading stage actor told me that he was 'absolutely embarrassed' watching himself in his first movie role. 'Everything seemed wrong. My posture, gesture and expression which have always felt natural behind the footlights, appeared strained, unnatural on the screen. I was depressed for weeks afterward. I took lessons in acting for the camera. I had to learn to act for the screen,' he said.

34. SEEK GUIDANCE OF YOUR DIRECTOR

Every actor, no matter how talented or experienced, needs the support and guidance of a competent director. This is especially so in motion picture acting, for film is a director's medium. Truffaut said the film director is the 'true author' of the finished film. He/she must know the basics of acting, writing, photography and editing. In films, it's the director who reigns supreme — ask any major star. Through the art of directing and editing, it is possible to turn a competent actor's performance into a brilliant one. This piece of magic is not possible on the theatre stage where an actor is required to give a sustained performance.

In film acting, an actor gets several tries to get it right. If he/she listens carefully to the advice of the director, chances are it will come out right when the 'bits and pieces' are put together. A simple scene can have as many as fifty or sixty takes. From these the director and editor can select the best and edit them in the correct tempo and rhythm to produce an exciting performance. Charlton Heston had this to say on the subject: 'In a film, how the scene plays on the floor isn't necessarily all that important. One of the first significant things you discover is that your best performance of an entire scene may not be the one that is used.'

A theatre actor who is capable of sustained performance will find this skill unused in picture making because scenes are shot out of sequence and in short bursts. A director's guidance is important. Veteran actor Don Ameche says a director has to be boss when scenes are shot out of sequence. 'If I don't listen to him, how can I make the picture flow on an even keel?' Sustained performance skill is an asset to the actor working on videotaped soap operas which record entire sequences of scenes without stopping the cameras.

If you are unsure of your part, feel insecure in the characterization, do not understand any part of the text, then seek the advice of your director. Don't be embarrassed about seeking help. If you would like a line reading, then ask for one. Nowadays many actors don't believe in line readings and some even fight against suggestions a director might offer in this regard. Laurence Olivier has made it a practice to request a line reading from a director when uncertain about text meaning. If any reader is of greater acting stature than Olivier, then ignore this suggestion.

Bette Davis maintains that it's the director who inspires the actor who is merely a 'puppet the director dangles'. And she says: 'The director is the best person to go to for guidance.' Charlton Heston adds: 'Seek help from a director where it's needed and listen to the advice when it's offered.' And Olivier maintains: 'Actor and director should understand the importance of their partnership. The director's word should be the final one.'

35. FROM DIRECTORS ON ACTORS AND ACTING

Actor-director **Hayes Gordon**, who has confined his career of late mostly to the Ensemble Theatre which he heads, would make an ideal film director. I worked under his skilled directorial hand in Terence Feely's play *Who Killed Santa Claus* and admire his ability to draw from actors that *extra* acting dimension which can mean so much to a performance. At a preview screening of a film we both appeared in, *The Return of Captain Invincible*, Hayes said to me: 'The camera is attracted to an actor's personality. For the stage, personality isn't as necessary as the skill to bring "life" to a characterization. Film lends itself to a separate acting approach than does the stage.'

Actor-director **Michael Blakemore**, whose distinguished career in the theatre includes working with Olivier and Peter Hall at the National Theatre as a director, returned to acting after an absence of 16 years to star in a mini-series, *The Last Bastion*. I worked under Blakemore's experienced direction in the Australian premiere run of Ira Levin's clever stage piece *Deathtrap*, which opened at Sydney's Theatre Royal before moving to

Melbourne's Comedy Theatre. I also worked with him in *The Last Bastion*. During a break in filming, he said to me: 'There is a feeling of total lack of control for the actor on the film set. An actor can readily assess a stage performance, but not so a film performance. He's in the hands of the director. It's an interesting difference, acting for the stage and acting for the camera.'

Film and television series director *Sam Newfield*, with whom I worked as an actor in a cowboy saga some years back, said to me: 'Theatre is the place an actor learns about acting. Film is done in fits and starts which doesn't allow any kind of sustained performance. You cannot learn the acting process in film in a short time, it sometimes takes years. Actors must learn to work with a film director, they've got to learn to "give" instead of restricting emotions and resenting a director as so many of them do.'

Director *Richard L. Bare*, who directed all 168 episodes of television's *Green Acres*, offers this advice to screen performers: 'If actors know anything about psychology, it will be apparent to them that the director's "suggestions" are really orders to be followed faithfully.'

Celebrated Hollywood director *George Cukor*, who brought us *Little Women, Romeo and Juliet, Born Yesterday, A Star Is Born, My Fair Lady* and so many other great films, offered this advise to an acting group he spoke to: 'Make film acting simple. Don't clutter it up with a lot of overly-physical gymnastics. Be natural and spontaneous. Speak with sincerity. If you are sincere in close-up you have nothing to worry about.'

Mervyn LeRoy, director of *The Wizard of Oz, Little Caesar, Waterloo Bridge, Mister Roberts, Gypsy*, etc, had this to say on the subject of film actors: 'If actors have talent, they're easy to shoot. If they don't, nothing helps.'

Vincente Minnelli, who directed the films *An American In Paris, Gigi, The Sandpiper, Goodbye Charlie*, etc, offered this advice: 'Spencer Tracy is the actor to study for good screen performance. There wasn't a better screen actor at comedy than Tracy. His instincts were infallible. He wasn't a mugger. He was subtle, clever, controlled and natural as an actor.'

King Vidor, director of *Northwest Passage, Duel in the Sun, The Fountain Head, War and Peace*, etc, made this point: 'An actor is at the mercy of the camera and the director. He shouldn't hesitate to communicate with his director if unsure about any aspect of what he's do do in front of the camera.'

Alfred Hitchcock, whose classic mystery and ghost stories have entertained and frightened audiences for scores of years — *The 39 Steps, Suspicion, Spellbound, Dial M for Murder, Rebecca, Psycho* — commented on acting thusly: 'My pictures are make-believe. Actors should do the same.'

Daniel Mann, who directed *Come Back, Little Sheba, The Rose Tattoo, A Streetcar Named Desire* and *Paint Your Wagon* on Broadway and the films *I'll Cry Tomorrow, The Last Angry Man, Butterfield 8*, etc, presented this point of view: 'If an actor doesn't have experience, I don't have the time on the set to teach him how to respond. My job is to direct a film, not coach an actor.'

Michael Curtiz, a director who had total disregard for any star's status, used his strong will to evoke many a good screen performance. Note his work in *Casablanca* and *Mildred Pierce*. I met him in 1957 at Paramount. About actors he said this: 'Actors have got to make themselves into people audiences can't take their eyes off. It's called charisma. It's screen presence that separates the stars from the also rans. It has to be there from the beginning, then developed. Actors have to learn how to speak, walk and project personality. They've got to be extraordinarily convincing in the roles they play.'

George Stevens, whom I met on the set of *The Diary of Anne Frank*, was rehearsing a scene with Shelly Winters. During a break, he said to me: 'This girl will win an Oscar for this role. When an actor has talent and can release it in performance in a controlled way, good acting occurs.' (Miss Winters won Best Supporting Actress Oscar in 1959 for *Diary of Anne Frank*.)

36. DON'T BE NERVOUS ABOUT DAY ONE ON THE SET

Some actors are terribly nervous of their first day on the set. In some ways this is understandable because cast and crew are probably meeting for the first time. As with starting any new job, meeting strangers in unfamiliar surroundings can be unnerving. Within an hour or so of meeting, cast and crew are hard at work, giving little chance of establishing more than a surface relationship. This tends to put people in an uneasy frame of mind which breeds insecurity.

I've overheard actors complaining about tough directors and unfriendly crews. I don't believe a member of a production unit consciously tries to be unfriendly or nasty toward an actor, unless the actor is deserving of it. Personally, I've found crews to be pleasant and helpful. Each member has an important function to perform, usually under pressure of time. Actors who get in the way and make a nuisance of themselves are rightly frowned upon. One of the most cheerful, friendly, patient and actor-conscious directors I've worked with is Don Sharp. He goes out of his way to be helpful to actors on the set.

Experienced screen actors become used to working with a production crew and do their best to become part of the whole production process, not separate to it. They are friendly, polite and professional in their work. And this helps to produce harmony instead of friction and assists in getting the job done faster and better because a *team* spirit is operative.

When arriving on the set for the first time, don't consider yourself as an 'outsider', a part-time worker of small importance. Your contribution, no matter how small your role, is vital to the whole production. If this were not the case, you would not be there. Be confident in your ability to get along well with people, to perform in a commendable and professional manner. Contribute what you are being paid to contribute. Become a team member. Take pride in your creative contribution and forget all about nervousness.

Barbra Streisand's supposed egomania is sometimes difficult to handle. Sinatra was known for his impatience when heavily into film acting. Brando was a nightmare to some directors and Bogart and George Sanders

Director *George Cukor* advised his actors to keep their work simple and unaffected for the camera. He liked to talk-through an actor's part so there would be understanding of the characterization.
◄

Alfred Hitchcock felt that actors required 'leading-through' their film roles. Hitchcock pre-planned very carefully his shots. His films are highly-respected for their precision and polish. Actors responded well to his direction. *Psycho,* released by Paramount Pictures in 1960, attests to the Hitchcock directorial genius. ►

often displayed rudeness. Bette Davis conjured up a reputation of being difficult as have many other stars past and present. Barbara Stanwyck was a complete professional on the set, a big favorite with all her co-workers. Don't become drugged by conceit. Don't make a first-class ass of yourself. In this way, you'll have nothing to be nervous about.

37. HELPFUL POINTERS FOR CAMERA ACTING

The following suggestions should prove helpful to actors working before the screen camera.

- Prior to the call for 'action', take deep breaths, wet the lips and swallow to ease throat dryness.
- Stand without slouching, place weight on the downstage foot.
- Reduce the tempo of movement, particularly when sitting and rising.
- Overlap emotions. Carry feelings into a scene when entering and hold feelings when exiting.
- Keep the body and head still in close-up.
- Keep the body in the 'open' position to camera unless otherwise directed.
- An on-camera turn means to turn *toward* the camera. An off-camera turn means to turn *away* from the camera.
- Refrain from exaggerated movement of jaw and lips. Exercise the jaw and tongue prior to performance to prevent 'fluffing' lines.
- The correct reading of a line will give you nearly all the accompanying facial and body expressions you need. Don't 'mug' to indicate feelings.
- Don't get 'hung up' on dialogue delivery. Speak conversationally.
- The camera is an infallible lie detector. Don't try to fake feelings.
- Allow thoughts and feelings to linger, don't chop them off.
- When writing, *write* — don't squiggle. When reading, *read*.
- Should you be told to 'save the food' during rehearsal of an eating scene, fake eating until the scene is actually shot.
- A request to 'hold' means to freeze your position while some adjustment to lights or camera is being made.
- Keep dialogue moving. Pause when it is *really* warranted.
- Interrupt some of your own actions with speech. Pick up a telephone, begin to dial, hesitate, deliver the line then complete the dialling action.
- Refer by *look* or *gesture* to a person or object you are referring to in your dialogue. To 'cheat the look' expose more of face to camera.
- For telephone scenes, allow enough time for answers to your questions. Hear answers in your mind. In some instances, cut your own lines, stopping on a consonant, *not* a vowel to give an abrupt cut.
- Throw a look in the direction you are about to move.
- Don't parrot the same mistake on retakes. Take your time.
- Save energy between scenes. Rest your eyes from the harsh lights. Sit if you can.
- If the scene is yours, take it. If it belongs to your partner, don't steal it.

- Is smoking in the scene necessary or are you doing it because of acting insecurity? Smoking dries the throat, causes coughing and makes the eyes squint. It can be upsetting to fellow players.
- Take *small* portions of food into the mouth in an eating scene and *sip* a drink.

38. AND FINALLY . . .

I made it Ma . . . the top of the world.

Jimmy Cagney, standing on top of a blazing petrol storage tank, arms upraised, shouted those lines as Cody Jarrett in *White Heat*. In Hollywood, making it to the top is what the television and motion picture industries are all about. Having been there and achieved reasonable, though not spectacular success, my advice to the ambitious acting aspirant is, *try*! Whatever the result, providing you do not allow frustration and disappointment to attract psychological and physical problems, the experience will leave you a wiser person and a lot clearer in your thinking as to what's best for you in regard to your future.

There is no way you can work out before you try whether you will make it to the top or not. The profession of acting is too unpredictable. However, you can assist your chances by learning the *process* of acting, writing and directing. Screen acting is an exciting adventure and sometimes financially rewarding. The profession deeply resents acting dilettantes. *Prepare* for the success you desire and go after it with enthusiasm. You can't do much more than that.

And a word of caution — don't worry yourself sick about reaching stardom or for that matter losing it once you've achieved it. Worry is self-defeating. Its emotional complications bring extra burdens to cope with. Use your mind and energy constructively. Care about the *quality* of your acting contributions rather than the quantity of roles that come your way. Not every actor seeking stardom will achieve it. And if you don't, then so what? It won't be the end of the world. You can still make other worthwhile contributions to society.

When Clark Gable was asked how he felt about being 'King of Hollywood', the world's number one movie star, he replied: 'There's only one place I can go from where they've got me now. I gave up worrying about staying a star years ago. It's not everything in life.' Add to Gable's philosophy Spencer Tracy's thoughts: 'It's just a job. Get there on time, know the lines, say them the best way you know how, collect your money then go home and forget about it until they call you again.' And a word from Bogart: 'All I owe anyone is a good performance.'

And *finally* . . . if you can get it all together, understand what's expected of you, refrain from worrying about your career and give good performances, you will indeed be a candidate to succeed in motion pictures and television.

SUMMARY OF IDEAS TO REVIEW

1: Screen work is a team effort. Actors have a duty to bring to the set their best manners and ability. Don't make the job more difficult for the director by unprofessional conduct.

2: Understand the functions of the producer, director and crew members. Know the process of producing a motion picture from pre-production to production shooting to post-production.

3: The three types of camera angles are: objective, subjective and point-of-view. Familiarize yourself with *subject* angles.

4: The key to playing in close-up is restraint. Don't force emotion-playing. Allow the *camera* to capture your feelings. Don't give a stage performance for the camera. Adjust for the closeness of the camera.

5: Switch on to the other players in the scene when the director calls 'action'. Channel nervous energy into your performance. Concentrate on speaking and listening.

6: Modify voice projection. Speak to one person, not a cast of thousands. Make dialogue conversational. Speak quietly but effectively.

7: Follow Greer Garson's advice and work with *efficiency*. Develop your talent so that you can get the job done with a minimum of fuss.

8: Seek the guidance of your director if you are unsure as to your role. Don't be timid in this regard.

9: Don't be nervous about day one on the set. The people and sur-roundings may be new to you. That's no reason to lose your confidence. Don't consider yourself an outsider. Your con-tribution, no matter how small, is important.

10: You won't discover before you begin an acting career whether or not you will succeed. If you want to be an actor then *try*. And if things don't go as desired, so what? There are other interesting ways to contribute your creativity.

TERMINOLOGY
FOR
TV-MOTION PICTURE
PRODUCTION

GLOSSARY OF SCREEN TERMS

ACTION: command of director to begin acting. Movement of players or objects in scene.

ANGLE: camera's viewpoint from a particular position.

ANIMATION: cartooning photographed frame-by-frame giving illusion of movement of figures.

ANSWER PRINT: first print of an edited, dubbed, scored motion picture.

BABY SPOT: smallest spotlight used to highlight part of a player's face.

BACK LIGHT: light played on actors or objects from back of set.

BACK TO SCENE: after an insert or cutaway shot, scene is picked-up from same position and angle as before interruption.

BACK WITH MUSIC: dialogue spoken *over* musical background.

BEAT: one count pause.

BILLBOARD: announcement prior to start of TV program giving information as to show title, cast, story highlights, etc.

BLOCKING: positions and moves given to actors by director at rehearsal.

BOOM: adjustable pole holding microphone extended above heads of players.

BREAK: time out for rest and refreshment.

BRIDGE: a connecting link between one scene and another or in dialogue one idea and another.

BUSINESS: a specific action by player such as writing, mixing drink, examining object, etc.

CENTER OF ATTENTION: person or object upon which camera focuses.

COMPOSITION: arrangement of players in setting pleasing to the eye. Framing of setting which is artistic.

COVERAGE: amount of angles and positions the camera records in addition to master scene for the editor to construct a story which flows.

CRANE SHOT: camera mounted on arm of crane allowing shots from extra height.

CUT: command of director to stop camera and acting.

CYCLORAMA: canvas backdrop around edge of studio floor.

DAILIES: film of previous day's shooting just as it comes from lab. Also called 'rushes'.

DAY FOR NIGHT: scene shot during day with filter and particular aperture setting to simulate night.

DISCOVERED: player is already in scene when it opens.

DOLLY SHOT: camera on wheels moves toward or away from subject or object.

DUBBING: re-recording of dialogue or several sound tracks onto final sound track.

DRESS REHEARSAL: final rehearsal before opening, with actors in full dress and makeup. Called a *FAX* rehearsal for television show. Use of full studio facilities.

DRY RUN: rehearsal minus studio cameras.

EYE LIGHT: small light near camera to bring out sparkle of actor's eyes

FADE IN: scene emerges from black to full image.

FADE OUT: scene gradually disappears to black.

FADE TO BLACK: method of ending a television program.

FILM CLIP: short highlight of a motion picture. Film inserted into a live television show.

FINAL CUT: completely edited print ready for dubbing and scoring.

FILTER MIKE: creates effect of voice coming through telephone.

FLAT: boards used in set construction to simulate walls.

FLOOR: television studio staging area.

FLOOR MANAGER: director's link with talent on studio floor. Floor manager is in charge of crew and players and is equal to assistant director of a film crew. Designation relates only to a television in-studio crew.

FOLLOW SHOT: camera follows moving player or object.

FORMAT: style or presentation of a television idea or script.

GRIPS: carpenters who move wild walls, persons who operate camera dolly or move camera from one position to another.

HAND PROPS: small items used by actors such as: gun, pen, letter, knife, keys, etc.

IDIOT CARDS: also called cue cards. Dialogue read by on-camera performer written on cards.

INSERT: close-up of a letter, sign, gun or object of importance needed to be seen in close-up.

INTERIOR: inside of building, any interior location or setting of scene.

KILL: remove a light, prop, set piece, etc. Also referred to as 'strike'.

LIMBO: area beyond the set.

LINE CUT: elimination of particular lines from script or during editing of scene.

LIP SYNC: recording session wherein actors match dialogue to screen characters' speech.

LOCALE: area where scene is to be staged.

LOOPING: dubbing by *syncing* to a loop of film run through projector continuously.

MAKEUP CALL: specific time to report to makeup *prior* to reporting to set.

MIDDLE BREAK: station identification about half-way point in program transmission.

MONITOR: television set which picks up images recorded by cameras.

NEGATIVE: film stock. Receives exposure through camera. Images are reversed when developed.

OPTICALS: optical tricks made in optical printer at laboratory: dissolves, fades, wipes, etc.

OUTLINE: story synopsis of about ten pages.

OUT TAKES: scenes not used in editing of film or television show.

OPEN END: pre-recorded show minus commercials. TV talk show having no set time to end.

P.A.: public address system.

PER DIEM: additional money paid to actors for meals, expenses while on location out of town.

PERSONALITY TEST: screen test. Actor is asked questions on-camera to view screen personality.

PRACTICAL: equipment or set piece which actually works: sink, stove, lights, radio, etc.

PRINT: satisfactory take which is to be processed at lab. Processed negative.

PROCESS SHOT: foreground action filmed against translucent screen onto which is projected from rear or front another background. Also called *rear* or *front* screen projection.

RED LIGHT: rotating light beacon outside studio entrance. When lit, indicates filming has begun and no admission until turned off. A bell, horn or buzzer sounds when scene is to begin and when scene is complete. This is a warning for 'quiet please' – 'all clear'.

SCENE: unit of action. One or more shots in sequence of shots in same location.

SHOOT AROUND YOU: re-arrangement of shooting schedule to accommodate an unavailable actor.

SHOT: single uninterrupted take of a scene. A *sequence* indicates several shots in same location setting and with no time lapses.

SLATE: board held in front of camera prior to a shot giving production information. For film, clapper sticks are attached and 'slapped' together to sync sound when editing. For television a *marker* board is used minus clapper sticks.

SPEED: relates to director that camera is running at correct speed. He then is free to give command for 'action'.

STAND BY: instruction from floor manager show is ready to begin. Voice call at *one minute,* then *30 seconds* and a countdown from *ten* to a hand signal for *action* follows.

STOCK SHOT: pre-filmed location shots. Also referred to as 'library' film.

STORYBOARD: drawings showing sequence of events to be shot.

SYNC: picture and sound correctly lined up.

TAG LINE: final important line of scene.

TAKE: completed action. Scene is successful and to be printed.

TELEPLAY: script of a *television* drama as opposed to a *screenplay* which represents a motion picture drama.

TD: television technical director assisting director in control room. Also called vision switcher.

TELEPROMPTER: device for visual prompting for news readers, narrators on live or recorded TV shows. Script is typed onto paper roll and electronically rolled in device under camera lens. When read, eyeline of player appears to be to camera.

TONE DEAF: said of an actor who cannot give correct reading of lines.

377

TREATMENT: detailed outline of about fifty pages of story and characters.

UNDERCRANK: slowing down of film *camera* speed to create increased *screen* action speed. *Overcrank increases* camera speed to give illusion of *slowing* down of screen action.

VOICE CUE: given by director or assistant to begin action.

VTR: video tape recording.

WILD CAMERA: camera filming without sound. An *MOS* shot means shooting scene without sound.

WILD TRACK: sound track made independently of camera.

WILD WALL: removable wall (flats) from set.

WRAP: finished at this location for the day, pack up shooting completed.

X: script abbreviation to indicate a stage cross.